School of Divinity

Gardner-Webb University
School of Divinity

This book donated
by

Mr. Lee Thomas

GEORGE ADAM SMITH'S
WORKS ON THE PROPHETS

THE BOOKS OF AMOS, HOSEA, MICAH

VOLUME I

GEORGE ADAM SMITH'S
WORKS ON THE PROPHETS

LIST OF NEW AND REVISED EDITIONS

THE BOOK OF THE TWELVE PROPHETS

COMMONLY CALLED THE MINOR

IN TWO VOLUMES—VOLUME I
AMOS, HOSEA, AND MICAH

BY

GEORGE ADAM SMITH

Kt., D.D., LL.D., Litt.D., F.B.A.

Principal of the University of Aberdeen

WITH AN INTRODUCTION AND A SKETCH OF
PROPHECY IN EARLY ISRAEL

REVISED EDITION

HARPER & BROTHERS Publishers

NEW YORK AND LONDON

CONTENTS

INTRODUCTION

AMOS

▼

CONTENTS

PREFACE

THE Prophets, to whom this and a following volume are dedicated, have, to our loss, been haunted for centuries by a peddling and an ambiguous title. Their Twelve Books are in size smaller than those of the great Three which precede them, and doubtless none of their chapters soar so high as the summits to which we are swept by Isaiah and the Prophet of the Exile. But in every other respect they are undeserving of the niggardly name of ' Minor.' Two of them, Amos and Hosea, were the first of written prophecy—rising cliff-like, with a sheer and magnificent originality, to a height and a mass sufficient to set after them the trend and slope of the whole prophetic range. The Twelve together cover the extent of that range, and illustrate the development of prophecy at almost every stage from the eighth century to the fourth. Yet even more than in the case of Isaiah or Jeremiah, the Church has been content to use a passage here and a passage there, leaving the rest of the books to absolute neglect or the almost equal oblivion of routine-reading. Among the causes of this disuse have been the more than usually corrupt state of the text ; the consequent disorder and in parts unintelligibleness of all the versions ; the ignorance

of the various historical circumstances out of which
the books arose ; the absence of successful efforts to
determine the periods and strophes, the dramatic
dialogues (with the names of the speakers), the lyric
effusions and the passages of argument, of all of which
the books are composed.

The following exposition is an attempt to assist the
bettering of this. As the Twelve Prophets illustrate
among them the whole history of written prophecy, I
have thought it useful to prefix a historical sketch of
the Prophet in early Israel, or as far as the appearance
of Amos. The Twelve are then taken in chronological
order. Under each of them a chapter is given of
historical and critical introduction to his book ; then
some account of the prophet himself as a man and
a seer ; then a complete translation of the various
prophecies handed down under his name, with textual
footnotes, and an exposition and application to the
present day ; finally, a discussion of the main doctrines
the prophet has taught, if it has not been found possible
to deal with these in the course of the exposition.

An exact critical study of the Twelve Prophets is
rendered necessary by the state of the entire text.
The present volume is based on a thorough examination of this in the light of the ancient versions and
of modern criticism. The emendations which I have
proposed are few and insignificant, but I have examined and discussed in footnotes all that have been
suggested, and in many cases my translation will be
found to differ widely from that of the Revised Version.
To questions of integrity and authenticity more space

is devoted than may seem to many to be necessary. But it is certain that the criticism of the prophetic books has now entered on a period of the same analysis and discrimination as in the case of the Pentateuch. Some hints were given of this in a previous volume on Isaiah, chapters xl–lxvi, which are evidently a composite work. Among the books now before us, the same fact has long been clear in the case of Obadiah and Zechariah, and also since Ewald's time with regard to Micah. But Duhm's *Theology of the Prophets*, which appeared in 1875, suggested interpolations in Amos. Wellhausen (in 1873) and Stade (from 1883 onwards) carried the discussion further both on those, and others, of the Twelve ; while a recent work by Andrée on Haggai proves that many similar questions may still be raised and have to be debated. The general fact must be admitted that hardly one book has escaped later additions—additions of justifiable nature, which supplement the point of view of a single prophet with the richer experience or the riper hopes of a later day, and thus afford to ourselves a more catholic presentment of the doctrines of prophecy and the Divine purposes for mankind. This general fact, I say, must be admitted. But the questions of detail are still in process of solution. It is obvious that settled results can be reached (as to some extent they have been already reached in the criticism of the Pentateuch) only after years of research and debate by all schools of critics. Meantime it is the duty of each of us to offer his own conclusions, with regard to every separate passage, on the understanding that, however final they may at present seem to him, the end is not yet. In previous criticism the defects, of which work in the same field has made me aware, are four : 1. A too rigid belief in the exact parallelism and symmetry of the prophetic style, which I feel has led, for instance, Wellhausen, to whom we otherwise owe so much on the Twelve Prophets, into many unnecessary emendations of the text, or, where some amendment is necessary, to absolutely unprovable changes. 2. In passages between which no connection exists, the forgetfulness of the principle that this fact may often be explained as justly by the hypothesis of the omission of some words, as by the favourite theory of the later intrusion of portions of the extant text. 3. Forgetfulness of the possibility, which in some cases amounts almost to certainty, of the incorporation, among the authentic words of a prophet, of passages of earlier as well as of later date. And, 4, depreciation of the spiritual insight and foresight of pre-exilic writers. These, I am persuaded, are defects in previous criticism of the prophets. Probably my own criticism will reveal many more. In the beginnings of such analysis as we are engaged on, we must be prepared for not a little arbitrariness and want of proportion ; these are often necessary for insight and fresh points of view, but they are as easily eliminated by the progress of discussion.

All criticism, however, is preliminary to the real work which the immortal prophets demand from scholars and preachers in our age. In a review of a previous volume I was blamed for applying a prophecy of Isaiah to a problem of our own day. This was

called 'prostituting prophecy.' *The* prostitution of
the prophets is their confinement to academic uses.
One cannot conceive an ending at once more pathetic
and more ridiculous to those great streams of living
water, than to allow them to run out in the sands of
criticism and exegesis, however golden these sands
may be. The prophets spoke for a practical purpose ;
they aimed at the hearts of men ; and everything that
scholarship can do for their writings has surely for its
final aim the illustration of their witness to the ways
of God with men, and its application to living questions
and duties and hopes. Besides, therefore, seeking to
tell the story of that wonderful stage in the history of
the human spirit—surely next in wonder to the story
of Christ Himself—I have not feared at every suitable
point to apply its truths to our lives to-day. The
civilisation in which prophecy flourished was in its
essentials marvellously like our own. To mark only
one point, the rise of prophecy in Israel came fast
upon the passage of the nation from an agricultural
to a commercial basis of society, and upon the appearance of the very thing which gives its name to civilisation—city-life, with its unchanging sins, problems, and
ideals.

A recent Dutch critic, whose exact scholarship is
known to readers of Stade's *Journal of Old Testament
Science*, has said of Amos and Hosea : ' These prophecies have a word of God, as for all times, so also
especially for our own. Before all it is relevant to
" the social question " of our day, to the relation of
religion and morality. . . . Often it has been hard for
me to refrain from expressly pointing out the agree-

ment between Then and To-day.'[1] This feeling will
be shared by all students of prophecy whose minds and
consciences are quick ; and I welcome the liberal plan
of the series in which this volume appears, because,
while giving room for the adequate discussion of
critical and historical questions, its chief design is to
show the eternal validity of the Books of the Bible
as the Word of God, and their meaning for ourselves
to-day.

Previous works on the Minor Prophets are almost
innumerable. Those to which I owe most will be
found indicated in the footnotes. The translation has
been executed upon the purpose, not to sacrifice the
literal meaning or exact emphasis of the original to
the frequent possibility of greater elegance. It produces every word with the occasional exception of a
copula. The reader will keep in mind that a line may
be destroyed by substituting our pronunciation of
proper names for the more musical accents of the
original. Thus, for instance, we obliterate the music
of ' Isra'el ' by making it two syllables and putting
the accent on the first : it has three syllables with the
accent on the last. We crush Yerushalayîm into
Jerúsalem ; we shred off Asshûr into Assyria, and dub
Miṣraîm Egypt. Hebrew has too few of the combina-
tions which sound most musical to our ears, to afford
the suppression of any one of them.

FREE CHURCH COLLEGE,
GLASGOW, 1896.

[1] J. J. P. Valeton. jun., *Amos en Hosea*, 1894; quoted by Budde in
the *Theologische Literaturzeitung*, September, 1894.

TO THE NEW AND REVISED EDITION

SINCE these two volumes first appeared in 1896 and 1898 respectively, the textual, literary, and historical criticism of *The Twelve Prophets* has vastly developed, as may be estimated from the Bibliography herewith appended, pages xvii–xix. In preparing this New and Revised Edition I have gone through the details of this later criticism and have made use of many of its suggestions and conclusions. Where I have disagreed with any of the rest of them I indicate my reasons for so doing either in the text of the volumes or in the footnotes to this.

In the light of our clearer knowledge of Hebrew Metre I have thoroughly revised and recast my translations of the Prophets' own words and of the additions to them from later pious hands.

I trust that such changes, bringing the results of Biblical Criticism down to this date, may continue the usefulness of a work, which during the last thirty-two years has maintained a wide circulation.

The First Edition I dedicated to my friend Henry Drummond, and to his memory, still vivid in the minds of all who knew, or were influenced by, him, I gratefully inscribe this new edition.

GEORGE ADAM SMITH.

UNIVERSITY OF ABERDEEN,
June, 1928.

BIBLIOGRAPHY

TRANSLATIONS AND COMMENTARIES

F. Hitzig—Die zwölf kleinen Propheten, 1838. 4th ed., Steiner, 1881.

E. B. Pusey—The Minor Prophets. 1865.

A. Wünsche—Der Prophet Hosea. 1868.

H. A. von Ewald—The Prophets of the O.T., translated by J. F. Smith, vols. i–iii and v. 1875–1881.

A. A. Vollers—Das Dodekapropheton der Alexandriner. 1880. (Not seen.)

T. K. Cheyne—Micah. 1882 ; Hosea. 1884 (Camb. Bible).

T. T. Perowne—Haggai and Zechariah. 1886; Obadiah and Jonah. 1889 ; Malachi (Camb. Bible).

C. von Orelli—Die zwölf kleinen Propheten. 1888, translated by Banks. 1893.

J. Wellhausen—Die kleinen Propheten ; Heft v. of Skizzen und Vorarbeiten. 1892. 3rd ed. 1898.

T. Andrée—Le Prophète Aggai, Introduction Critique et Commentaire. 1893.

A. B. Davidson—Nahum, Habakkuk, and Zephaniah (Camb. Bible). 1896.

H. Guthe, K. Marti, E. Kautzsch, J. W. Rothstein—Das Zwölfprophetenbuch in Kautzsch's Die Heilige Schrift des A.T. 1896. 3rd ed. 1910.

S. R. Driver—Joel and Amos (Camb Bible). 1897.

W. Nowack—Die kleinen Propheten, Hand-kommentar Zum A.T. 1897. 2nd ed. 1903.

T. K. Cheyne—Critica Biblica, pt. ii. pp. 119–198. 1903.

K. Marti—Das Dodekapropheton (Kurzer Hand-Commentar zum A.T.). 1904.

W. R. Harper—Amos and Hosea (International Critical Commentary). 1905.

P. Haupt—The Bk. of Micah, a new metrical translation. 1910 ; also Notes on Micah (Amer. Jour. of Semitic Lang. and Liter.). 1910.

B. Duhm—Die zwölf Propheten in den Versmassen der Urschrift übersetzt. 1910 ; and Anmerkungen zu den zwölf Propheten in Z.A.T.W. 1911.

J. M. P. Smith, W. H. Ward, J. A. Bewer—Micah, Zephaniah, Nahum, Habakkuk, Obadiah, Joel (International Critical Commentary). 1911 ; H. G. Mitchell, J. M. P. Smith, J. A. Bewer—Zechariah to Jonah.

A. R. Gordon—The Prophets of the O.T. 1916.
G. W. Wade—Micah, Obadiah, Joel, and Jonah (Westminster Commentary). 1925.
A. von Bulmerincq—Der Prophet Maleachi, Band i Einleitung. 1926.
R. M. Gwynn—The Book of Amos. 1927.
In the Century Bible the corresponding volumes are undated : R. F. Horton—Hosea to Micah ; S. R. Driver—Nahum to Malachi.

Other Relevant Works

A list of historical works upon the period of the Prophets, on prophecy in general, and on introduction to the Old Testament will be found on pp. xviii, xix of my Isaiah, Vol. I. The following deal with the Twelve Prophets, in whole or in part.

1. *General* :—

W. Robertson Smith—The Prophets of Israel. 1882.
F. W. Farrar—The Minor Prophets (Men of the Bible Series. No date)
P. Volz—Die vorexilische Yahweprophetie. 1897.
W. Riedel—A. T. Untersuchungen, Heft i. 1902.
W. O. E. Oesterley—The Development of Monotheism in Israel Expositor. 1902.
E. A. Edghill—Evidential Value of Prophecy. 1906.
E. Sievers—Metrische Studien, in Abhandlungen der philol. histor Classe der K. Sächsischen Gesellschaft der Wissenschaften. 1907.
W. Cossmann—Die Entwicklung des Gerichtgedankens bei den A.T Propheten. Z.A.T.W., Beiheft 29. 1915.
A. C. Welch—The Prophets and the World Order. Expositor. 1919.
K. Budde—Eine folgenschwere Redaktion des Zwölfprophetenbuchs Z.A.T.W. 1921.
W. L. Wardle—The Origins of Hebrew Monotheism. Z.A.T.W. 1925.
S. A. Cooke—The Prophets of Israel (Cambridge Ancient History, chap. xx). 1925.
K. Budde—Alttestamentliche Forschungen. 1925.

2. *On Amos* :—

A. B. Davidson—The Prophet Amos. Expositor. 1887.
K. Budde—Die Ueberschrift des Buches Amos u. des Propheten Heimath ; in Semitic Studies in memory of A. Kohut. 1897.
H. G. Mitchell—Amos an Essay in Exegesis. 1900.
M. Löhr—Untersuchungen zum Buch Amos. Z.A.T.W., Beiheft 4. 1901.
E. Baumann—Der Aufbau der Amosreden. Z.A.T.W., Beiheft 7. 1903.
F. Prätorius—Zum Texte des Amos. Z.A.T.W., 1914 ; also 1915.
K. Budde—Zur Geschichte des Buches Amos. Z.A.T.W., Beiheft 27, pp. 63 ff. 1914 ; also Zu Text und Auslegung des Buches Amos. J.B.L. 1924-1925.
Köhler—Articles on Amos in der Schweizerischen Theol. Zeitschrift. 1917. (Not seen.)

BIBLIOGRAPHY xix

L. I. Newman—Parallelism in Amos (University of California Publications). 1918.
K. Marti—Zur Komposition von Amos i. 3–ii. 3.   Z.A.T.W., Beiheft 33, pp. 323 ff. 1918.

3. *On Hosea :—*

A. B. Davidson—Expositor. 1879.
W. R. W. Gardner—Notes on Certain Passages in Hosea. A.J.S.L. xviii. 1902.
J. Bewer—Some Ancient Variants in Hosea. J.B.L. 1911.
K. Budde—Der Schluss des Buches Hosea (in Studies on the History of Religions presented to C. H. Toy). 1912.
W. W. Cannon—The Text of Hosea. Expositor.
J. M. P. Smith—The Marriage of Hosea (in the Biblical World). 1913.
L. Waterman—The Marriage of Hosea. J.B.L. 1918.
C. H. Toy—Notes on Hosea, i–iii. J.B.L. 1918.
A. Heermann—Ehe und Kinder des Propheten Hosea. Z.A.T.W. 1922.
H. Schmidt—Die Ehe des Hosea. Z.A.T.W. 1924.
P. Humbert—La Logique de la Perspective Nomade chez Osée et l'Unite d'Osée ii. 4–22 ; in *Vom Alten Testament*, dedicated to K. Marti. 1925.
O. R. Sellers—Hosea's Motives. A.J.S.L. 1925.

On Micah :—

C. P. Caspari—Ueber Micha . . . und seine prophetische Schrift. 1851–1852.
V. Ryssel—Untersuchungen über die Textgestalt und die Echtheit des Buches Micha. 1887.
S. R. Driver—Micah, ii. 7, 12 ff. Expositor. 1887.
P. Volz—Die vorexilische Yahweprophetie, pp. 63–67. 1897.
B. Stade—Z.A.T.W. 1903.
K. Budde—Das Räthsel von Micha i. Z.A.T.W 1917–1918. Micha ii, iii, *ibid.* 1919–1920. Verfasser und Stelle von Mi. iv. 1–4 (Jes. ii. 2–4), Zeitschrift der Deutscher Morgenländischen Gesellschaft. 1927.
F. C. Burkitt—Micah vi and vii, a Northern Prophecy. J.B.L. 1926.

The literature relevant to the rest of the Twelve Prophets will be found at the beginning of Vol. II of this work.

THE GEOGRAPHY

For illustration of the geographical names and statements in the Book of the Twelve Prophets the reader is referred to the relevant maps and letterpress in the Atlas of the Historical Geography of the Holy Land (designed and edited by myself and prepared under the direction of J. G. Bartholomew, LL.D., and published by Messrs. Hodder & Stoughton, especially Maps 1–8, 15–30, 35–37.

ABBREVIATIONS

A.J.S.L.	= American Journal of Semitic Languages and Literature.
A.T.	= Alte Testament.
Enc. Bibl.	= Encyclopædia Biblica.
Hist. Geog. or H.G.H.L.	= Historical Geography of the Holy Land.
J.B.L.	= Journal of Biblical Literature.
K.A.T.[3]	= Die Keilinschriften und das A.T. 3rd ed.
LXX.	= The Septuagint or Greek Version of the O.T.
S.B.O.T.	= Haupt's Sacred Books of the Old Testament (Polychrome Bible).
Syr.	= Syriac Version of the O.T.
Targ.	= Targum.
Vulg.	= Vulgate.
Z.A.T.W.	= Zeitschrift für Alttestamentliche Wissenschaft.

INTRODUCTION

Καὶ τῶν ιβ' προφητῶν τὰ ὀστᾶ
    ἀναθάλοι ἐκ τοῦ τόπου αὐτῶν,
Παρεκάλεσαν δὲ τὸν Ἰακώβ
    καὶ ἐλυτρώσαντο αὐτοὺς ἐν πίστει ἐλπίδος.

And of the Twelve Prophets may the bones
    Flourish again from their place,
For they comforted Jacob
    And redeemed them by assurance of hope.'

ECCLESIASTICUS xlix. 10.

CHAPTER I

THE BOOK OF THE TWELVE

IN the order of our English Bible the Minor Prophets, as they are usually called, form the last
twelve books of the Old Testament. They are immediately preceded by Daniel, and before him by the
three Major Prophets. Isaiah, Jeremiah (with Lamentations), and Ezekiel. Why all sixteen were thus
gathered at the end of the other sacred books, we do
not know. Perhaps, because it was held fitting that
prophecy should occupy the last outposts of the Old
Testament towards the New.

In the Hebrew Bible, however, the order differs, and
is more significant. The Prophets[1] form the second
division of the threefold Canon—Law, Prophets, and
Writings—and Daniel is not among them. The Minor
follow immediately after Ezekiel. Moreover, they are
not twelve books, but one. They are gathered under
the common title *Book of the Twelve ;*[2] and although
each of them has the usual colophon detailing the
number of its own verses, there is also one colophon

---

[1] Including, of course, the historical books, Joshua to 2 Kings, which
were known as ' the Former Prophets ' ; while what we call the prophets
Isaiah to Malachi, were known as ' the Latter.'

[2] ספר תרי עשר, the Aramaic form of the Hebrew שנים עשר, which
appears with the other in the colophon to the book. A later contraction
is תריסר. This is the form transliterated in Epiphanius : δαθαριασαρά.

for all the twelve, placed at the end of Malachi and reckoning the sum of their verses from the first of Hosea onwards. This unity, which there is reason to suppose was given to them before their reception into the Canon,[1] they have never since lost. However much their place has changed in the order of the books of the Old Testament, however much their own internal arrangement has differed, the Twelve have always stood together. There has been every temptation to scatter them because of their various dates. Yet they never have been scattered ; and in spite of the fact that they have not preserved their common title in any Bible outside the Hebrew, that title has lived on in literature and common talk. Thus the Greek canon omits it ; but Greek Jews and Christians always counted the books as one volume,[2] calling them ' The Twelve Prophets,' or ' The Twelve-Prophet ' Book.[3] It was the Latins who designated them ' The Minor Prophets ' : ' on account of their brevity as compared with those who are called the Major because of their ampler volumes.'[4] And this name has passed into most modern languages,[5] including our own. But it is better to revert to the original, canonical, and unambiguous title of ' The Twelve.'

The collection and arrangement of ' The Twelve '

---

[1] See Ryle, *Canon of the O.T.*, p. 105.

[2] So Josephus, *Contra Apion*, i. 8 (*circa* 90 A.D.), reckons the pro-phetical books as thirteen, of which the Minor Prophets could only have been counted as one—whatever the other twelve may have been. Melito of Sardis (*c.* 170 A.D.), quoted by Eusebius (*Hist. Eccl.*, iv. 26), speaks of τῶν δώδεκα ἐν μονοβίβλῳ. To Origen (*c.* 250 ; *apud ibid.*, vi. 25) they could only have been one out of the twenty-two he gives for the O.T. Cf. Jerome (*Prolog. Galeatus*), ' Liber duodecim Prophetarum.'

[3] Οἱ Δώδεκα Προφῆται : Jesus son of Sirach, xlix. 10 ; Τὸ δωδεκαπρόφητον.

[4] Augustine, *De Civ. Dei*, xviii. 29 : cf. Jerome, *Proem. in Esaiam.*

[5] The German usage generally preserves the numeral, ' Die zwölf kleinen Propheten.'

are matters of obscurity, from which, however, three or four facts emerge that are tolerably certain. The inseparableness of the books is a proof of the ancient date of their union. They must have been put together before they were received into the Canon. The Canon of the Prophets—Joshua to Second Kings and Isaiah to Malachi—was closed by 200 B.C. at the latest, and perhaps as early as 250 [1]; but if we have (as seems probable) portions of ' The Twelve,' [2] which must be assigned to a little later than 300, this may be held to prove that the whole collection cannot have long preceded the fixing of the Canon of the Prophets. On the other hand, the fact that these latest pieces have not been placed under a title of their own, but are attached to the Book of Zechariah, is pretty sufficient evidence that they were added after the collection and fixture of twelve books—a round number which there would be every disposition not to disturb. That would give us for the date of the first edition (so to speak) of our Twelve some year before 300 ; and for the date of the second edition some year towards 250. This is a question, however, which may be reserved for final decision after we have examined the date of the separate books, and especially of Joel and the second half of Zechariah. That there was a previous collection, as early as the Exile, of the books written before then, may be regarded as more than probable. But we have no means of fixing its exact limits. Why the Twelve were all ultimately put together is reasonably suggested by Jewish writers. They are small, and, as separate rolls, might have been lost. [3] It is possible that the desire

[1] ' The *collection*—we might also say the *canon*—of the Prophets took place in course of the third century ' (Budde art. ' Canon ' 41 in *Enc. Bibl.*).

[2] See vol. ii, on Zech. ix ff.

[3] *Talmud :* Baba Bathra, 14 : cf. Rashi's Commentary.

of the round number twelve is responsible for the admission of Jonah,[1] a book very different in form from all the others ; just as we have hinted that the fact of there being already twelve may account for the attachment of the late fragments to the Book of Zechariah. But all this is only to guess, where we have no means of certain knowledge.

The Book of the Twelve has not always held the place which it now occupies in the Hebrew Canon, at the end of the Prophets. The rabbis taught that Hosea, but for the comparative smallness of his prophecy, should have stood first of all the writing prophets, of whom they regarded him as the oldest.[2] And doubtless it was for the same chronological reasons, that early Christian catalogues of the Scriptures, and various editions of the Septuagint, placed the whole of the Twelve in front of Isaiah.[3]

The internal arrangement of the Twelve in our English Bible is the same as that of the Hebrew Canon, and was probably determined by what the compilers thought to be the respective ages of the books. Thus, first we have six, all supposed to be of the earlier Assyrian period, before 700—Hosea, Joel, Amos, Obadiah, Jonah, and Micah ; then three from the late Assyrian and the Babylonian periods—Nahum, Habbakuk, and Zephaniah ; and then three from the Persian period after the Exile—Haggai, Zechariah, and Malachi. The Septuagint have altered the order of the first six, arranging Hosea, Amos, Micah, Joel, and Obadiah according to their size, and setting Jonah after

[1] So also Budde, *Gesch d. althebr. Litteratur*, 1906.
[2] *Talmud, ibid.*
[3] So the Codices Vaticanus and Alexandrinus, but not Cod. Sin. So also Cyril of Jerusalem († 386), Athanasius (365), Gregory Naz. († 390), and the spurious Canon of the Council of Laodicea (*c.* 400) and Epiphanius (403). See Ryle, *Canon of the O.T.*, pp. 215 ff.

them, probably because of its different form. The remaining six are left as in the Hebrew.

Recent criticism, however, has made it clear that the Biblical order of ' The Twelve Prophets ' is no more than a very rough approximation to the order of their real dates ; and, as it is obviously best for us to follow in their historical succession prophecies, which illustrate the whole history of prophecy from its rise with Amos to its fall with Malachi and his successors, I propose to do this. Detailed proofs of the separate dates must be left to each book. All that is needful here is a general statement of the order.

Of the first six prophets the dates of Amos, Hosea, and Micah (but of the latter's book in part only) are certain. The Jews have been able to defend Hosea's priority only on fanciful grounds.[1] Whether or not he quotes from Amos, his historical allusions are more recent. With the exception of a few fragments incorporated by later authors, the Book of Amos is thus the earliest example of prophetic literature, and we take it first. The date we shall see is about 755. Hosea begins five or ten years later, and Micah just before 722. The three are in every respect—originality, comprehensiveness, influence upon other prophets—the greatest of our Twelve, and will therefore be treated with most detail, occupying the whole of this first volume.

The rest of the first six are Obadiah, Joel, and Jonah. But the Book of Obadiah, although it opens with an early oracle against Edom, is in its present form from after the Exile. The Book of Joel is of uncertain date, but, as we shall see, the great probability is that it also is post-exilic ; and the Book of Jonah belongs to a form

---

[1] By a forced interpretation of the phrase in chap. i. 2, *When the Lord spake at the first by Hosea* (R.V.), *Talmud :* Baba Bathra, 14.

of literature so different from the others that we may.
most conveniently, treat of it last.

This leaves us to follow Micah, at the end of the
eighth century, with the group Zephaniah, Nahum, and
Habakkuk from the second half of the seventh century ;
and finally to take in their order the post-exilic Haggai,
Zechariah I–IX, Malachi, and the other writings which
we feel obliged to place about or even after that date.

One other word is needful. This assignment of the
various books to different dates is not to be held as
implying that the whole of a book belongs to such
a date or to the author whose name it bears. We
shall find that hands have been busy with the texts
of the books long after the authors of these must have
passed away ; that besides early fragments incorporated
by later writers, prophets of Israel's new dawn mitigated the judgements and lightened the gloom of the
watchmen of her night ; that here and there are passages
which are evidently intrusions, both because they interrupt the argument and because they reflect a much
later historical environment than their context. This,
of course, will require discussion in each case, and
such discussion will be given. The text will be subjected to an independent examination. Some passages
hitherto questioned we may find to be unjustly so ;
others not hitherto questioned we may see reason to
suspect. But in any case we shall keep in mind, that
the results of an independent inquiry are uncertain ;
and that in this new criticism of the prophets, which
is comparatively recent, we cannot hope to arrive for
some time at even such a comparative consensus, as
has been reached in the far older and more elaborated
criticism of the Pentateuch.[1]

Such is the extent and order of the journey which

[1] For further considerations on this point see later chapters.

lies before us. If it is not to the very summits of Israel's outlook that we climb—Isaiah, Jeremiah, and the great Prophet of the Exile—we are yet to traverse the range of prophecy from beginning to end. We start with its first abrupt elevations in Amos. We are carried by the side of Isaiah and Jeremiah, yet at a lower altitude, on to the Exile. With the returned Israel we pursue an almost immediate rise to vision, and then by Malachi and others are conveyed down dwindling slopes to the very end. Beyond the land is flat. Though Psalms are sung and brave deeds done, and faith is strong and bright, there is no height of outlook ; *there is no more any prophet* [1] in Israel.

But our Twelve do more than thus carry us from beginning to end of the Prophetic Period. Of second rank as are most of the heights of this mountain range, they yet bring forth and speed on their way not a few of the streams of living water which have nourished later ages, and are flowing to-day. Impetuous cataracts of righteousness—*let it roll on like water, and justice as an everlasting stream ;* the irrepressible love of God to sinful men ; the perseverance and pursuits of His grace ; His mercies that follow the exile and the outcast ; His truth that goes forth richly upon the heathen ; the hope of the Saviour of mankind ; the outpouring of the Spirit ; counsels of patience ; impulses of tenderness and of healing ; melodies innumerable— all sprang from these lower hills of prophecy, and sprang so strongly that the world hears and feels them still.

And from the heights of our present pilgrimage there are also clear those great visions of the Stars and the Dawn, of the Sea and the Storm, concerning which it is true, that as long as men live they shall seek out the places whence they can be seen, and thank God for His prophets.

[1] Psalm lxxiv. 9.

CHAPTER II

THE PROPHET IN EARLY ISRAEL

OUR Twelve Prophets will carry us, as we have seen, across the whole extent of the Prophetical period—the period when prophecy became literature, assuming the form and rising to the intensity of an imperishable influence on the world. The earliest of the Twelve, Amos and Hosea, were the inaugurators of this period. They were not only the first (so far as we know) to commit prophecy to writing, but we find in them the germs of all its subsequent development. Yet Amos and Hosea were not unfathered. Behind them lay an older dispensation, and their own was partly a product of this, and partly a revolt against it. Amos says of himself: *The Lord Yahweh hath spoken, who can but prophesy ?*—but again : *No prophet I, nor prophet's son !* Who were those earlier prophets, whose office Amos assumed while repudiating their spirit—whose name he abjured, yet could not escape from it ? And, while we are about the matter, what do we mean by ' prophet ' in general ?

In common use the name ' prophet ' has degenerated to the meaning of ' one who foretells the future.' Of this meaning it is the first duty of every student of prophecy earnestly to rid himself. In its native Greek ' prophet ' meant not ' one who speaks before,' but ' one who speaks for, or on behalf of,' another. At the

Delphic oracle ' The Prophetēs ' was the title of the official, who received the utterances of the frenzied Pythoness and expounded them to the people ; [1] but Plato says that this is a misuse of the word, and that the true prophet is the inspired person himself, he who is in communication with the Deity and who speaks directly for the Deity.[2] So Tiresias, the seer, is called by Pindar the ' prophet ' or ' interpreter of Zeus,' [3] and Plato even styles poets ' the prophets of the Muses.' [4] It is in this sense that we must think of the ' prophet ' of the Old Testament. He is a speaker for God. The sharer of God's counsels, as Amos calls him, he becomes the bearer and preacher of God's Word. Prediction of the future is only a part, and often a subordinate and accidental part, of an office whose full function is to declare the character and the will of God. But the prophet does this in no systematic or abstract form. He brings his revelation point by point, in connection with some occasion in

---

[1] Herodotus, viii. 36, 37.

[2] *Timæus*, 71, 72. The whole passage is worth transcribing :—

' No man, when in his senses, attains prophetic truth and inspiration ; but when he receives the inspired word either his intelligence is enthralled by sleep, or he is demented by some distemper or possession. And he who would understand what he remembers to have been said, whether in dream or when he was awake, by the prophetic and enthusiastic nature, or what he has seen, must recover his senses ; and then he will be able to explain rationally what all such words and apparitions mean, and what indications they afford, to this man or that, of past, present, or future, good and evil. But, while he continues demented, he cannot judge of the visions which he sees or the words which he utters ; the ancient saying is very true that " only a man in his senses can act or judge about himself and his own affairs." And for this reason it is customary to appoint diviners or interpreters as discerners of the oracles of the gods. Some persons call them prophets ; they do not know that they are only repeaters of dark sayings and visions, and are not to be called prophets at all, but only interpreters of prophecy ' (Jowett's *Translation*).

[3] *N.*, i. 91.   [4] *Phædrus*, 262 D.

the history of his people, or phase of their character. He is not a philosopher nor a theologian with a system of doctrine (at least before Ezekiel), but the messenger of God at some crisis in the life or conduct of His people. His message is never out of touch with events. These form either the subject-matter or the proof or the execution of every oracle he utters. It is, therefore, God not merely as Truth, but even more as Providence, whom the prophet reveals. And although that Providence includes the full destiny of Israel and mankind, the prophet brings the news of it, for the most part, piece by piece, with reference to some present sin or duty, or some impending crisis. Yet he does all this, not merely because the word needed for the day has been committed to him by itself, and as if he were only its mechanical vehicle ; but because he has come under the overwhelming conviction of God's presence and of His character, a conviction often so strong that God's word breaks through him and God speaks in the first person to the people.

I. FROM THE EARLIEST TIMES TO SAMUEL

There was no ancient people but believed in the power of certain personages to consult the Deity and to reveal His will. Every man might sacrifice ; but not every man could render in return the oracle of God. This pertained to select individuals or orders. So the prophet seems to have been an older specialist than the priest, though in every tribe he frequently combined the latter's functions with his own.[1]

The matters on which ancient man consulted God

---

[1] It is still a controversy whether the original meaning of the Semitic root KHN is prophet, as in the Arabic KâHiN, or priest, as in the Hebrew KôHeN (Wellhausen, *Skizzen*, iii. 130 ff.).

were as wide as life. But naturally at first, in a rude state of society and at a low stage of mental development, it was in regard to the material defence and necessities of life, the bare law and order, that men almost exclusively sought the Divine will. And the whole history of prophecy is just the effort to substitute for these elementary provisions a more personal standard of the moral law, and more spiritual ideals of the Divine Grace.

By the Semitic race—to which we may now confine ourselves, since Israel belonged to it—Deity was worshipped, in the main, as the god of a tribe. Every Semitic tribe had its own god ; it would appear that there was no god without a tribe : [1] the traces of belief in a supreme and abstract Deity are few and ineffectual. The tribe was the medium by which the god made himself known, and became an effective power on earth : the god was the patron of the tribe, the supreme magistrate and the leader in war. The piety he demanded was little more than loyalty to ritual ; the morality he enforced was mainly a matter of police. He took no cognisance of the character or inner thoughts of the individual. But the tribe believed him to stand in very close connection with all the practical interests of their common life. They asked of him the detection of criminals, the discovery of lost property, the settlement of civil suits, sometimes when the crops should be sown, and always when war should be waged and by what tactics.

The means by which the prophet consulted the Deity on these subjects were for the most part primitive

[1] Cf. Jer. ii. 10 : *For pass over to the isles of Kittim, and see ; and send unto Kedar, and consider diligently ; and see if there be such a thing. Hath a nation changed their gods ?* From the isles of Kittim unto Kedar—the limits of the Semitic world.

and rude.   They may be summed up under two kinds :
Visions either through falling into ecstasy or by
dreaming in sleep, and Signs or Omens.   Both kinds
are instanced in Balaam.[1]   Of the signs some were
natural, like the whisper of trees, the flight of birds,
the passage of clouds, the movements of stars.   Others
were artificial, like the casting or drawing of lots.
Others were between these, like the shape assumed
by the entrails of the sacrificed animals when thrown
on the ground.   Again, the prophet was often obliged
to do something wonderful in the people's sight, in
order to convince them of his authority.   In Biblical
language he had to work a miracle or give a sign.
One instance throws a flood of light on this habitual
expectancy of the Semitic mind.   There was once an
Arab chief, who wished to consult a distant soothsayer
as to the guilt of a daughter.   But before he would
trust the seer to give him the right answer to such
a question, he made him discover a grain of corn
which he had concealed about his horse.[2]   He required
the physical sign before he would accept the moral
judgement.

To us the crudeness of the means employed, the
opportunities of fraud, the inadequacy of the tests for
spiritual ends, are very obvious.   But do not let us,
therefore, miss the numerous moral opportunities which
lay before the prophet even at that early stage of his
evolution.   He was trusted to speak in the name of
Deity.   Through him men believed in God and in the
possibilty of a revelation.   They sought from him the
discrimination of evil from good.   The highest possibilities of social ministry lay open to him ; the tribal

[1] Num. xxiv. 4, *falling but having his eyes open*.   Ver. 1, *enchantments*
ought to be *omens*.   See my *Early Poetry of Israel*.
[2] Instanced by Wellhausen. *Skizzen u. Vorarb.*. No. v.

existence often hung on his word for peace or war ;
he was the mouth of justice, the rebuke of evil, the
champion of the wronged. Where such opportunities
were present, can we imagine the Spirit of God to have
been absent—the Spirit Who seeks men more than
they seek Him, and as He condescends to use their poor
language for religion must also have stooped to the
picture language, to the rude instruments, symbols
and sacraments, of their early faith ?

In an office of such mingled possibilities everything
depended—as we shall find it depend to the very end
of prophecy—on the moral insight and character of the
prophet himself, on his conception of God and whether
he was so true to this as to overcome his professional
temptations to self-indulgence, fraud and avarice, malice
towards individuals, subservience to the powerful, or,
worst snares of all, the slothfulness and insincerity of
routine. We see this moral issue put very clearly in
such a story as that of Balaam, or in such a career as
that of Mohammed.

So much for the Semitic soothsayer in general. Now
let us turn to Israel.

Among the Hebrews the *man of God*,[1] to use his
widest designation, is at first called *Seer*,[2] or *Gazer*,[3]
the word which Balaam uses of himself. In con-
sulting the Divine will he employs the same external
means, he offers the people for their evidence the
same signs, as do the seers or soothsayers of other
Semitic tribes. He gains influence by the miracles,
the wonderful things, which he does.[4] Moses himself is
represented after this fashion. He meets the magicians
of Egypt on their own level. His use of *rods ;* the

[1] אִישׁ אֱלֹהִים   [2] רֹאֶה .   [3] חֹזֶה .

[4] Deut. xiii. 1 ff. admits that heathen seers were able to work miracles
and give signs, as well as the prophets of Yahweh.

holding up of his hands that Israel may prevail against
Amalek ; Joshua's casting of lots to discover a criminal ;
Samuel's dream in the sanctuary ; his discovery for a
fee of the lost asses of Saul ; David and the images in his
house, the ephod he consulted ; the sign to go to battle
*what time thou hearest the sound of a going in the tops of
the mulberry trees ;* Solomon's inducement of dreams by
sleeping in the sanctuary at Gibeah,—these are a few of
the many proofs, that early prophecy in Israel employed
not only the methods but even much of the furniture
of the kindred Semitic religions. But then those tools
and methods were at the same time accompanied by
the noble opportunities of the prophetic office to which
I have just alluded—opportunities of religious and
social ministry—and, still more, these opportunities
were at the disposal of moral influences which, it is a
matter of history, were not found in any other Semitic
religion to nearly the same degree as in Israel's. However you will explain it, that Divine Spirit, which we
have felt unable to conceive as absent from any Semitic
prophet who truly sought after God, that Light which
lighteth every man who cometh into the world, was
present to an unparalleled degree with the early prophets of Israel. He came to individuals, and to the
nation as a whole, in events and in influences which may
be summed up as the impression of the character of
their national God, Yahweh : to use Biblical language,
as *Yahweh's spirit* and *power*. It is true that in many
ways the God of early Israel reminds us of other
Semitic deities. Like some of them He appears with
thunder and lightning ; like all of them He is the God
of one tribe who are His peculiar people. He bears
the same titles—Melek, Adon, Baal (*King, Lord,
Possessor*). He is propitiated by the same offerings.
To choose one striking instance, captives and spoil of

war are sacrificed to Him with the same relentlessness, and by a process which has even the same names given to it, as in the votive inscriptions of Israel's heathen neighbours.[1] Yet notwithstanding all these elements, the religion of Yahweh from the very first evinced, by the confession of all critics, an ethical force shared by no other Semitic creed. From the first there was in it the promise and the potency of that sublime mono-theism, which in the period of our Twelve it afterwards reached.[2] Its earliest effects of course were chiefly political ; it welded the twelve tribes into the unity of a nation ; it preserved them as one amid the many temp-tations to scatter along those divergent lines of culture and of faith, which the geography of their country placed so attractively before them.[3] It taught them to prefer religious loyalty to material advantage, and so inspired them with high motives for self-sacrifice and every other duty of patriotism. But it did even better than thus teach them to bear one another's burdens. It inspired them to care for one another's sins. The last chapters of the Book of Judges prove how strong a national conscience there was in early Israel. Even then Israel was a moral unity.[4] Gradually there grew up, but still unwritten, a body of Torah, or revealed law, which, though its framework was the common custom of the Semitic race, was inspired by ideals of humanity and justice not elsewhere in that race dis-cernible by us, to the same degree.

When we analyse this ethical distinction of early

[1] Cf. Mesha's account of himself and Chemosh on the Moabite Stone, with the narrative of the taking of Ai in the Book of Joshua.

[2] Cf. Kuenen : *Gesammelte Abhändlungen* (trans. by Budde), p. 461.

[3] So in Deborah's Song. Cf. Jer. ii. 28: *as many as thy cities are thy gods, O Judah.*

[4] On this whole subject, see the writer's essay, on ' The Hebrew Genius ' in *The Legacy of Israel* ' 1927), pp. 1-10.

Israel, this indubitable progress which the nation were
making while the rest of their world was morally
slow, we find it ascribed to their impressions of the
character of their God.   This character did not affect
them as Righteousness only.   At first it was even a
more wonderful Grace.   Yahweh had chosen them when
they were no people, had redeemed them from servitude,
had brought them to their land ; had borne with their
stubbornness, and had forgiven their infidelities.   Such
a Character was partly manifest in the great events of
their history, and partly communicated itself to their
finest personalities—as the Spirit of God does com-
municate with the spirit of man made in His image.
Those personalities were the prophets from Moses to
Samuel.   They inspired the nation to believe in God's
purposes for itself ; they rallied it to war for the common
faith, and war was then the pitch of self-sacrifice :
they gave justice to it in God's name, and rebuked its
sinfulness without sparing.   Criticism has proved that
we do not know nearly so much about those first
prophets, as perhaps we thought we did.   But under
their God they made Israel.   Out of their work grew
the monotheism of their successors whom we are
now to study, and later the Christianity of the New
Testament.   For myself I cannot but believe, that in
the influence of Yahweh which Israel owned in those
early times, there was the authentic revelation of a
real Being.

2. FROM SAMUEL TO ELISHA

Of the oldest order of Hebrew prophecy, Samuel
was the last representative   Till his time, we are told,
the prophet in Israel was known as the Seer,[1] but

[1] 1 Sam. ix. 9.   See above, p. 15.

now, with other tempers and other habits, a new order appears, whose name—and that means to a certain extent their spirit—is to displace the older name and the older spirit.

When Samuel anointed Saul he bade him, for a sign that he was chosen of the Lord, go forth to meet *a company of prophets*—Nebi'îm, the singular is Nabi' [1]— coming down from the high place or sanctuary with viols, drums, and pipes, and *prophesying. There,* he added, *the spirit of Yahweh shall come upon thee, and thou shalt prophesy with them, and shalt be turned into another man.* So it happened ; and the people *said one to another, What is this that is come to the son of Kish ? Is Saul also among the prophets ?* [2] Another story, probably from another source, tells us that later, when Saul sent troops of messengers to the sanctuary at Ramah to take David, they saw *the company of prophets prophesying and Samuel standing appointed over them, and the spirit of God fell* upon one after another of the troops ; as upon Saul himself when he followed them up. *And he stripped off his clothes also, and prophesied before Samuel in like manner, and lay down naked all that day and all that night. Wherefore they say, Is Saul also among the prophets ?* [3]

All this is very different from the habits of the Seer, who had hitherto represented prophecy. He was solitary, but these went about in bands. They

---

[1] Hebrew נָבִיא, lit. *spokesman, speaker,* from the root נבא, which in other Semitic languages means *to utter, announce, speak.* But some take נבא to be ' a weakened form of נבע, *to bubble up, pour forth* (of flow of words under excitement of inspiration).' See the *Heb. Engl. Lexicon of the O.T.,* by Brown, Driver, Briggs, p. 611.

[2] 1 Sam. x. 1-16, xi. 1-11, 15. Chap. x. 17-27, xi. 12-14, belong to other and later documents. Cf. Robertson Smith, *Old Testament in the Jewish Church,* pp. 135 ff.

[3] 1 Sam. xix. 20-24.

were filled with an infectious enthusiasm, by which
they excited each other and all sensitive persons whom
they touched. They stirred up this enthusiasm by
singing, playing upon instruments, and dancing : its
results were frenzy, the tearing of their clothes, and
prostration. The same phenomena have appeared in
every religion—in Paganism often, and several times
within Christianity. They may be watched to-day
among the dervishes of Islam, who by singing (as
one has seen them in Cairo), by swaying of their
bodies, by repeating the Divine Name and dwelling
on the love and ineffable power of God, work themselves into an excitement which ends in prostration
and often in insensibility.[1]   The whole process is due to
an overpowering sense of the Deity—crude and unin-
telligent if you will, but sincere and authentic—which
seems to haunt the early stages of all religions, and to
linger to the end with the stagnant and unprogressive.
The appearance of this prophecy in Israel has given
rise to a controversy as to whether it was purely a
native product, or was induced by infection from the
Canaanite tribes around.   Such questions are of little
interest in face of these facts : that the ecstasy sprang
up in Israel at a time when the spirit of the people was
stirred against the Philistines, and patriotism and religion were equally excited ; that it is represented as
due to the Spirit of God ; and that the last of the old
order of Yahweh's prophets recognised its harmony with
his own dispensation, presided over it, and gave Israel's
first king as one of his signs, that he should come under
its power.   These things being so, it is surprising that

[1] What seemed most to induce the frenzy of the dervishes whom I
watched was the fixing of their attention upon, the yearning of their
minds after, the love of God.   ' Ya habeebi ! '—' O my beloved ! '—
they cried over and over again.

one [1] should see in the dancing prophets nothing but
eccentrics into whose company it was shame for so
good a man as Saul to fall. He reaches this conclusion only by supposing that the reflexive verb used
for their *prophesying—hithnabbē'*—had at this time that
equivalence to mere madness to which it was reduced
by the excesses of later generations of prophets. With
Samuel we feel that the word had no reproach : the
Nebi'îm were recognised by him as standing in the
prophetical succession. They sprang up in sympathy
with a national movement. The king who joined himself to them was the same who sternly banished from
Israel all the baser forms of soothsaying and traffic with
the dead. But, indeed, we need no other proof than
this ; the name Nebi'îm so establishes itself in the
popular regard that it displaces the older names of
Seer and Gazer, and becomes the classical term for the
whole body of prophets from Moses to Malachi.

One very remarkable change was effected by this
new order of prophets, probably the greatest relief
which prophecy experienced in the course of its evolution. This was separation from the ritual and from
the implements of soothsaying. Samuel had been both
priest and prophet. But after him the names and
the duties were specialised, though the specialising was
incomplete. While the new Nebi'îm remained in connection with the ancient centres of religion, they do not
appear to have exercised any part of the ritual. The
priests, on the other hand, did not confine themselves
to sacrifice and other forms of public worship, but
exercised many of the so-called prophetic functions.
They also, as Hosea tells us, were expected to give

[1] For example, Cornill, in the first of his lectures on *Der Israelitische Prophetismus*, one of the very best popular studies of prophecy, by a master on the subject. See below, p. 71.

Tôrôth—revelations of the Divine will on points of conduct and order. There remained with them the ancient forms of oracle—the Ephod, or plated image, the Teraphim, the lot, and the Urim and Thummim,[1] all of these apparently still regarded as indispensable elements of religion.[2] From such rude forms of ascertaining the Divine Will, prophecy in its new order was free. And it was free of the ritual of the sanctuaries. As has been justly remarked, the ritual of Israel always remained a peril to the people, the peril of relapsing into Paganism. Not only did it materialise faith and engross affections in the worshipper which were meant for moral objects, but very many of its forms were actually the same as those of the other Semitic religions, and it tempted its devotees to the confusion of their God with the gods of the heathen. Prophecy was now independent of ritual, and we may see in such independence the possibility of its subsequent career along moral and spiritual lines. Amos condemns the ritual, and Hosea brings the message from God, *I will have mercy and not sacrifice.* This is the glory of prophecy in that era in which we are to study it. But do not let us forget that this became possible through the ecstatic Nebi'îm of Samuel's time, and through their separation from the national ritual and the material forms of soothsaying. It is the way of Providence to prepare for the revelation of moral truths, by the enfranchisement, sometimes centuries before, of an order

---

[1] It is now past doubt that these were two sacred stones used for decision in the case of an alternative issue. This is plain from the amended reading of Saul's prayer in 1 Sam. xiv. 41, 42 (after the LXX) : *O Yahweh, God of Israel, wherefore hast Thou not answered Thy servant this day ? If the iniquity be in me or in Jonathan my son, O Yahweh God of Israel, give Urim : and if it be in Thy people Israel, give, I pray Thee, Thummim.*

[2] Hosea iii. 4. See next chapter, p. 35.

or a nation of men from political or professional interests which would have rendered it impossible for their descendants to appreciate those truths without prejudice or compromise.

We may conceive then of these Nebi'îm, these prophets, as enthusiasts for Yahweh and for Israel. For Yahweh—if to-day we see men cast by the adoration of the despot-deity of Islam into transports so excessive that they lose all consciousness of earthly things and fall into a trance, can we not imagine a like effect produced on the same sensitive natures of the East by the contemplation of such a God as Israel's, so mighty in earth and heaven, so faithful to His people, so full of grace ?   Was not such an ecstasy of worship most likely to be born of the individual's ardent devotion in the hour of the nation's despair ? [1]   Of course there would be swept up by such a movement the volatile and unbalanced minds of the day—as these always have been swept up by powerful religious excitement— but that is not to discredit the sincerity of the main volume of the feeling nor its authenticity as a work of the Spirit of God, the impression of the character and power of Yahweh.

These ecstatics were also enthusiasts for Israel ; and this saved the movement from morbidness. They worshipped God neither out of physical sympathy with nature, like the Phœnician devotees of Adonis or the Greek Bacchantes ; nor out of terror at the approaching end of all things, like some of the ecstatic sects of the Middle Ages ; nor out of a selfish passion for their own salvation, like so many a modern Christian fanatic ; but in sympathy with their nation's aspirations for freedom and her whole political life.   They

[1] Cf. Deut. xxviii. 32–34.

were enthusiasts for their people. The ecstatic prophet was not confined to his body nor to nature for
the impulses of Deity. Israel was his body, his atmosphere, his universe. Through it all he felt the thrill
of Deity. Confine religion to the personal, it tends
to grow morbid. Wed it to patriotism, it lives in the
open air and its blood is pure. So in days of national
danger the Nebi'îm would be inspired like Saul to
battle for their country's freedom ; in more settled
times they would be lifted to the responsibilities of
educating the people, counselling the governors, and
preserving the national traditions. This is what actually took place. After the critical period of Saul's
time has passed, the prophets still remain enthusiasts ;
but they are enthusiasts for affairs. They counsel and
they rebuke David.[1] They prepare Jeroboam, and they
justify Northern Israel's revolt.[2] They overthrow and
they set up dynasties.[3] They offer the king advice on
campaigns.[4] Like Elijah, they take up against the
throne the cause of the oppressed ; [5] like Elisha, they
stand by the throne its trusted counsellors in peace and
war.[6] That all this is no new order of prophecy in
Israel, but the developed form of the ecstasy of Samuel's
day, is plain from the continuance of the name Nebi'îm
and from these two facts besides : that the ecstasy survives and that the prophets still live in communities.
The greatest figures of the period, Elijah and Elisha,
have upon them *the hand of Yahweh*, as the influence
is now called : Elijah when he runs before Ahab's
chariot across Esdraelon, Elisha when by music he
induces upon himself the prophetic mood.[7] Another

[1] 2 Sam. xii. 1 ff.   [2] 1 Kings xi. 29 ; xii. 22.
[3] 1 Kings xiv. 2, 7–11 ; xix. 15 f. ; 2 Kings ix. 3 ff.
[4] 1 Kings xxii. 5 ff. ; 2 Kings iii. 11 ff.   [5] 1 Kings xxi. 1 ff.
[6] 2 Kings vi–viii. etc.   [7] 1 Kings xviii. 46 ; 2 Kings iii. 15.

ecstatic figure is the prophet who was sent to anoint
Jehu ; he swept in and he swept out again, and the
soldiers called him *that mad fellow*.[1]   But the roving
bands had settled down into more or less stationary
communities, who partly lived by agriculture and partly
by the alms of the people or the endowments of the
crown.[2]   Their centres were either the centres of national
worship, like Bethel and Gilgal, or the centres of government, like Samaria, where the dynasty of Omri supported prophets both of Baal and of Yahweh.[3]   They
were called prophets, but also *sons of the prophets*, the
latter name not because their office was hereditary, but
by the Oriental fashion of designating every member
of a guild as the son of the guild.   In many cases the
son may have succeeded his father ; but the ranks
could be recruited from outside, as we see in the case
of the young farmer, Elisha, whom Elijah anointed
at the plough.   Probably all wore the mantle which
is distinctive of some of them, the mantle of hair, or
skin of a beast.[4]

The risks of degeneration, to which this order of
prophecy was liable, arose both from its ecstatic temper
and from its connection with public affairs.

Religious ecstasy is always dangerous to the moral
and intellectual interests of religion.   The largest
prophetic figures of the period, though they feel the
ecstasy, attain their greatness by rising superior to it.
Elijah's raptures are impressive ; but nobler are his
defence of Naboth and his denunciation of Ahab.   And
so Elisha's inducement of the prophetic mood by music

---

[1] 2 Kings ix. 11.   *Mad fellow*, not necessarily a term of reproach.
[2] 1 Kings xviii. 4, cf. 19 ; 2 Kings ii. 3, 5 ; iv. 38–44 ; v. 20 ff. ; vi.
1 ff. ; viii. 8 f. etc.
[3] 1 Kings xviii. 19 ; xxii. 6.
[4] So Elijah, 2 Kings i 8 : cf. John the Baptist, Matt. iii. 4.

is the least attractive element in his career : his greatness lies in his combination of the care of souls with
political insight and vigilance for the national interests.
Doubtless many of the sons of the prophets with smaller
abilities cultivated a religion as rational and moral.
But for the herd ecstasy would be everything. It was
so easily induced or imitated that much of it cannot
have been genuine. Even where the feeling was at
first sincere we understand how readily it became
morbid ; how fatally it might fall into sympathy with
that drunkenness from wine and that sexual passion
which Israel saw already cultivated as worship by the
surrounding Canaanites. We must feel these dangers
of ecstasy if we would understand why Amos cut himself off from the Nebi'îm, and why Hosea laid emphasis
on the moral and intellectual sides of religion : *My people
perish for lack of knowledge.* Hosea indeed considered
the degeneracy of ecstasy as a judgement : *the prophet
is a fool, the man of the spirit is mad—for the multitude of
thine iniquity.*[1] A later age derided the ecstatics, and
took one of the forms of the verb *to prophesy* as equivalent to the verb *to be mad.*[2]

But temptations as gross beset the prophet from that
which should have been the discipline of his ecstasy—
his connection with public affairs. Only some prophets
were brave rebukers of the king and the people. The
herd which fed at the royal table—four hundred under
Ahab—were flatterers, who could not tell the truth,
who said Peace, peace, when there was no peace. These
were false prophets. Yet it is curious that the very

---

[1] Hosea ix. 7.
[2] Jer. xxix. 26 : *Every man that is mad and worketh himself into
prophesying* (מתנבא, the same form as is used without moral reproach
in 1 Sam. x. 10 ff.).

early narrative which describes them [1] does not impute their falsehood to any base motives of their own, but to the direct inspiration of God, who sent forth a lying spirit upon them. So great was the reverence still for the *man of the spirit!* Rather than doubt his inspiration, they held his lies to be inspired. One does not of course mean that these consenting prophets were conscious liars ; but that their dependence on the king, their servile habits of speech, disabled them from the truth. Subserviency to the powerful was their temptation. In the story of Balaam we see confessed the base instinct that he who paid the prophet should have the word of the prophet in his favour. In Israel prophecy went through the same struggle between the claims of its God and the claims of its patrons. Nor were those patrons always the rich. The bulk of the prophets were dependent on the charitable gifts of the common people, and in this we may find reason for that subjection of so many of them to the vulgar ideals of the national destiny, to signs of which we are pointed by Amos. The priest at Bethel only reflects public opinion when he takes for granted that the prophet is a thoroughly mercenary character : *Seer, get thee gone to the land of Judah ; eat there* thy *bread, and play the prophet there !* [2] No wonder that Amos separates himself from such hireling craftsmen !

Such was the course of prophecy up to Elisha, and the borders of the eighth century. We have seen how even for the ancient prophet, mere soothsayer though we might regard him in respect of the rude instruments of his office, there were present moral opportunities from which, if he only proved true to them, we cannot conceive the Spirit of God to have been absent. In

[1] 1 Kings xxii.   [2] Amos vii. 12

early Israel we are sure that the Spirit did meet such strong and pure characters, from Moses to Samuel, creating by their means the nation of Israel, welding it to a unity, which was not only political but moral— and moral to a degree not elsewhere realised in the Semitic world. We saw how a new race of prophets arose under Samuel, separate from the older forms of prophecy by lot and oracle, separate, too, from the ritual ; and therefore free for a moral and spiritual advance of which the priesthood, still bound to images and the ancient rites, proved themselves incapable. But this new order of prophecy, besides its moral opportunities, had also its moral perils : its ecstasy was dangerous, its connection with public affairs was dangerous too. Again, the test was the personal character of the prophet himself. And so once more we see raised above the herd great personalities, who carry forward the work of their predecessors. The results are, besides the discipline of the monarchy and the defence of justice and the poor, the firm establishment of Yahweh as the one and only God of Israel, and the impression on Israel both of His omnipotent guidance of them in the past, and of a destiny, still vague but brilliant, which He had prepared for them in the future.

This brings us to Elisha, and from Elisha there are but forty years to Amos. During those forty years, however, there was rising in Israel a new civilisation ; beyond her there opened up a new world ; and with Assyria there entered the resources of Providence, a new power. It was these three facts—the New Civilisation, the New World, and the New Power— which made the difference between Elisha and Amos, and raised prophecy from a national to a universal religion.

CHAPTER III

THE EIGHTH CENTURY IN ISRAEL

THE long life of Elisha fell to rest on the margin of the eighth century.[1] He had seen much evil upon Israel. The people were smitten in all their coasts. None of their territory across Jordan was left ; and not only Hazael and his Syrians, but bands of their own former subjects, the Moabites, periodically raided Western Palestine, up to the gates of Samaria.[2] Such a state of affairs determined the activity of the last of the older prophets. Elisha spent his life in the duties of the national defence, and in keeping alive the spirit of Israel against her foes. When he died they called him *Israel's chariot and the horsemen thereof*,[3] so incessant had been both his military vigilance [4] and his political insight.[5] But Elisha was able to leave behind him the promise of a new day of victory.[6] It was in the peace and liberty of this day that Israel rose a step in civilisation ; that prophecy, released from the defence, became the criticism, of the national life ; and that the people, no longer absorbed in their own borders, looked out, and for the first time realised the world, of which they were only a part.

---

[1] He died in 798 or 797.
[3] 2 Kings xiii. 14.
[5] viii, etc.

[2] 2 Kings x. 32, xiii. 20, 22.
[4] vi. 12 ff., etc.
[6] xiii. 17 ff.

King Joash, whose arms the dying Elisha had blessed, won back in the sixteen years of his reign (798–783) the cities which the Syrians had taken from his father.[1] His successor, Jeroboam II, came in, therefore, with a flowing tide. He was strong, and he took advantage of it. During his long reign of about forty years (783–743) he restored the border of Israel from the Pass of Hamath between the Lebanons to the Dead Sea, and occupied at least part of the territory of Damascus.[2] This means that the constant raids to which Israel had been subjected now ceased, and that by the time of Amos, about 755, a generation was grown up who had not known defeat, and the most of whom had perhaps no experience even of war.

Along the same length of years Uzziah (*circa* 778–740) had dealt similarly with Judah.[3] He had pushed south to the Red Sea, while Jeroboam pushed north towards Hamath ; and while Jeroboam had taken the Syrian towns he had crushed the Philistine. He had reorganised the army, and invented new engines of siege for casting stones. On his frontiers opposed to the desert he had built towers : there is no better means of keeping the nomads in subjection.

All this meant such security across broad Israel as had not been known since the days of Solomon. Agriculture must have revived : Uzziah, the Chronicler tells us, *loved husbandry*. But we hear most of Trade and Building. With quarters in Damascus and a port on the Red Sea, with allies in the Phœnician towns and tributaries in the Philistine, with command of the main routes between Egypt and the North as between the Desert and the Levant, Israel, during those forty years of Jeroboam and Uzziah, must have be-

---

[1] 2 Kings xiii 23–25.   [2] xiv. 28, if not Damascus itself.
[3] Uzziah or Azariah, 2 Kings xv : cf. 2 Chron. xxvi.

come a somewhat commercial people. Hosea calls the
Northern Kingdom a very Canaan [1]—Canaanite being
the Hebrew term for trader—as we should say a very
Jew ; and Amos exposes the restlessness, greed, and
indifference to the poor of a community making haste
to be rich. The first effect of this was an increase of
the towns and of town-life. Every document of the
time—up to 720—speaks of its buildings.[2] In ordinary
building houses of ashlar seem to be novel enough
to be mentioned. Vast *palaces*—the name of them first
heard of in Israel under Omri and his Phœnician alliance,
and then only as that of the king's citadel [3]—are now
built by wealthy grandees out of money extorted from
the poor ; they can have risen only since the Syrian
wars. There are summer houses in addition to winter
houses ; and it is not only the king, as in the days of
Ahab, who furnishes his buildings with ivory. When
an earthquake comes and cities are overthrown, the
vigour and wealth of the people are such that they
build more strongly than before.[4] With all this we
have the characteristic tempers and moods of city-
life : the fickleness and liability to panic possible only
where men are in crowds ; the luxury and false art
which are engendered by artificial conditions of life ;
the poverty which in all cities, from the beginning to
the end of time, lurks by the side of the most brilliant
wealth.

[1] xii. 7 (Heb. ver. 8). Trans., *As for Canaan, the balances, etc.*
[2] Amos, *passim*. Hosea viii. 14, etc. ; Micah iii. 10 ; Isa. ix. 10.
[3] ארמון, a word not found in the Pentateuch, Joshua, Judges, or
Samuel, is used in 1 Kings xvi. 18, 2 Kings xv. 25, for a citadel within
the palace of the king. Similarly in Isa. xxv. 2 ; Pro. xviii. 19. But
in Amos generally of any large or grand house. That the name first
appears in the time of Omri's alliance with Tyre, points to a Phœnician
origin. Probably from root ארם, *to be high*.
[4] Isa. ix. 10.

In short, in the half-century between Elisha and Amos, Israel rose from one to another of the great stages of culture. Till the eighth century they had been but a kingdom of fighting shepherds and husbandmen. Under Jeroboam and Uzziah city-life and civilisation, in the proper sense of the word, was developed. Only once before had Israel taken so long a step : when they crossed Jordan, leaving the nomadic life for the agricultural ; and that had been momentous for their religion. They came among new temptations : the use of wine, and the shrines of local gods who were believed to have more influence on the fertility of the land than Yahweh who had conquered it for His people. But this further step, from the agricultural stage to the mercantile and civil, was equally fraught with danger. There was the closer intercourse with foreign nations and their cults. There were all the temptations of rapid wealth, the dangers of an equally increasing poverty. The growth of comfort among the rulers meant the growth of thoughtlessness. The upper classes were lifted away from feeling the woes of the people. There was a well-fed and sanguine patriotism, but at the expense of indifference to social sin and want. Religious zeal and liberality increased, but were coupled with the proud's misunderstanding of God : an optimist faith without moral insight or sympathy.

It is all this which makes the prophets of the eighth century so modern, while Elisha's life is still so ancient. With him we are back in the times of our own border wars—of Wallace and Bruce, with their struggles for the freedom of the soil. With Amos we stand among the conditions of our own day. The City has arisen. For the development of the highest form of prophecy, the universal and permanent form. there was needed

that marvellously unchanging mould of human life,
whose needs and sorrows, whose sins and problems,
are to-day the same as they were those thousands of
years ago.

With Civilisation came Literature. The long peace
gave leisure for writing ; and the just pride of the
people in boundaries broad as Solomon's own, determined that this writing should take the form of
heroic history. In the parallel reigns of Jeroboam and
Uzziah many critics have placed the great epics of
Israel : the earlier documents of our Pentateuch which
trace God's purposes to mankind by Israel, from the
creation of man to the settlement of the Promised
Land ; the histories which contribute to the Books
of Judges, Samuel and Kings. But whether all these
were composed now or earlier, it is certain that the
nation lived in the spirit of them, proud of its past,
aware of its vocation, and confident that its God, who
had created the world and so mightily led itself, would
bring it from victory by victory to a complete triumph
over the heathen. Israel of the eighth century were
devoted to Yahweh; and although passion or self-
interest might lead individuals or even communities to
worship other gods, He had no possible rival upon the
throne of the nation.

As they delighted to recount His deeds by their
fathers, so they thronged the scenes of these with
sacrifice and festival. Bethel and Beersheba, Dan and
Gilgal, were the principal ; [1] but Mispeh, the top of
Tabor,[2] and Carmel,[3] perhaps Penuel,[4] were also conspicuous among the countless *high places* [5] of the land.

---

[1] 1 Kings xii. 28 ff., and Amos and Hosea, *passim.*
[2] Hosea v. 1.   [3] 1 Kings xviii. 30 ff.   [4] 1 Kings xii. 25.
[5] Originally so called from their elevation (though oftener on the
flank than on the summit of a hill) ; but like the name High Street

Of those in Northern Israel Bethel was the chief. It enjoyed the proper site for an ancient shrine, which was nearly always a market as well—near a frontier and where many roads converged ; where traders from the East could meet with traders from the West, the wool-growers of Moab and the Judæan desert with the merchants of Phœnicia and the Philistine coast. Here, on the spot on which the father of the nation had seen heaven open,[1] a great temple was now built, with a priesthood endowed and directed by the crown,[2] but supported also by the tithes and free-will offerings of the people.[3] *It is a sanctuary of the king and a house of the Kingdom.*[4] Jeroboam had ordained Dan, at the other end of the kingdom, to be the fellow of Bethel ; [5] but Dan was far away from the bulk of the people, and in the eighth century Bethel's real rival was Gilgal.[6] Whether this was the Gilgal by Jericho, or either of the other two Gilgals on the Samarian hills —one, the present Jiljiliyeh, near Shiloh, the other, the present Juleijil, on the Makhna plain, one mile east of the foot of Mount Gerizim—is uncertain. One of the latter had been a sanctuary in Elijah's day, with a settlement of the prophets ; but the former must have proved a great attraction to a people so devoted to the sacred events of their past. Was it not the first

or the Scottish High Kirk, the term came to be dissociated from physical height and was applied to any sanctuary, even in a hollow, like so many of the sacred wells.

[1] The sanctuary itself was probably on the present site of the Burj Beitin (with the ruins of an early Christian Church), some few minutes to the south-east of the present village of Beitin, which probably represents the city of Bethel that was called Luz at the first.

[2] I Kings xii. 25 ff. ; Amos vii.

[3] Amos iv. 4.   [4] Amos vii. 13.   [5] I Kings xii. 25 ff.

[6] Curiously enough conceived by many of the early Christian Fathers as containing the second of the calves. Cyril, *Comm. in Hoseam*, 5 : Epiph., *De Vitis Proph.*, 237 ; *Chron. Pasc.*, 161.

resting-place of the Ark after the passage of Jordan, the scene of the reinstitution of circumcision, of the anointing of the first king, of Judah's second submission to David ? [1] As there were many Gilgals in the land—literally *cromlechs*, ancient *stone-circles* sacred to the Canaanites as well as to Israel—so there were many Miṣpehs, *Watch-towers*, *Seers' stations :* the one mentioned by Hosea was probably in Gilead. [2] To the southern Beersheba, to which Elijah had fled from Jezebel, pilgrimages were made by northern Israelites traversing Judah. The sanctuary on Carmel was the ancient altar of Yahweh which Elijah had rebuilt ; but Carmel seems at this time to have lain, as it did so often, in the power of the Phœnicians, for it is imagined by the prophets only as a hiding-place from the face of Yahweh. [3]

At all these sanctuaries it was Yahweh and no other who was sought : *thy God, O Israel, which brought thee up out of the land of Egypt.* [4] At Bethel and at Dan He was adored in the form of a calf ; probably at Gilgal also, for there is a strong tradition to that effect ; [5] and elsewhere men still consulted the other images which had been used by Saul and by David : the Ephod and the Teraphim. [6] With these there was the old Semitic

---

[1] Josh. iv. 20 ff., v. 2-10, etc. ; 1 Sam. xi. 14, 15, xiii. 4, 7 ; 2 Sam. xix. 15, 40. This Gilgal by Jericho fell to N. Israel after the Disruption ; but there is nothing in Amos or Hosea to tell us, whether it or either of the Gilgals in the Samarian highlands, which seem to have absorbed the sanctity of the latter, is the shrine which they couple with Bethel —except that they never talk of *going up* to it. The passage from Epiphanius cited in the previous note speaks of the Gilgal with the calf as the ' Gilgal which is in Shiloh.' On all these three Gilgals see the present writer's article ' Gilgal,' in the *Enc. Bibl.*

[2] Site uncertain. See *Hist. Geog.*, pp. 579, 586.

[3] Amos ix. 3. But cf. i. 2.   [4] 1 Kings xii. 28.

[5] See above, p. 34, n. 6.

[6] The Ephod, *the plated thing ;* presumably a wooden image covered either with a skin of metal or a cloak of metal. The Teraphim were images in human shape.

symbol of the Maṣṣebah, or upright stone on which oil was poured.[1] All had been used in the worship of Yahweh by the examples and leaders of the past ; all had been spared by Elijah and Elisha : it was no wonder that the common people of the eighth century felt them to be indispensable elements of religion, the removal of which, like that of the monarchy or of sacrifice would mean divorce from the nation's God.[2]

One exception must be made. Compared with the sanctuaries we have mentioned, Ṣion itself was modern. But it contained the main repository of Israel's religion, the Ark, and in connection with the Ark the worship of Yahweh was not a worship of images. It is significant that from this, the original sanctuary of Israel, with a pure worship, the new prophecy derived its first inspiration. But to that we shall return later with Amos.[3] Apart from the Ark, Jerusalem was not free from images, nor even from the altars of foreign deities.

Where the externals of the ritual were thus so much the same as those of the Canaanite cults, still practised in and around the land, it is not surprising that the worship of the God of Israel should be invaded by pagan practices, or that Yahweh Himself should be regarded with imaginations steeped in pagan ideas of the Godhead. That even the foulest tempers of the

[1] The *menhir* of modern Palestine—not a hewn pillar, but oblong natural stone narrowing a little towards the top (cf. W. R. Smith, *Religion of the Semites*, pp. 183–188). From Hosea x. 1, 2, it would appear that the maṣṣeboth of the eighth century were artificial. *They make good* maṣṣeboth (A.V. wrongly *images*).

[2] So indeed Hosea iii. 4 implies. The Asherah, the pole or symbolic tree of Canaanite worship, does not appear to have been used as a part of the ritual of Yahweh's worship. But, that there was constantly a temptation so to use it, is clear from Deut. xvi. 21, 22. See Driver on that passage, or my *Deuteronomy* (Camb. Bible).

[3] See below, p. 79.

Canaanite ritual, those inspired by wine and the sexual
passion, were licensed in the sanctuaries of Israel,
both Amos and Hosea testify. But the worst of the
evil was wrought in the popular conception of God.
Let us remember again that Yahweh had no real
rival at this time in the devotion of His people, and
that their faith was expressed both by the legal forms
of His religion and by a liberality which exceeded these.
The tithes were paid to Him, and paid, it would appear,
with more than legal frequency.[1] Sabbath and New
Moon, as days of worship and rest from business,
were observed with a Pharisaic scrupulousness for the
letter if not for the spirit.[2] The prescribed festivals
were held and thronged by zealous devotees who
rivalled each other in the amount of their free-will
offerings.[3] Pilgrimages were made to Bethel, to Gilgal,
to far Beersheba, and the very way to the latter appeared as sacred to the Israelite as the way to Mecca
does to a pious Moslem of to-day.[4] Yet, in spite of
this devotion to their God, Israel had not true ideas
of Him. To quote Amos, they sought His sanctuaries,
but Him they did not seek ; in the words of Hosea's
frequent plaint, they *did not know Him*. To the mass
of the people, to their governors, their priests, and
the most of their prophets, Yahweh was but the characteristic Semitic deity—patron of His people, and caring
for them alone—who had helped them in the past, and
was bound to help them still—jealous as to the correct-
ness of His ritual and the amount of His sacrifices,
but indifferent about morality. Nay, there were still
darker streaks in their views of Him. A god, figured
as an ox, could not be adored by a cattle-breeding
people without starting in their minds thoughts too

---

[1] Amos iv. 4 ff.
[2] Amos viii. 5 ; cf. 2 Kings iv. 23.
[3] Amos iv. 4 f.
[4] See below, p. 194.

akin to the tempers of the Canaanite faiths. These things it is almost a shame to mention ; but without knowing that they fermented in the life of that generation, we shall not appreciate the vehemence of Amos or of Hosea.

Such a religion had no discipline for the mercenary life of the day. Injustice and fraud were rife in the precincts of the sanctuary. Magistrates and priests alike were smitten with their generation's love of money, and did everything for reward. Again and again the prophets speak of bribery. Judges took gifts and perverted the cause of the poor ; priests drank the mulcted wine, and slept on the pledged garments of religious offenders. There was no disinterested service of God or of the commonweal. The influence of the commercial character of the age appears in another very remarkable result. An agricultural community is always sensitive to the religion of nature. They are awed by its chastisements—droughts, famines, and earthquakes. They feel its majestic order in the course of the seasons, the procession of day and night, the march of the great stars, all the host of the Lord of Hosts. But Amos seems to have had to break into passionate reminders of Him that maketh Orion and the Pleiades, and turneth the murk into morning.[1] Several physical calamities visited the land. The locusts are bad in Palestine every sixth or seventh year : one year before Amos began they had been very bad. There was a monstrous drought, followed by a famine. There was a long-remembered earthquake—*the earthquake in the days of Uzziah.* With Egypt so near, the home of the plague, and with much war afoot in Northern Syria, there were probably

---

[1] But whether these be by Amos, see Ch. XI.

more pestilences in Western Asia than those recorded in 80ż, 765 and 759. A total eclipse of the sun took place in 763. But of all these, except perhaps the pestilence, a commercial people are more independent than an agricultural. Israel speedily recovered from them, without any moral improvement. Even when the earthquake came *they said in pride and stoutness of heart, The bricks are fallen down, but we will build with hewn stones ; the sycomores are cut down, but we will change to cedars*.[1]   It was a marvellous generation— so joyous, so energetic, so patriotic, so worshipful ! But its strength was the strength of cruel wealth, its peace the peace of an immoral religion.

I have said that the age is very modern, and we shall indeed go to its prophets feeling that they speak to conditions of life not unlike our own. But if we wish a closer analogy from our history, we must travel back to the fourteenth century in England—Langland's and Wyclif's century, which, like this one in Israel, saw both the first real attempts towards a national literature, and the first real attempts towards moral and religious reform. Then as in Israel a long victorious reign was drawing to a close, under the threat of disaster when it should have passed. Then as in Israel there had been droughts, earthquakes and pestilences with no moral effect upon the nation. Then also city life was developing at the expense of country life. Then also the wealthy began to draw aloof from the people. Then also there was a national religion, zealously culti- vated and endowed by the liberality of the people, but superstitious, mercenary, and corrupted by sexual disorder. Then too were many pilgrimages to popular shrines, and the land was rife with mendicant priests

[1] Isa. ix. 10.

and hireling preachers. And then too prophecy raised its voice, for the first time fearless in England. As we study the verses of Amos we shall find exact parallels to them in the verses of Langland's *Vision of Piers the Plowman*, which denounce the same vices in Church and State, and enforce the same principles of religion and morality.

It was when the reign of Jeroboam was at its height of assured victory, when the nation's prosperity seemed impregnable after the recovery from those physical calamities, when the worship and the commerce were in full course throughout the land, that the first of the new prophets broke out against Israel in the name of Yahweh, threatening judgement alike upon the new civilisation of which they were so proud and the old religion in which they were so confident. These prophets were inspired by feelings of the purest morality, by the passionate conviction that God could no longer bear such impurity and disorder. But, as we have seen, no prophet in Israel ever worked on the basis of principles only. He came always in alliance with events. These first appeared in the shape of the great physical disasters. But a more powerful instrument of Providence, in the service of judgement, was appearing on the horizon. This was the Assyrian Empire. So vast was its influence on prophecy that we must devote to it a separate chapter.

CHAPTER IV

THE INFLUENCE OF ASSYRIA UPON PROPHECY

BY far the greatest event in the eighth century before Christ was the appearance of Assyria in Palestine. To Israel, since the Exodus and Conquest, nothing had happened capable of so enormous an influence at once upon their national fortunes and their religious development. But while the Exodus and Conquest had advanced the political and spiritual progress of Israel in equal proportion, the effect of the Assyrian invasion was to divorce these two interests, and destroy the state while it refined and confirmed the religion. After permitting the Northern Kingdom to reach an extent and splendour unrivalled since the days of Solomon, Assyria overthrew it in 721 and left all Israel scarcely a third of their former magnitude. But while Assyria proved so disastrous to the state, her influence upon the prophecy of the period was little short of creative. Humanly speaking, this highest stage of Israel's religion could not have been achieved by the prophets except in alliance with the armies of that heathen empire. Before we turn to their pages it may be well for us to make clear in what directions Assyria performed this service for Israel. While pursuing this inquiry we may be able to find answers to the scarcely less important questions : why the prophets were at first doubtful of the part

Assyria was destined to play in the providence of the Almighty ? and why, when the prophets were at last convinced of the certainty of Israel's overthrow, the statesmen of Israel and the bulk of the people still remained unconcerned about her coming, or sanguine of their power to resist her ? This requires, to begin with, a summary of the details of the Assyrian advance upon Palestine.

In the far past Palestine had often been the hunting-ground of the Assyrian kings. But after 1100 B.C., and for nearly two centuries and a half, her states were left to themselves—and to Egypt. Then Assyria resumed the task of breaking down that disbelief in her power with which her long withdrawal seems to have inspired their politics. In 870 Assurnasirpal reached the Levant, and took tribute from Tyre and Sidon. Omri was reigning in Samaria, and must have come into close relations with the Assyrians, for during more than a century and a half after his death they still called the land of Israel by his name.[1] In 854 Shalmaneser II defeated at Karkar the combined forces of Ahab and Benhadad. In 850, 849, and 846 he conducted campaigns against Damascus. In 842 he received tribute from Jehu,[2] and in 839 again fought Damascus under Hazael. After this there passed a whole generation during which Assyria came no farther south than Arpad, some sixty miles north of Damascus ; and Hazael employed the respite in those campaigns which proved so disastrous for Israel, by robbing her of the provinces across Jordan, and ravaging the country about Samaria.[3] In 803 Assyria returned,

[1] Bit-Ḫumria = Beth-'Omri, ' the house of Omri ' : so even in Sargon's time, 722–705. See *K.A.T.*[3], 59, 247, 265.

[2] The Black Obelisk of Shalmaneser in the British Museum, on which the messengers of Jehu are portrayed.

[3] 2 Kings x. 32 f. ; xiii. 3.

and accomplished the siege and capture of Damascus.
The first consequence to Israel was that restoration
of her hopes under Joash, at which the aged Elisha
was still spared to assist,[1] and which reached its fulfilment in the recovery of all Eastern Palestine by
Jeroboam II.[2] Jeroboam's own relations to Assyria
have not been recorded either by the Bible or by the
Assyrian monuments.   It is hard to think that he paid
no tribute to the ' king of kings.'   At all events it
is certain that, while Assyria again overthrew the
Arameans of Damascus in 773 and their neighbours
of Hadrach in 772 and 765, Jeroboam was himself
invading Aramean land, and the Book of Kings even
attributes to him an extension of territory, or at least
of political influence, up to the northern mouth of
the great pass between the Lebanons.[3] For the next
twenty years Assyria only once came as far as Lebanon
—to Arpad and Hadrach in 754—and it may have been
this long quiescence which enabled the rulers and people
of Israel to forget, if indeed their religion and sanguine
patriotism had ever allowed them to realise, how much
the conquests and splendour of Jeroboam's reign were
due, not to themselves, but to the heathen power which
had maimed their oppressors.   Their dreams were brief.
Before Jeroboam himself was dead, a new king had
usurped the Assyrian throne (745 B.C.) and inaugurated
a more vigorous policy.   Borrowing the name of the
ancient Tiglath-Pileser, he followed that conqueror's
path across the Euphrates.   At first it seemed as if he
was to suffer check.   His forces were engrossed by the

[1] 2 Kings xiii. 14 ff.
[2] The phrase in 2 Kings xiii. 5, *Yahweh gave Israel a saviour*, is interpreted by certain scholars as if the saviour were Assyria.   In xiv. 27 he is
plainly said to be Jeroboam.
[3] The entering in of Hamath (2 Kings xiv. 25).

siege of Arpad for three years (c. 743), and this delay, along with that of two years more, during which he had to return to the conquest of Babylon, may well have given cause to the courts of Damascus and Samaria to believe that the Assyrian power had not revived.   Combining, they attacked Judah under Ahaz But Ahaz appealed to Tiglath-Pileser, who within a year (734–733) overthrew Damascus and carried captive the populations of Gilead and Galilee.   There could now be no doubt as to what the Assyrian power meant for the political fortunes of Israel.   Before this resistless empire, the people of Yahweh were as the most frail of their neighbours—sure of defeat, and sure, too, of that terrible captivity in exile which formed the novel policy of the invaders against the tribes who withstood them. Northern Israel dared to withstand.   The vassal Hoshea, whom the Assyrians had placed on the throne of Samaria in 730, kept back his tribute.   The people rallied to him ; and for more than three years this little tribe of highlanders resisted in their capital the Assyrian siege. Then came the end.   Samaria fell in 721, and Israel went into captivity beyond the Euphrates.

In following the course of this tragedy, the heart cannot but feel that *all* the splendour and the glory did not lie with the prophets, in spite of their being the only actors in the drama who perceived its moral issues and predicted its actual end.   Who can withhold admiration from those few tribesmen, who accepted no defeat as final, but so long as they were left to their fatherland rallied their ranks and defied the huge empire.   Nor was their courage always as blind, as in the time of Isaiah Samaria's so fatally became.   For one cannot fail to notice, how fitful and irregular was Assyria's advance, at least up to the reign of Tiglath-Pileser ; or how prolonged and doubtful were her

sieges of some of the towns. The Assyrians themselves
do not always record spoil or tribute after what they
call their victories in Palestine. To the same campaign
they had often to return for several years in succession.[1]
It took Tiglath-Pileser himself three years to reduce
Arpad; Shalmaneser IV besieged Samaria for three
years, and was slain before it yielded. These facts
enable us to understand that, apart from the moral
reasons which the prophets urged for the certainty
of Israel's overthrow by Assyria, it was possible that
Assyria would not come back, and that while she was
engaged with other portions of her huge and disorganised
empire, a combined revolution of her Assyrian vassals
would be successful. The prophets themselves felt
these chances. They were not always confident, as we
shall see, that Assyria was to be the means of Israel's
overthrow. Amos, and in his earlier years Isaiah,
describe her with a cautious vagueness for which there
is no other explanation than the political uncertainty
that hung over the future of her advance upon Syria.
If, then, even in those high minds, to whom the moral
issue was clear, the political form which that issue
would assume was yet temporarily uncertain, what
reason must the mere statesmen of Syria have often
felt for the security which filled the intervals between
the Assyrian invasions, or the sanguine hopes which
inspired their resistance to these.

We must not cast over the Assyrian advance the
triumphant air of the annals of such kings as Tiglath-
Pileser or Sennacherib. Campaigning in Palestine was
dangerous even to the Romans; and for the Assyrian
armies there was possible besides some sudden recall
by the rumour of a revolt in a distant province. Their

[1] Shalmaneser II in 850, 849, 846 to war against Dad'idri or Hadad-
ezer of Damascus, and in 842 and 839 against Hazael, his successor.

own annals supply us with good reasons for the resistance offered to them by the tribes of Palestine. No
defeat, of course, is recorded ; but the annals are full
of delays and withdrawals. Then the Plague would
break out ; we know how in the last year of the century it turned Sennacherib, and saved Jerusalem.[1] In
short, up almost to the end the Syrian chiefs had
fair reasons for resistance to a power which had often
defeated them ; while at the very end, when no such
reason remained and our political sympathy is exhausted, we feel it replaced by an even warmer admiration for their desperate defence. Mere mountain-cats
of tribes as some of them were, they held their poorly
furnished rocks against one, two or three years of siege.

In Israel these political reasons for courage against
Assyria were enforced by the instincts of the popular
religion. The century had felt a new outburst of enthusiasm for Yahweh.[2] This was consequent, not only
upon the victories over Aram, but upon the literature
of the peace which followed those victories : the collection of the stories of the ancient miracles of Yahweh
in the beginning of His people's history, and of
His purpose of bringing Israel to supreme rank in
the world. Such a God, so anciently manifested, so
recently proved, could never surrender His nation to
a mere Goî [3]—a heathen people. Add this dogma of
the popular religion of Israel to those substantial hopes
of Assyria's withdrawal from Palestine, and you see
cause for the complacency of Jeroboam and his people
to the fact that Assyria had at last, by the fall of
Damascus, reached their own borders, as well as for
the courage with which Hoshea in 725 threw off the

[1] See in this series *Isaiah*, vol. i, pp. 374 ff.
[2] See above, pp. 33 ff.
[3] To use the term which Amos adopts with such ironical force : vi. 14.

Assyrian yoke, and, with a willing people, for three years defended Samaria against the great king. Let us not think that the opponents of the prophets were fools or puppets of fate. They had reasons for their optimism ; they fought for their hearths and altars with a valour and patience which proves that the nation as a whole was not so corrupt, as we are sometimes, by the language of the prophets, tempted to suppose.

But all these—the reasonableness of the hope of resisting Assyria, the valour which stubbornly fought her, the religious faith which sanctioned both valour and hope—the more vividly illustrate the independence of the prophets, who took an opposite view, who consistently affirmed that Israel must fall, and foretold that she should fall to Assyria.

The reason of this conviction was, of course, a fundamental faith in the righteousness of their God. That was a belief independent of the course of events. As a matter of history, the ethical reasons for Israel's doom were manifest to the prophets within Israel's own life, before the signs grew clear on the horizon that the doomster was to be Assyria.[1] We may go further, and say that it could not possibly have been otherwise. For except the prophets had been previously furnished with the ethical reasons for Assyria's resistless advance on Israel, that advance must have been to them a paralysing problem. But they nowhere treat it as a problem. By them Assyria is always either welcomed as a proof or summoned as a means

---

[1] When we get down among the details we shall see evidence for this fact, that Amos prophesied against Israel at a time when he thought that the Lord's anger was to be exhausted in natural chastisements of His people, and before it was revealed to him that Assyria was required to follow up these chastisements with a heavier blow.   See Ch. VI, section 2

—the proof of their conviction that Israel requires humbling, the means of effecting that humiliation. The faith of the prophets is ready for Assyria from the moment that she becomes ominous for Israel, and every footfall of her armies on Yahweh's soil becomes the corroboration of the purpose He has already declared to His servants in the terms of their moral consciousness. The spiritual service which the advance of Assyria rendered to Israel was therefore secondary to the prophets' native convictions of the righteousness of God, and could not have been performed without these. This will become more clear if we look at the exact nature of that service.

In its broadest effects, the Assyrian invasion meant for Israel a considerable change in the intellectual outlook. Hitherto Israel's world had virtually lain between the borders promised of old to their ambition —*the river of Egypt,*[1] *and the great river, the River Euphrates*. These had marked not merely the sphere of Israel's politics, but the horizon within which Israel had been accustomed to observe the action of their God and to prove His character, to feel the problems of their religion rise and to grapple with them. But now from the outside of this little world there burst that awful power, sovereign and inexorable, which effaced all distinctions and treated Israel in the same manner as her heathen neighbours. This was more than a widening of the world : it was a change of the poles. At first sight it appeared merely to have increased the scale on which history was conducted ; it was really an alteration of the whole character of history. Religion itself shrivelled up, before a force so much vaster than anything it had yet encountered, and so

[1] That is, of course, not the Nile, but the great Wady, at present known as the Wady el 'Arish, which divides Palestine from Egypt

contemptuous of its claims. *What is Yahweh,* said the Assyrian in his laughter, *more than the gods of Damascus, or of Hamath, or of the Philistines ?* In fact, for the mind of Israel, the crisis, though less in degree, was in quality not unlike that produced in the religion of Europe by the revelation of the Copernican astronomy. As the earth, previously believed to be the centre of the universe, the stage on which the Son of God had achieved God's eternal purposes to mankind, was discovered to be but a satellite of one of innumerable suns, a mere ball swung beside millions of others by a force which betrayed no sympathy with the great transactions that took place on it, and thus faith in the Divine worth of these was rudely shaken—so Israel, who had believed themselves to be the peculiar people of the Creator, the interpreters of the God of Righteousness to all mankind,[1] and who now felt themselves brought to an equality with other tribes by this sheer force, which, indifferent to spiritual distinctions, swayed the fortunes of all alike, must have been tempted to unbelief in the spiritual facts of their history, in the power of their God and the destiny He had promised them. Nothing could have saved Israel, as nothing could have saved Europe, but a conception of God which rose to this new demand upon its powers—a faith which said : ' Our God is sufficient for this greater world and its forces that dwarf our own ; the discovery of these only excites in us a more awful wonder of His power.' The prophets had such a conception of God. To them He was absolute righteousness—righteousness wide as the world, stronger than the strongest force. To the prophets, therefore, the rise of Assyria increased the possibilities of Providence. But it could

[1] So already in the JE narratives of the Pentateuch.

not have done this had Providence not already been invested by their faith in a God mighty by His character to rise to such possibilities.

Assyria, however, was not only Force : she was also the symbol of a great Idea—the Idea of Unity. We have just ventured on one historical analogy. We may try another and a more exact one. The Empire of Rome, grasping the world and reducing all races of men to much the same level of political rights, powerfully assisted Christian theology in imposing upon the human mind a clearer imagination of unity in the government of the world and of spiritual equality among men of all nations. Not dissimilar service to the faith of Israel was performed by the Empire of Assyria. History, that hitherto had been but a series of angry pools, became as the ocean, swaying in tides to one almighty impulse. It was far easier to imagine a sovereign Providence when Assyria reduced history to a unity by overthrowing all the rulers and all their gods, than when history was broken up into the independent fortunes of many states, each with its own religion valid only in its own territory. By shattering the tribes Assyria shattered the tribal theory of religion, which we have seen to be the characteristic Semitic theory—a god for every tribe, a tribe for every god. The field was cleared of the many ; there was room for the One. That He appeared, not as the God of the conquering race, but as the Deity of one of their many victims, was due to Yahweh's righteousness. At this juncture, when one throne was suggested for the world and that throne was empty, there was a great chance, if we may so put it, for a god with a character. And the only God in the Semitic world who had a character was Yahweh.

It is true that the Assyrian Empire was not constructive, like the Roman, and, therefore, could not assist the prophets to the idea of a Catholic Church. But there can be no doubt that it did assist them to a feeling of the moral unity of mankind. A great historian has made the just remark that, whatsoever widens the imagination, enabling it to realise the actual experience of other men, is a powerful agent of ethical advance.[1] Now Assyria widened the imagination and the sympathy of Israel in precisely this way. Consider the universal Pity of the Assyrian conquest : how state after state went down before it, how all things mortal yielded and were swept away. The mutual hatreds and ferocities of men could not persist before a common Fate, so sublime, so tragic. And thus we understand how in Israel the old envies and rancours of that border warfare with her foes which had filled the last four centuries of her history are mitigated by a tenderness and compassion towards the national efforts, the achievements and all the busy life of the Gentile peoples. Isaiah is especially distinguished by this in his treatment of Egypt and of Tyre ; and even where he and others do not, as in these cases, appreciate the sadness of the destruction of so much brave beauty and serviceable wealth, their tone in speaking of the fall of the Assyrian on their neighbours is one more of compassion than of exultation.[2] As the rivalries and hatreds of individuals are stilled in the presence of death, so even that factious, ferocious world of the Semites ceased to *fret its anger and watch it for ever* (to quote Amos' phrase) in face of the universal Assyrian Fate. But in that Fate there was more than

Lecky, *History of European Morals*, I.
[1] The present writer has already pointed out this with regard to Egypt and Phœnicia in *Isaiah*, I, Chs. XXII and XXIII, and with regard to Philistia in *Hist. Geog.*, p. 178.

Pity. On the data of the prophets Assyria was afflicting
Israel for moral reasons : it could not be for other
reasons that she was afflicting their neighbours. Israel
and the heathen were suffering for the same righteousness' sake. What could have better illustrated the
moral equality of all mankind ! No doubt the prophets were already theoretically convinced[1] of this—
for the righteousness they believed in was nothing
if not universal. But it is one thing to hold a belief
on principle and another to have practical experience
of it in history. To a theory of the moral equality
of mankind Assyria enabled the prophets to add sympathy and conscience. We shall see all this illustrated
in the opening prophecies of Amos against the foreign
nations.

But Assyria did not help to develop monotheism in
Israel only by contributing to the doctrines of a moral
Providence and of the equality of all men beneath it.
The influence must have extended to Israel's conception
of God in Nature. Here, of course, Israel was already
possessed of great beliefs. Yahweh had created man ;
He had divided the Red Sea and Jordan. The desert,
the storm, and the seasons were subject to Him. But
at a time when the superstitious mind of the people
was still feeling after other Divine powers in the earth,
the waters and the air of Canaan, it was a valuable
antidote to such dissipation of their faith to find one
God swaying, through Assyria, all families of mankind.
The Divine unity to which history was reduced must
have reacted on Israel's views of Nature, and made
it easier to feel one God also there. Now, as a matter

[1] I put it this way only for the sake of making the logic clear ; for
it is a mistake to say that the prophets at any time held merely theoretic
convictions. All their conviction was really experimental—never held
apart from some illustration or proof of principle in actual history.

of fact, the imagination of the unity of Nature, the belief in a reason and method pervading all things, was powerfully advanced in Israel throughout the Assyrian period.

We may find an illustration of this in the greater, deeper meaning in which the prophets use the old national name of Israel's God—Yahweh Seba'oth, *Yahweh of Hosts.* This title, which came into frequent use under the early kings, when Israel's vocation was to win freedom by war, meant then (as far as we can gather) only *Yahweh of the armies of Israel*—the God of battles, the people's leader in war,[1] whose home was Jerusalem, the people's capital, and His sanctuary their battle emblem, the Ark. Now the prophets hear

---

[1] יהוה צבאות: 1 Sam. i. 3 ; iv. 4 ; xvii. 45, where it is explained by the parallel phrase *God of the armies of Israel ;* 2 Sam. vi. 2, where it is connected with Israel's battle emblem, the Ark ; and so throughout Samuel and Kings, and also Chronicles, the Psalms and some prophets. The plural צבאות is never used in the Old Testament except of human hosts, and generally of the armies or hosts of Israel. The theory therefore which sees the same meaning in the Divine title is probably the correct one. It was first put forward by Herder (*Geist der Eb. Poesie*, ii. 84, 85), and after some neglect it has been revived by Kautzsch (*Z.A.T.W.*, vi. ff.) and Stade (*Gesch.*, i. 437, *n.* 3). The alternatives are that the hosts originally meant those of heaven, either the angels (so, among others, Ewald, *Hist.*, Eng. Ed., iii. 62) or the stars (so Delitzsch, Kuenen, Baudissin, Cheyne (*Prophecies of Isaiah*, i. 11). In the former of these two there is some force ; but the reason given for the latter, that the name came to the front in Israel when the people were being drawn into connection with star-worshipping nations, especially Aram, seems baseless. Israel had not been long in touch with Aram in Saul's time, yet even then the name is accepted as if one of much earlier origin. A clear account of the argument on the other side to that taken in this note will be found in Smend, *Alttestamentliche Religionsgeschichte*, pp. 185 ff. But see especially Kautzsch, *Enc. Bibl.*, art. ' Names,' § 123 : ' The most probable conclusion is that in prophetic usage Yahwe Sebaôth—agreeably to its original meaning [the armies of Israel]— suggested in the first place the angelic hosts of war, but that finally the starry host, as the grandest proof of divine omnipotence and infinity, prevailed.'

Yahweh go forth (as Amos does) from the same place. but to them the Name has a far deeper significance. They never define it, but they use it in associations where *Hosts* must mean something different from the armies of Israel. To Amos the hosts of Yahweh are not the armies of Israel, but those of Assyria : they are also the nations whom He marshals and marches across the earth, Philistines from Caphtor, Aram from Kir, as well as Israel from Egypt. Nay, more ; according to those Doxologies which either Amos or a kindred spirit has added to his lofty argument,[1] Yahweh sways and orders the powers of the heavens : Orion and Pleiades, the clouds from the sea to the mountain peaks where they break, day and night in constant procession. It is in associations like these that the Name is used, either in its old form or slightly changed as *Yahweh God of Hosts*, or *the Hosts ;* and we cannot but feel that the hosts of Yahweh are now looked upon as all the influences of earth and heaven—human armies, stars and powers of nature, which obey His word and work His will.[2]

[1] See below, Ch. XI.

[2] This general meaning is supported by the LXX renderings of the name ' Lord of the powers ' (κύριος τῶν δυνάμεων) or ' Almighty God (ὁ θεὸς ὁ παντοκράτωρ) or ' Lord Almighty ' (κύριος παντοκράτωρ).

AMOS

' Towers in the distance, like an earth-born Atlas . . . such a man in such a historical position, standing on the confines of light and darkness, like day on the misty mountain-tops.'

CHAPTER V

THE BOOK OF AMOS

THE genuineness of the bulk of the Book of Amos
is accepted by virtually all critics. When this
volume was first published in 1896, the only passages
of the Book (besides the title) which were suspected
as interpolations were the three references to Judah,
the three famous outbreaks in praise of the might
of Yahweh the Creator, the final prospect of a hope
that does not gleam in any other part of the book,
and the judgements on Tyre and Edom with other
clauses alleged to reflect a stage of history later than
that in which Amos worked. But since 1896 critics
have also suspected or denied the authenticity of the
Exordium to the prophecies, of the judgement on the
Philistine cities, and of other scattered verses held to
reflect a later stage of the history or the language
or the theology of Israel, or to be mere expansions of,
or glosses on, the original.[1]   And some of these criticisms

---

[1] The full list of questioned or rejected passages is this : (1) References
to Judah—ii. 4, 5 ; (iii. 1b, *the whole family*) ; vi. 1, in *Sion ;* ix., 11, 12
(2) The three outbreaks of Praise of the Creator—iv. 13 ; v. 8, 9 ; ix.
5, 6.   (3) The Final Hope—ix. 8–15, including vv. 11, 12 already mentioned.   (4) Other passages alleged to reflect a later stage either of the
language or the history, or the theology of Israel—i. 2, 6–12 ; iii. 7, 14b ;
v. 26 ; vi. 2, 14 ; viii. 11–14.   (5) Other alleged expansions or glosses
in ii. 10, 12, 14 f. ; iii. 1, 3 ; iv. 7 f., 10 ; v. 6, 13, 16, 22 ; vi. 9–11a ;
vii. *d.* 1 ; viii. 6, 8, 13, etc.

are supported by reasons drawn from the metrical structure of the verses with which they deal; the study of which structure has been greatly developed since 1896. But each of all these questions can be discussed separately as we reach the verse which it concerns, and we may now pass to consider the general course of the prophecy which is independent of them.

The Book of Amos consists of Three Groups of Oracles, under one title, which is evidently meant to cover them all.

The title runs as follows :—

> Words of 'Amos—who was among the herdsmen from Tekôa'—which he saw concerning Israel in the days of 'Uzziah king of Judah, and in the days of Yarob'am son of Yoash,[1] king of Israel : two years before the earthquake.

That this title is composite and of gradual construction has been argued from its fulness ; from its two relative clauses of which the first is clearly an intrusion between *the words of Amos* and the second, *which he saw ;* from the awkward position of *from Tekoa'* which more naturally follows *Amos* than *shepherds ;* and from the curious date, *two years before the earthquake,* which implies that the earthquake predicted by Amos, viii. 8, ix. 5, was already past, perhaps a considerable time.[2] Though many judge the full title to be post-exilic, this

---

[1] So designated to distinguish him from the first Jeroboam, the son of Nebat.

[2] This line of argument started by Hoffmann (*Z.A.T.W.*, 1883, p. 123) has been developed by König (*Einleitung*, 307), Budde (*Semitic Studies in Memory of A. Kohut*, 1897), Nowack, Löhr, Cheyne, Marti, Duhm, W. Cossmann (*Z.A.T.W.*, Beiheft 29, 1915), and others. Duhm (*Z.A.T.W.*, 1911, p. 1) supposes a biography of Amos as a possible source of the data in the title. Budde (*Z.A.T.W.*, Beiheft 27, 1914) argues that these data were drawn from the original opening of the fragmentary narrative, vii. 10–17, which he holds originally stood at the beginning of the book. See below, p. 69.

is very far from clear. An earlier date is perfectly possible, and Wellhausen gives some reason for supposing it to be by a contemporary (or near contemporaries ?) of Amos. But whatever its date or dates may have been, the title is 'entirely consistent with the contents of the book and is to be accepted as historical.' [1]

The Three Sections, with their contents, are as follows :—

FIRST SECTION : CHAPS. I, II. THE HEATHEN'S CRIMES AND ISRAEL'S

A series of oracles of similar form, directed against the crimes of all the states of Palestine, and culminating in a detailed denunciation of the social evils of Israel, whose doom is foretold, beneath the same flood of war as shall overwhelm her neighbours.

SECOND SECTION : CHAPS. III–VI. ISRAEL'S CRIMES AND DOOM

A series of various oracles of denunciation, which have no further logical connection than is supplied by a general sameness of subject, and a perceptible increase of detail and articulateness from beginning to end of the section. They are usually grouped according to the recurrence of the formula *Hear this word*, which stands at the head of our present chaps. iii, iv and v ; and by the two cries of *Woe* at v. 18 and vi. 1. But even more obvious than these commencements are the various climaxes to which they lead. These are all threats of judgement, each more strenuous or explicit than the one that has preceded it : iii. 15, iv. 3, iv. 12, v. 17, v. 27 and vi. 14 ; and according to them the oracles may be divided into six groups.

1. iii. 1–15. After the main theme of judgement is stated in 1, 2, we have in 3–8 a parenthesis on the prophet's right to threaten doom ; after which 9–15, following directly on 2, emphasise the social disorder, threaten the land with invasion, the people with extinction and the overthrow of their civilisation.

[1] Harper, *in loco*.

2. iv. 1–3, beginning *Hear this word*, is against women **and** describes the siege of the capital and their captivity.

3. iv. 4–12, with no opening formula, contrasts the people's vain propitiation of God by ritual with His treatment of them by physical chastisements—drought, blight, and locusts, pestilence, earthquake—and summons them to prepare for another, unnamed, visitation. *Yahweh God of Hosts is His Name*.

4. v. 1–17, beginning with the formula *Hear this word*, and a dirge over a vision of the nation's defeat, attacks, like the previous group, the lavish ritual, sets in contrast Yahweh's demands for justice and civic purity ; and, offering a reprieve if Israel will repent, closes with the prospect of an universal mourning (vv. 16, 17), which, though introduced by a *therefore*, has no logical connection with what precedes it.

5. v. 18–26 is the first of the two groups that open with *Woe*. Affirming that the eagerly expected *Day of Yahweh* will be darkness and disaster on disaster inevitable (18–20), it again emphasises God's desire for righteousness rather than worship (21–26), and closes with the threat of captivity beyond Damascus. *Yahweh God of Hosts is His Name*, as at the close of 3.

6. vi. 1–14. The second *Woe*, on them *that are at ease in Ṣion* (1, 2) : a satire on the rich and their indifference to the national suffering (3–6) : captivity must come, with the desolation of the land (7–10) ; and the prophet reiterates a downfall of the nation because of its perversity. *A Nation* —needless to name it !—will oppress Israel from Hamath to the River of the Arabah.

THIRD SECTION : CHAPS. VII–IX. VISIONS WITH INTERLUDES

The Visions betray traces of development ; but they are interrupted by a piece of narrative and addresses on the same themes as chaps. iii–vi. The FIRST TWO VISIONS (vii. 1–6) are of disasters—locusts and drought—in the realm of nature ; they are averted by prayer from Amos. The THIRD (7–9) is in the sphere not of nature, but history : Yahweh, standing with a plumbline, as if to show the nation's fabric to be utterly twisted, announces that it shall be overthrown, and that the dynasty of Jeroboam must be put to the sword. Upon this mention of the king, the first in the book, there starts the NARRATIVE (10–17) of how Amaṣiah, priest at Bethel—obviously upon hearing the prophet's threat—sent word to Jeroboam ; and then (whether before or after getting a reply) proceeded to silence Amos, who, however, reiterates his prediction of doom, again described as captivity in a foreign land, and adds a FOURTH VISION (viii. 1–3), of the Ḳaits or *Summer Fruit*, which suggests Ḳêts, or *End* of the Nation. Here it would seem Amos' discourses at Bethel take end. Then comes viii. 4–6, another exposure of the sins of the rich ; followed by a triple pronouncement of doom (7), again in the terms of physical calamities—earthquake (8), eclipse (9, 10), and famine (11–14), in the last of which the public worship is again attacked. A FIFTH VISION, of the Lord by the Altar commanding to smite (ix. 1), is followed by a powerful threat of the hopelessness of escape from God's punishment (ix. 1b–4) ; the third of the great apostrophes to the might of Yahweh (5, 6) ; another statement of the equality in judgement of Israel with other peoples, and of their utter destruction (7–8a). Then (8b) we meet the first qualification of the hitherto unrelieved sentence of death. Captivity is described, not as doom, but as discipline (9) : the sinners of the people, scoffers at doom, shall die (10). And this seems to leave room for two final oracles of restoration and glory, the only two in the book, which are couched in the exact terms of the promises of later prophecy (11–15) and are by many denied to Amos.

Such is the course of the Book of Amos. To have traced it must have made clear to us the unity of the book,[1] as well as the character of the period to which Amos belonged. But it also furnishes us with evidence towards the answer of such questions as these— whether we can fix an exact date for the whole or any part, and whether we can trace a logical or historical development through the chapters, either as these now stand, or in some such re-arrangement as we saw to be necessary for the authentic prophecies of Isaiah.

Let us take first the simplest of these tasks—to ascertain the general period of the book. Twice—by the title and by the portion of narrative [2]—we are pointed to the

---

[1] Apart from the suspected parentheses already mentioned.
[2] Ch. vii. 10 ff.

reign of Jeroboam II, *circa* 783–743 ; other historical allusions suit the same years. The principalities of Palestine are all standing, except Gath ;[1] but the great northern cloud which carries their doom has risen and is ready to burst. Now Assyria, we have seen, had become fatal to Palestine as early as 854. Infrequent invasions of Syria had followed, in one of which, in 803, Rimmon Nirari III had subjected Tyre and Sidon, besieged Damascus, and received tribute from Israel. So far then as the Assyrian data are concerned, the Book of Amos might have been written early in the reign of Jeroboam. Even then was the storm lowering as he describes it. Even then had the lightning broken over Damascus. There are other symptoms, however, which demand a later date. They seem to imply, not only Uzziah's overthrow of Gath,[2] and Jeroboam's conquest of Moab [3] and of Aram,[4] but that establishment of Israel's political influence from Lebanon to the Dead Sea, which must have taken Jeroboam several years to accomplish. With this agree other features of the prophecy—the sense of political security in Israel, the large increase of wealth, the ample and luxurious buildings, the gorgeous ritual, the easy ability to recover from physical calamities, the consequent care-

[1] And, if vi. 2 be genuine, Hamath.

[2] 2 Chron. xxvi. 6. In the list of the Philistine cities, Amos i. 6–8, Gath does not occur, and in harmony with this in vi. 2 it is said to be overthrown ; see Ch. IX, Section 3.

[3] 2 Kings xiv. 25, *to the sea of the Arabah ;* Amos vi. 14, *to the Wady of the Arabah* or *Arabim*, given in Isa. xv. 7 as the S. border of Moab, probably Wady el Hesy. In Amos ii. 3 the ruler of Moab is called, not king, but שׁוֹפֵט , or regent, such as Jeroboam substituted for the king Moab.

[4] According to Grätz's emendation of vi. 13 : *we have taken Lo-Debar and Karnaim*. Perhaps too in iii. 12, though the verse is very obscure, some settlement of Israelites in Damascus is implied. For Jeroboam's conquest of Aram (2 Kings xiv. 28), see pp. 30, 43.

lessness and pride of the upper classes. All these
imply that the last Syrian invasions of Israel in the
beginning of the century were at least a generation
behind the men into whose careless faces the prophet
hurled his words of doom. During this interval Assyria
had again advanced—in 775, in 773, and in 772.[1] None
of these expeditions, however, had come south of
Damascus, and this, their invariable arrest at some
distance from the proper territory of Israel, may have
further flattered the people's sense of security, though
possibly Jeroboam, like some of his predecessors,
bought his peace by tribute to the emperor. In 765,
when the Assyrians for the second time invaded
Hadrach, in the neighbourhood of Damascus, their
records mention a pestilence, which, both because their
armies were then in Syria, and because the plague
generally spreads over the whole of Western Asia, may
well have been the pestilence mentioned by Amos. In
763 a total eclipse of the sun took place, and is perhaps
implied by the ninth verse of his eighth chapter. If
this double allusion to pestilence and eclipse be correct,
it brings the book down to the middle of the century
and the latter half of Jeroboam's long reign. In 755
the Assyrians came back to Hadrach ; in 754 to Arpad :
with these exceptions Syria was untroubled by them
till after 745. It was probably these quiet years in
which Amos found Israel *at ease in Sion.*[2] If we
went down further, within the more forward policy of
Tiglath-Pileser, who ascended the throne in 745 and
besieged Arpad from 743 to 740, we should find an
occasion for the urgency with which Amos warns Israel
that the invasion of her land and the overthrow of

---

[1] In 775 to Erini, ' the country of the cedars '—that is, Mount Amanus,
near the Gulf of Antioch ; in 773 to Damascus ; in 772 to Hadrach.
[2] vi. 1.

the dynasty of Jeroboam is certain.[1]   But Amos might
have spoken as urgently even before Tiglath-Pileser's
accession ; and the probability that Hosea, who prophesied within Jeroboam's reign, quotes from Amos
seems to imply that the prophecies of the latter had
been current for some time.

Towards the middle of the eighth century is, therefore, the most definite date to which we are able to
assign the Book of Amos.[2]   At so great a distance the
difference of a few unmarked years is invisible.   It is
enough that we know the moral dates—the state of
national feeling, the personages alive, the great events
behind the prophet, and the still greater imminent.
We can see that Amos wrote in the political pride of
the latter years of Jeroboam's reign, after the pestilence and eclipse of the sixties, and before the advance
of Tiglath-Pileser in the last forties, of the eighth
century.

A particular year is indeed offered by the title of the
book, which, if not by Amos himself, cannot be much
later : *Words of 'Amos, which he saw in the days of
Uzziah and of Jeroboam, two years before the earthquake.*
This was the great earthquake of which other prophets
speak as having happened in the days of Uzziah.[3]
But we do not know what was the year of the earthquake, and are still far from a definite date.

The mention of the earthquake, however, introduces

---

[1] vii. 9.

[2] Critics ' are all but unanimous in agreeing that Amos delivered these
sermons between 765 and 750 B.C.'   So Harper, whose review of the whole
question of date (*Commentary*, pp. cii–civ) is admirable.   See too Marti,
pp. 146 f.   Conclusive are their answers to other theories :—Day's and
Chapin's that the book is post-exilic, later than Joel (*Amer. Journal of
Semitic Lang. and Literature*, xviii. 66 ff.) ; Elhorst's that it dates from
the beginning of Josiah's reign.

[3] Zech. xiv. 5, and probably Isa. ix. 9, 10 (Eng.).

us to the answer of another of our questions—whether, with all its unity, the Book of Amos reveals any lines of progress, either of event or of idea, either historical or logical.

Granting the truth of the title, that Amos had his prophetic eyes opened two years before the earthquake, it will be a sign of historical progress if we find in the book itself any allusions to the earthquake. Now these are present. In the First Section we find none, unless the threat of God's visitation in the form of a shaking of the land be considered as a tremor communicated to the prophet's mind from the recent upheaval. But in the Second Section there is an obvious reference : the last of the unavailing chastisements, with which Yahweh has chastised His people, is described as a *great overturning*.[1] And in the Third Section, in two passages, the judgement, which Amos has already stated will fall in the form of an invasion, is also figured in the terms of an earthquake.[2] Nor does this exhaust the tremors which that convulsion had started ; but throughout the Second and Third Sections there is a sense of instability, of the liftableness and breakableness of the very ground of life. Of course, as we shall see, this was due to the prophet's knowledge of the moral explosiveness of society in Israel ; but he could hardly have described the results of that in the terms he has used, unless himself and his hearers had recently felt the ground quake under them, and seen whole cities topple over. If, then, Amos began to prophesy two years before the earthquake, the bulk of his book

---

[1] iv. 11 ; on earthquakes in Palestine see the present writer's *Jerusalem*, vol. i, ch. iv. Again this year, 1927, violent shocks have visited the land, ruining many buildings large and small.

[2] viii. 8 ; ix. 5.

was spoken, or at least written down, after the earthquake had left all Israel trembling.[1]

This proof of progress in the boo: is confirmed by another feature. In the abstract given above it is easy to see that the judgements of the Lord upon Israel were of a twofold character. Some were physical—famine, drought, blight, locusts, earthquake ; and some were political—battle, defeat, invasion, captivity. Now it is significant—and I do not think the point has been previously remarked—that not only are the physical represented as happening first, but that at one time the prophet seems to have understood that no others would be needed, that indeed God did not reveal to him the imminence of political disaster till He had exhausted the discipline of physical calamities. For this we have double evidence. In chap. iv Amos reports that the Lord has sought to rouse Israel out of the moral lethargy into which their religious services have soothed them, by withholding bread and water ; by blighting their orchards ; by a pestilence, a thoroughly Egyptian one ; and by an earthquake. But these having failed to produce repentance, God must visit the people once more : how, the prophet does not say, leaving the imminent terror unnamed, but

[1] Of course it is always possible to suspect—and let us by all means exhaust the possibilities of suspicion—that the title has been added by a scribe, who interpreted the forebodings of judgement which Amos expresses in the terms of earthquake as if they were the predictions of a real earthquake, and was anxious to show, by inserting the title, how they were fulfilled in the great convulsion of Uzziah's days. But to such a suspicion we have a complete answer. No later scribe, who understood the book he was dealing with, would have prefixed to it a title, with the motive just suspected, when in ch. iv he read that an earthquake had just taken place. The very fact that such a title appears over a book which speaks of the earthquake as past, surely attests the *bona fides* of the title. With that mention in ch. iv of the earthquake as past, none would have ventured to say that Amos began to prophesy before the earthquake unless they had known this to be the case.

we know that the Assyrian is meant.   Parallel to this
is the course of the Visions in chap. vii.   The Lord
caused Amos to see (whether in fancy or in fact we
need not now stop to consider) the plague of locusts.
It was so bad as to threaten Israel with destruction.
But Amos interceded, and God answered, *It shall not
be.*   Similarly with a plague of drought.   But then the
Vision shifts from the realm of nature to that of
politics.   The Lord sets the plumbline to the fabric
of Israel's life : this is found hopelessly bent and unstable.   It must be pulled down, and the pulling down
shall be political : the family of Jeroboam is to be
slain, the people are to go into captivity.   The next
Vision, therefore, is of the End—the Final Judgement
of war and defeat, which is followed only by Silence.

Thus, by a double proof, we see not only that the
Divine method in that age was believed to act first
by physical chastisement, and only then by an ultimate
doom of war and captivity ; but that the experience
of Amos himself, his own intercourse with the Lord,
passed through these two stages.   The significance of
this for the picture of the prophet's life we shall see
in our next chapter.   Here we are concerned to ask
whether it gives us any clue as to the extant arrangement of his prophecies, or justification for rearranging
them, as the prophecies of Isaiah have to be re-arranged,
according to the various stages of historical development at which they were uttered.

We have just seen that the progress from the physical chastisements to the political doom is reflected in
both the last two Sections of the book.   But the same
gradual, cumulative method is attributed to the Divine
Providence by the First Section : *for three transgressions.
yea, for four, I will not turn it back ;* and then follow
the same disasters of war and captivity as are threatened

in Sections II and III. But each Section does not only
thus end similarly ; each also begins with the record of
an immediate impression made on the prophet by his
God (chaps. i. 2 ; iii. 3–8 ; vii. 1–9).

To sum up : The Book of Amos consists of three
Sections, which seem to have received their present
form towards the end of Jeroboam's reign ;[1] and which,
after emphasising their origin as due to the immediate
influence of Yahweh Himself on the prophet, follow
much the same course of the Divine dealings with
that generation of Israel—a course which began with
physical chastisements, that failed to produce repentance, and ended with the irrevocable threat of the
Assyrian invasion. Each Section, that is to say, starts
from the same point, follows much the same direction,
and arrives at the same conclusion. Chronologically
one cannot be put before the other ; but from each
it is possible to learn the stages of experience through
which Amos himself passed—to discover how God
taught the prophet, not only by the original intuitions
from which all prophecy starts, but by the gradual
events of his day both at home and abroad.

A cardinal question is that of the source and the
proper position of the passage of narrative, vii. 10–17.
Till towards the end of last century its present position
between the third and fourth visions of Amos was
generally regarded as its proper and original position,
Amasiah's report to Jeroboam, vii. 10, naturally following the prophet's declaration of doom on the house
of Jeroboam, vii. 9.[2] Then the feeling arose that,

---

[1] Except for the later additions, not by Amos ; see p. 3.

[2] So, for example, Wellhausen ; Driver, ' a historical episode intimately
connected with the preceding visions and arising out of them ; ' and the
first edition of the present volume. Compare Nowack, 1st ed., 1897,
p. 150 ; and Harper, 1905, p. cxxix.

whether belonging to the original Book of Amos or borrowed for this from another biographical work, the passage ' interrupts ' the visions and is out of place where it now stands ; and several attempts have been made to find for it another place in the Book—immediately before the visions, or immediately after them, or at the very end of the Book, or at the very beginning.[1] These great differences of opinion, as well as the hesitancy with which some of them are advanced, show the difficulty and uncertainty of the questions both of the source and of the original position of vii. 10–17. Fortunately the questions do not affect the reliability of the narrative which is still generally accepted. ' The passage furnishes for us the background to the whole Book.' [2]

This decides our plan for us. We shall first trace the life and experience of Amos, as his book, and especially the narrative portion of it, enables us to do ; and then we shall examine, in the order in which they lie, the three parallel forms in which, when he was silenced at Bethel, he or some one else collected the fruits of that experience, and gave them their final expression.

---

[1] Cheyne, *Enc. Bibl.*, 1899, col. 155, ' from a partly biographic, partly prophetic work written or dictated by the prophet himself' ; Riedel, *A.T. Untersuchungen*, Heft 1, 1902, from a collection of tales of the prophets like those of Elijah and Elisha ; Duhm, *Z.A.T.W.*, 1911, p. 1, from a biography of Amos from which the data in the title, i. 1, were also taken ; Budde, *Z.A.T.W.*, Beiheft 27, 1914, p. 71, considering it as a fragment without proper introduction or end, supposes that the data in the title were taken from the now lost introduction to it, and that the whole originally stood at the beginning of the Book ; Löhr, *Z.A.T.W.*, Beiheft 4, 1901, puts it after the visions, Baumann, *Z.A.T.W.*, Beiheft 7, 1903, before them between chs. vi and vii ; Marti, *Comm.*, 1904, after ix. 7, at the close of the original Book ; and Duhm, *op. cit.*, attaches it to vi. 11, vii. 7, viii. 3, which he takes to be one song. Löhr, Baumann, and Harper read all or most of the passage as equally metrical with the oracles of the Book. Others read it as prose. See below, p. 106

[2] Budde, *op. cit.*, p. 1.

The style of the book is simple and terse. The fixity of the prophet's aim—upon a few moral principles and the doom they demand—keeps his lines firm and sharp, and sends his periods or strophes rapidly to their climax. That he sees nature only under moral light renders his poetry austere and occasionally savage. His language is very pure. There is no ground for Jerome's charge that he was ' imperitus sermone ' : we shall have to notice only a few irregularities in spelling, due perhaps to the dialect of the deserts in which he passed his life.[1]

The text of the book is for the most part well preserved ; but there are a number of evident corruptions. Of the Greek Version the same holds good as we have said in more detail of the Greek of Hosea.[2] It is sometimes correct where the Hebrew text is not, sometimes suggestive of the emendations required, and sometimes hopelessly astray.

[1] Cf. ii. 13 ; v. 11 ; vi. 8, 10 ; vii. 9, 16 ; viii. 8 (?).
[2] See below, Ch. XII

CHAPTER VI

THE MAN AND THE PROPHET

THE Book of Amos opens one of the greatest stages in the religious development of mankind. Its originality is due to a few simple ideas, which it propels into religion with an almost unrelieved abruptness. But, like all ideas which ever broke upon the world, these also have flesh and blood behind them. Like every other Reformation, this one in Israel began with the conscience and the protest of an individual. We have found in the Book not only a personal adventure of a heroic kind, but a progressive series of visions, with some other proofs of a development both of facts and ideas. Behind the book there beats a life, and our first duty is to attempt to trace its spiritual history. 'Amos,' says a critical writer,[1] 'is one of the most wonderful appearances in the history of the human spirit.'

1. THE MAN AND HIS DISCIPLINE

Amos i. 1 ; iii. 3–8 ; vii. 14, 15

When charged at the crisis of his career with being but a hireling-prophet, Amos disclaimed the official name and took his stand upon his work as a man : *No*

[1] Cornill : *Der Israelitische Prophetismus. Five Lectures for the Educated Laity.* 1894.

prophet I, nor prophet's son, but a herdsman and a dresser of sycamores. Yahweh took me from behind the flock.[1] We shall enhance our appreciation of this manhood, and of the new order of prophecy which it asserted, if we look at the soil on which it was so bravely nourished.

Six miles south from Bethlehem, as Bethlehem is six from Jerusalem, there rises on the edge of the Judæan plateau, towards the desert, a commanding hill, the ruins on which are still known by the name of Teḳôaʻ.[2]

In the time of Amos Tekoa was a place without sanctity and almost without tradition. The name suggests that the site may at first have been that of a camp. Its fortification by Rehoboam, and the mission of its wise woman to David, are its only previous appearances in history. Nor had nature been less grudging to it than fame. The men of Tekoa looked out upon a desolate and haggard world. South, west, and north the view is barred by a range of limestone hills, on one of which directly north the grey towers of Jerusalem are hardly to be discerned from the grey mountain lines. Eastward the prospect is still more desolate, but open ; the land slopes for nearly eighteen miles to a depth of four thousand feet. Of this long descent, the first step, immediately below the hill of Tekoa, is a shelf of stony moorland with the ruins of vineyards.

---

[1] Amos vii. 14 f. See further, pp. 74 ff., 116.

[2] Khurbet Taḳûaʻ, Hebrew Teḳôaʻ, תְּקֹועַ, from תקע, *to blow a trumpet* (cf. Jer. vi. 1, *Blow the trumpet in Tekoa*) or *to pitch a tent*. The latter seems the more probable derivation of the name, and suggests a nomadic origin, which agrees with the position of Tekoa on the borders of the desert. Tekoa does not occur in the list of the towns taken by Joshua. —There are no reasons for supposing that some other Tekoa is meant. The two alleged are (1) that Amos exclusively refers to the Northern Kingdom, (2) that sycomores do not grow at such levels as Tekoa. These are dealt with on pp. 74 ff.

It is the lowest ledge of the settled life of Judæa. The eastern edge drops suddenly by broken rocks to slopes spotted with bushes of 'retem,' the broom of the desert, and with patches of poor wheat. From the foot of the slopes the land rolls away in a maze of low hills and shallow dales, that flush green in spring, but for the rest of the year are brown with withered grass and scrub. This is the *Wilderness* or *Pastureland of Tekoa*,[1] across which by night the wild beasts howl, and by day the blackened sites of deserted camps, with the loose cairns that mark the nomads' graves, reveal a human life almost as vagabond and nameless as that of the beasts. Beyond the rolling land is Jeshimon, or Devastation—a chaos of hills, none of whose ragged crests are tossed as high as the shelf of Tekoa, while their flanks shudder down some further thousands of feet, by crumbling precipices and corries choked with debris, to the coast of the Dead Sea. The northern half of this is visible, bright blue against the red wall of Moab, and the level top of the wall, broken only by the valley of the Arnon, constitutes the horizon. Except for the blue water—which shines in its gap between the torn hills like a bit of sky through rifted clouds—it is a dreary world. Yet the sun breaks over it, perhaps the more gloriously; mists, rising from the sea simmering in its great vat, drape the nakedness of the desert noon; and through the dry desert night the planets ride with a majesty they cannot assume in our troubled atmospheres. It is also a very empty and silent world, yet every stir of life upon it excites, therefore, the greater vigilance, and man's faculties, relieved from the rush and confusion of events, form the instinct of marking, and reflecting upon, every single phenomenon. And it is

[1] 2 Chron xx. 20.

a very wild world. Across it, the towers of Jerusalem give the only signal of the spirit, the one token that man has a history.

Upon this wilderness, where life is full of poverty, and danger—where nature starves the imagination, but excites the faculties of perception and curiosity ; with the mountain tops and the sunrise in his face, and with Jerusalem so near—Amos did the work which made him a man, heard the voice of God calling him to be a prophet, and gathered those symbols and figures in which his prophet's message still reaches us with so fresh and so austere an air.

Amos was *among the shepherds from Tekoa.* The word for *shepherd* is unusual, and means the herdsman of a breed of desert sheep, still under the same name prized in Arabia for the excellence of their wool.[1] And he was *a dresser of sycomores.* The tree, which is not our sycamore, is very easily grown in sandy soil with a little water. It reaches a great height and mass of foliage. The fruit is like a small fig, with a sweet but watery taste, and is eaten only by the poor. Born not of the fresh twigs, but of the trunk and older branches, the sluggish lumps are provoked to ripen by pinching or piercing, which seems to be the literal meaning of the term that Amos uses of himself—*a dresser of sycomores.*[2] The sycomore does not grow

[1] i. 1, נֹקֵד, nôḳêd, is doubtless the same as the Arabic ' naḳḳâd,' or keeper of the ' naḳad,' defined by Freytag as a short-legged and deformed race of sheep in the Bahrein province of Arabia, from which comes the proverb ' viler than a naḳad ' ; yet the wool is very fine. The king of Moab is called נֹקֵד in 2 Kings iii. 4 (A.V. *sheep-master*). In vii. 14 Amos calls himself בּוֹקֵר, cattleman, which there is no reason to alter, as some do, to נֹקֵד.

[2] בּוֹלֵס, bôlês, probably from a root (found in Æthiopic) balas, *a fig ;* hence one who *had to do with figs, handled them, ripened them.* LXX. κνίζων, *nipping* or *pricking*, Vulg. *vellicans.*

at so high a level as Tekoa ; [1] and this fact, taken along with the limitation of the ministry of Amos to the Northern Kingdom, has been held to prove that he was originally an Ephraimite, a sycomore-dresser, who had migrated and settled down, as the peculiar phrase of the title says, *among the shepherds of Tekoa*.[2] We shall see, however, that his familiarity with life in Northern Israel may easily have been won in other ways than through citizenship in that kingdom ; while the general nature of the definition, *among the shepherds from Tekoa*, does not oblige us to place either him or his sycomores so high as the village itself. The most easterly township of Judæa, Tekoa commanded the wilderness beyond, to which indeed it gave its name, *the wilderness of Tekoa*. The shepherds of Tekoa were therefore, in all probability, scattered across the region down to the oases on the Dead Sea, which have generally been owned by one or other of the settled communities in the hill-country above, and may at that time have belonged to Tekoa, just as in Crusading times they

---

[1] The Egyptian sycomore, *Ficus sycomorus*, is not found in Syria above one thousand feet above the sea, while Tekoa is more than twice as high as that. Cf. 1 Kings x. 27, *the sycomores that are in the vale* or *valley land*, עֵמֶק; 1 Chron. xxvii. 28, *the sycomores that are in the low plains*. ' The sycomore grows in sand on the edge of the desert as vigorously as in the midst of a well-watered country. Its roots go deep in search of water, which infiltrates as far as the gorges of the hills, and they absorb it freely even where drought seems to reign supreme ' (Maspero on the Egyptian sycomore : *The Dawn of Civilisation*, translated by McClure, p. 26). ' Everywhere on the confines of cultivated ground, and even at some distance from the valley, are fine single sycomores flourishing as though by miracle amid the sand. . . . They drink from water, which has infiltrated from the Nile, and whose existence is nowise betrayed upon the surface of the soil ' (*ib.*, p. 121). Always and still reverenced by Moslem and Christian.

[2] So practically Oort (*Th. Tijdsch.*, 1891, 121 ff.), when compelled to abandon his previous conclusion (*ib.*, 1880, 122 ff.) that the Tekoa of Amos lay in Northern Israel.

belonged to the monks of Hebron, or were in 1891
cultivated by the Rushaideh Arabs, who pitched their
camps not far from Tekoa itself. As you will still
find everywhere on the borders of the Syrian desert
shepherds nourishing a few fruit-trees round the chief
well of their pasture, in order to vary their milk diet,
so in some low oasis in the wilderness of Judæa Amos
cultivated the poorest, but the most easily grown of
fruits, the sycomore.[1] All this pushes Amos and his
dwarf sheep deeper into the desert, and emphasises
what has been said above, and still remains to be
illustrated, of the desert's influence on his discipline
as a man and on his speech as a prophet. In the same
desert another prophet was bred, who was also the
pioneer of a new dispensation, and whose ministry,
both in its strength and its limitations, is recalled by
the ministry of Amos. John the son of Zacharias *grew
and waxed strong in spirit, and was in the deserts till the
day of his showing unto Israel.*[2] Here, too, our Lord
was *with the wild beasts.*[3] How much Amos had been
with them may be seen from many of his metaphors.
*The lion roars, who shall not fear? . . . As when the
shepherd rescues from the mouth of the lion two shin-
bones or a bit of an ear. . . . It shall be as when one
is fleeing from a lion, and a bear comes upon him; and
he enters a house, and leans his hand on the wall, and a
serpent bites him.*

As a wool-grower, however, Amos must have had
his yearly journeys among the markets of the land;
and to such were probably due his opportunities of

---

[1] In 1891 we met the Rushaideh, who cultivated Engedi, encamped
just below Tekoa.   But at other points between the hill-country of Judæa
and the desert, and between Moab and the desert, we found round some
of the herdsmen's central wells a few fig-trees or pomegranates, or even
apricots.

[2] Luke i. 80.   [3] Mark i. 13.

familiarity with Northern Israel, the originals of his
vivid pictures of her town-life, her commerce and the
worship at her sanctuaries. One hour westward from
Tekoa would bring him to the high-road between
Hebron and the North, with its troops of pilgrims
passing to Beersheba.[1] It was but half-an-hour more
to the watershed and an open view of the Philistine
plain. Bethlehem was only six, Jerusalem twelve
miles from Tekoa. Ten miles farther, across the
border of Israel, lay Bethel with its temple, seven
miles farther one of the Gilgals, and twenty miles
farther still Samaria the capital, in all but two days'
journey from Tekoa. These had markets as well as
shrines;[2] their annual festivals would also be great
fairs. It is certain that Amos visited them; it is even
possible that he went to Damascus, in which the Israelites had their own quarters for trading. By road and
market he would meet with men of other lands.
Phœnician pedlars, or Canaanites as they were called,
came up to buy the homespun for which the house-
wives of Israel were famed[3]—hard-faced men who were
also willing to purchase slaves, and haunted even the
battle-fields of their neighbours for this sinister purpose.
Men of Moab, at the time subject to Israel; Aramean
hostages; Philistines who held the export trade to
Egypt—these Amos must have met and may have
talked with; their dialects scarcely differed from his
own. It is no distant, desert echo of life which we
hear in his pages, but the noisy rumour of caravan
and market-place: how the plague was marching up
from Egypt;[4] ugly stories of the Phœnician slave-
trade;[5] rumours of the advance of the awful Power,
which men were hardly yet accustomed to name, but

---

[1] v. 5; viii. 14.   [2] See p. 34.   [3] Prov. xxxi. 24.
[4] iv. 10.   [5] i. 9.

which had already twice broken from the North upon Damascus. Or it was the progress of some national mourning—how lamentation sprang up in the capital, rolled along the highways, and was re-echoed from the husbandmen and vinedressers on the hill-sides.[1] Or, at closer quarters, we see and hear the bustle of the great festivals and fairs—the *solemn assemblies*, the reeking holocausts, the *noise of songs and viols;*[2] the brutish zeal kindling into drunkenness and lust on the very steps of the altar ; the embezzlement of pledges by the priests, the restlessness of the traders, their false measures, their entanglement of the poor in debt ;[3] the careless luxury of the rich, their *banquets, buckets of wine, ivory couches*, pretentious music.[4] These things are described as by an eyewitness. Amos was not a citizen of the Northern Kingdom, to which he almost exclusively refers ; but it was because he went up and down in it, using those eyes which the desert air had sharpened, that he so thoroughly learned the wickedness of its people, the corruption of Israel's life in every rank and class of society.[5]

But the convictions which he applied to this life Amos learned at home. They came to him over the desert, and without further material signal than was flashed to Tekoa from the towers of Jerusalem. This is placed beyond doubt by the figures in which he describes his call from his God. Contrast his story so far as he reveals it, with that of another. Some twenty years later, Isaiah of Jerusalem saw the Lord in the Temple, high and lifted up, and all the inaugural vision of this greatest of the prophets was conceived in the figures of the Temple—the altar, the smoke the burning coals. But to his predecessor *among the*

---

[1] v. 16. [2] v. 21 ff. [3] ii. 7, 8 ; viii. 4 ff.
[4] vi. 1, 4–7. [5] Chs. ii ff.

shepherds of Tekoa, although revelation also starts from Jerusalem, it reaches him, not in the sacraments of her sanctuary, but across the bare pastures, and as it were in the roar of a lion

> *Yahweh from Sion roareth,*
> *And uttereth His voice from Jerusalem.*[1]

We read of no formal process of consecration for this first of the prophets. Through his clear desert air, the word of God breaks upon him without medium or sacrament. And the native vigilance of the man is startled, is convinced by it, beyond all argument or question. *The lion hath roared, who shall not fear? Yahweh hath spoken, who can but prophesy?*

These words are taken from a passage in which Amos illustrates prophecy from other instances of his shepherd life. We have seen what a school of vigilance the desert is. Upon the bare surface all that stirs is ominous. Every shadow, every noise— the shepherd must know what is behind and be warned. Such a vigilance Amos would have Israel apply to his own message, and to the events of their history. Both of these he compares to certain facts of desert life, behind which his shepherdly instincts have taught him to feel an ominous cause.

iii. 3. *Do two walk together*
> *Except they have trysted?*[2]

—except they have made an appointment? Hardly in the desert for there men meet and take the same road as seldom as ships at sea.

---

[1] ii. 2. I am not convinced that the denial of this verse to Amos by most recent critics is right. But see Harper and Budde (*Z.A.T.W.*, **1910**, 37 ff.) for reasons against its authenticity.

[2] The argument that this is a gloss because a platitude, and meaningless compared with what follows (Marti) is baseless.

iii. 4. *Does a lion roar in the jungle*
    And have no prey ?
    Or a young lion let out his voice from his den [1]
    Except he have captured ?

The hunting lion is silent till his quarry be in sight ; when the lonely shepherd hears the roar across the desert, he knows the lion leaps upon his prey, and he shudders as Israel ought to do when they hear God's voice by the prophet, for this also is never loosened but for some grim fact, some leap of doom.

    5. *Falls a bird to the earth* [2]
    And no noose be upon her ?
    Or a snare spring up from the ground,
    And not be a-catching, catching ?

No one ever saw a bird pulled down when trying to fly off, but knew that there was a loop or mesh about her, nor does a trap or net rise except there be something in it to flutter, struggle, and so lift it up. Or, turning now from animal to human life, take what happens in a town when the alarm-trump sounds.

    6. *Or the horn* [3] *be blown in a town*
    And the people not tremble ?
    Or calamity hap in a town,
    And Yahweh not do it ?
    7. *Yea, the Lord Yahweh*
    Doth nothing at all,
    But His counsel He hath revealed
    To His servants the prophets. [4]

[1] Some omit *from his den* as rendering the line too long.

[2] So LXX. A Heb. scribe has added *the snare* inadvertently as from the next couplet.

[3] שׁוֹפָר in early Israel was the trump or horn blown as a summons to war or defence : only later was the word used of the temple trumpet.

[4] Verse 7 is regarded by Löhr, Baumann, Budde, Marti, and Duhm as a late gloss. I agree with Harper that their reasons (language and awkwardness of metre) are indecisive.

8. *The lion has roared,*
 Who shall not fear ?
 The Lord Yahweh hath spoken
 Who can but prophesy ?

My voice of warning and these events of evil have the same cause. God is behind them both.[1]

We cannot miss the personal note which rings through this triumph in the reality of things unseen. Not only does it proclaim a man of sincerity and conviction : it is resonant with the discipline by which that conviction was won—were won, too, the freedom from illusion and the power of looking at facts in the face, which Amos alone of his contemporaries possessed.

St. Bernard describes the first stage of the Vision of God as the Vision Distributive, in which the eager mind distributes her attention upon common things and common duties in themselves. It was in this elementary school that the earliest of the new prophets passed his apprenticeship and received his gifts. Others may excel Amos in the powers of the imagination and the intellect. But by the habits of his shepherd's life, by daily wakefulness to its alarms and daily faithfulness to its opportunities, he was trained in that simple power of appreciating facts and causes, which, applied to the great phenomena of the spirit and of history, forms his distinction among his peers. In this we find perhaps the reason why he records of himself no solemn hour of cleansing and initiation. *Yahweh took me from following the flock, and Yahweh said unto me, Go, prophesy unto My people Israel.*[2] Amos was of them of whom it is written, ' Blessed are those servants whom

---

[1] See further on this important passage, iii. 3–8, pp. 87 ff.
[2] vii. 15

the Lord when He cometh shall find watching.'
Throughout his hard life, this shepherd had kept
his mind open and his conscience quick, so that when
the word of God came to him he knew it, as fast as he
knew the roar of the lion across the moor. Certainly
there is no habit, which, so much as this of watching
facts with a single eye and a responsible mind, is indispensable alike in the humblest duties and in the
highest speculations of life. When Amos gives those
naïve illustrations of how real the voice of God is to
him, we receive them as the tokens of a man, honest
and awake. Little wonder that he refuses to be reckoned
among the professional prophets of his day, who found
their inspiration in excitement and trance. Upon him
the impulses of the Deity come in no artificial or morbid
ecstasy, removed far from real life. They come upon
him, as it were, in the open air. They appeal to the
senses of his healthy and expert manhood. They convince him of their reality with the same force as do
the most startling events of his lonely shepherd watches.
*The lion hath roared, who shall not fear ? Yahweh hath
spoken, who can but prophesy ?*

The influence of the same discipline is visible when
Amos passes from the facts of his own consciousness
to the facts of his people's life. His day in Israel
sweltered with optimism. The glare of wealth, the
fulsome love of country, the rank incense of a religion
that was without morality—these thickened all the
air, and neither the people nor their rulers had any
vision. But Amos carried with him his clear desert
atmosphere and his desert eyes. He saw the raw
facts : the poverty, the cruel negligence of the rich,
the injustice of the rulers, the immorality of the priests.
The meaning of these things he questioned with as
much persistence as he questioned every suspicious

sound or sight upon those pastures of Tekoa.   He had
no illusions : he knew a mirage when he saw one.
Neither the military pride of the people, fostered by
recent successes over Syria, nor the dogmas of their
religion, which asserted their God's swift triumph upon
the heathen, could prevent him from knowing that the
immorality of Israel meant Israel's political downfall.
He was one of those recruits from common life, by
whom religion and the state have been reformed.
Springing from the laity and often from the working
classes, their freedom from dogmas and routine, as
well as from the compromising interests of wealth, rank,
or party, renders them experts in life to a degree that
almost no professional priest, statesman, or journalist,
however honest or sympathetic, can hope to rival.   Into
politics they bring facts, but into religion they bring
vision.

It is of the utmost significance that this reformer,
this founder of the highest order of prophecy in Israel,
should not only thus begin with facts, but to the very
end be occupied with almost nothing else, than the
vision and record of them.   In the Book of Amos there
is but one prospect of the Ideal.   It does not break till
the close, and then in such contrast to the plain and
final indictments, which constitute nearly all the rest
of the Book, that many have not unnaturally denied
to him the verses which contain it.   Throughout the
other chapters we have but the exposure of present
facts, material and moral, nor the sight of any future
more distant than to-morrow and the immediate consequences of to-day's deeds.   Let us mark this.   The
new prophecy which Amos started in Israel reached
Divine heights of hope, unfolded infinite powers of
moral and political regeneration—dared to blot out
all the past, dared to believe all things possible in the

future.   But it started from the truth about the moral
situation of the present.   Its first prophet not only
denied popular dogmas and ideals, but appears not to
have substituted for these any others.   He spent his
gifts of vision on the discovery and appreciation of
facts.   Now this is necessary, not only in great re-
formations of religion, but at almost every stage in
her development.   We are constantly disposed to abuse
even the most just and necessary of religious ideals as
substitutes for experience or as escapes from duty, and
to boast about the future before we have understood
or mastered the present.   Hence the need of realists
like Amos.   Though they are destitute of dogma, of
comfort, of hope, of the ideal, let us not doubt that
they also stand in the succession of the prophets of
the Lord.

Nay, this is a stage of prophecy on which may be
fulfilled the prayer of Moses : *Would to God that all
the Lord's people were prophets !*   To see the truth and
tell it, to be accurate and brave about the moral
facts of our day—to this extent the Vision and the
Voice are possible for every one of us.   Never for us
may the doors of heaven open, as they did for him
who stood on the threshold of the earthly temple,
and he saw the Lord enthroned, while the Seraphim
of the Presence sang the glory.   Never for us may
the skies fill with that tempest of life which Ezekiel
beheld from Shinar, and above it the sapphire throne,
and on the throne the likeness of a man, the likeness
of the glory of the Lord.   Yet let us remember that
to see facts as they are and to tell the truth about
them—this also is prophecy.   We may inhabit a sphere
which does not prompt the imagination, but is as
destitute of the historic and traditional as was the
wilderness of Tekoa.   All the more may our un-

glamoured eyes be true to the facts about us. Every common day leads forth her duties as shining as every night leads forth her stars. The deeds and the fortunes of men are in our sight, and spell, to all who will honestly read, the very Word of the Lord. If only we be loyal, then by him who made the rude sounds and sights of the desert his sacraments, and whose vigilance for things seen and temporal became the vision of things unseen and eternal, we also shall see God, and be sure of His ways with men.

Before we pass from the desert discipline of the prophet, we must notice one of its effects, which, while it greatly enhanced the clearness of his vision, undoubtedly disabled Amos for the highest prophetic rank. He who lives in the desert lives without patriotism—detached and aloof. He may see the throng of men more clearly than those who move among it. He cannot possibly so much feel for them. Unlike Hosea, Isaiah, and Jeremiah, Amos was not a citizen of the kingdom against which he prophesied, and indeed no proper citizen of any kingdom, but a nomad herdsman, hovering on the desert borders of Judæa. He saw Israel from the outside. His message to her is achieved with scarcely one sob in his voice. For the sake of the poor and the oppressed among the people he is indignant. But with the erring, staggering nation as a whole he has no real sympathy. His pity for her is exhausted in one elegy and two brief intercessions ; hardly more than once does he even call her to repentance. His sense of justice, in fact had almost never to contend with his love. This made Amos the better witness, but the lesser prophet. He did not rise so high as his great successors, because he did not so feel himself one with the people whom he was forced to condemn, because he did not bear their fate as his own nor travail for their new birth. ' Ihm fehlt die Liebe.' Love is the element lacking in his prophecy ; and therefore the words are true of him, which were uttered of his great follower across this same wilderness of Judæa, that mighty as were his voice and his message to prepare the way of the Lord, yet *the least in the Kingdom of Heaven is greater than he.*

2. The Word and its Origins

Amos i. 2 ; iii. 3–8 ; and *passim*

We have seen the preparation of the Man for the Word. We are now to ask, Whence came the Word to the Man ?—the Word that made him a prophet. What were its sources and sanctions outside himself ? These involve other questions. How much of his message did Amos inherit from the previous religion of his people ? And how much did he teach for the first time in Israel ? And again, how much of this new element did he owe to the great event of his day ? And how much implies some other source of inspiration ?

To these inquiries outlines of the answers ought by this time to be visible. We have seen that the contents of the Book of Amos consist of two kinds : facts, actual or imminent, in the history of his people ; and certain moral principles of an elementary order. Amos appeals to no dogma nor form of law, nor to any religious or national institution. Still more re- markably, he does not rely upon miracle nor any so- called ' supernatural sign.' To employ the terms of Mazzini's famous formula, Amos draws his materials solely from ' conscience and history.' Within himself he hears certain moral principles speak in the voice of God, and certain events of his day he recognises as the judicial acts of God. The principles condemn the living generation of Israel as morally corrupt ; the events threaten the people with political extinction. From this agreement between inward conviction and outward event Amos draws his confidence as a prophet, and enforces on the people his message of doom as God's own word.[1]

The passage in which Amos most explicitly illustrates this harmony between event and conviction is one whose metaphors we have already quoted in proof of the desert's influence upon the prophet's life. When Amos asks, *Can two walk together except they have made an appointment ?* his figure is drawn, as we have seen, from the wilderness in which two men will hardly meet except they have arranged to do so ; but the truth he would illustrate by the figure is that two sets of phenomena which coincide must have sprung from a common purpose. Their conjunction forbids mere chance. What kind of phenomena he means, he lets us see in his next instance : *Does a lion roar in the jungle and have no prey ? Doth a young lion let forth his voice except he have captured* something ? That is, those ominous sounds never happen without some fell deed happening along with them. Amos thus plainly hints that the two phenomena on whose coincidence he insists are an utterance on one side, and on the other side a deed fraught with destruction. The reading of the next metaphor about the bird and the snare is uncertain ; at most what it means is that you never see signs of distress or a vain struggle to escape without there being, though out of sight, some cause for them.[2]

---

[1] See Harper in confirmation, p. cx.

[2] *Shall a bird fall earthwards and there be no noose about her ? Shall a snare spring from the ground and not be taking* something ? On this see p. 80. Its meaning seems to be equivalent to the Scottish **proverb :** ' There's aye some water whaur the stirkie droons.'

But from so general a principle he returns in his fourth metaphor to the special coincidence between utterance and deed. *Is the alarum-trumpet blown in a city and do the people not tremble ?* Of course they do ; they know such sound is never made without the approach of calamity. But who is the author of every calamity ? God Himself : *Shall there be calamity in a city and Yahweh not have done it ?* Very well then ; we have seen that common life has many instances in which, when an ominous sound is heard, it is because it is linked with a fatal deed. These happen together, not by mere chance, but because the one is the expression, the warning, or the explanation of the other. And we also know that fatal deeds which happen to any community in Israel are from God. He is behind them. But they, too, are accompanied by a warning voice from the same source as themselves. This is the voice which the prophet hears in his heart—the moral conviction which he feels as the Word of God. *The Lord Yahweh doeth nothing but He hath revealed His counsel to His servants the prophets.*[1] Mark the grammar : the revelation comes first to the prophet's heart ; then he sees and recognises the event, and is confident to give his message about it. So Amos, repeating his metaphor, sums up his argument. *The lion hath roared, who shall not fear ?*—certain that there is more than sound happening or to happen. *The Lord Yahweh hath spoken, who can but prophesy ?*—certain that what his God has spoken to him inwardly is likewise no mere sound, but that deeds of judgement are about to happen, as the ominous voice requires they should.[2]

[1] ' Which Amos could hardly have written, unless he had had the most vivid and ocular evidence of a true prophetic impulse, even before his own time came to receive one ' (Cheyne, *Enc. Bibl.*, 157).

[2] There is thus no reason to alter the words *who shall not prophesy* to *who shall not tremble*—as Wellhausen does. To do so is to blunt the point of the argument.

The prophet is thus made sure of his message by the agreement between the inward convictions of his soul and the outward events of the day. When these walk together, it proves that they have come of a common purpose. He who causes the events—it is God Himself, *for shall there be calamity in a city and Yahweh not have done it ?*—must be author also of the inner voice or conviction which agrees with them. *Who* then *can but prophesy ?* Observe again that no support is here derived from miracle ; nor is claim made for the prophet on the ground of his ability to foretell the event. It is the agreement of the idea with the fact, their evident common origin in the purpose of God, which makes a man sure that he has in him the Word of God. Both are necessary, and together are enough. Are we then to leave the origin of the Word in this coincidence of fact and thought—as it were an electric flash produced by the contact of conviction with event ? Hardly : there are questions behind this coincidence. For instance, as to how the two react on each other—the event provoking the conviction, the conviction interpreting the event ? The argument of Amos seems to imply that the ethical principles are experienced by the prophet prior to the events which justify them. Is this so, or was the shock of the events required to awaken the principles ? And if the principles were prior, whence did Amos derive them ? These questions lead us to the very origins of revelation.

The greatest of the events with which Amos and his contemporaries dealt was the Assyrian invasion. In a previous chapter we have tried to estimate the intellectual effects of Assyria on prophecy.[1] Assyria widened the horizon of Israel, put the world to Hebrew

[1] See Ch. IV.

eyes in a new perspective, vastly increased the possibilities of history and set to religion a novel order of
problems. We can trace the effects upon Israel's con-
ceptions of God, of man, and even of nature.[1] Now
it might be plausibly argued that the new prophecy
in Israel was first stirred and quickened by all this
mental shock and strain, and that even the loftier ethics
of the prophets were thus due to the advance of Assyria.
For, as the most vigilant watchmen of their day, the
prophets observed the rise of that empire, and felt its
fatality for Israel. Turning then to seek the Divine
reasons for such a destruction, they found these in
Israel's sinfulness, to the full extent of which their
hearts were at last awakened. According to such a
theory the prophets were politicians first and moralists
afterwards : alarmists to begin with, and preachers of
repentance only second. Or—to recur to the language
employed above—the prophets' experience of the historical event preceded their conviction of the moral
principle which agreed with it.

In support of such a theory it is pointed out that
after all the most original element in the prophecy of
the eighth century was the announcement of Israel's
fall and exile. The Righteousness of Yahweh had
previously often been enforced in Israel, but never had
any voice drawn from it this awful conclusion that
the nation must perish. The first in Israel to dare this
was Amos, and surely what enabled him to do so was
the imminence of Assyria upon his people. Again,
such a theory might plausibly point to the opening verse
of the Book of Amos, with its unprefaced, unexplained
pronouncement of doom upon Israel (i. 2) :—

---

[1] See pp. 48 ff.

Yahweh roareth from Ṣion,
And giveth voice from Jerusalem ;
And the pastures of the shepherds mourn,
And the summit of Carmel is withered ! [1]

Here, it might be averred, is the earliest prophet's earliest utterance.   Is it not audibly the voice of a man in a panic—such a panic as, ever on the eve of historic convulsions, seizes the more sensitive minds of a doomed people ?   The distant Assyrian thunder has reached Amos, on his pastures, unprepared—unable to articulate its meaning, and with only faith enough to hear in it the voice of his God.   He needs reflection to unfold its contents ; and the process of this reflection we find through the rest of his book.   There he details for us, with increasing clearness, both the ethical reasons and the political results of that Assyrian terror, by which he was at first so wildly shocked into prophecy.

But the panic-born are the still-born ; and it is impossible that prophecy, in her ethical and religious vigour, can have been the daughter of so fatal a birth. If we look again at the evidence which is quoted from Amos in favour of such a theory, we shall see how contradicted it is by other features of his book.

To begin with, we are not certain that the terror of the opening verse of Amos is the Assyrian terror.   Even if it were, the opening of a book does not necessarily represent the writer's earliest feelings.   The rest of the chapters contain visions and oracles which obviously date from a time when Amos was not yet startled by

---

[1] See above, p. 79, n. 1, on the authenticity of this verse. *Withered,* וְיָבֵשׁ *is withered*, should possibly be pointed וְיֵבשׁ , *is abashed* (Duhm), the effect described being perhaps that of the threat of a political invasion, and not of a physical calamity : drought, or the like.

Assyria, but believed that the punishment which Israel
required might be accomplished through a series of
physical calamities—locusts, drought, and pestilence.[1]
Nay, it was not even these earlier judgements, preceding the Assyrian, which stirred the word of God in
the prophet. He introduces them with a *now* and a
therefore. That is to say, he treats them only as the
consequence of certain facts, the conclusion of certain
premises. These facts and premises are moral—they
are exclusively moral. They are the sins of Israel's
life, regarded without illusion and without pity. They
are certain simple convictions, which fill the prophet's
heart, about the impossibility of the survival of any
state which is so perverse and so corrupt.

This origin of prophecy in moral facts and moral
intuitions, which are in their beginning independent of
political events, may be illustrated by several other
points. For instance, the sins which Amos marked in
Israel were such as required no ' red dawn of judgement ' to expose their flagrance and fatality. The
abuse of justice, the cruelty of the rich, the shameless
immorality of the priests, are not sins which we feel
only in the cool of the day, when God Himself draws
near to judgement. They are such things as make men
shiver in the sunshine. And so the Book of Amos,
and not less that of Hosea, tremble with the feeling
that Israel's social corruption is great enough of itself,
without the aid of natural convulsions, to shake the
very basis of national life. *Shall not the land tremble
for this*, Amos says after reciting some sins, *and every
one that dwells therein?* [2] Not drought nor pestilence
nor invasion is needed for Israel's doom, but the
elemental force of ruin which lies in the people's own

----

[1] See pp. 65 ff.   [2] viii. 8.

wickedness. This is enough to create gloom long before the political skies be overcast—or, as Amos puts it, this is enough

> *To cause the sun to go down at noon,*
> *And to darken the earth in clear day.*[1]

And once more—in spite of Assyria the ruin may be averted, if only the people will repent : *Seek good and not evil, and Yahweh of Hosts will be with you, as you say.*[2] Assyria, however threatening, becomes irrelevant to Israel's future from the moment that Israel repents.

Such beliefs, then, are obviously not the results of experience, nor of a keen observation of history. They are primal convictions of the heart, deeper than all experience, and themselves contain sources of historical foresight. With Amos it was not the outward event which inspired the inward conviction, but the conviction which anticipated and interpreted the event, though when the event came there can be no doubt that it confirmed, and articulated the conviction.[3]

But when we have thus tracked the stream of prophecy as far back as these elementary convictions we have not reached the fountain-head. Whence did Amos derive his simple and absolute ethics ? Were they original to him ? Were they new in Israel ? Such questions start an argument which touches the origins of revelation.

---

[1] viii. 9.   [2] v. 14.

[3] How far Assyria assisted the development of prophecy we have already seen. But we have been made aware, at the same time, that Assyria's service to Israel in this respect presupposed the possession by the prophets of certain beliefs in the character and will of their God, Yahweh. The prophets' faith could never have risen to the magnitude of the new problems set to it by Assyria if there had not been already inherent in it that belief in the sovereignty of a Righteousness of which all things material were but the instruments.

It is obvious that Amos not only takes for granted the laws of righteousness which he enforces : he takes for granted also the people's conscience of them. New, indeed, is the doom which sinful Israel deserves, and original to himself is the proclamation of it ; but Amos appeals to the moral principles which justify the doom, as if they were not new, and as if Israel ought always to have known them. This attitude of the prophet to his principles has, in our time, suffered judgement. It has been called an anachronism. So absolute a morality, some say, had never before been taught in Israel ; nor had righteousness been so exclusively emphasised as the purpose of Yahweh. Amos and the other prophets of his century were the virtual ' creators of ethical monotheism ' : it could only be by a prophetic licence or prophetic fiction that he appealed to his people's conscience of the standards he promulgated, or condemned his generation to death for not having lived up to them.

Let us see how far this criticism is supported by the facts.

To no sane observer can the religious history of Israel appear as anything but a course of gradual development. Even in the moral standards, in respect of which it is confessedly often difficult to prove growth, the signs of the nation's progress are very manifest. Practices come to be forbidden in Israel and tempers to be mitigated, which in earlier ages were sanctioned to their extreme by the explicit decrees of religion. In the nation's attitude to the outer world sympathies arise, along with ideals of spiritual service, where previously only war and extermination had been enforced in the name of the Deity. Now in such an evolution it is equally indubitable that the longest and most rapid stage was the prophecy of the eighth century. The prophets of that time condemn acts which had been inspired by their immediate predecessors ; [1] they abjure, as impeding morality, a ceremonial which the leaders of earlier generations had felt to be indispensable to religion ; and they unfold ideals of the nation's moral destiny, of which older writings give us only hints. Yet, while the fact of a religious evolution in Israel is thus certain, we must not fall into the vulgar error which interprets evolution as if it were mere addition, nor forget that even in the most creative periods of religion nothing is brought forth which has not already been promised, and, at some earlier stage, placed, so to speak, within reach of the human mind. After all it is the mind which grows ; the moral ideals which become visible to its more matured vision are so Divine that, when they present themselves, the mind cannot but think that they were always real and always imperative. If we remember these commonplaces we shall do justice both to Amos and to his critics.

In the first place it is clear that most of the morality which Amos enforced is of that fundamental order which can never have been recognised as the discovery or invention of any prophet. Whatever be their origin, the conscience of justice, the duty of kindness to the poor, the horror of wanton cruelty towards one's enemies, which form the chief principles of Amos, are discernible in man as far back as history allows us to search for them. Should a generation have lost them, they can be brought back to it, never with the thrill of a new lesson, but only with the shame of an old and an abused memory. To neither man nor people can

---

[1] Compare, for instance, Hosea's condemnation of Jehu's murder of Joram, with Elisha's command to do it ; also 2 Kings iii. 19, 25, with Deut. xx. 19.

the righteousness which Amos preached appear as a discovery, but always as a recollection and a remorse. And this is most true of the people of Moses and of Samuel, of Nathan, of Elijah, and of the Book of the Covenant. Ethical elements had been characteristic of Israel's religion from the very first. They were not due to a body of written law, but rather to the character of Israel's God, appreciated by the nation in all the great crises of their history.[1] Yahweh had won for Israel freedom and unity. He had been a spirit of justice to their lawgivers and magistrates.[2] He had raised up a succession of consecrated personalities,[3] who by life and word had purified the ideals of the whole people. The results had appeared in the creation of a strong national conscience, which avenged with horror, as *folly in Israel*, the wanton crimes of any person or section of the commonwealth ; in the gradual formation of a legal code, based indeed on the common custom of the Semites, but greatly more moral than that ; and even in the attainment of certain profoundly ethical beliefs about God and His relations, beyond Israel, to all mankind. Now, let us understand once for all, that in the ethics of Amos there is nothing which is not rooted in one or other of these achievements of the previous religion of his people. To this religion Amos felt himself attached in the closest possible way. The word of God comes to him across the desert, as we have seen, yet not out of the air. From the first he hears it rise from that one monument of his people's past which we have found visible on his physical horizon [4]—*from Sion, from Jerusalem,*[5] from the city of David, from the Ark, whose ministers were Moses and Samuel, from the repository of the

---

[1] See above, pp. 16 ff.   [2] Isa. xxviii. 6.   [3] Amos ii. 11.
[4] *Ante*, p. 72.   [5] i. 2. See p. 79.

main tradition of Israel's religion.[1] Amos felt himself
in the sacred succession ; his feeling is confirmed by
the contents of his book. The details of that civic
justice which he demands from his generation are found
in the Book of the Covenant—the only one of Israel's
great codes which appears by this time to have been
in existence ; [2] or in those popular proverbs which
almost as certainly were found in early Israel. [3]

Nor does Amos go elsewhere for the religious sanctions of his ethics It is by the ancient mercies of
God towards Israel that he shames and convicts his
generation—by the deeds of grace which made them a
nation, by the organs of doctrine and reproof which have
inspired them, unfailing from age to age. *I destroyed
the Amorite before them. . . . Yea, I brought you up out
of the land of Egypt, and I led you forty years in the
wilderness, to possess the land of the Amorites. And I
raised up of your sons for prophets, and of your young men
for Nazirites. Was it not even thus, O ye children of
Israel ? saith Yahweh.* [4] We cannot even say that the
belief which Amos expresses in his God as the supreme
Providence of the world [5] was a new thing in Israel,
for a belief as universal inspires those portions of the
Book of Genesis which, like the Book of the Covenant,
were already extant.

[1] Therefore we see how inadequate is Renan's comparison of Amos
to a modern revolutionary journalist (*Histoire du Peuple Israel*, II).
Journalist indeed ! This would-be cosmopolitan and impartial critic's
judgements somewhat smack of the boulevards !

[2] Exod. xx ; in the JE book of history, and, according to nearly all
critics, complete by 750 ; the contents must have been familiar in Israel
before that. There is no trace in Amos of influences peculiar to the
Deuteronomic or the Levitical legislation. See below on ii. 4, 5.

[3] See especially Schultz, *O.T. Theol.*, Eng. Trans. by Paterson, I, 214.

[4] ii. 9-11. On this passage see further, in Ch. VII.

[5] If iv. 13, v. 8 and ix. 6 be genuine, this remark equally applies to
belief in Yahweh as Creator.

We see, therefore, what right Amos had to present his ethical truths to Israel, as if they were not new, but had been within reach of his people from of old.

We could not, however, commit a greater mistake, than to confine the inspiration of our prophet to the past, and interpret his doctrines as inferences from the earlier religious ideas of Israel, inferences forced by his own passionate logic, or more naturally ripened for him by the progress of events. A writer has thus summarised the work of the prophets of the eighth century : ' In fact they laid hold upon that bias towards the ethical, which dwelt in Yahwism from Moses onwards, and they allowed it alone to have value as corresponding to the true religion of Yahweh.'[1] But this is too abstract to be an adequate statement of the prophets' own consciousness. What overcame Amos was a Personal Influence—the Impression of a Character ; and it was this not only as it was revealed in the past of his people. The God who stands behind Amos is indeed the ancient Deity of Israel, and the facts which prove Him God are those which made the nation—the Exodus, the guidance through the wilderness, the overthrow of the Amorites, the gift of the land. *Was it not even thus, O ye sons of Israel ?* But what beats and burns through the pages of Amos is not the memory of those wonderful works, so much as a fresh vision and understanding of the Living God who worked them. Amos has himself met with his God on the conditions of his own time—on the moral situation provided by the living generation of Israel. By an intercourse conducted, not through the distant signals of the past, but here and now, through the events of the prophet's own day, Amos has re-

[1] Kayser, *Old Testament Theology*

ceived an original and overpowering conviction of his people's God as absolute righteousness. What prophecy had hitherto felt in part, and applied to one or other of the departments of Israel's life, Amos is the first to feel in its fulness, and to every extreme of its consequences upon the worship, the conduct and the fortunes of the nation. To him God not only commands this and that righteous law, but God and righteousness are identical. *Seek Yahweh and ye shall live . . . seek good and ye shall live.*[1] The absoluteness with which Amos conceived this principle, the courage with which he applied it, carry him along those two great lines upon which we most clearly trace his originality as a prophet. In the strength of this principle he does what is really new in Israel : he discards the two elements which had hitherto existed alongside the ethical, and had warped it.[2]

Up till now the ethical spirit of the religion of Yahweh [3] had to struggle with two beliefs which we can trace back to the Semitic origins of the religion—the belief, namely, that, as the national God, Yahweh would always defend their political interests, irrespective of morality ; and the belief that a ceremonial of rites and sacrifices was indispensable to religion. These principles were mutual : as the deity was bound to succour the people, so were the people bound to supply the deity with gifts, and the more of these they brought the more they made sure of his favours. Such views were not devoid of moral benefit. In the formative

---

[1] v. 6, 14.

[2] Cf. Cossmann (*Z.A.T.W.*, Beiheft 29, p. 26) : ' Jahwe ist dem Amos eine durchaus sittliche Macht. Kein Prophet hat diese Wesensbestimmtheit Jahwe's schärfer betont und stärker in Jahwe's Wirken zur Darstellung kommen lassen als er.' Cornill (*The Prophets of Israel*, p. 42) : ' In Amos we have the incorporation of the moral law.'

[3] See above, p. 16.

period of the nation they had contributed both discipline and hope. But of late they had between them engrossed men's hearts, and crushed out of religion both conscience and common sense. By the first of them, the belief in Yahweh's predestined protection of Israel, the people's eyes were so holden they could not see how threatening were the times ; by the other, the confidence in ceremonial, conscience was dulled, and that immorality permitted which they mingled shamelessly with their religious zeal. Now the conscience of Amos did not merely protest against the predominance of the two, but was so exclusive, so spiritual, that it boldly banished both from religion. Amos denied that Yahweh was bound to save His people ; he affirmed that ritual and sacrifice were no part of the service He demands from men. This is the measure of originality in our prophet. The two religious principles inherent in the fibre of Semitic religion, which till now had gone unchallenged in Israel, Amos cast forth from religion in the name of an absolute righteousness. On the one hand, Yahweh's peculiar connection with Israel meant no more than jealousy for their holiness : *You only have I known of all the families of the earth, therefore will I visit upon you all your iniquities.*[1] And, on the other hand, all their ceremonial was abhorrent to Him : *I hate, I despise your festivals. . . . Though ye offer Me burnt offerings and your meal offerings, I will not accept them. . . . Take thou away from Me the noise of thy songs ; I will not hear the music of thy viols. But let justice run down as waters, and righteousness as a perennial stream.*[2]

It has just been said that emphasis upon morality as the sum of religion, to the exclusion of sacrifice, is the original element in the prophecies of Amos. He himself, however, does not regard this as proclaimed for the first time in Israel, and the precedent he quotes is so illustrative of the sources of his inspiration that we do well to look at it for a little. In the verse next to the one last quoted he reports these words of God : *Did ye offer unto Me sacrifices and gifts in the wilderness, for forty years, O house of Israel ?* An extraordinary challenge ! From the present blind routine of sacrifice Yahweh appeals to the beginning of His relations with the nation : did they then perform such services to Him ? Of course, a negative answer is expected. No other agrees with the main contention of the passage. In the wilderness Israel had not offered sacrifices and gifts to Yahweh. Jeremiah quotes a still more explicit word of his God : *I spake not unto your fathers in the day that I brought them out of the land of Egypt concerning burnt offerings and sacrifices : but this thing I commanded them, saying, Obey My voice, and I will be your God, and ye shall be My people.*[1]

To these Divine statements we shall not be able to do justice if we hold by the traditional view that the Levitical legislation was proclaimed in the wilderness. Discount that legislation, and the statements become clear. It is true, of course, that Israel must have had a ritual of some kind from the first ; and that both in the wilderness and in Canaan their spiritual leaders must have performed sacrifices as if these were acceptable to their God. But even so the Divine words which Amos and Jeremiah quote are historically correct ; for while the ethical contents of the religion of Yahweh were its original and essential contents— *I commanded them, saying, Obey My voice*—the ritual

[1] Jer. vii. 22 f. See the present writer's *Jeremiah.*

was but a modification of the ritual common to all
Semites ; and ever since the occupation of the land,
it had, through the infection of the Canaanite rites on
the high places, grown more and more Pagan, both
in its functions and in the ideas which these were
supposed to express.[1] Amos was right. Sacrifice had
never been the Divine, the revealed element in the
religion of Israel. Nevertheless, before Amos no
prophet in Israel appears to have said so. And what
enabled this man in the eighth century to offer testimony, so novel but so true, about the beginnings of
his people's religion in the fourteenth, was plainly
neither tradition nor historical research, but an overwhelming conviction of the spiritual and moral character
of God—of Him Who had been Israel's God both then
and now, and Whose righteousness had been, just as
much then as now, exalted above all national interests
and susceptibility to ritual. When we thus see the prophet's knowledge of the Living God enabling him, not
only to proclaim an ideal of religion more spiritual
than Israel had yet dreamed, but to perceive that such
an ideal had been the essence of the religion of Yahweh
from the first, we understand how thoroughly Amos
was mastered by that knowledge. If we need any
further proof of his ' possession ' by the character of
God, we find it in those phrases in which his own
consciousness disappears, and we have no longer the
herald's report of the Lord's words, but the accents
of the Lord Himself, fraught with personal feeling of
the most intense quality. *I Yahweh hate, I despise
your feast days. . . . Take thou away from Me the noise
of thy songs ; I will not hear the music of thy viols.*[2]
. . . I abhor the arrogance of Jacob, and hate his palaces.[3]

---

[1] See above, pp. 21 f.   [2] v. 21–23.   [3] vi. 8.

. . . The eyes of the Lord Yahweh are upon the sinful kingdom.[1] *. . . Yahweh sweareth, I will never forget any of their works.*[2] Such sentences reveal a Deity who is not only manifest Character, but surging and importunate Feeling. We have traced the prophet's word to its ultimate source. It springs from the righteousness, the vigilance, the urgency of the Eternal. The intellect, imagination, and heart of Amos—the convictions he has inherited from his people's past, his conscience of their evil life to-day, his impressions of current and coming history—are enforced and illuminated, made impetuous and radiant, by the Spirit, that is to say the Purpose and the Energy, of the Living God. Therefore, as he says in the title of his book, or as some one says for him, Amos *saw* his words. They stood out objective to himself. And they were not mere sound. They glowed and burned with God Himself.

When we realise this, we feel how inadequate it is to express prophecy in the terms of evolution. No doubt, as we have seen, the ethics and religion of Amos represent a large and measurable advance upon those of earlier Israel. And yet with Amos we do not seem so much to have arrived at a new stage in a Process, as to have penetrated to the Idea which has been behind the Process from the beginning. The change and growth of Israel's religion are realities—their fruits can be seen, defined, catalogued—but a greater reality is the unseen Purpose which impels them. They have been expressed only now. He has been unchanging from of old and for ever—from the first absolute righteousness in Himself, and absolute righteousness in His demands from men.

[1] ix. 8.   [2] viii. 7.

3. The Prophet and his Ministry

Amos vii, viii. 1–4

We have seen the preparation of the Man for the Word ; we have sought to trace to its source the Word which came to the Man. It now remains for us to follow the Prophet, Man and Word combined, upon his Ministry to the people.

For reasons given in a previous chapter [1] there must be some doubt as to the actual course of the ministry of Amos before his appearance at Bethel. Most authorities, however, agree that the visions recounted in the beginning of the seventh chapter form the substance of his address at Bethel, which was interrupted by the priest Amasiah. These visions furnish a probable summary of the prophet's experience up to that point. While they follow the same course, which we trace in the two series of oracles that now precede them in the book, the ideas in them are less elaborate. At the same time it is evident that Amos must have already spoken upon other points than those which he puts into the first three visions. For instance, Amasiah reports to the king that Amos had predicted the exile of the whole people [2]—a conviction which, as we have seen, the prophet reached only after some length of experience. It is equally certain that Amos had already exposed the sins of the people in the light of the Divine righteousness. Some sections of the book which deal with this subject appear to have been originally spoken ; and it is unnatural to suppose that the prophet announced the chastisements of God without having previously justified these to the consciences of men.

[1] Ch. V, p. 69.   [2] vii. 11.

If this view be correct, Amos, having preached for some time to Israel concerning the evil state of society, appeared at a great religious festival in Bethel, determined to bring matters to a crisis, and to announce the doom which his preaching threatened and the people's continued impenitence made inevitable. Mark his choice of place and of audience. It was no mere king he aimed at. Nathan had dealt with David, Gad with Solomon, Elijah with Ahab and Jezebel. But Amos sought the people, with whom resided the real forces and responsibilities of life : the wealth, the social fashions, the treatment of the poor, the spirit of worship, the ideals of religion.[1] And Amos sought the people upon what was not only a great popular occasion, but one on which was arrayed, in pomp and lavishness, the very system he essayed to overthrow. The religion of his time—religion as mere ritual and sacrifice—was what God had sent him to expose, and he faced it at its headquarters, and upon one of its high days, in the royal and popular sanctuary where it enjoyed at once the patronage of the crown, the lavish gifts of the rich, and the thronged devotion of the multitude. As Savonarola at the Duomo in Florence, as Luther at the Diet of Worms, as our Lord Himself at the feast in Jerusalem, so was Amos at the feast in Bethel. Perhaps he was still more lonely. He speaks nowhere of having made a disciple, and in the sea of faces which turned on him when he spoke, it is probable that he could not welcome a single ally. They were officials, or interested traders, or devotees ; he was a stranger and a wild man, with a word that spared the popular dogma as little as the royal

---

[1] On the ministry of eighth-century prophets to the people, see the author's *Isaiah*, I, p. 117.

prerogative. Well for him was it that over all those
serried ranks of authority, those fanatic crowds, that
lavish splendour, another vision commanded his eyes.
*I saw the Lord standing over the altar, and He said,
Smite.*[1]

I render the whole of the following section, vii. 1–
viii. 3, as prose. Several attempts have been made to
reduce it to metrical form throughout.[2] But these seem
to me forced and fanciful and, in view of the prevailing
narrative, unnatural ; while the differences from each
other that they exhibit are a further reason for regarding them with doubt. Some clauses in the text
of the visions may be read as metre ; but the section
is narrative as a whole and best read as prose.[3]

Amos told the pilgrims at Bethel that the first events
of his time in which he felt a purpose of God in harmony with his convictions about Israel's need of
punishment were calamities of a physical kind. Of
these, which in chap. iv he describes as successively
drought, blasting, locusts, pestilence, and earthquake,
he selected at Bethel only two—locusts and drought—
and he began with the locusts. This may have been
either the same visitation as he specifies in chap. iv,
or a previous one ; for of all the plagues of Palestine
locusts have been the most frequent, occurring every
six or seven years. Chap. vii. 1–3 : *Thus the Lord Yahweh*

---

[1] ix. 1.

[2] Especially by Löhr, Baumann, Harper, and Haupt (*J.B.L.*, **xxxv**,
1916, p. 284) ; cf. Duhm, p. 14.

[3] Cf. Marti, p. 207 : ' Das unterscheidende Merkmal dieses . . .
Teiles ist dass er in der Hauptsache *erzählende* Abschnitte und dem
entsprechend *Prosa* bietet ; ' and Budde, p. 68 : ' Alle Änderungsvor-
schläge auf Grund einer angenommenen metrischen Gliederung des
Stückes fallen mit dieser irrigen Annahme von selbst dahin.' See also
Geschichte der althebr. Litteratur, 70, for wise remarks on the necessity
of allowing to the prophets more freedom in their verse than is shown
in the lyrical poets.

gave me to see : and, behold, a brood [1] *of locusts at the beginning of the coming up of the spring crop.* In the Syrian year there are practically two tides of verdure : one which starts after the early rains of October and continues through the winter, checked by the cold ; and one which comes away with greater force under the influence of the latter rains and more genial airs of spring.[2] Of these it was the later and richer which the locusts had attacked. *And, behold, it was the spring crop after the king's mowings.*[3] These seem to have been a tribute which the kings of Israel levied on the spring herbage, and which the Roman governors of Syria used annually to impose in the month Nisan.[4] *After the king's mowings* would be a phrase to mark the time when everybody else might turn to reap their own crops. It was thus the crisis of the year when the locusts appeared ; the April crops devoured, there was no hope of further fodder till December. Still, the calamity had happened before, and had been survived ; a nation so vigorous and wealthy as Israel was under Jeroboam II need not have been frightened to death. But Amos felt it with a conscience. To him it was the beginning of that destruction of his

---

[1] So LXX, followed by Hitzig, Wellhausen, and others, by reading יֹצֵר for יֹצֵר. *Locusts*, Heb. גֹּבַי, perhaps locusts in the larva-stage, see Driver, pp. 84, 201.

[2] Cf. *Hist. Geography of the Holy Land*, pp. 64 ff. The word translated *spring crop* above is לֶקֶשׁ, and from the same root as the name of the latter rain, מַלְקוֹשׁ, which falls in the end of March or beginning of April. Cf. *Zeitschrift des deutschen Palästina-Vereins*, IV, 83 ; VIII, 62.

[3] But some read with the LXX, ילק (βροῦχος), locusts at a more advanced stage of development. But the clause may be a gloss or explanatory note on the preceding clause (Nowack, Baumann, Duhm, Harper, Marti).

[4] Cf. 1 Kings xviii. 5 with 1 Sam. viii. 15, 17 ; 1 Kings iv. 7 ff. See Robertson Smith, *Religion of the Semites*, p. 228.

people which the spirit within him knew that their sin
had earned.   So *it came to pass, when the locusts were
making an end*[1] *of devouring the herb of the land, that
I said, Lord Yahweh remit, I pray Thee,* or *pardon*—
a proof that there already weighed on the prophet's
spirit something more awful than loss of grass—*how
shall Jacob rise again ?*[2] *for he is little.*   The prayer
was heard.   *Yahweh relented for this : It shall not be,
said Yahweh.*   The unnameable *it* must be the same
as in the frequent phrase of the first chapter : *I will
not turn It back*—namely, the final doom on the people's
sin.   The reserve with which this is mentioned, both
while there is still chance for the people to repent and
after it has become irrevocable, is impressive.

The next example which Amos gave at Bethel of
his permitted insight into God's purpose was a great
drought, vii. 4–6 : *Thus the Lord Yahweh gave me to
see : and, behold, the Lord Yahweh was calling fire into
the quarrel.*[3]   There was, then, already a quarrel between
God and His people—another sign that the prophet's
moral conviction of Israel's sin preceded the rise of the
events in which he recognised its punishment.   *And* the
fire *devoured the Great Deep, yea, it was about to devour*[4]
the Portion.   Severe drought in Palestine might well
be described as fire, even when it was not accompanied

---

[1] So most now render, following the emendation of the Heb. text
by Torrey (*Journ. of Bibl. Lit.*, 1894, p. 63), וַיְהִי הָא מְכַלֶּה.

[2] LXX : *Who shall raise up Jacob again ?*

[3] So Professor A. B. Davidson.   But the grammar might equally
well afford the rendering *one calling that the Lord will punish with
the fire*, the ל of לְרִיב marking the introduction of indirect speech
(cf. Ewald, § 338*a*).   But Hitzig for קְרָא reads קָרָה (Deut. xxv. 18),
to *occur, happen.*   Similarly Wellhausen, *es nahte sich su strafen mit
Feuer der Herr Jahve.*   All these renderings yield practically the same
meaning.

[4] A. B. Davidson, *Syntax*, § 57, Rem. 1.

by the flame and smoke of those forest and prairie fires which Joel describes as its consequences.[1] But to have the full fear of such a drought, we should need to feel beneath us the curious world which the men of those days felt. To them the earth rested on a great deep, from whose stores all her springs and fountains burst. When these failed it meant that the unfathomed floods below were burnt up. But how fierce the flame that could effect this ! And how certainly able to devour next the solid land which rested above the deep —the very *Portion* [2] assigned by God to His people. Again Amos interceded : *And I said, Lord Yahweh, I pray Thee forbear : how shall Jacob rise ? for he is little.* And for the second time Jacob was reprieved. *Yahweh relented for this : It also shall not come to pass, said the Lord Yahweh.*

We have treated these visions, not as the imagination or prospect of possible disasters,[3] but as insight into the meaning of actual plagues. Such a treatment is justified, not only by the habit of Amos to deal with real facts, but also by the occurrence of these same plagues among the series by which, as we are told, God had already sought to move the people to repentance.[4] The general question of sympathy between

[1] i. 19 f.
[2] Cf. Micah ii. 4. חֵלֶק is the word used, and according to the motive given above stands well for the climax of the fire's destructive work. This meets the objection of Wellhausen, who proposes to omit חֵלֶק, because the heat does not dry up first the great deep and then the fields (*Ackerflur*). This is to mistake the obvious point of the sentence. The drought was so great that, after the fountains were exhausted, it seemed as if the solid framework of the land, described with apt pathos as the *Portion*, would be the next to disappear. Some take חלק as *divided*, therefore *cultivated, ground*.
[3] So, for instance, Von Orelli.   [4] Ch. IV.

such purely physical disasters and the moral evil of a people we may postpone, confining ourselves here to the part played in the events by the prophet himself.

Surely there is something wonderful in the attitude of this shepherd to the fires and plagues that Nature sweeps upon his land.   He is ready for them.   And he is ready not only by the general feeling of his time that such things happen of the wrath of God.   His sovereign and predictive conscience recognises them as God's ministers.   They are sent to punish a people already condemned.   Yet, unlike Elijah, Amos does not summon the drought, nor welcome its arrival.   How far has prophecy travelled since the violent Tishbite !   With all his conscience of Israel's sin, Amos yet prays that their doom may be turned.   We have here some evidence of the struggle through which these later prophets passed, before they accepted their awful messages to men.   Even Amos, desert-bred and living aloof from Israel, shrank from the judgement which it was his call to punish.   For two moments—they would appear to be the only two in his ministry—his heart contended with his conscience, and twice he entreated God to forgive.   At Bethel he told the people all this, in order to show how unwillingly he took up his duty against them, and how inevitable he found that duty to be.   But still more shall we learn from his tale, if we feel in his words about the smallness of Jacob not pity only but sympathy.   We shall learn that prophets are never made solely by the bare word of God, but that even the most objective and judicial of them has to earn his title to proclaim judgement by suffering with men the agony of the judgement he proclaims.   Never to a people came there a true prophet who had not first prayed for them.   To have entreated for men, to have represented them in the highest courts of Being, is to have also earned judicial rights upon them. And thus it is that our Judge at the Last Day shall be none other than our great Advocate who continually maketh intercession for us. It is prayer, let us repeat, which, while it gives us all power with God, endows us at the same time with moral rights over men. Upon his mission of judgement we shall follow Amos with the greater sympathy that he thus comes forth to it from the mercy-seat and the ministry of intercession.

The first two visions which Amos told at Bethel were of disasters in the sphere of nature, but his third lay in the sphere of politics. The two former were, in their completeness at least, averted ; and the language Amos used of them seems to imply that he had not even then faced the possibility of a final overthrow. He took for granted *Jacob* was *to rise again :* he only feared as to *how* this should be. But the third vision is so final that the prophet does not even try to intercede. Israel is measured, found wanting, and doomed. Assyria is not named, but is obviously intended ; and the fact that the prophet arrives at certainty with regard to the doom of Israel, just when he thus comes within sight of Assyria, is instructive as to the influence exerted on prophecy by the rise of that empire.[1]

vii. 7–9 : *Thus He gave me to see : and, behold, the Lord had taken His station*—'tis a more solemn word than the *stood* of our versions—*upon a city wall* once built to *the plummet,*[2] *and in His hand a plummet. And Yahweh said unto me, What art thou seeing, Amos ?*

---

[1] See Ch. IV, p. 47.

[2] Literally *of the plummet*, an obscure expression. It cannot mean plumb-straight, for the wall is condemned. Harper thinks *plummet* 'has crept in here by mistake' and with many others omits it. Duhm omits *the Lord* and reads the verb with *plummet—a plummet was set to the wall.*

The question betrays some astonishment by the pr
phet at the vision or some difficulty he felt in maki
it out.   He evidently does not feel it at once, as t
natural result of his own thinking : it is objective a
strange to him ; he needs time to see into it.   *A
I said, A plummet.   And the Lord said, Behold, I a
setting a plummet in the midst of My people Israel.
will not again pass them over.*   To set a measuring-li
or a line with weights attached to any building mea
to devote it to destruction ; [1] but here it is uncerta
whether the plummet threatens destruction, or mea
that God will at last clearly prove to the prophet t
insufferable obliquity of the fabric of the nation's li
originally set straight by Himself—originally *a wall o
plummet*.   For God's judgements are never arbitrar
by a standard we men can read He shows us the
necessity.   Conscience itself is no mere voice of autho
ity : it is a convincing plummet, and plainly lets
see *why* we should be punished.   But whichever inte
pretation we choose, the result is the same.   *The hi
places of Isaac* [2] *shall be desolate, and the sanctuaries
Israel laid waste ; and I will rise against the house
Jeroboam with the sword.*   A declaration of war ! Isra
is to be invaded, her dynasty overthrown.   Every o
who heard the prophet would know, though he name
them not, that the Assyrians were meant.

It was apparently at this point that Amos wa

---

[1] 2 Kings xxi. 13 : *I will stretch over Jerusalem the line of Samar
and the plummet* or *weight* (מִשְׁקֹלֶת) *of the house of Ahab.* Isa. xxx
11 : *He shall stretch over it* (Edom) *the measuring-line of confusi
and the weights* (literally *stones*) *of emptiness.*

[2] As in verse 16. Amos is the only prophet who uses this name f
the people of Yahweh. Does he mean by it N. Israel only or does
include Judah in it, or mean by it Judah only ? Isaac himself dw
in S. Palestine, and there Beersheba was one of the sanctuaries whi
Amos condemned along with Bethel and Gilgal in N. Israel, v. 5.

interrupted by Amasiah. The priest, who was conscious of no spiritual power with which to oppose the prophet, gladly grasped the opportunity given him by the mention of the king, and fell back on the invariable resource of a barren and envious sacerdotalism : *He speaketh against Cæsar.*[1] There follows one of the great scenes of history—the scene which, however fast the ages and the languages, the ideals and the deities may change, repeats itself with the same two actors. Priest and Man face each other—Priest with King behind, Man with God—and wage that debate in which the warfare and progress of religion largely consist. But the story is only typical by being real. Many subtle traits of human nature prove that we have here an exact narrative of fact. Take Amasiah's report to Jeroboam. He gives to the words of the prophet just that exaggeration and innuendo which betray the wily courtier, who knows how to accentuate a general denunciation till it feels like a personal attack. And yet, like every Caiaphas of his tribe, the priest in his exaggerations expresses a deeper meaning than he is conscious of ; vii. 10 ff. : *And Amasiah the priest of Bethel sent unto Jeroboam the king of Israel saying : Amos*—the mere mention of the name without description proves that the prophet was already known in Israel, perhaps was one on whom the authorities had long kept their eye—*Amos hath conspired against thee*—yet God was his only fellow-conspirator !—*in the midst of the house of Israel*—this royal temple at Bethel. *The land is not able to hold all his words*—it must burst ; yes, but in another sense than thou meanest, O Caiaphas-Amasiah ! *For thus hath Amos said, By the sword shall Jeroboam die*—Amos had spoken only of the dynasty, but the

[1] John xix. 12.

twist which Amasiah lends to the words is calculated
—*and Israel going shall go into exile from off his own
ground.* This was the one unvarnished spot in the
report.

Having fortified himself, as little men will do, by
his duty to the powers that be, Amasiah dares to turn
upon the prophet; and he does so, it is amusing
to observe, with that tone of intellectual and moral
superiority which it is extraordinary to see some men
derive from a merely official station or touch with
government. *And Amasiah said unto Amos, Visionary,[1] begone! Get thee off to the land of Judah; and earn[2]
bread there, and there play the prophet. But at Bethel*
—mark the rising accent of the voice—*thou shalt not
again prophesy. The King's Sanctuary it is, and the
House of the Kingdom.*[3] With the official mind this is
more conclusive than that it is the House of God!
In fact the speech of Amasiah justifies the hardest
terms which Amos uses of the religion of his day. In
all this priest says there is no trace of the spiritual
—only fear, pride, and privilege. Divine truth is
challenged by human law, and the Word of God
silenced in the name of the King.

We have here a conception of religion, which is not
merely due to the unspiritual character of the priest
who utters it, but has its roots in the far back origins
of Israel's religion. The pagan Semite identified absolutely State and Church; and on that identification
was based the religious practice of early Israel. It had
many healthy results: it kept religion in touch with

[1] The word *seer* is here used in a contemptuous sense, and has therefore to be translated by some such word as *visionary*.

[2] Literally *eat*.

[3] בֵּית מַמְלָכָה—that is, a *central* or *capital sanctuary.* Cf. עִיר
הַמַּמְלָךְ (1 Sam. xxvii. 5), *city of the kingdom, i.e.* chief or capital town

public life ; order, justice, patriotism, self-sacrifice for the common weal, were devoutly held to be matters of religion. So long, therefore, as the system was inspired by spiritual ideals, nothing for those times could be better. But we see in it an almost inevitable tendency to harden to sheer officialism. That it was more apt to do so in Israel than in Judah, is intelligible from the political origin of the Northern Schism, and the erection of the national sanctuaries from motives of statecraft.[1] Erastianism could hardly be more flagrant or more ludicrous in its opposition to true religion than at Bethel. And yet how often have the ludicrousness and the flagrancy been repeated, with far less temptation ! Ever since Christianity became a state religion, she that needed least to use the weapons of this world has done so again and again in a Pagan fashion. The attempts of Churches by law established, to stamp out by law religious dissent ; or where such attempts were no longer possible, the charges now of fanaticism and now of sordidness and religious shopkeeping, which have been so frequently made against dissent by little men who fancied their state connection, or their higher social position, to mean an intellectual and moral superiority ; the claims which many a minister of religion makes upon the homes and the souls of a parish, by virtue not of his calling in Christ, but of his position as official priest of the parish—all these are the sins of Amaṣiah, priest of Bethel. But they are not confined to an established Church. The Amaṣiahs of dissent are also many. Wherever the official masters the spiritual ; wherever mere dogma or tradition is made the standard of preaching ; wherever new doctrine is silenced, or programmes of reform condemned, as

[1] 1 Kings xii. 26, 27.

in Free Churches they have sometimes been, not by spiritual argument, but by the *ipse dixit* of the dogmatist, or by ecclesiastical rule or expediency—there you have the same spirit. The dissenter who checks the Word of God in the name of some denominational law or dogma is as Erastian as the churchman who would crush it, like Amaṣiah, by invoking the State. Such things in whatever Church are the beggarly rudiments of Paganism ; and religious reform is achieved, as it was that day at Bethel, by the abjuring of officialism.

But Amos answered and said unto Amaṣiah, No prophet I, nor prophet's son. But a herdsman [1] *I, and a dresser of sycomores ; and Yahweh took me from behind the flock, and Yahweh said unto me, Go, prophesy unto My people Israel.*

On such words we do not comment ; we give them homage. The answer of this shepherd to this priest is no mere claim of personal disinterestedness. It is the protest of a new order of prophecy,[2] the charter of a spiritual religion. As we have seen, the *sons of the prophets* were guilds of men who had taken to prophesying because of certain gifts of temper and natural disposition, and they earned their bread by the exercise of these. Among such craftsmen Amos will not be reckoned. He is a prophet, but not of the kind with which his generation was familiar. An ordinary member of society, he has been suddenly called by

---

[1] *Prophet* and *prophet's son* are equivalent terms, the latter meaning one in the professional guilds of prophets. There is no need to change herdsman, בוקר, as Wellhausen and others do, into נוקד, shepherd, the word used in i. 1. (On sycomores see above, pp. 74 f.) Haupt's attempt (*J.B.L.*, xxxv, 1916, p. 282) to prove that Amos was not a shepherd by translating נוקד *piercer* and reading *from a life of peace* for *from after the flock* is fanciful and forced.

[2] Cf. Wellhausen, *Hist.*, Eng. Ed., § 6 : ' Amos was the founder and the purest type of a new order of prophecy.'

God from his civil occupation for a special purpose and by a call which has not necessarily to do with either gifts or a profession. This was something new, not only in itself, but in its consequences upon the general relations of God to men. What we see in this dialogue at Bethel is, therefore, not merely the triumph of a character, however heroic, but also a step forward— one of the greatest and most potential—in the history of religion.

There follows a denunciation of the man who sought to silence this fresh voice of God. *Now therefore hearken to the Word of Yahweh*[1] *thou that sayest, Prophesy not against Israel, nor let drop* thy words *against the house of Israel ; therefore thus saith Yahweh.* . . . Thou hast presumed to say ; *Hear what God will say.* Thou hast dared to set thine office and system against His word and purpose. See how they must be swept away. Against its usual order the grammar flings forward to the beginnings of its clauses each detail of the priest's estate then giving the scene of its desecration. *Thy wife—in the city shall play the harlot ; and thy sons and thy daughters—by the sword shall fall ; and thy ground —by the measuring rope shall be divided ; and thou on ground unclean shalt die.* Do not let us blame the prophet for cruelty in the first of these details. He did not invent it. With the rest it formed an ordinary consequence of defeat in the warfare of the times— an inevitable item of that general overthrow which, with bitter emphasis, the prophet describes in Amasiah's own words : *Israel going shall go into exile from off his own ground.*

There is added, viii. 1–3, a vision in line with the three which preceded the priest's interruption. We are

---

[1] This clause is omitted as superfluous by Baumann, Budde, and others

therefore justified in supposing that Amos spoke **it** also on this occasion, and in taking it as the close of his address at Bethel. *Thus the Lord Yahweh gave me to see : and, behold, a basket of Ḳaiṣ, that is summer fruit. And He said, What art thou seeing, Amos ? And I said, A basket of Ḳaiṣ. And Yahweh said unto me, The Ḳeṣ—the End—has come upon My people Israel. I will not again pass them over.* This does not carry the prospect beyond the third vision, but it stamps its finality, and there is therefore added, viii. 4, a vivid realisation of the result. By four disjointed lamentations, we are made to feel the shocks of the final collapse, and in the utter end an awful silence. *And the songs of the temple shall be howlings in that day, Rede of the Lord Yahweh. Multitude of corpses ! In every place ! He hath cast out ! Hush !* [1]

These then were perhaps the last words which Amos spoke to Israel. If so, they form a curious echo of what was enforced upon himself, and he may have meant them as such. He was *cast out ;* he was *silenced.* They might almost be the verbal repetition of the priest's orders. In any case the silence is appropriate. But Amaṣiah little knew what power he had given to prophecy the day he forbade it to speak. The gagged prophet began to write ; and those accents which, humanly speaking, might have died out with the songs of the temple of Bethel were clothed upon with the immortality of literature. Amos silenced wrote a book—first of prophets to do so—and this is the book we have now to study.

---

[1] For *songs,* Hoffmann, Wellhausen, etc., read *singing women,* which better agrees with the verb, lit. *shall howl. Temple* may equally well be *palace* which some prefer. Some consider the text hopelessly corrupt. Duhm proposes to read *I will cast them out* for *He hath cast out, hush* As said above, he attaches the verse to vi. 11 ; vii. 9.

CHAPTER VII

ATROCITIES AND ATROCITIES

AMOS I. 3–II

LIKE other prophets of Israel, Amos receives oracles for foreign nations. Unlike them he arranges the oracles not after, but before, his indictment of his own people, and so as to lead up to this. His reason is obvious and characteristic. If his aim be to enforce a religion independent of his people's interests and privileges, how can he better do so than by exhibiting its principles at work outside his people, and then, with the impetus drained from many areas, sweep in upon the vested iniquities of Israel herself? This is the course of the first section of his book— chaps. i and ii. One by one the neighbours of Israel are cited and condemned in the name of Yahweh; one by one they are told they must fall before the still unnamed engine of the Divine Justice. But when Amos has stirred his people's conscience and imagination by his judgement of their neighbours' sins, he turns with the same formula on themselves. Are they morally better? Are they more likely to resist Assyria? With greater detail he shows them worse and their doom the heavier for all their privileges. Thus is achieved an oratorical triumph, by tactics in harmony with the principles of prophecy and suited to the tempers of that time.

But Amos achieves another feat, which extends

beyond his own day. The sins he condemns in the heathen are at first sight very different from those which he exposes within Israel. Not only are they sins of foreign relations, of treaty and war, while Israel's are civic and domestic ; but they are what we call the atrocities of Barbarism—wanton war, massacre, and sacrilege ; while Israel's are rather the sins of Civilisation—the pressure of the rich upon the poor, the bribery of justice, the seduction of the innocent, impurity, and other evils of luxury. So great is this difference that a critic more gifted with ingenuity than with insight might plausibly distinguish in the section before us two prophets with different views of national sin—a ruder prophet, and an earlier, who judged nations only by the flagrant drunkenness of their war, and a more subtle prophet, and a later, who exposed the masked corruptions of their religion and their peace. Such a theory would be as false as it would be plausible. For not only is the diversity of the objects of the prophet's judgement explained by this, that Amos had no familiarity with the interior life of other nations, and could only arraign their conduct at those points where it broke into light in their foreign relations, while Israel's civic life he knew to the core. But Amos had besides a deliberate aim in placing the sins of civilisation as the climax to a list of the atrocities of barbarism. He would recall what men always forget, that the former are even more cruel and criminal than the latter ; that luxury, bribery, and intolerance, the oppression of the poor, the corruption of the innocent and the silencing of the prophet—what Christ calls offences against His little ones—are even more awful atrocities than the wanton horrors of barbarian warfare. If we keep in mind this moral purpose, we shall study with more interest than we could otherwise do the somewhat

foreign details of this section. Horrible as the outrages are which Amos describes, they were repeated
only yesterday by Turkey : many of the crimes with
which he charges Israel blacken the life of Turkey's
chief accuser, Great Britain.

In his survey—if indeed it be all his own—Amos
includes the six states of Palestine that bordered upon
Israel, and lay in the way of the advance of Assyria :
Aram of Damascus, Philistia, Tyre, Edom, Ammon,
and Moab. They are not arranged in geographical
order. The list begins with Aram in the north-east,
then leaps to Philistia in the south-west, comes north
again to Tyre, crosses to the south-east and Edom,
leaps Moab to Ammon, and then comes back to Moab.
Nor is any other explanation of the order visible.
Damascus heads the list, no doubt, because her cruelties
had been most felt by Israel, and perhaps too because
she lay most open to Assyria. It was also natural to
take next to Aram Philistia,[1] as Israel's other greatest
foe ; and nearest to Philistia lay Tyre. The three
south-eastern principalities come together. There may
also have been other reasons unknown to us.

These considerations make us hesitate to accept the
objections to the authenticity of the oracles on Philistia,
Tyre, and Edom, which are based on the fact that they
do not lie in the natural course of the Assyrian invasion
which is threatened to all the states included by the
oracles. To suppose that Amos must have followed
a strictly geographical order in threatening the states
which were neighbours to Israel seems a precarious
hypothesis ; unless there are other, intrinsic objections
to the authenticity of these oracles. Such intrinsic
objections will be discussed in each case as we come
to it.

[1] As in chs. vi. 2 ; ix. 7.

Each oracle is introduced by the declaration : *Thus saith*, or *hath said, Yahweh : Because of three crimes* or *transgressions of . . . yea, because of four, I will not turn It back*. In harmony with the rest of the book, God is represented as moving to punishment, not for a single sin, but for repeated and cumulative guilt. The unnamed *It* which God will not recall is not the word of judgement, but the Divine anger and the hand stretched forth to smite.[1] After the formula, an instance of the nation's guilt is given, and then in almost identical terms the destruction is decreed of all by war and captivity. Assyria is not mentioned, but it is the Assyrian fashion of dealing with conquered states which is described. Except in the case of Tyre and Edom, the oracles conclude as they have begun, by asserting themselves to be the *word of Yahweh*, or of *Yahweh the Lord*. It is no abstract righteousness which condemns these foreign peoples, but the God of Israel, and their evil deeds are described by the characteristic Hebrew word for sin—*crimes, revolts* or *treasons* against Him.[2]

1. Damascus of Aram

i. 3. *Thus sayeth Yahweh :*
    For three transgressions of Damascus,
    Yea for four I will not turn It back,
    For their threshing with thresh-drags of basalt,[3]
    The Gilead . . . (?) [4]

  4. *So I will send fire on the House of Hazael,*
    And it shall devour Ben-Hadad's palaces.

---

[1] So Isa. v. 25 ; cf. Ezek. xx. 22.
[2] פְּשָׁעִים.   [3] See next page.
[4] Extraordinarily short line, but Heb. gives no sign of a slip.

5. *I will shatter the bars* [1] *of Damascus*
   And cut off the dwellers [1] *from Bik'ath-'Aven*
   With the sceptre-bearer out of Beth-'Eden,
   And Aram's folk shall be exiled to Ḳir,
   Yahweh hath said.

In the text *basalt* is *iron*, but Arabs still call basalt iron, and the threshing-drags or sledges of Hauran, curved slabs [2] of wood drawn by horses, are studded below with basalt teeth which thresh out the grain and chop up the straw. So cruelly had Gilead been *threshed* by Hazael and his son Ben-hadad in the century before that of Amos. Fortresses were burned, soldiers slain without quarter, and women with child put to a horrible end. [3] Hazael and Ben-hadad are named here because they were thus Israel's worst oppressors and not merely because their names are typical of the dynasty of Damascus. [4] Are Bik'ath-'Aven and Beth-'Eden actual place-names, in which case they have not been certainly identified? Or have they been coined by the prophet, *Vale of Vanity* or *Idolatry* for the valley between the Lebanons, still called the Beka' in which Baalbek (Baal of the Beka'?) stands; and *House of Pleasure*, as if some royal paradise about Damascus whose surroundings are still 'Paradise' to the Arab world? [5] Ḳîr or Ḳôr was in the north from which the Arameans had originally come. [6]

---

[1] Heb. singular but collective ; LXX plural. So too in vv. 7, 8, etc.

[2] Arab. lûh, ' a slab ': description with drawings in Driver, p. 227 ; see also Musil, *Arabia Petræa*, iii. 302 ff.

[3] 2 Kings viii. 12 ; xiii. 3, 7.

[4] So Wellhausen.

[5] Wellhausen suggests that Aven may have been a god's name. Assyrian inscriptions mention a Bit-Adini on the Euphrates, too far north to be relevant here. See *K.A.T.*,[3] 39 f., 273.

[6] See ix. 7 ; Isa. xxii. 6.

2. THE PHILISTINES

i. 6. *Thus sayeth Yahweh :*
For three transgressions of Gaza,
Yea for four I will not turn It back,
For their exiling a whole population,[1]
To deliver them *up to Edom.*

7. *So I will send fire on the walls of Gaza,*
And it shall devour her palaces,

8. *I will cut off the dwellers from Ashdod*
And the sceptre-bearer from Ashkelon,
I will turn [2] *My hand against Ekron*
And the rest of the Philistines shall perish.
Yahweh [3] *hath said.*

I have little hesitation in agreeing with those who take this oracle as from Amos himself.[4] The critics who deny it to him [5] do so on the ground that Gath is omitted from the oracle's list of Philistine towns, for they suppose that Gath did not disappear from history till after Sargon's conquest of Philistia in 711. But this is not certain. It is true that the statement that Hazael *took Gath* [6] long before Amos' time does not by itself imply the destruction of the city, but when besides, in Sargon's account of his campaign, we read that Gath then belonged to Ashdod,[7] we may not unreasonably believe it possible that Gath had lost its independence by the time of Amos and that this was why the prophet omitted its name from his oracle on Philistia. A further reason offered for the late date of the oracle,

---

[1] So Driver ; Ewald, *whole villages.* Heb. lit. *exile a whole exile.*

[2] Some would render *bring again and again ;* cf. Isa. i. 25 ; Ps. lxxxi. 15.

[3] So LXX ; Heb. *the Lord Yahweh.*

[4] The older critics and of recent ones Winckler, Driver, Cheyne (*Enc. Bibl.*), Nowack, Baumann, Harper, Moffatt, Newman.

[5] Wellhausen, Marti.   [6] 2 Kings xii. 17.

[7] Winckler, *Geschichte Israels*, p. 225, *K.A.T.*[3], pp. 69-71. On the Philistine towas see my *Hist. Geog.*, ch. ix.

ATROCITIES AND ATROCITIES   125

that it is dependent on Joel iii. 4–6, seems to me groundless. In chap. vi. 2 Amos implies that Gath has already fallen ; Micah i. 10 is merely the repetition of an old proverb.

By all tribes of the ancient world the captives of their bow and spear were regarded as legitimate property : it was no offence to the public conscience that they should be sold into slavery. But the Philistines seem, without excuse of war, to have descended upon certain districts and swept the whole of the population before them, for purely commercial purposes. It was professional slave-catching. The Philistines were like the Arabs in Africa—not warriors who win their captives in honourable fight, but slave-traders pure and simple. In warfare in Arabia itself it is still a matter of conscience with the nomads not to extinguish a hostile tribe, however bitter they be against it.[1] Gaza is chiefly blamed by Amos, for she was the emporium of the trade on the border of the desert, with roads and regular caravans to Petra and Elah on the Gulf of Akaba, both of them places in Edom and depots for the traffic with Arabia.[2]

3. Tyre

i. 9. *Thus sayeth Yahweh :*
   For three transgressions of Tyre,
   Yea for four I will not turn It back,
   For their delivering over whole populations [3] *to Edom,*
   And they did not remember the covenant of brothers.
  10. *So I will send fire on the walls of Tyre*
   And it shall devour her palaces.

---

[1] Doughty, *Arabia Deserta*, i. 335.
[2] On the close connection of Edom and Gaza see my *Hist. Geog.*, pp. 182 ff.
[3] Lit. *a whole exile* (*i.e. body of exiles*) or *captivity*.

This oracle, like those on Edom and Judah, differs considerably from the others in structure, and we can hardly attribute this difference to the wish of an author to avoid repetition, for then ' it would be impossible to understand why the condensation is made in one case rather than in another.' [1]   On this ground, added to the fact that in view of the Assyrian invasion threatened upon all the neighbours of Israel the oracle of Tyre stands out of its proper geographical order, the most of recent critics have doubted or denied its authenticity and taken it to be a late addition to the prophecies of Amos. These critics form indeed an imposing body of opinion.[2]   At the same time it would have been strange if from a list of states so liable to the Assyrian doom Tyre had been omitted, Tyre which lay on the natural path of the avenger and was actually visited by him.

It is a difficult question, for the oracle contains no definite historical allusion, which might enable us to decide one way or another.   We do not know to what *the covenant of brothers* refers.   Some understand by it that the captives were Hebrews and the brotherhood that between Israel and Edom ; others that the captives were Hebrews and the brotherhood one between Israel and Tyre ; others that the captives were Phœnicians and the brotherhood that between Tyre and the other Phœnician cities.   But of these alternatives the first is impossible, for in such a case the crime would have been not Tyre's in selling but Edom's in buying. Nor is the second any more likely, for though there once had been an alliance between Israel and Tyre, and Kings Solomon and Hiram had called each other

[1] Harper, p. 28

[2] Wellhausen, Nowack, Löhr, Baumann, Cheyne, Marti, Budde, Harper, Duhm, Newman, Moffatt.

brothers,[1] Israel felt themselves of a wholly different race and religion from Canaan, and, besides, during the prophetic period before Amos their political and religious hostility had been so violent that we can hardly think of him or another prophet as conceiving of any sort of brotherhood between them. We are therefore left to the great probability of the third alternative, that the covenant of brotherhood refers to the close kinship between the Phœnician cities.[2] This, however, hardly carries us to a definite date. For while in the scrappy records of Phœnician history before the time of Amos we find no instance of so gross an outrage by Tyre, it is possible for such to have occurred. During the next century Tyre twice basely took sides with Assyria in the latter's suppression of the revolts of other Phœnicians,[3] and it is also possible that her baseness may then have extended to the crime with which this oracle charges her.

But whoever may have been the author of the oracle, note that it expresses not resentment against a betrayal of Israel but indignation at an outrage upon natural rights and feelings with which Israel's interests were not concerned. This certainly suits the lofty spirit, if it does not belong to the original form, of the prophecies of Amos.

---

[1] I Kings ix. 13.

[2] This is the more probable that the other Phœnician cities are not mentioned in the oracle. It is curious that Wellhausen, after allowing that Tyre's crime was probably committed against those cities, should find a reason for doubting the authenticity of the oracle in the fact of their omission as contrasted with the list of Philistine towns in the preceding oracle.

[3] Under Asarhaddon, 678–676 B.C., and later under Assurbanipal (Pietschmann, *Gesch. der Phonizier*, pp. 302 f.).

4. EDOM

i. 11. *Thus sayeth Yahweh :*
For three transgressions of Edom,
Yea for four I will not turn It back,
For his pursuing his brother with the sword.
And he stifled his natural feelings,
And was ever fretting [1] *his anger,*
And his wrath he kept [2] *for aye.*

12. *So I will send fire upon Teman,*
And it shall devour the palaces of Boṣrah.

The objections to the authenticity of this oracle are more serious than those in the case of the oracle on Tyre. It has been remarked [3] that before the Jewish Exile so severe a tone could not have been adopted by a Jew against Edom, who had been mostly under the yoke of Judah, and not leniently treated. What were the facts ? Joab subdued Edom for David with great cruelty. [4] Jewish governors were set over the conquered people, and this state of affairs seems to have lasted, in spite of an Edomite attempt against Solomon, [5] till 850. In Jehoshaphat's reign, 873–850, *there was no king of Edom, a deputy was king,* who towards 850 joined the kings of Judah and Israel in an invasion of Moab through his territory. [6] But, soon after this invasion and perhaps in consequence of its failure, Edom revolted from Joram of Judah (849–842), who unsuccessfully attempted to put down the revolt. [7] The Edomites appear to have remained independent

---

[1] There is no need to amend *was fretting* with Olshausen (Marti and others) to the *kept* of Ps. ciii. 9, even though Syr. and Vulg. support this.

[2] Read with LXX שמר לנצח, though throughout the verse the LXX translation is very vile.

[3] Wellhausen, *in loco.*

[4] 2 Sam. viii. 13, with 1 Kings xi. 16.

[5] 1 Kings xi. 14–25.

[6] 1 Kings xxii. 47 ; 2 Kings iii.

[7] 2 Kings viii. 20–22.

for fifty years at least, though they paid tribute to
Ramman-Nirari III (812–783)[1] Amaṣiah of Judah
(797–779) smote them,[2] but not it would seem into
subjection, for, according to the Chronicler, Uzziah
had to win back Elath for the Jews after Amasiah's
death.[3] The history, therefore, of the relations of
Judah and Edom before the time of Amos was of such
a kind as to make credible the existence in Judah at
that time of the feeling about Edom which inspires
this oracle. Edom had shown the vigilant, implacable
hatred here described. But was the right to blame
them for it Judah's, who herself had persistently waged
war, with confessed cruelty, against Edom? Could
a Judæan prophet be just in blaming Edom and saying
nothing of Judah? It is true that in the fifty years of
Edom's independence—the period, we must remember,
from which Amos seems to draw the materials of all
his other charges—there may have been events to
justify this oracle as spoken by him ; and our ignorance
of that period is reason why we should pause before
rejecting the oracle so dogmatically as Wellhausen
does. But we have at least serious grounds for sus-
pecting it. To charge Edom, whom Judah has conquered and treated cruelly, with restless hate towards
Judah seems to fall below that high impartial tone
which prevails in the other oracles of this section.
The charge was much more justifiable at the time
of the Exile, when Edom did behave shamefully towards Israel.[4] Wellhausen points out that Teman and
Bosrah are names which do not occur in the Old
Testament before the Exile, but this is uncertain and

[1] Buhl, *Gesch. der Edomiter*, p. 65.
[2] 2 Kings xiv. 10   [3] 2 Chron. xxvi. 2.
[4] See, however, Buhl, *op. cit.*, 6.

inconclusive.[1] The oracle wants the concluding formula
of the rest.

5. AMMON

i. 13. *Thus sayeth Yahweh :*
For three transgressions of the sons of Ammon,
Yea for four I will not turn It back,
For their ripping up Gilead's women with child,
For the sake of enlarging their border.

14. *So I will set fire to the walls of Rabbah*
And it shall devour her palaces,
With clamour in the day of battle
And storming in the day of the whirlwind.

15. *And their king shall go into exile,*
He and his princes [2] together—
Yahweh hath said.

To enlarge their border—for such an end they committed such an atrocity, upon women with child !
The crime has been more or less frequent in Semitic
warfare.   Wellhausen [3] refers to several instances in
the feuds of Arab tribes about their borders.   In our
own day the Turks have been guilty of it.[4]   The historian of Israel puts the same charge into the mouth
of Elisha against Hazael of Aram,[5] and probably the
war was the same, when Gilead was attacked simul-

---

[1] Teman is etymologically *south-land ;* Gen. xxx. 34, etc. Boṣrah,
now Buṣeirah, thirty-five miles N.N.E. of Petra. See Doughty,
Arabia Deserta, vol. i, pp. 31, 38 (with map attached to the vol. ; A.
Musil, *Arabia Petræa*, ii, Edom i, pp. 158, 337. In two passages Boṣrah,
the city, is parallel as here to a region ; Isa. xxxiv. 6 ; lxiii. 1. Teman
need not be taken here as a city, as which it does not appear before
Eusebius.

[2] LXX, *their priests and their princes*, due to taking (as Syr. and Vulg.
do) Malkam, *their king*, as Milkom the Ammonite god. See Jer. xlix. 3.

[3] P. 70.   [4] Notably in the Armenian massacres.

[5] 2 Kings viii. 12.

taneously by Arameans from the north and Ammonites from the east.   Rabbah is Rabbath-Ammon, *chief town* or *capital* of Ammon.[1]   As we speak of ' storming ' a city, Amos and Isaiah [2] use the tempest and whirlwind to describe the overwhelming invasion by Assyria.   The oracle concludes with the characteristic Assyrian policy towards defeated peoples—exile.

6. MOAB.

ii. 1.   *Thus sayeth Yahweh :*
    For three transgressions of Moab,
    Yea for four I will not turn It back,
    For his burning down of the bones
    Of the King of Edom to lime.[3]

  2.   *So I will send fire upon Moab,*
    And it shall devour Keriyoth's palaces,
    And Moab shall die in tumult,
    With clamour, with the sound of the trumpet.

  3.   *I will cut off the regent from his* [4] *midst*
    And slay all his [4] *princes with him—*
    Yahweh hath said.

---

[1] Ammon and Rabbath-Ammon, *H.G.H.L.*, 578, 593.

[2] Isa. xxvii. 7 f. ; xxviii. 2.

[3] The proper division of the lines of this couplet is uncertain.   I give it in the order of the words in the text.   Marti would place *to lime* after *burning* as the end of the first line.   Baumann leaves *to lime* alone as the second line which recalls *the Gilead* as the last line of i. 3 ; see above, p. 122.

> ' Imperial Cæsar dead and turned to clay
> Might stop a hole to keep the wind away.'

But some by altering לשׂיד (*to lime*) to לשׁדד and bringing up to it the line *and Moab shall die in tumult* and changing some of its letters obtain the reading *in order to desecrate the dead because of violence done to Moab* (see Harper and Moffatt).

[4] *His* (by slight emendation) for *her* of the text ; Moab is masculine. If the feminine is retained it means the land.

In the invasion of Moab by Israel, Judah, and Edom, about 850, the rage of Moab seems to have been directed chiefly against Edom.[1] Whether the opportunity to appease that rage occurred on the withdrawal of Israel we cannot say. But either then or later, balked of their attempt to get the King of Edom alive, Moab wreaked their vengeance on his corpse and burned his bones to lime. This was a sacrilege in the belief of all antiquity. A parallel case is found in Asshurbanipal's vindictive violation of the tombs of the King of Elam : ' I carried off their bones to the land of Ashur, I prevented their manes from resting ; I deprived them of the funeral offering and the libation of water.'[2]

Keriyoth, with the definite article, *The-Cities*, where Chemosh had his shrine,[3] may be the present Kureiyat on the Moab plateau, but this is claimed by many for Kiriathaim. *In tumult shall Moab die*, to Israel the Moabites were the *sons of tumult*.[4] *Regent*, literally *judge*, a deputy for either a disabled or a deposed king,[5] or possibly a vassal-king appointed by Jeroboam II on his conquest of Moab.[6]

These then are the charges which the prophet brings against the heathen neighbours of Israel.

If we look across the details through which we have been working, we see a picture of the Semitic world so summary and so vivid that we get the like of it nowhere else—the Semitic world in its characteristic turbulence ; its factions and ferocities, causeless raids and quarrels, tribal disputes about boundaries flaring up into the

[1] 2 Kings iii. 26 ; so rightly Pusey.
[2] *The Rassam-Cylinder*, vi. 74 ; Rogers, *Hist. of Bab. and Assyria*, ii. 273 ; Dhorme, *Revue Biblique*, 1911, p. 357.
[3] Moabite stone, line 13.   [4] Jer. xlviii. 25.
[5] 2 Kings xv 5.   [6] 2 Kings xiv. 25.

most terrible massacres, vengeance that wreaks itself alike on the embryo and the corpse—*cutting up women with child in Gilead*, and *burning to lime the bones of the king of Edom*. And the commerce which binds these ferocious tribes together is the slave-trade in its wholesale and most odious form.

Amos treats none of the atrocities subjectively. It is not because they have been inflicted upon Israel that he feels or condemns them. The appeals of Israel against the tyrant become many as the centuries go on ; the later parts of the Old Testament are full of the complaints of God's people, conscious of their mission to the world, against the heathen who prevented them from it. Here we find none of these complaints, but a strictly objective and judicial indictment of the crimes of heathen men against each other ; and though this is made in the name of Israel's God, it is not in the interests of His people or of any of His purposes through them, but solely by the standard of an impartial righteousness which, as we are soon to hear, must descend in equal judgement on Israel.[1]

Again, for the moral principles which Amos enforces no originality can be claimed. He condemns neither war as a whole nor slavery as a whole, but limits his curse to wanton and deliberate aggravations of them : to the slave-trade in cold blood, in violation of treaties and for purely commercial ends ;[2] to war for selfish causes, that wreaks itself on pregnant women and dead

[1] Similarly Löhr who sees in the Yahweh of these oracles ' the guardian of the moral order in the world of nations.' Baumann is wrong in contradicting this statement and seeing in the Yahweh of the oracles only ' the avenger of his horribly treated people. The inhumanity of the warfare does not constitute the crime but aggravates it ' (*op. cit.*, p. 11, n.). Marti: ' Yahweh guards the fulfilment of the humane moral duties ' (*Comm.*, p. 164). See also his *Geschichte der Israel. Religion*, 4th ed., p. 170.

[2] See above, p. 125.

men ; to national hatreds, that never will be still. Now
against such things there has always been in mankind
a strong conscience, of which the word ' humanity ' is
in itself a sufficient proof. We need not here inquire
into the origin of such a common sense—whether it be
some native impulse of tenderness which asserts itself
as soon as the duties of self-defence are exhausted, or
some rational notion of the needlessness of excesses,
or whether, in committing these, men are visited by
fear of retaliation from the wrath they have unnecessarily exasperated. Certain it is, that warriors
of many races have hesitated to be wanton in their war,
and have foreboded the judgement of heaven upon
every blind extravagance of hate or cruelty. It is
well known how ' fey ' the Greeks felt the insolence
of power and immoderate anger ; they are the fatal
element in many a Greek tragedy.[1] But the Semites
themselves, whose racial ferocity is notorious, are not
without the same feeling. ' Even the Beduins' old
cruel rancours are often less than the golden piety of
the wilderness. The danger past, they can think of the
defeated foeman with kindness, . . . putting only their
trust in Ullah to obtain the like at need for themselves.
It is contrary to the Arabian conscience to extinguish
a Kabîla.' [2] Similarly in Israel some of the earliest
ethical movements were revolts of the public conscience against horrible outrages, like that, for instance,
done by the Benjamites of Gibeah.[3] Therefore in these
oracles on his wild Semitic neighbours Amos discloses
no new ideal for either tribe or individual. Our view
is confirmed that he was intent only upon rousing

---

[1] ἰδυσσεβίας μὲν ὕβρις τέκος (Æschylus, *Eumen.*, 534): cf. *Odyssey*, xiv. 262 ; xvii. 431.

[2] *I.e.*, a tribe ; Doughty, *Arabia Deserta*, i. 335.

[3] Judges xix, xx.

the natural conscience of his Hebrew hearers in order to engage this upon other vices to which it was less impressionable—that he was describing those deeds of war and slavery, whose atrocity all men admitted, only that he might proceed to bring under the same condemnation the civic and domestic sins of Israel.

We turn with him, then, to Israel. But in his book as it now stands in our Bibles, Israel is not immediately reached. Between her and the foreign nations two verses are bestowed upon Judah :—

> ii. 4. *Thus sayeth Yahweh :*
> *For three transgressions of Judah,*
> *Yea for four I will not turn It back*
> *For their despising the Torah of Yahweh*
> *And they kept not His statutes,*
> *And their falsehoods led them astray,*
> *Which their fathers had followed.*
> 5. *So I will send fire upon Judah*
> *And it shall devour the palaces of Jerusalem.*

These verses have been suspected as a later insertion,[1] on the ground that every reference to Judah in the Book of Amos must be late, that the language is very formal, and that the phrases in which the sin of Judah is described sound like echoes of Deuteronomy, while the term *falsehoods* for *idols* is late, after Jeremiah, the syntax awkward, and the structure of the verse unlike that of the genuine oracles. The first of these

---

[1] Duhm was the first to publish reasons for rejecting the passage (*Theol. der Propheten*, 1875, p. 119), but Wellhausen had already reached the same conclusion (*Kleine Propheten*, p. 71). Oort and Stade adhere. On the other side see Robertson Smith, *Prophets of Israel*, p. 398, and Kuenen, who adheres to Smith's arguments (*Onderzoek*) ; also Driver, p. 117. More recently Budde, Nowack, Volz, Cheyne, Marti, and Harper deny the authenticity of the oracle.

reasons may be dismissed ; it would have been more strange if Amos had never referred to Judah.[1] The charges, however, are not like those which Amos elsewhere makes, and though the phrases may be quite as early as his time, which is very doubtful, the reader of the original, and even the reader of the English version, is aware of a certain tameness and vagueness of statement, which contrasts remarkably with the usual pungency of the prophet's style. We are forced to suspect the authenticity of theses verses.

We ought to pass, then, straight from the third to the sixth verse of this chapter, from the oracles on foreign nations to that on Northern Israel. It is introduced with the same formula as they are. But there follow a greater number of details, for Amos has come among his own people whom he knows to the heart, and he applies to them a standard more exact and an obligation more heavy than any he could lay to the life of the heathen.

7. ISRAEL

ii. 6. *Thus sayeth Yahweh :*
For three transgressions of Israel
Yea for four I will not turn It back,
For their selling the honest [2] *for silver,*
And the poor [3] *for a pair of shoes ;*

---

[1] 'It is plain that Amos could not have excepted Judah from the universal ruin which he saw to threaten the whole land, or at all events such exception would have required to be expressly made on special grounds' (Robertson Smith, *The Prophets of Israel*, p. 398).

[2] Heb. saddik, *righteous* : hardly, as most take it, the *legally* (as distinguished from the *morally*) *righteous*.

[3] Literally *the needy*.

7. *Who tramp to the dust the head of the feeble (?)* [1]
And the way of the humble pervert.
A man and his father frequent the same maid [2]
To the abuse of My Holy Name. [3]

8. *On garments in pledge they stretch them out*
By the side of every altar,
And the wine of the fined they drink
In the house of their god. [4]

So vicious and unashamed a society ! The rich oppress the poor not, it would seem, by corrupting justice with bribes, but as creditors selling their needy debtors into slavery for the proverbial *pair of shoes*, or, as we should say, ' for an old song,' unless *pair of shoes* is to be taken here in the sense in which it is used elsewhere as a token or symbol in the conveyance of property, and so ' cheating the needy out of his land.' [5] The feeble

---

[1] Heb. and the English versions : *that pant after the dust of the earth on the head of the poor*, so improbable a hyperbole (though accepted by Hitzig, Pusey, and Duhm) that many emendations of the text have been proposed. The most certain of these is the reading הַשֹּׁפִים or הַשֹּׁאֲפִים, participle of שׁוּף, *who trample* or *crush* (Gen. iii. 15) instead of הַשֹּׁאֲפִים, *who pant after ;* so with Jerome most moderns ; the LXX πατοῦντα though applied to *shoes* of the previous line lends this some support. Jerome, approved by Driver, would delete *on* before *the head ;* others, Wellhausen, Nowack, Torrey, Löhr, Marti, delete as an ancient gloss *the dust of the earth*, but ' if these words are not genuine it is difficult to understand how they found their way into the text ' (Driver) ; the LXX read them. Moffatt : *tramp like dust. Feeble*, Heb. דַּל, *thin*, often rendered *poor*. The emendations proposed for the next line are quite unnecessary ; cf. Job xxiv. 4.

[2] *The same*, LXX ; Heb. *the maid*, the definite article expressing not a definite individual but a member of a well-known class or genus.

[3] LXX, *the name of their God.*

[4] Löhr transfers ver. 8 to between 7*a* and 7*b* ; Harper wholly transposes vv. 7 and 8 and certainly effects a better climax for the strophe.

[5] Hoffmann, *Z.A.T.W.*, iii, pp. 97 ff. ; Box, *Expository Times*, 1901, 377 f. ; Harper, 49 ; basing their opinion on the LXX version of 1 Sam. xii. 8 confirmed by the restored Heb. text of Ecclus. xlvi. 19.

are crushed, and the meek prevented from pursuing their own quiet ways of faith and conduct ; with flouting of the humane law that a creditor must return by sunset the clothes given him in pledge by his poor neighbour,[1] for the rich creditor uses these to stretch himself on either feasting or sleeping ; the use of fines (therefore public moneys ?) to buy wine with for revelling in the house of *their god* or *gods ;* and shameless public unchastity, possibly also practised in the sanctuaries as among other peoples of the time. A riot of sin, exploiting the misery of the poor, profaning religion ; a religion feverish and sensual.

By one of the sudden contrasts that he loves Amos sweeps out of all this into God's ideal of religion—a great historical movement, told in the language of the open air : national deliverance, guidance on the highways of the world, the inspiration of prophecy and of pure consecrated lives. What contrast to sanctuaries filled with revellings and hot with lust !

ii. 10.[2] *Yet I brought you up from the land of Egypt,*
Through the desert I led you for forty years
To possess the land of the Amorite.

9. *And I destroyed the Amorite [3] before you,[4]*
Whose height was as the height of cedars,
And strong was he as the oaks ;
Yet his fruit I destroyed from above,
And his roots from below.

---

[1] Ex. xxii. 6.

[2] Logically and chronologically **vv. 9, 10** should be transposed as above ; so Löhr, Harper, Moffatt. Marti takes 10 as interpolated, because of the greater roughness and heaviness of its rhythm which are obvious.

[3] On *Amorite*, used for all the inhabitants of Canaan, see Driver's *Deuteronomy*, pp. 11 f. and Harper *in loco.*

[4] So some Heb. MSS ; Heb. text has *them.*

11. *And I raised from your sons for Prophets,*
     And from your youths for Nazirites.
     Was it not even thus, O sons of Israel !—
     'Tis the Rede of Yahweh—
12. *But you gave the Nazirites wine to drink*
     And charged the Prophets, Prophesy not ! [1]

We are out on open history with God Himself—the
I, I, of vv. 9, 10 are very emphatic. For Israel religion is history : their deliverance, by His grace and
Power, from servitude ; His guidance and training of
them ; His gift of a land and a home, and upon that
stage and shelter His raising of spiritual guides and
examples. Yet these the people had done their worst
to silence and corrupt. Their doom must come.

Before we take the prophet's utterance of this let
us remind ourselves how far beyond his own day and
people his words are needed, that the social sins of a
civilised and enlightened nation are just as bad as
the atrocities of barbarian war and slave-trading and
as certain of Divine punishment.

In the nineteenth Christian century, Britain, the
destroyer of the slave-traffic and champion of oppressed
nationalities, suffered its own children to work in
factories and clay-pits sometimes for sixteen hours a
day, and in mines set women to tasks for which horses
were deemed too valuable. After 1848 things improved
somewhat, but how slowly and against what callousness
of Christians Lord Shaftesbury's long and often dis-
appointed labours testify. Our religious public, which
cursed the Turk and cried out in righteous indignation
against his atrocities upon the Armenians, has by the
avarice of some, the passion for enjoyment of many

---

[1] Harper, Marti, etc., take this verse as interpolated, but not, I think,
on sufficient grounds.

more, and the thoughtlessness of others contributed
to conditions of life and fashions of society which
bear cruelly on the poor, taint our literature, increase
temptation both in town and country, and render pure
childlife hardly possible among masses of our population.   Along some of the lines of our Christian civilisation men are just as cruel and lustful as Turk or
Kurd.

Amos heard God sentence Israel as follows :—

ii. 13   *Behold I am to bear down upon you*
         As a waggon bears down full of sheaves.

Or, as alternative readings render, with the same impression of a general judgement :—

         I make the ground under you quake,
         As a waggon full of sheaves makes it quake.

Or *as a waggon* itself *quakes* or *groans* under its load.
The shock is to be War—War and all its panic.

    14.   *And flight shall fail from the swift,*
           And the strong shall not prove his power,
           Nor the mighty escape with his life.

    15.   *He that grasps the bow shall not stand,*
           Nor the swift of foot escape,
           Nor the rider on horse escape with his life.

    16.   *And the stoutest of heart of the mighty (?)*
           Shall flee away stripped in that day—
           The Rede of Yahweh.

NOTE ON THE SENTENCE OF DOOM (II. 13)

The verb עוק of the Massoretic text is not found elsewhere,
and whether we retain it, or take it as a variant of, or mistake
for, צוק, or adopt some other reading, the whole phrase is
uncertain, and the exact meaning has to be guessed, though
the general sense remains much the same.   The following is a
complete note on the subject, with reasons for adopting the
above version : *I am to bear down on you, etc.*

(1) LXX : *Behold, I roll* (κυλίω) *under you as a waggon full of straw is rolled ;* A.V.: *I am pressed under you as a cart is pressed ;* Pusey : *I straiten myself under you, etc.* These versions take עוק in the sense of צוק, *to press,* and תחת in its usual meaning of *beneath ;* conformably to the well-known figure by which God is said to be laden with the transgressions of His people. But this does not mean an actual descent of judgement, and yet vv. 14–16 imply that such an intimation has been made in ver. 13 ; besides מעיק and תעיק are both in the Hiphil, *to press,* or *make to press.* (2) Accordingly some, adopting this sense of the verb, take תחת as *down upon.* Ewald : *I press down upon you as a cart full of sheaves presseth.* Guthe (in Kautzsch): *Ich will euch quetschen.* Rev. Eng. Ver. : *I will press you in your place.*—But עוק has been taken in other senses. (3) Hoffmann (*Z.A.T.W.,* iii, 100) renders it *groan* like Arab. 'îk, so Aquila's τρίζειν and Jerome's *stridens ;* Marti, *I will make it crack under you.* (4) Wetzstein (*ibid.,* 278 ff.) quotes Arab. 'âk, to *stop, hinder,* and suggests *I will bring to a stop.* (5) Buhl (12th ed. of Gesenius, sub עוק), in view of possibility of עֲגָלָה being threshing-roller, recalls Arab. 'akk, *to cut in pieces.* (6) Hitzig proposed to read מפיק and תפיק : *I will make it shake under you, as the laden waggon shakes* (the ground). So rather differently Wellhausen : *I will make the ground quake under you, as a waggon quakes under its load of sheaves.*

I have only to add that, in the Alex. Cod. of LXX, which reads κωλύω for κυλίω, we have an interesting analogy to Wetzstein's proposal ; and that in support of the rendering of Ewald, and its interpretation of תחתיכם which seems to me on the whole the most probable, we may compare Job xxxvi. 16, לֹא מוּצַק תַּחְתֶּיהָ. That, it is true, suggests rather the choking of a passage than the crushing of the ground ; but this sense is even more applicable to a harvest waggon laden with sheaves.

Waggon full of sheaves,—Wellhausen goes too far when he suggests that Amos would have to go outside Palestine to see such a waggon. That a people who already knew the use of chariots for travelling (cf. Gen. xlvi. 5, JE) and waggons for agricultural purposes (1 Sam. vi. 7 ff.) did not use them at least in the lowlands of their country is extremely improbable. Cf. *Hist. Geog.,* Appendix on *Roads and Wheeled Vehicles in Syria.*

CHAPTER VIII

CIVILISATION AND JUDGEMENT

AMOS III–IV. 3

WE now enter the Second Section of the Book
of Amos: chaps. iii–vi. It is a collection
of various oracles of denunciation, grouped partly by
the recurrence of the formula *Hear this word*, which
stands at the head of our present chapters iii, iv, and v,
which are therefore probably due to it ; partly by two
cries of *Woe* at v. 18 and vi. 1 ; and also by the fact
that each of the groups thus started leads up to an
emphatic, though not at first detailed, prediction of
the nation's doom (iii. 11–15 ; iv. 3 ; iv. 12 ; v. 16,
17 ; v. 26, 27 ; vi. 14). Within these divisions lie a
number of short indictments, sentences of judgement
and the like, which have no further logical connection
than is supplied by their general sameness of subject
and a perceptible increase of articulateness from beginning to end of the Section. The sins of Israel are
more detailed, and the judgement of war, coming from
the North, advances gradually till we discern the
unmistakeable ranks of Assyria. But there are parentheses and interruptions, which cause the student of
the text no little difficulty. Some of these, however,
may be only apparent : it will always be a question
whether their want of immediate connection with what
precedes them is not due to the loss of several words

from the text rather than to their own intrusion into it. Of others it is true that they are obviously out of place as they lie ; their removal brings together verses which evidently belong to each other. Some of these parentheses, however, may be from Amos himself. It is only where a verse, besides interrupting the argument, seems to reflect a historical situation later than the prophet's day, that we can be sure it is not his own And in this textual criticism we must keep in mind, that the obscurity of the present text of a verse, so far from being an adequate proof of its subsequent insertion, may be the very token of its antiquity, scribes or translators of later date having been unable to understand it. To reject a verse, only because *we* do not see the connection, would be as arbitrary, as the opposite habit of those who, missing a connection, invent one, and exhibit their artificial joint as evidence of the integrity of the whole passage. In fact we must avoid headstrong surgery, for to a great extent we work in the dark.

The general subject of the Section may be indicated by the title, Religion and Civilisation. A vigorous community, wealthy, cultured, and honestly religious, are, at a time of settled peace and growing power, threatened, in the name of the God of justice, with their political overthrow. Their civilisation is counted for nothing ; their religion, on which they base their confidence, is denounced as false and unavailing. These two subjects are not, and could not have been, separated by the prophet in any of his oracles. But in the first, the briefest and most summary of these, iii–iv. 3, it is mainly with the doom of the civil structure of Israel's life that Amos deals ; and it will be more convenient for us to take them first, with all due reference to the echoes of them in later parts of the

Section. In iv. 4–vi he assaults the Religion and its
false peace ; and we shall take that in the next chapter.
First, then, Civilisation and Judgement (iii–iv. 3) ;
Second, The False Peace of Ritual (iv. 4–vi).

These few brief oracles open upon the same note as
that on which the previous Section closed—that the
crimes of Israel are greater than those of the heathen ;
and that the people's peculiar relation to God means,
not their security, but their heavier doom. It is then
affirmed that Israel's wealth and social life are so
sapped by luxury and injustice that the nation must
perish. And, as in every luxurious community the
women deserve especial blame, the last of the group
of oracles is reserved for them (iv. 1–3).

iii. 1. *Hear this word, which Yahweh hath spoken
against you, O sons of Israel, against the whole kindred
which I brought up from the land of Egypt* [1]—Judah as
well as North Israel, so that we see the precariousness
of a criticism which would cast out of the Book of
Amos as unauthentic every reference to Judah.

> 2. *Only you have I known
> Of all kindreds of the ground,
> Therefore on you will I visit
> All your iniquities.*

Ground, not world, as if to stamp the meanness and
mortality of them all.

---

[1] These clauses some have sought to reduce to metre by eliding some
of them thus : *against the whole kindred . . . land of Egypt* (Löhr, cf.
Marti) or only *against the whole kindred* (Baumann) or *Sons of Israel*
(Harper). It is, of course, possible that later additions have here padded
a metrical verse into a piece of prose ; but the proposed variations show
the inability of us moderns to distinguish the original verse from the
additions. LXX confirms the Hebrew text, except that it reads *House*
for *sons* See Duhm, *Z.A.T.W*, 1911, p. 4.

This famous text has been called 'the keynote,' the licence,' and 'the charter' of prophecy. But the names are too petty for what is not less than the fulmination of an element. It is thunder we hear. It is, in a moment, the explosion and discharge of the full storm of prophecy. As when from a burst cloud the streams below rise suddenly and all their banks are overflowed, so the prophecies that follow surge and rise clear of the old limits of Israel's faith by the unconfined, unmeasured flood of heaven's justice which breaks through this single verse. Once for all are submerged the lines of custom and tradition within which the course of religion has hitherto flowed; and, as it were, the surface of the world is altered. It is a crisis which has happened more than once again in history: when helpless man has felt the relentlessness of the moral issues of life; their renunciation of the past, however much they have helped to form it; their sacrifice of every development however costly, and of every hope however pure; their deafness to prayer, their indifference to penitence; when no faith saves a Church, no courage a people, no culture or prestige even the most exalted order of men; but at the bare hands of a judgement, uncouth of voice and often unconscious of a Divine mission, the results of a great civilisation are for its sins swept remorselessly away.

Before the storm bursts, we learn by its lightnings some truths from the old life that is to be destroyed. *You alone have I known of all the kindreds of the ground : therefore will I visit your iniquities upon you.* Religion is no insurance against doom, no mere atonement and escape from consequences. Escape! Religion is only opportunity—the greatest moral opportunity which men have, and which if they violate nothing remains for them but a certain fearful looking forward unto judgement. You only have I known; and because you did not take the moral advantage of My intercourse, because you felt it only as privilege and pride, pardon for the past and security for the future, therefore doom inexorable awaits you.

Then as if the people had interrupted him with the question, What sign do you give us that this judgement is near?—Amos goes into that noble digression (vv. 3–8) on the harmony between the prophet's word and the imminent events of the time, which we have already studied.[1] From this apologia, ver. 9 returns to the note of vv. 1 and 2 and develops it. Not only is Israel's responsibility greater than that of other people's. Her crimes themselves are more heinous.

> iii. 9. *Make it heard o'er the palaces in Asshûr*[2]
> *O'er the palaces in the land of Miṣraim,*
> *Say, Gather on the Mount*[3] *of Samaria*
> *And disorders see rife in her midst,*
> *And cruelties to the core of her.*
> 10 *For they know not how to deal straight,*
> *['Tis the Rede of Yahweh]*[4]
> *Who are storing up wrong*
> *And ruin in their palaces.*

'To their crimes,' said the satirist of the Romans, 'they owe their gardens, palaces, stables, and fine old plate.'[5]　And William Langland declared of the rich English of his day:—

> 'For toke thei on trewly · they tymbred not so heigh,
> Ne boughte non burgages · be ye full certayne.'[6]

---

[1] See above, pp. 79 ff. and pp. 87 ff.
[2] With the LXX באשור for באשדד, *in Ashdod* of the text, which is retained by many.
[3] Singular as in LXX, and not plural as in Heb.
[4] Possibly an editorial addition.　　[5] Juvenal, *Satires*, I
[6] *Vision of Piers Plowman*.　Burgages = tenements

11. *Therefore thus saith the Lord Yahweh :*
     A Foe [1] shall blockade thy [2] land,
     And pull down [3] thy strength from off thee,
     And thy palaces be plundered.

12. *[Thus sayeth Yahweh]*
     Just as the shepherd from the mouth of the lion
     Saves two legs or the bit of an ear,
     So saved shall the sons of Israel be,
     They who now *sit in Samaria*
     In the corners [4] of diwans,
     And on the . . . (?) of couches.

The description, as will be seen from the note below,[5]

---

[1] Some render *distress.*   [2] So LXX ; Heb. *the.*

[3] Some read the passive, *brought down shall be.*

[4] Some read צָפִית , *rug* or *cushion* (*Enc. Bibl.*, 511, Marti).

[5] *In Damascus on a couch : on a Damascus couch : on a Damascus-cloth couch :* or *Damascus-fashion on a couch*—equally probable and equally beyond proof. The text is difficult, nor do the versions help. (1) The consonants of the word before *a couch* spell *in Damascus,* and so LXX take it. This would be parallel to *in Samaria.* But although Jeroboam II is said to have taken Damascus (2 Kings xiv. 28), this is not necessarily the town itself, of whose occupation by Israel we have no evidence, while Amos always assumes it to be Aramean, and here he is addressing Israelites. Still retaining the name, we can take it with *couch* as parallel, not to *in Samaria,* but to *in the corner of the diwan ;* in that case the meaning may have been *a Damascus couch* (though as the two words stand it is impossible to parse them, and Gen. xv. 2 cannot be quoted in support of this, for it is too uncertain, being possibly a gloss ; yet it is curious that as the two passages run the name Damascus should be in the same strange grammatical conjunction in each) ; or possibly *Damascus-fashion on a couch,* which (if the first half of the clause, as some maintain, refers to some affected posture then in fashion) is a possible rendering. (2) The Massoretes have pointed, not *bedammesek* = *in Damascus,* but *bedemeshek,* a form not found elsewhere, by which some (Ges., Hitz., Ew., R.V.) understand some Damascene stuff (as possibly, but not certainly, our Damask and the Arabic dimshaḳ originally meant), *e.g., silk* or *velvet cushions.* (3) Others rearrange the text : *e.g.,* Hoffmann (*Z.A.T.W.*, III, 102) transfers the clause from ver. 12 to ver. 13, reading, *O those who sit in Samaria on the edge of the diwan and in Damascus on*

is obscure. Some think it is intended to satirise a novel and affected fashion of sitting adopted by the rich More probably it means that idle security in the luxuries of civilisation which Amos threatens more than once in similar phrases.[1] The corner of the diwan is in Eastern houses the seat of honour.[2] To this desert shepherd, with the hard ground to rest on, the couches and ivory-mounted diwans of the rich must have seemed symbols of extravagance. But the pampered bodies that loll their lazy lengths upon them shall be left like the crumbs of a lion's meal—*two legs and the bit of an ear!* Their civilisation shall perish with them.

> iii. 13. *Hear and bear witness on Jacob's House—*
> *Rede of Lord Yahweh, God of the Hosts—*
>
> 14. *On the day I visit on Israel his crimes*
> *I make visitation on the altars [3] of Bethel,*
> *Hewn off shall the horns of the altar be*
> *And shall fall to the earth.*
>
> 15. *And I will smite the winter-houses,*
> *Along with the houses of summer,*
> *And the houses of ivory [4] shall perish,*
> *Yea houses manifold come to an end—*
> *The Rede of Yahweh.*

The genuineness of these verses in part or in whole is

---

a couch, hearken and testify against the house of Jacob. But those addressed in ver. 13 are the same as those addressed in ver. 9, cf. Wellhausen who prefers to believe that after sons of Israel something has fallen out. Duhm and Marti read דבשת, *hump* or *bolster*. LXX translators, who make several blunders in this passage, instead of translating ערש *couch* merely transliterate into ἱερεῖς.

[1] vi. 4, *that lie on ivory diwans and sprawl on their couches*
[2] Van Lennep, *Bible Lands and Customs*, p. 460.
[3] For *altars* Stade and Marti read *the Maṣṣebah* without reason enough.
[4] That is *inlaid with ivory.*

denied by most moderns.[1]   At least it is probable that
editorial additions to the first three lines have rendered
them nearer prose than metre.   But to assert that the
title, *Jacob's House*, is foreign to Amos, and that here
he is concerned only with the sins of the Samarian
rich, which have nothing to do with *Bethel's altars*, is
not convincing.

But the luxury of no civilisation can be measured
without its women, and to the women of Samaria Amos
now turns with the most scornful of all his words.

> iv. 1. *Hear this word, ye kine of Bashan,*
> *Who are on the Mount of Samaria,*
> *Who oppress the feeble,*
> *Who crush the needy,*
> *Who say to their lords :*
> *Bring, let us drink !*
> 2. *Yahweh* [2] *hath sworn by His holiness,*
> *Lo, days come upon you*
> *When they carry you off* [3] *with hooks,*
> *And with fish-hooks the last of you.*

They put hooks [4] in the nostrils of unruly cattle, and
the figure is often applied to human captives ; [5] but
so many should these cattle of Samaria be that for
the *last of them fish-hooks* must be used.

[1] See Wellhausen, Löhr, Duhm, Marti and in reply to Wellhausen
Harper.   Moffatt makes ver. 15 follow ver. 12.

[2] Heb. adds *the Lord*, which LXX has not.

[3] Duhm and Marti read *lift your nose* (Isa. xxxvii. 29), and in parallel
to this render *last of you* by *your hinder part*, as though they were carried
off dead.

[4] The words for hook in Hebrew—the two used above, צִנּוֹת and סִירוֹת
and a third, חוֹחַ—all mean originally *thorns*, doubtless the first hooks
of primitive man ; but by this time they would signify metal hooks—a
change analogous to the English word *pen*.

[5] Cf. Isa. xxxvii. 29 ; 2 Chron. xxxiii. 11.   On the use of fish-hooks,
Job xl. 25, 26 (Heb.), xli. 1, 2 (Eng.) ; Ezek. xxix. 4.

iv. 3. *And by the breaches out shall ye go,*
    Every one headlong,
    And be cast forth . . . ——[1]
    The Rede of Yahweh.

It is a cowherd's rough picture of women : a troop
of kine—heavy, heedless animals, trampling in their
anxiety for food upon every frail and lowly object in
in the way, but when their city has been stormed to
be hurried away captive through the *breaches* in its
walls.   Yet there is a prophet's insight into character.
Not of Jezebels, or Messalinas, or Lady-Macbeths is
it spoken, but of the ordinary matrons of Samaria.
Thoughtlessness and luxury are able to make brutes
out of women of gentle nurture, with homes and a
religion.[2]

Such are these three or four short oracles of Amos,
probably among his earliest—the first challenges of
prophecy to that great stronghold which before forty
years she is to see thrown down according to her word.

---

[1] The verb, which in the text is active, must be taken in the passive.
The word not translated above is הַהַרְמוֹנָה , *unto the Harmôn*, which
name does not occur elsewhere.   LXX read εἰς τὸ ὄρος τὸ ῾Ρομμάν, which
Ewald renders *ye shall cast the Rimmon to the mountain* (cf. Isa. ii. 20),
and he takes Rimmon to be the Syrian goddess of love.   Steiner (quoted
by Wellhausen) renders *ye shall be cast out to Hadad Rimmon*, that is,
violated as קְדֵשׁוֹת.   Hitzig separates הַהַר from מוֹנָה , which he takes
as contracted from מַעֲנָה , and renders *ye shall fling yourselves out on the
mountains as a refuge*.   Marti transfers from ver. 2 to 3, דּוּגָה , *fish*, reads
it דֹּמֶן , *dung*, and פְּרָצִים , *breaches*, פֶּרֶשׁ , *filth ;* and on the strength
of the word γυμναί in LXX reads עֲרֻמּוֹת , *naked*, for הַהַרְמוֹנָה ; which
latter Duhm suggests reading הַמַּדְמֵנָה , *the dungheap*.   All these are
but conjectures.

[2] I have treated this passage in connection with Isaiah's prophecies or
women in *Isaiah i-xxxix*, Ch. XVI.

As yet, however, there seems to be nothing to justify the menaces of Amos. Fair and stable rises the structure of Israel's life. A nation, who know themselves elect, who in politics are prosperous and in religion proof to doubt, build high their palaces, see the skies above them unclouded, and bask in their pride, heaven's favourites without a fear. This man, solitary and sudden from his desert, springs upon them in the name of God and their poor. Straighter word never came from Deity : *Yahweh hath spoken, who can but prophesy ?* The insight of it, the justice of it, are alike convincing. Yet at first it appears as if it were sped on the personal and very human passion of its herald. For Amos not only uses the desert's cruelties—the lion's to the sheep— to figure God's impending judgement upon His people, but enforces the latter with all a desert-bred man's horror of cities and civilisation. It is their costly furniture, their lavish and complex building, on which he sees the storm break. We seem to hear again that frequent phrase of the previous section : *the fire shall devour the palaces thereof.* The palaces, he says, are storehouses of oppression ; the palaces will be plundered. Here, as throughout his book,[1] couches and diwans draw the scorn of a man accustomed to the simple furniture of the tent. Observe his especial hatred of houses. Four times in one verse he smites them : *winter-house on summer-house, and the ivory houses shall perish—yea, houses manifold.* So in another oracle : *Houses of ashlar ye have built, and ye shall not inhabit ; vineyards of delight have ye planted, and ye shall not drink of their wine.*[2] And in another : *I loathe the pride of Jacob, and his palaces I hate ; and I will give up a city and all that is in it. . . . For, lo,*

---

[1] Cf. ch. vi. 4. [2] v. 11;

Yahweh is about to command, and He will smite the great house into ruins and the small house into splinters.[1]   No wonder that such a prophet found war with its breached walls insufficient, and welcomed, as the full ally of his word, the earthquake itself.[2]

Yet all this is no mere desert 'razzia' in the name of the Lord, a nomad's hatred of cities and of the culture of settled men.   It is not a temper ; it is a vision of history.   In the only argument which these early oracles contain, Amos claims to have events on the side of his word.   *Shall the lion roar and not be catching* something ?   Neither does the prophet speak till he knows that God is ready to act.   History accepted this claim.   Amos spoke about 755.   In 734 Tiglath-Pileser swept Gilead and Galilee ; in 724 Shalmaneser overran the rest of Northern Israel : *blockade of thy land !*   For three years the Mount of Samaria was invested, and then taken ; the houses overthrown, the rich and the delicate led away captive.   It happened as Amos foretold ; for it was not the shepherd's rage within him that spoke.   He had *seen the Lord standing, and He said, Smite.*

But this assault of a desert nomad upon the structure of a nation's life raises many echoes in history and some questions in our own minds to-day.   Again and again have civilisations far more powerful than Israel's been threatened by the desert in the name of God, and in good faith it has been proclaimed by the prophets of Christianity and other religions that God's kingdom cannot come on earth till the wealth, the culture, the civil order, which men have taken centuries to build, have been swept away by some great political convulsion.   To-day Christianity herself suffers the same

---

[1] vi. 8, 11.   [2] Cf. what was said on building above, p. 31.

assaults. and is told by many, the high life and honest intention of whom cannot be doubted, that till the civilisation which she has helped to create is destroyed, there is no hope for the purity or the progress of the race. And Christianity, too, has doubts within herself. What is the world which our Master refused in the Mount of Temptation, and so often and so sternly told us that it must perish ?—how much of our wealth, of our culture, of our politics, of the whole fabric of our society ? No thoughtful and religious man, when confronted with civilisation, not in its ideal, but in one of those forms which give it its very name, the life of a large city, can fail to ask, How much of this deserves the judgement of God ? How much must be overthrown, before His will is done on earth ? All these questions rise in the ears and the heart of a generation, that more than any other has been brought face to face with the ruins of empires and civilisations, which have endured longer, and seemed each in its day more stable, than their own.

In face of the confused thinking and fanatic speech which have risen on such topics, it seems to me that the Hebrew prophets supply us with four cardinal rules.

First, they insist that it is the moral question upon which the fate of a civilisation is decided. By what means has this system grown ? Is justice observed in essence as well as in form ? Is there freedom, or is the prophet silenced ? Does luxury or self-denial prevail ? Do the rich make life hard for the poor ? Is childhood sheltered and innocence respected ? By these, claim the prophets, a nation stands or falls ; and history has proved the claim on wider worlds than they dreamt of.

But by themselves moral reasons are never enough

to justify a prediction of speedy doom upon **any** system or society. None of the prophets began to foretell the fall of Israel till they read, with keener eyes than their contemporaries, the signs of this in current history. And that, I take it, was the point which made a notable difference between them, and one who like them scourged the social wrongs of his civilisation, yet never spoke a word of its fall. Juvenal nowhere calls down judgements, except upon individuals. In his time there were no signs of the decline of the empire, even though, as he marks, there was a flight from the capital of the virtue which was to keep the empire alive. But the prophets had political proof of the nearness of God's judgement, and they spoke in the power of its coincidence with the moral corruption of their people.

Again, if conscience and history (both of them, to the prophets, being witnesses of God) thus combine to announce the early doom of a civilisation, neither the religion that may have helped to build it, nor any remanent virtue in it, nor its ancient value to God, can avail to save. We are tempted to deem that the long and costly development of ages is cruelly thrown away by the convulsion and collapse of an empire ; it feels impious to think that the patience, the providence, the millennial discipline of the Almighty are to be in a moment abandoned to some rude and savage force. But we are wrong. *You only have I known of all the kindreds of the ground*, yet I must *visit upon you your iniquities*. Nothing is too costly for justice. And God finds some other way of conserving the honest results of the past.

It is a corollary of this, that the sentence upon civilisation must often seem to come by voices that are insane, and its execution by means that are criminal.

Of course, when civilisation is arraigned as a whole, and its overthrow demanded, there may be nothing behind the attack but jealousy or greed, the fanaticism of ignorant men or the madness of disordered lives. But this is not necessarily the case. For God has often in history chosen the outsider as the herald of doom, and sent the barbarian as its instrument. By the statesmen and patriots of Israel, Amos must have been regarded as a savage, with a savage's hate of civilisation. But we know what he answered when Amasiah called him rebel. And it was not only for its suddenness that the apostles said the *day of the Lord should come as a thief*, but also because of its methods. For over and over again has doom been pronounced, and pronounced truly, by men who in the eyes of civilisation were criminals and monsters.

Apply these four principles to the question of ourselves. It will scarcely be denied that our civilisation tolerates, and in part lives by, the existence of vices which, as we admit, ruined the ancient empires. Are the political possibilities of overthrow also present ? That there exist among us means of new historic convulsions is a thing hard for us to admit. But the signs cannot be hid. When we see the jealousies of the Christian peoples, and their preparations for battle ; the arsenals of Europe which a few sparks may explode ; the millions of soldiers one man's word may mobilise ; when we imagine the opportunities which a general war would furnish to the discontented masses of the European proletariat,[1]—we must surely acknowledge the existence of forces capable of inflicting calamities, so severe as to affect not merely this nationality or

[1] This, written in 1896, has surely been realised since the Great War of 1914–1918.

that type of culture, but the vigour and progress of
civilisation herself ; and this without looking beyond
Christendom, or taking into account the rise of the
yellow races to a consciousness of their approach to
equality with ourselves. If, then, in the eyes of the
Divine justice Christendom merits judgement,—if life
continue to be left so hard to the poor ; if innocence
be still hardly possible for so much of the childhood
of the Christian nations ; if with many of the leaders
of civilisation prurience be lifted to the level of an art,
and licentiousness followed as a cult ; if we continue
to pour the evils of our civilisation upon the barbarian,
and ' the vices of our young nobles,' to paraphrase
Juvenal, ' are aped in ' Hindustan—then let us know
that the means of a judgement more awful than any
which has yet scourged a delinquent civilisation are
extant and actual among us. And if one should reply,
that our Christianity makes all the difference, that God
cannot undo the development of nineteen centuries,
or cannot overthrow the peoples of His Son—let us
remember that God does justice at whatever cost ;
that as He did not spare Israel at the hands of Assyria,
so He did not spare Christianity in the East when the
barbarians of the desert found her careless and corrupt.
*You only have I known of all the kindreds of the ground,
therefore will I visit upon you all your iniquities.*

CHAPTER IX

THE FALSE PEACE OF RITUAL

Amos iv. 4–vi

THE next four groups of oracles [1]—iv. 4–13, v.
1–17, v. 18–27, and vi—treat of many different
details, and each of them has its own emphasis ; but
all are alike in this, that they vehemently attack the
national worship and the sense of political security
which it has engendered. Let us at once make clear
that this worship is the worship of Yahweh. It is true
that it is mixed with idolatry, but, except possibly in
one obscure verse,[2] Amos does not concern himself with
the idols. What he strikes at, what he would sweep
away, is his people's form of devotion to their own
God. The cult of the national God, at the national
sanctuaries, in the national interest and by the whole
body of the people, who practise it with a zeal unparalleled by their forefathers—this is what Amos
condemns. And he does so absolutely. He has nothing but scorn for the temples and the feasts. The
assiduity of attendance, the liberality of gifts, the
employment of wealth and art and patriotism in worship—he tells his generation that God loathes it all.
Like Jeremiah he even seems to imply that God never
instituted in Israel any sacrifice or offering.[3] It is all

[1] See p. 144.   [2] v. 26.   [3] v. 25.

this which gives these oracles their interest for us ; and that interest is not merely historical.

It is indeed historical to begin with. When we find, not idolatry, but all religious ceremony—temples, public worship, tithes, sacrifice, the praise of God by music, in fact every material form in which man has been wont to express his devotion to God—scorned and condemned with the same uncompromising passion as idolatry itself, we receive a needed lesson in the history of religion. For when one is asked, What is the distinguishing characteristic of heathenism ? one is always ready to say, Idolatry, which is not true. The distinguishing characteristic of heathenism is the stress which it lays upon ceremonial. To the pagan religions, both of the ancient and of the modern world, rites were the indispensable element in religion. The gifts of the gods, the abundance of fruits, the security of the state, depended upon the full and accurate performance of ritual. In Greek literature we have innumerable illustrations of this : the *Iliad* itself starts from a god's anger, roused by an insult to his priest, whose prayers for vengeance he hears because sacrifices have been assiduously offered to him. And so too with the systems of paganism from which the faith of Israel, though at first it had so much in common with them, broke away to its supreme religious distinction. The Semites laid the stress of their obedience to the gods upon traditional ceremonies ; and no sin was held by them so heinous as the neglect or infringement of a religious rite. By the side of this offences against one's fellow-men or one's own character were deemed mere misdemeanours. In the day of Amos this pagan superstition penetrated the religion of Yahweh, and so absorbed the attention of men, that without the indignant and complete repudiation of it prophecy could not have started on her task of identifying morality with religion, and of teaching men more spiritual views of God. But even when we are thus aware of ceremonialism as the characteristic quality of the pagan religions, we have not measured the full reason of that uncompromising attack on it, which is the chief feature of this part of the permanent canon of our religion. For idolatries die everywhere ; but everywhere a superstitious ritualism survives. It has continued with philosophies that have ceased to believe in the gods who enforced it. Upon ethical movements which have gained their freedom by breaking away from it, in the course of time it has made up, and laid its paralysing weight. With offers of help it flatters religions the most spiritual in theory and intention. The Pharisees, than whom few parties had at first purer ideals of morality, tithed mint, anise and cummin, to the neglect of the essence of the Law ; and even some Christians, who have assimilated the Gospel of St. John, find it hard and sometimes impossible to believe in salvation apart from their own sacraments, or outside their own denominational forms. Now this is because ritual is a thing which appeals both to the baser and to the nobler instincts of man. To the baser it offers itself as a mechanical atonement for sin, and a substitute for all moral and intellectual effort in connection with faith ; to the nobler it insists on a man's need in religion of order and routine, of sacrament and picture. Plainly then the words of Amos have significance for more than the immediate problems of his day. And if it seem to some, that Amos goes too far with his cry to sweep away all ceremonial, let them remember, besides the crisis of his times, that the temper he exposes and seeks to dissipate is a rank and obdurate error of the human heart. Our Lord, Who recognised the place of ritual in worship, Who said, *Thus it behoveth us to fulfil all righteousness*, which righteousness in the dialect of His day was not the moral law, but man's due of rite, sacrifice, tithe, and alms,[1] said also, *I will have mercy and not sacrifice*. There is an irreducible minimum of rite and routine in worship ; there is an invaluable loyalty to traditional habits ; there are holy and spiritual uses in symbol and sacrament. But these are all dispensable ; and because they are all constantly abused, the voice of the prophet is ever needed which tells us that God will have none of them ; but let justice roll on like water, and righteousness like an unfailing stream.

For the superstition that ritual is the indispensable bond between God and man, Amos substitutes two other aspects of religion. They are history as God's discipline of man ; and civic justice, as man's duty to God. The first of them he contrasts with religious ceremonialism in chap. iv. 4–13, and the second in chap. v ; while in chap. vi he assaults once more the false political peace which the ceremonialism engenders.

1. FOR WORSHIP CHASTISEMENT

Amos iv. 4–13

In chap. ii Amos contrasted the popular conception of religion as worship with God's conception of it as history. He placed a picture of the sanctuary, hot with religious zeal, but hot too with passion and the fumes of wine, side by side with a great prospect of the national history : God's guidance of Israel from Egypt onwards. That is, as we said at the time, he placed an

---

[1] Another proof o how the spirit of ritualism tends to absorb morality.

indoors picture of religion side by side with an open-air one. He repeats that arrangement here. The religious services he sketches are more pure, and the history he takes from his own day ; but the contrast is the same. Again we have on the one side the temple worship—artificial, exaggerated, indoors, smoky ; but on the other a few movements of God in Nature, which, though they all be calamities, have a moral majesty upon them. The series opens with a scornful call to worship, which the prophet, letting out his whole heart at the beginning, shows to be equivalent to sin. Note next the caricature of their exaggerated zeal : sacrifices every morning instead of once a year, tithes every three days instead of every three years.[1] To offer leavened bread was a departure from the older fashion of unleavened.[2] To publish their liberality was like the later Pharisees, who were not dissimilarly mocked by our Lord : *When thou doest alms, cause not a trumpet to be sounded before thee, as the hypocrites do in the synagogues and in the streets, that they may have glory of men.*[3]

Verses 4–11 fall into seven strophes of four lines each, but the third strophe, vv. 7–8, has had lines added to it the genuineness of which is doubtful, and the sixth strophe as it stands has five lines.

iv. 4. *Come away to Bethel* [4] *and transgress,*
To Gilgal [4] *and multiply transgression !*
And bring each morning your sacrifices,
Every three days your tithes !

---

[1] Ver. 4 : cf. 1 Sam. i ; Deut. xiv. 28. Wellhausen offers another exegesis : Amos is describing exactly what took place at Bethel—sacrifice on the morning, *i.e.*, next to the day of their arrival, tithes on the third day thereafter. So Guthe and Marti.

[2] See Wellhausen's note, and compare Lev. vii. 13.   [3] Matt. vi. 2.

[4] On Bethel and Gilgal, see pp. 33 f. *To Gilgal* so LXX.

iv. 5. *Burn with leaven your offering of praise,*
Proclaim, make heard your freewill gifts,
For thus ye love to, O sons of Israel !—
Rede of Yahweh the Lord.

6 *But I for My part have given you*
Cleanness of teeth in all your towns,
And in all your localities lack of bread.
Yet to Me ye returned not—Rede of Yahweh.

7. *And I held from you the winter-rain,*[1]
[While yet were three months from the harvest,
I would cause it to rain on one town
And not to rain on another,
One lot would be rained upon
And the lot I rained not upon would wither.][2]

8. *And two or three towns would straggle to one*
To drink water and would not be filled.
Yet to Me ye returned not—Rede of Yahweh.

9. *I smote you with blasting and mildew,*
I wasted[3] *your gardens and vineyards,*

---

[1] בֶשֶׁם : *Hist. Geog.*, p. 64. In 1895 the same was threatened, according to the *Mittheilungen u. Nachrichten des D.P.V.*, p. 44 : ' Nachdem es im December einigemal recht stark geregnet hatte besonders an der Meeresküste ist seit kurz vor Weihnachten das Wetter immer schön u. mild geblieben, u. wenn nicht weiterer Regen fällt, so wird grosser Wassermangel entstehen denn bis jetzt (16 Febr.) hat Niemand Cisterne voll.' The harvest is in April-May.

[2] While the other strophes in this series have four lines each, this one has nine ; and the five bracketed above are prosaic and less metrical than the rest. By leaving them out the strophe becomes of the same size and regular metre as the others. So Marti. Other elisions have been proposed, Löhr going so far as to elide all vv. 7, 8 ! But this is to destroy the strophe. That some places have a full rainfall, while others suffer drought not infrequently happens in Palestine. On the tenses in vv. 7, 8 see Davidson's *Hebrew Syntax*, § 54*b* ; and Driver *in loco*.

[3] So after Wellhausen most moderns, reading הֶחֱרַבְתִּי for הַרְבּוֹת, *multitude* of the text.

And your figs and your olives the locust devoured,
Yet to Me ye returned not—Rede of Yahweh.

10. *I sent among you the pestilence [by way of Egypt]* [1]
     I slew your choice youths with the sword
     Along with your captured horses, [2]
     And brought up the stench of your camps in your
        nostrils,
     Yet to Me ye returned not—Rede of Yahweh.

11. *I have overthrown among you*
     Like God's overthrow of Sĕdōm and Gomorrah, [3]
     Ye were as a brand snatched from the burning,
     Yet to Me ye returned not—Rede of Yahweh.

This recalls a passage in that English poem of which
we are again and again reminded by the Book of Amos,
The Vision of Piers Plowman. It is the sermon of
Reason in Passus V (Skeat's edition) :—

' He preved that thise pestilences · were for pure synne.
 And the southwest wynde · in saterday et evene
 Was pertliche [4] for pure pride · and for no poynt elles.
 Piries and plomtrees · were puffed to the erthe,
 In ensample ze segges [5] · ze shulden do the bettere.

[1] The bracketed words may be a later note. They refer not to the
plagues on the eve of the Exodus (as some think), but because plague
generally visited Palestine from the direction of Egypt : see my *Hist.
Geog.*, pp. 157 ff. Note the connection of plague and war.
[2] Lit. *with the captivity of your horses*—either that their horses, so
invaluable in Palestine, were taken by the foe (Wellhausen), or, because
of the following line, that they also were slain (Driver). Newman proposes to omit the line, and so reduce the strophe to the same four-line
form as the others.
[3] The same formula as in Deut. xxix. 23, Isa. xiii. 19, Jer. xlix. 18,
l. 40. Marti takes these convulsions here not as of earthquake but as of
war !
[4] Apertly, openly.   [5] Men

Beches and brode okes · were blowen to the grounde.
Torned upward her tailles · in tokenynge of drede,
That dedly synne at domesday · shal fordon [1] hem alle.'

In the ancient world the settled belief was that
natural calamities like these were the effects of the
deity's wrath. When Israel suffers from them the
prophets take for granted that they are for the people's
punishment. I have elsewhere shown how the climate
of Palestine lent itself to these convictions ; in this
respect the Book of Deuteronomy contrasts it with
the climate of Egypt.[2] And although some have
rightly scoffed at the exaggerated form of the belief,
that God is angry with the sons of men every time
drought or floods happen, yet the instinct is sound which
in all ages has led religious people to feel that such
things are inflicted for moral purposes. In the economy
of the universe there may be physical ends served by
such disasters, apart from their meaning to man. But
man at least learns from them that nature does not
exist solely for feeding, clothing, and keeping him
wealthy ; nor is it anything else than his monotheism,
his faith in God as the Lord both of his moral life
and of nature, which moves him to believe, as Hebrew
prophets taught and as our early English seer heard
Reason herself preach. Amos had the more need to
explain those disasters as the work of the God of
righteousness, that his contemporaries, while willing
to grant Yahweh leadership in war, were tempted to
attribute to the Canaanite gods of the land all power
over the seasons.

What, however, more immediately concerns us in
this passage is its effective contrast between men's
treatment of God and God's treatment of men. They

---

[1] Undo.   [2] *Hist. Geog.*, ch. iii, pp. 73 f.

lavish on Him gifts and sacrifices. He, *for His part*, sends them cleanness of teeth, drought, blasting of their fruits, pestilence, war, and earthquake. That is to say, they regard Him as a being to be flattered and fed. He regards them as creatures with characters to discipline, even at the expense of their material welfare. Their views of Him, if religious, are sensuous and gross; His views of them, if austere, are moral and ennobling. All this may be grim, but it is grand; and short as the efforts of Amos are, we begin to perceive in him something already of the greatness of an Isaiah.

And have not those, who have believed as Amos believed, ever been the strong spirits of our race, making the very disasters which crushed them to the earth the tokens that God has great views about them ? Laugh not at the simple peoples, who have their days of humiliation and their fast-days after floods and stunted harvests. For they take these, not like other men, as signs of their frailty and helplessness; but as measures of the greatness God sees in them, His provocation of their souls to the infinite possibilities which He has prepared for them.

Israel, however, did not turn even at the fifth call to penitence, and there remained nothing for her but a fearful looking forward to judgement, the more terrible that the prophet does not define what the doom shall be.

iv. 12. *Therefore thus shall I do to thee Israel,*
      And because I shall do to thee this,
      Make ready to meet thy God, Israel !

The integrity of this verse has of recent years been

widely denied,[1] and some critics, conceiving it to be defective, attach to the first of it lines from other parts of the Book. But as it stands, and indeed by its very vagueness, it forms as striking a climax to the preceding strophes, as could well be imagined. Nor does prophecy lack an analogy to it. In Isaiah ix the judgements recounted conclude with a Divine warning as vague and therefore as impressive : *For all this His wrath is not turned away but His Hand is stretched out still.* For Amos as for Isaiah, in their cautious conception of the Assyrian advance, it was natural to be still indefinite with regard to the form of the Divine judgement, which their consciences told them was certain, because required by the righteousness of God and the sin of Israel. Such indefiniteness we might expect from each of them at an early stage of his prophesying. However this may be, do not let us forget that to Amos the Doomster of Israel is neither the Assyrian, nor any other force in history or nature, but God Himself ; and that it is in consonance with all the rest of his teaching on this subject that the prophet here leaves his people face to face with their God and with Him alone. As Ewald remarks, ' there cannot be a more forcible conclusion than this.' [2]

Much more reasonable is doubt about the genuineness of the next verse, but we shall deal with this and like passages later on, in Chap. XI :—

---

[1] Duhm, Oort, Guthe, Nowack, Cheyne, Marti, Harper, Newman agree that at least part of ver. 12 is a later addition. Löhr would attach to the first line of it iii. 14, ix. 1, 7 ; Baumann v. 21 ff. ; Cheyne (*Enc. Bibl.*), v. 8 f.

[2] With Ewald all the older critics and Davidson, Driver, W. R. Smith, Edghill, Moffatt retain ver. 12 as genuine. Wellhausen says, ' One can at least put up with it ' !

iv. 13. *For behold, He who formed the mountains*
And created the wind,
And declareth to man what His mind is,
Turning the dawn into darkness,
And He treadeth the heights of the earth,
Yahweh, God of Hosts,[1] is His Name.

2. FOR WORSHIP JUSTICE

Amos v

In the next group of oracles Amos continues his attack on the national ritual, and now contrasts it with the service of God in public life—the relief of the poor, the discharge of justice. But he does not begin with this. The group opens with an elegy, which bewails the nation as already fallen. In this short wail, we catch the well-known measure of the Hebrew dirge or Ḳinah ; not so artistic as in later poems, yet with at least the characteristic couplet of a long and a short line, with three and two stresses respectively.

v. 1. *Hear this word which I lift up against you—a* *Dirge, O house of Israel :—*

2. *Fallen, no more shall she rise,*
Virgin of Israel !
Flung is she down on her own ground,
No one to raise her !

The *Virgin*, which with Isaiah is a standing title for Jerusalem and occasionally used of other cities, is here probably the nation of Northern Israel. The explanation follows. It is War.

[1] On this Divine Name see above, p. 53.

v. 3. *For thus saith the Lord Yahweh to the House of Israel :—*

> *The town that goes forth a thousand*
> *Shall have a hundred left,*
> *And the town that goes forth a hundred*
> *Shall have left but ten.*[1]

But judgement is not yet irrevocable. There break forthwith the only two promises which lighten the lowering darkness of the book. Let the people turn to Yahweh Himself—and that means let them turn from the ritual, and instead of it purge their civic life, restore justice in their courts and help the poor. For God and moral good are one. It is *seek Me and ye shall live*, and *seek good and ye shall live*. Omitting for the present a discussion as to whether the interruption of praise to the power of Yahweh be from Amos or another, we read the oracle as follows :—

> 4. *Thus saith Yahweh to the House of Israel :*
> *Seek Me* [2] *and live !*
> 5. *And seek not Bethel,*
> *And come not to Gilgal,*
> *Nor cross to Beersheba !* [3]
> *For to Gilgal the gall of exile,*
> *And Bethel becomes* Beth-*Aven* [4]

---

[1] The text adds *to the house of Israel,* but this destroys the metre here and properly belongs to the introduction to the verse, as above.

[2] Some read *Yahweh.*

[3] There is no need to omit this line with Baumann and Newman.

[4] Except in some such clumsy way it is not possible to echo the play upon words, which the prophet's curse contains—*ha-gilgal galoh yigleh*; and *Beth-El, House of God becomes* House of *idolatry.* Ewald, *Gilgal wird Galle weinen ;* Wellhausen, *Gilgal wird zum Galgen gehen* The next line Moffatt renders *and Bethel sinks to be bethral.*

This rendering, however, scarcely gives the rude force
of the original ; for Aven, *idolatry*, means also wickedness and perdition, so that we should not exaggerate
the antithesis if we employed a phrase which once
was not vulgar : *And Bethel, house of God, shall go to
the Devil !* [1] The epigram was the more natural that
near Bethel, on a site now uncertain, but close to the
edge of the desert to which it gave its name, there lay
from ancient times a village called Beth-Aven, however the form may have risen. And we shall find
Hosea stereotyping this epigram of Amos, and calling
the sanctuary Beth-Aven oftener than he calls it
Beth-El. He begins again :—

> 6. *Seek Yahweh and live*
>   *Lest He break forth like fire on the House of*
>   *Joseph*,[2]
>   *And it devour with none to quench [in Bethel]*,[3]
> 8. *He [4] Who made the Seven Stars and Orion* [5]

[1] LXX βαιθὴλ ἔσται ὡς οὐχ ὑπάρχουσα.

[2] A forceful figure and an awkward construction which LXX seeks to
remedy by taking *House of Joseph* as nominative to the verb. Many
emendations have been proposed : *send fire on, set fire to*, etc. Marti
proposes four lines by reading *lest a flame break out, a fire in the House
of Joseph.*

[3] Perhaps an interpolation : LXX *in the House of Israel.*

[4] Ver. 7 is clearly out of place here ; as the LXX perceived and tried
to give it another rendering to make it seem in place. Ewald, Wellhausen, Harper, and Moffatt remove it to between vv. 9 and 10. There
it well begins another oracle ; perhaps הוי should be inserted before it
as in v. 18, vi. 1. On vv. 8, 9 see below, Ch. XI.

[5] *Seven Stars and Orion*, כימה and כסיל. כימה, *Kimah*, means
perhaps *group* or *cluster*. Here it is rendered by Aq. and in Job ix. 9
by LXX Ἀρκτοῦρος, and here by Theod. and in Job xxxviii. 31 by
LXX *chain* or *cluster of the Pleiades*, or *Seven Stars* ; so most moderns
here. But Stern takes it for Sirius (Canis Major, Great Dog), brightest
of stars and a more suitable fellow to Orion than the dimmer Pleiades.
כסיל, *Fool*, or *Giant* (?) is Hebrew for Orion by which LXX render it ;
Targ. נפלא. To the ancients this constellation seemed like a giant
fettered in heaven, 'a fool so far as he trusted in his bodily strength'

> *Turning the murk [1] into morning*
> *And day into night He darkeneth,*
> *Calling for the waters of the sea*
> *And He poureth them out on the face of the earth,*
> *Yahweh His Name.*
>
> **v. 9.** *Who flasheth out ruin [2] on the stronghold*
> *And bringeth [3] destruction on the fortress.*

This rendering of the last verse is uncertain, but there is no alternative so probable, and it returns to the note from which the passage started, that God should break forth like fire.

> 7. Ah, *they that turn justice to wormwood*
> *And righteousness press [4] to the earth ;*
> 10. *They hate who reproves in the gate,[5]*
> *And who honestly speaks they abhor.*

Thus, in the vision of the English Mystic Peace complains of Wrong :—

> ' I dar noughte for fear of hym · fyhte ne chyde.' [6]

> 11. *So because ye trample the feeble,*
> *And take of him lifts of grain,[7]*
> *Houses of ashlar ye builded,*

(Dillmann). His identification in later ages with Nimrod may have behind it some ancient belief (Budde, *Urgeschichte*, pp. 395 ff. ; Zimmern *K.A.T.*[3], 581, n. 3). By altering one consonant and some vowels Hoffmann reads in ver. 9 the names of other constellations ; so also Guthe and Duhm.

[1] *Murk*, abstract noun, meaning *deep shadow*, LXX σκιά ; rendered *shadow of death* by modern versions.

[2] *Ruin*, so LXX reading שֹׁבֶר for שֹׁד ; avoiding the awkward repetition of the latter as in the next line and improving the rhythm.

[3] So LXX, reading the active or factitive form of the verb.

[4] Possible alternative, *make stagnant*.

[5] The city gate was both law-court and place of the people's council

[6] *Vision of Piers Plowman*, Passus IV, line 52 ; see the whole passage

[7] Uncertain : Hitzig takes it as the apodosis of the preceding line *He shall have to take from him a present of corn*, *i.e.*, as alms.

> *But ye shall not inhabit them ;*
> *Vineyards of pleasure ye planted*
> *But shall not drink of their wine.*

12. *For I know how many your crimes,*
> *How powerful* [1] *your sins,*
> *Who browbeat the righteous, take bribes*
> *And thrust off the needy in the gate.* [2]

13. *So in such a time the prudent is dumb,*
> *For an evil time it is.* [3]

14. *Seek good and not evil,*
> *That ye may live,*
> *And so Yahweh* [4] *be with you—*
> *As ye have said.*

15. *Hate the evil and love the good,*
> *Set justice on her feet in the gate !*
> *It may be that Yahweh the God of Hosts*
> *Will show grace to the remnant of Joseph.*

If in the Book of Amos there are any verses out of their proper place it is surely these. They break the connection between those on either side of them. The initial line, therefore, of 16 follows upon 13 more naturally than upon 15. If this be correct the question arises : Are 14, 15 by Amos himself or a later addition to his prophecies ? In previous editions of this volume I have hesitated to leave them to Amos because of the phrase *a remnant of Joseph ;* for Northern Israel was not reduced to a remnant till years after Amos prophesied, the years subsequent to 734–731 when Tiglath-

[1] Cp. ' Pecca fortiter.'
[2] The city gate was both law-court and place of the people's council.
[3] Marti and Duhm dismiss this verse as not by Amos. But Wellhausen : ' a remark by the way ' and surely a natural one !
[4] Heb. adds *God of Hosts* which, though confirmed by LXX is redundant, unduly loads the metre, and may be a later insertion; if it be retained the words *be with you* fall into the next line.

Pileser swept into exile Gilead and Galilee and left
only Ephraim to *the House of Joseph*. Yet foreboding
as he did a drastic invasion of Israel by the Northern
Power Amos might well have hoped for the survival
of a remnant of its people, however small, which
indeed he grimly hints at in iii. 12. Verses 14, 15
may therefore be from himself though now removed
from their proper place either after vv. 4–6 or elsewhere. It is rash to deny him so natural a mitigation of
the doom he was forced to pass on a people which had
so many good elements in it that it shortly produced
a prophet like Hosea. And the rest of the two verses
are full of the spirit of Amos.[1]

Verse 13 had said the time was so evil that the
prudent man kept silence. All the more must God
Himself speak.[2]

> **v. 16.** *Therefore thus Yahweh sayeth,*
> *The God of Hosts, the Lord :* [3]
> *On all the squares lamentation*
> *In all streets they are saying Woe ! Woe !* [4]
>
> *The ploughmen* [5] *are calling to mourning,*
> *To laments the kenners of dirges,*

[1] Marti and Duhm plausibly attach them to vv. 4-6, making of the
combination four stanzas of four lines each. Guthe divides them by
8 f. Löhr, Nowack, and Cheyne take them with 13 as a later interpolation. Moffatt puts them in brackets after 27. Oort takes 15 as added
after the fall of Samaria.

[2] Löhr attaches these stanzas to vv. 11, 12 but deletes the last line ;
Baumann deletes 17*a* and attaches 16 and 17*b* to vv. 2, 3. Harper takes
the third last line as an interpolation.

[3] LXX and some moderns omit the Lord, אֲדֹנָי, for which Harper
would read אַרְנִין, *I will cause shouting*, but this verbal form is hardly
appropriate for a day of mourning.

[4] Heb. *Hō! Hō!* To-day mourners in Urmia say in their Syriac
dialect, ûhû, ûhû.

[5] Taking with Ewald and Harper אִכָּר as nominative not accusative,
and with Harper as collective.

17. *In all the vineyards lamenting !—*
    As I pass through thy midst saith Yahweh.

It is the solemn cry of the Great Passover, when Egypt
was filled with wailing and the dead lay in every house.
This is what shall come on Ephraim ; town and country,
rustic and artist alike will wail for their dead.   The
Plague is implied.

The next verse starts another, but kindred, theme.
As blind as Israel's confidence in ritual, so blind their
confidence in dogma, and the popular dogma was that
of the *Day of Yahweh.*

All popular hopes expect their victory to come in
a single sharp crisis—a day.   And again, the day of
any one means either the day he has appointed, or
the day of his display and triumph.   So Yahweh's day
meant to the people the day of His judgement, or of
His triumph : His triumph in war over their enemies,
His judgement upon the heathen.[1]   But Amos, whose
keynote has been that judgement begins at home, cries
woe upon such hopes, and tells his people that for them
the day of Yahweh is not victory over their foes, but
insidious, importunate, inevitable death for themselves
And this he describes as a man who has lived alone
with wild beasts, from the jungles of the Jordan where
lions lurked to the huts of the desert infested with
snakes.

18. *Woe to them who long for the day of Yahweh,*
    What is it for you—this day of Yahweh ? [2]

---

[1] Wellhausen aptly quotes from Tolstoy : ' You know what kind of a
people we Russians are.   We hope ever that something, or some one
will come, to heal at once all our wounds, to free us at once from all our
infirmities as from a bad tooth.'   Similarly Demosthenes of the
Athenians, ' They trusted that in two or three days all would be realised
that they might wish for.'

[2] Harper takes this line as interpolated, I think without reason.

> *Darkness it is and not light.*
>
> **v. 19.** *As when a man flees from a lion,*
> *And a bear falls upon him,*
> *Or gets into the house, leans his hand on the wall*
> *And a serpent bites him.*
>
> **20.** *Is it not darkness the day of Yahweh ?—*
> *Storm-dark* [1] *and never a ray upon it.*

The last line of 18 and the first of 20 seem redundant, and some, not unreasonably, suggest the elision of the one or the other.[2] Some too would take all ver. 19 as a later interpolation,[3] but this seems a vain proposal, for would such a verse more likely be due to some literary editor than to the desert-shepherd himself ? The LXX confirms the Hebrew text of all three verses.

Then Amos returns to the worship, that nurse of vain hopes, that false prophet of peace, and hears God speak more strongly than ever of its futility and hatefulness. For with pagan folly they still believed that the smoke of their burnt-offerings went up to heaven and flattered the nostrils of Deity. How ingrained was this belief may be judged from the fact that the terms of it had to be adopted by the apostles of a spiritual religion, if they would make themselves understood to Jewish and heathen converts alike, and are now the metaphors of the sacrifices of the Christian heart.[4]

> **21.** *I hate, I loathe your feasts,*
> *Nor savour your solemn assemblies.*

---

[1] LXX, γνόφος, fitly.

[2] Löhr the former, Marti and Harper the latter, while Marti transfers the last line of all as a fourth line for 18.

[3] Löhr and Duhm.   [4] Ephesians v. 2, etc.

22. *Though you bring Me up your holocausts* [1]
    And oblations, I will not accept them,
    Nor look at your peace-gifts of fatlings. [2]

23. *O spare Me the noise of your songs,*
    To the play of your viols I list not.

24. *But let justice roll on like waters,*
    And right an unfailing stream.

The verb *nor savour* or *have taste for* is literally *smell*—the smoke and scent of the burning sacrifices which alike to the Hebrews and their neighbours ascended to the nostrils of the hungry Deity, as, for instance, the Babylonians coarsely expressed it : ' A peace-offering I made . . . the gods inhaled the savour . . . the gods like flies gathered around the sacrifice.' [3] To the later Jews the ascending smoke of the holocausts was a more ethical symbol, ' the people's confession of their sin, their surrender through death and fire of the lives God was pleased to take in place of their guilty and forfeit selves.' [4]

There follows the remarkable appeal from the habits of the age which Amos addressed to those of the times of Israel's simplicity.

25. *Was it flesh- or meal-offerings ye brought Me*
    In the wilderness forty years long ?—
    O House of Israel. [5]

---

[1] Duhm and Marti delete this line as a later addition, but gratuitously. Löhr suggests that a line has fallen out after it, but this is also groundless.

[2] So too, is Harper's opinion that this line has been interpolated.

[3] See *K.A.T.*[3], p. 550.

[4] See my *Jerusalem*, vol. ii, pp. 528 f.

[5] No one doubts that this verse is interrogative. But A.V. puts it in a form—*Have ye brought unto Me ?* etc.—which implies blame that they did not do so. Ewald was first to see that, as rendered above, an appeal to the forty years was the intention of the verse. So after him nearly all critics, also R.V. : *Did ye bring unto Me ?* On the whole question of

It is a question to which a negative answer is obviously
expected. This is clear both from its form and the
whole argument into which it is put, that sacrifices are
vain ; and is in agreement with the conclusion of
Jeremiah that in the wilderness wanderings no system
of sacrifice was instituted. At the very time when
God made Israel His people, and led them to the
promised land—the time when of all others He did
most for them—He was not moved to such love and
deliverance by the propitiatory bribes, which this
generation imagine to be availing and indispensable
Nay, those still shall not avail, for exile from the land
shall now as surely come in spite of them, as the
possession of the land in old times came without them.
This at least seems to be the drift of the very obscure
verse which follows, and is the unmistakable statement
of the close of the oracle.

> 26. *But ye shall take up Sakkuth*
> *Your king, and Kewan your god,*
> *Images ye made for yourselves.*[1]

the possibility of such an appeal see above, pp. 100 f., and cf. Jer. vii. 22.
To avoid this conclusion Macdonald (*J.B.L.*, xviii, 214 f.) and Harper
wrest the meaning of the verse to ' ye brought me these but also true
worship.' Impossible ! Guthe and Marti delete *meal-offering* and
forty years. Duhm brings down the first clause of 22 to after wilderness.

[1] Ver. 26 is very difficult, for both the text and the rendering of the
possible alternatives to this are uncertain. (1) As to the *text*, the present
division into words must be correct ; at least no other is possible But
the present order of the words is obviously wrong. For *your images* is
evidently described by the relative clause *which you have made*, and
ought to stand next it. What then is to be done with the two words
that at present come between—*star of your god ?* Are they both a mere
gloss, as W. R. Smith held ? or should they precede the pair of words,
כיון צלמיכם, which they now follow ? Such is the text which the
LXX translator had before him, only for כון he misread ריפן or ריון :

καὶ ἀνελάβετε τὴν σκηνὴν τοῦ Μωλὸχ καὶ τὸ ἄστρον τοῦ Θεοῦ ὑμῶν 'Ραιφάν

[Ῥεφάν, Q], τοὺς τύπους αὐτῶν [om. AQ] οὓς ἐποιήσατε ἑαυτοῖς. This arrangement has the further evidence, that it brings *your god* into proper parallel with *your king*. The Hebrew text would then run thus :—

ונשאתם את סכות מלככם ואת [כוכב אלהיכם]
כיון צלמיכם אשר עשיתם לכם

(2) The translation of this text is equally difficult : not in the verb ונשאתם, for both the grammar and the argument oblige us to take it as future, *and ye shall lift up* (though Harper renders, *but now ye lift up*), but in the two words סכות and כיון. Are these common nouns, or proper names of deities in apposition to *your king* and *your god ?* The LXX takes סכות as = *tabernacle*, and כיון as a proper name (Theodotion takes both as proper names). A.V. partly follows the LXX. Schrader (*Stud. u. Krit.*, 1874, 324 ; *K.A.T.*[1], pp. 442 f.) takes them as the consonants of Sakkut, a name of the Assyrian god Adar, and of Kewan, the Assyrian name for the planet Saturn : *Ye shall take up Sakkut your king and Kewan your star-god, your images which* . . . Baethgen goes further and takes both the מלך of מלכיכם and the צלם of צלמיכם as Moloch and Selam, proper names, in combination with Sakkut and Kewan (*Beitr. z. Sem. Rel.*, 239). On all these deities see Zimmern in *K.A.T.*[3], pp. 409 f., 475 f., 622 ff. Now it is true that Second Kings implies that the worship of the host of heaven existed in Samaria before its fall (2 Kings xvii. 16), but the introduction to Samaria of Assyrian gods (among them Adar) is placed by it after the fall (2 Kings xvii. 31), and besides, Amos does not elsewhere speak of the worship of foreign gods, nor is the mention of them necessary to the argument here. On the contrary, even if Amos were to mention the worship of idols by Israel, would he have selected at this point the Assyrian ones ? (See, however, Tiele, *Revue de l'Histoire des Religions*, iii. p. 211, who makes Koun and the planet Keiwan purely Phœnician deities.) Some critics take סכות and כיון as common nouns in the construct state. So Ewald, and W. R. Smith (*O.T.J.C.*, 294) *the shrine of your king and the stand of your images*. This is more in harmony with the absence from the rest of Amos of any hint as to the worship of idols, but a strong objection to it is that the alleged common nouns are not found elsewhere in Hebrew. It is just possible that the words may themselves be later insertions, for the verse would read very well without them : *And ye shall lift up your king and your images* (Harper, *the image of your god) which you have made yourselves.* Wellhausen and others take כוכב and צלמיכם as glosses respectively to כיון and אלהיכם. The whole verse, however, may be an interpolation ; so Wellhausen, Nowack, Duhm (who would remove the verse to after 27), Löhr, Cheyne, and Marti. Guthe (except for *your images, the star*), Baumann (except for *star of your God*), Harper (as above) and Moffatt accept the verse as from Amos

v. 27. *But I will exile you beyond Damascus*
Saith Yahweh, God of Hosts is His Name.[1]

Thus like the previous one this chapter closes with the marshalling of God's armies. But as there His hosts were the movements of Nature and the Great Stars, so here they are the nations of the world. By His rule of both He is the God of Hosts. In this case the host intended is, of course, the Assyrian, which exiled whole peoples, carrying them north-eastwards—*beyond* Damascus.

3. AT EASE IN ṢION

Amos vi [2]

The evil of the national worship was the false political confidence which it engendered. Leaving the ritual, Amos proceeds to assault this confidence. We are taken from the worship of the people to the banquets of the rich, but again in order to have their security and extravagance contrasted with the pestilence, war, and exile that are rapidly approaching. The *ease* which is condemned means a proud overweening *ease*; the third line is ironical.

---

[1] The text is confirmed by LXX, and accepted in whole by Ewald, Driver, Baumann, Harper, and others. The last clause is peculiar. Two clauses seem to have run into one—*saith Yahweh, God of Hosts*, and *God of Hosts is His Name*. The word שְׁמוֹ = *His Name*, may have been added (Löhr, Duhm, Marti) to give the oracle the same conclusion as that at the end of the preceding chapter; and it is not to be overlooked that שְׁמוֹ at the end of a clause does not occur elsewhere in the book outside the three questioned Doxologies iv. 13, v. 8, ix. 6. Further, see below, pp. 214-216.

[2] On vi. 5, H. S. Elhorst, *Z.A.T.W.*, 1913.

vi. 1. *Woe to them that are at ease in Şion,*[1]
And that trust in the Mount of Samaria !
Men of mark [2] *of the first of the nations*
And to them the House of Israel resort . . .[3]. [4]

3. *Who put off the day of calamity,*[5]
And draw near the sessions of injustice,[6]

[1] *In Şion*: 'very suspicious,' Cornill and others; Löhr, Cheyne, **Marti**, Moffatt reject or read differently. Wellhausen, Driver, Duhm, and Harper retain.

[2] Lit. *pricked off, noted ;* cf. Arab. nakîb, a chief.

[3] Feeling this line feeble some change the reading ; *e.g.*, Duhm : *their food is the House of Israel ;* he takes the pricked off of the previous line as referring to the *marked* bell-wethers of the flock.

[4] I remove ver. 2 to a note, not that I am certain that it is not by Amos —who can be dogmatic on such a point ?—but because the text of it, the place it occupies, and its relation to the facts of current history, raise doubts. It is easily detached from the context, without disturbing the flow of the chapter, which runs more equably without it. The Massoretic text gives : *Pass over to Calneh, and see ; and go thence to Hamath Rabbah, and come down to Gath of the Philistines : are they better than these kingdoms, or is their territory larger than yours ?* Presumably *these kingdoms* are Judah and Israel. But that can only mean that Israel *is* the best of peoples, a statement out of harmony with the irony of ver. 1, and impossible in the mouth of Amos. Geiger, therefore, proposes to read : ' Are you better than these kingdoms—*i.e.*, Calneh, Hamath, Gath—or is your territory larger than theirs ? ' But this is also unlikely, for Israel's territory was much larger than Gath's. Besides, the question would have force only if Calneh, Hamath, and Gath had already fallen. Gath had, but it is at least very questionable whether Hamath had. Therefore Schrader (*K.A.T.*, p. 444) rejects the whole verse ; and Kuenen agrees that if we are to understand Assyrian conquests, it is hardly possible to retain it ; so Wellhausen, Löhr, Marti, Harper, Moffatt. Bickell's argument against the verse, that it does not fit into the metrical system of Amos vi. 1-7, is precarious.

[5] Davidson, *Syntax*, § 100, R. 5.

[6] שֶׁבֶת חָמָס ; LXX σαββάτων ψευδῶν, on which hint Hoffmann renders : ' you that daily demand the tribute of evil (cf. Ezek. xvi. 33), and every Sabbath extort by violence.' But this is unnecessary and opposed to viii. 5, which tells us no trade was done on the Sabbath. שֶׁבֶת is to be taken in the common sense of sitting in judgement rather than (with Wellhausen) in the sense of the enthronement of wrong-doing. Duhm thinks the text corrupt and reads by changing some consonants,

vi. 4. *Who lie upon ivory diwans,*
And sprawl on their couches,
Who eat off the lambs from the flock,
And calves from the midst of the stall.[1]

It is the way of men to wish and fancy far off the crisis their sins are hastening on ; Isaiah described the same generation as drawing iniquity with cords of hypocrisy and sin as it were with a cart-rope. The luxuries described in ver. 4 filled the hardy shepherd with contempt ; the meats are the most delicate, but perhaps in his irony he also means that the consumption by the rich was so extravagant as to finish off the lambs and calves.

5. *Who babble*[2] *to the sound of the viol,*
And like David[3] *devise them melodies,* (?)[4]
6. *Who drink up wine by the bason,*
And anoint with the finest of oil,
Yet grieve not over the ruin of Joseph.[5]

---

who vow (after the εὐχομενοι of LXX A) *the evil day and bring near ruin and violence ;* cf. Guthe.

[1] To this day, in some parts of Palestine, the general fold into which the cattle are shut contains a portion railed off for calves and lambs (cf. M. Blanckenhorn in the *Mittheilungen u. Nachrichten* of the D.P.V., 1895, p. 37). It may be this to which Amos refers. But it is not ' the usual word for lambs and denotes apparently such as, from their age or kind, were a special delicacy ' (Driver).

[2] Heb. *paraṭ* like its Arabic fellow *faraṭa* may mean either *to sing extravagantly*, or *to improvise idly* (Ewald *in loco* and Driver, p. 236) : the latter meaning is suitably parallel to the *devise* of the next line. Marti : ' phantasieren.'

[3] A gloss according to Guthe, Löhr, Duhm, Cheyne, and Harper, but retained as genuine by Driver, Marti, and Moffatt.

[4] Heb. reads *instruments of song ;* for which many emendations have been proposed. In any case David is here remembered not for sacred, but for secular music (W. R. Smith, *O.T. in the Jewish Church*, pp. 223 f.).

[5] Marti removes this line to after the first of ver. 13.

The *ruin of Joseph* is the moral ruin, for the social structure of Israel is obviously still secure.[1]   The rich are indifferent to it ; they have wealth, art, patriotism, religion, but neither heart for the poverty nor conscience for the sin of their people.   We know their kind !   Who live well and imagine they are clever and refined.   They have their political zeal, will rally to an election when the interests of their class or trade are in danger.   They have a robust and exuberant patriotism, talk grandly of commerce, empire, and the national destiny ; but for the real woes and sores of the people, the poverty, the overwork, the dissoluteness, which more affect a nation's life than anything else, they have no pity and no care.

The next stanza opens with the double initial of judgement, *therefore now*, repeats the doom of exile, and echoes the word *sprawlers* of ver. 4, yet here in a moral rather than a physical sense, *dissolutely indifferent* to the ruinously sinful condition of Israel.

7. *Therefore now shall they go into exile*
   At the head of the exiles,
   And stilled be the revel of the dissolute—
   Rede of Yahweh, the God of Hosts.[2]
8. *Sworn by Himself hath Yahweh*
   I am loathing [3] *the pride of Jacob*
   And his palaces I hate,
   And I give up the town and its fulness.

[1] It is possible that here, as in v. 15 and 16, we have prophecy later than the disaster of 734, when Tiglath-Pileser made a great *breach* or *havoc* in the body politic of Israel by taking Gilead and Galilee.   But this is scarcely probable, for Amos almost everywhere lays stress upon the moral corruption of Israel, as her real danger.

[2] With Wellhausen, Marti, Harper, and Moffatt I bring this line up here from 8 to complete the stanza of four lines.

[3] מתאב for מתעב , which should be read.

vi. 11.[1] *For behold Yahweh commanding*

.   .   .   .[2]

> *And He smites the great house to ruins,*
> *And the small house to splinters.*

The collapse must come, postpone it as their fancy will, for it has been worked for and is inevitable. How could it be otherwise ?

12. *Shall horses run up a cliff,*
    Or the sea be ploughed by oxen ?[3]
    That ye should turn justice to poison
    And the fruit of right to wormwood.

13. *Who exult in Lo-Debar,*
    Who say, Is it not by our strength
    We have taken to us Ḳarnaim ?

So Grätz and most moderns rightly read the verse. The Hebrew text and all the versions take these names as if they were common nouns—Lo-Debar, *a thing of nought ;* Ḳarnaim, *a pair of horns*—and doubtless it was just because of this possible play upon their names, that Amos selected these two out of all the recent conquests of Israel. Karnaim, in full Ashteroth-Ḳarnaim, *Astarte of Horns*, was that immemorial fortress and sanctuary which lay out upon the great plateau of Bashan towards Damascus ; so obvious and cardinal a site that it appears in the sacred history both in the earliest recorded campaign in Abraham's time and in one of the latest under the Maccabees.[4]

---

[1] For vv. 9 and 10 on the pestilence see pp. 184 ff.

[2] A line may have dropped here.

[3] So Michaelis, בְּבָקָר יָם for בִּבְקָרִים , and so all moderns.

[4] Gen. xiv. 5 ; 1 Macc. v. In the days of Eusebius and Jerome (4th century) there were two places of the name : one of them doubtless

Lo-Debar was of Gilead, and probably lay on that last rampart of the province northward, overlooking the Yarmuk ; a strategical point which must have often been contested by Israel and Aram, and with which no other Old Testament name has been identified.[1] These two fortresses, with many others, Israel had lately taken from Aram ; but not as they boasted, *by their own strength.* It was only Aram's pre-occupation with Assyria now urgent on the northern flank, which allowed Israel these easy victories. And that same northern foe would soon overwhelm themselves.

> 14. *For lo, I am to raise against you,*
> *A nation, O House of Israel,*[2]
> *And they shall oppress you from the entry to Hamath,*
> *Even to the vale of the 'Arabah.*

Every one knows the former, the Pass between the Lebanons, at whose mouth stands Dan, northern limit of Israel ; but it is hard to identify the latter. If Amos means to include Judah, we should have expected the Torrent of Egypt, the present Wady el'Arish ; but the Wady of the 'Arabah may be a corresponding valley in the eastern watershed issuing in the 'Arabah. If Amos threatens only the Northern Kingdom, he intends

the present Tell Ashtara south of El-Merkez, the other distant from that fourteen Roman miles.

[1] Along this ridge ran, and still runs, one of the most important high-ways to the East, that from Beth-Shan by Gadera to Edrei. About seven miles east from Gadera lies a village, Ibdar, ' with a good spring and some ancient remains ' (Schumacher, *N. Ajlun,* 101). Lo-Debar is mentioned in 2 Sam. ix. 4, 5 ; xvii. 27 ; and doubtless the Lidebir of Josh. xiii. 26 on the north border of Gilead is the same (R.V. note).

[2] The clause, *Rede of Yahweh God of the hosts* (with the article, an unusual form of the title) is to be omitted with codd. A and Q of the LXX.

some wady running down to that Sea of the 'Arabah, the Dead Sea, which is elsewhere given as the limit of Israel.[1]

The Assyrian flood, then, was about to break, and the oracles close with the hopeless prospect of the whole land submerged beneath it.

4. A FRAGMENT FROM THE PLAGUE

In the above exposition, I have omitted two curious verses, 9 and 10, which are held by some not to be from Amos himself,[2] and by others [3] to be at least out of place, interrupting the current of the chapter, reflecting another kind of calamity than it does, and cast in a style difficult to harmonise with that of the context. For reasons which will appear I cannot agree that the two verses are not by Amos, nor am I even sure that they are out of place ; but they are so distinct and remarkable that it is convenient to deal with them specially. The text and consequently its division into lines are more than usually uncertain ; and from the time of the codices of the Septuagint to our own day textual emendations have been rife. But not only do these, by their number and differences, cast doubt on the probability of each other ; the most of them also rob the vivid little piece of its atmosphere and spirit. These are natural and urgent enough, along with such details as the breathlessness of the piece spares us, to justify a conjectural metrical arrangement,

---

[1] 2 Kings xiv. 25. The Torrent of the 'Arabah can scarcely be the Torrent of the 'Arabim of Isa. xv. 7, for the latter was outside Israel's territory, and the border between Moab and Edom. The LXX render *Vale* or *wady of the West*, τῶν δυσμῶν.

[2] Nowack, Löhr, Harper, Moffatt.

Wellhausen, Guthe, Cheyne, Baumann.

especially if we take the piece along with the couplet immediately preceding it.[1]

   VI. 8. *Sworn by Himself hath Yah-weh,*
       I am loathing the pride of Jacob,
       And I hate his palaces,
       So I give up a town and its fulness . . . (?) [2]
     9. *And it shall be if ten* [3] *be left,*
       In a single house, they shall die, [4]
       And their kinsmen [5] *and burner (?)* [6] *lift them*
       To bring forth their bones [7] *from the house,*
  10. *And they say to one back* [8] *in the house,* [9]
       Are there yet with thee ?—and he says, None !
       Says also, Hush !—for one must not
       Mention the Name of Yahweh.

But the death of so large a household as ten, and it may be (though this is not certain) the funeral left to a distant relation and the disposal of the bodies by burning instead of the burial customary among the Hebrews [10] sufficiently reflect the kind of calamity.

[1] As Marti and Duhm, retaining the whole for Amos, reasonably do.
[2] The verb almost invariably requires a sequence. See below.
[3] So LXX B; Heb. and LXX AQ add *men*.
[4] LXX adds καὶ ὑπολειφθήσονται οἱ κατάλοιποι.
[5] LXX *their kinsmen ;* Heb. *his kinsman* or *uncle*, but perhaps collective.
[6] So Heb., LXX B καὶ παραβιῶνται as if reading ויפצרו, *and press*, but LXX A καὶ οἱ παραβιωται.
[7] So LXX ; Heb. *the bones*, that is *bodies*.
[8] Lit. *in the two sides* or *corner*, *inmost recess ;* cf. Isa. xiv. 14 f.
[9] Duhm transfers *in the house* to after *with thee* in the next line.
[10] The burning of a body was regarded, as we have seen (Amos ii. 1), as a sacrilege ; and practised outside pestilence only on great criminals : Lev. xx. 14; xxi. 9; Josh. vii. 25. Doughty (*Arabia Deserta*, 68) mentions that, in Medina, a Persian pilgrim was burned to death by an angry crowd for defiling Mohammed's tomb.

It is a weird bit of memory, the recollection of an eye-witness, from one of those pestilences which, during the first half of the eighth century, happened in Western Asia.[1]   But what does it do here ?   Wellhausen says that there is nothing to lead up to the incident ; that before it the chapter speaks, not of pestilence, but only of destruction by an enemy.   This is not accurate. The phrase immediately preceding may mean either *I will shut up a city and its fulness*, in which case a siege is meant, and a siege was the possibility both of famine and pestilence ; or *I will give up the city and its fulness* . . . , in which case a word or two may have been dropped, and one ought perhaps to add *to the pestilence*.[2] The latter alternative is the more probable, and this may be one of the passages, already alluded to,[3] in which the want of connection with the preceding verses is to be explained, not upon the theory that there has been an intrusion into the text, but upon the hypothesis that some words have been lost.

The uncertainty of the text, however, does not weaken the impression of its ghastly realism : the unclean and haunted house ; the kinsman and the body-burner afraid to search through the infected rooms, and calling in muffled voice to a single survivor crouching in some far corner of them, *Are there any more with thee ?* his reply, *None*—himself the next ! Yet these details are not the most weird.   Over all hangs a terror darker than the pestilence.   *Shall there be evil in a city and Yahweh not have done it ?*   Such,

---

[1] The Assyrian inscriptions record at least three—in 803, 765, 759.

[2] As in Psalm lxxviii. 50.   הִסְגִּיר, to give up, is so seldom used absolutely (Deut. xxxii. 30 is poetry and elliptic) that we may well believe it was followed by words signifying to what the city was to be given up.

[3] Pp. 142 f.

as we have heard from Amos, was the faith of the age.
But in times of woe this was held with a craven and
awful superstition. The whole of life was believed to
be overhung with loose accumulations of Divine anger.
And as in some fatal hollow in the high Alps, where
any noise may bring down the impending masses of
snow, and the fearful traveller hurries along in silence,
so the men of that superstitious age feared, when an
evil like the plague was imminent, even to utter the
Deity's name, lest it should loosen some avalanche of
His wrath. *And he said, Hush! for*, adds the comment,
one must not make mention of the name of Yahweh.

This reveals another side of the popular religion
which Amos has been attacking. We have seen it as
the superstition of routine; but we now know that
this was a routine broken by panic. The God who in
times of peace was propitiated by regular supplies of
sacrifice and flattery, is conceived, when His wrath is
roused and imminent, as kept quiet only by the silence
of its miserable objects. The false peace of ritual is
tempered by panic.

CHAPTER X

DOOM OR DISCIPLINE?

AMOS VIII. 4–IX

WE enter the Third Section of the Book: chaps. vii–ix. As we have already treated the first part of it—the group of four visions, which probably formed the prophet's discourse at Bethel, with the interlude of his adventure there (vii–viii. 3) [1]—we may pass to what remains: from viii. 4 to the end of the book. This portion consists of groups of oracles obscure in their relations to each other, and per-haps containing verses not from Amos himself. They open in a denunciation of the rich, which echoes previous oracles, and soon pass to judgements of a kind already threatened, but now with greater relentlessness. Then, just as all is at the darkest, lights break; exceptions are made; the inevitable exile is described not as doom, but as discipline; and, with only this preparation for a change, we are swept on a scene, in which, though the land is strewn with the ruins that have been threatened, the sunshine of a new day floods them; the promise of restoration is given; Nature will be regenerated, and the life of Israel replanted on its own ground.

Whether it was given to Amos himself to behold

[1] See Ch. VI, section 3.

this day—whether these last verses of the book were his ' Nunc Dimittis,' or the hope of a later generation, which found his book intolerably severe, and mingled with its judgements their own new mercies—we shall try to discover. Meanwhile, there is no doubt, we start with the authentic oracles of the prophet. We know the ring of his voice. To the tyranny of the rich, which he has often lashed, he adds the greed and fraud of the traders ; and paints Israel's doom in those shapes of earthquake, eclipse, and famine with which his own generation had recently become familiar. Note that in this first group Amos employs only physical calamities, and says nothing of war and captivity. If the standard which we have applied to the growth of his doctrine be correct, these ought to be counted among his earlier utterances. War and captivity follow in chap. ix. That is to say, this Third Section follows the same development as both the First and the Second.

1. Earthquake, Eclipse, and Famine

Amos viii. 4–14

In vv. 4–6 the order of the lines is questionable and the genuineness of them contested. But in the speed of his scorn Amos may well have interrupted the greedy words he puts into the mouth of the traders by flinging at them the frauds (5b–6a) by which they fed their greed. But see Ewald's plan of the passage.

viii. 4. *Hear this, ye who trample the needy,*
And oppress [1] *the poor of the land,*

---

[1] So LXX καταδυναστεύοντες ; Heb. *put an end to*. Löhr thinks that a line has slipped out after this one.

viii. 5. *Saying, when will the New-Moon be over*
That we may be selling grain ?
And the Sabbath that we may open ?
—Making small the measure and large the weight,[1]
And warping the fraudulent scales,
   6. *Buying the poor for silver*
And the needy for a pair of shoes [2]—
And that we may sell refuse for grain.[3]

The existence at this date of the New-Moon and Sabbath as days of rest from business is interesting ; even more interesting is the peril to which they lie open. As in the case of the Nazirites and the prophets, we see how the religious institutions and opportunities of the people are threatened by worldliness and greed. And, as in every other relevant passage of the Old Testament, we have the interests of the Sabbath bound up in the same cause with the interests of the poor. The Fourth Commandment enforces the day of rest on behalf of the servants and bondsmen. When a later prophet substitutes for religious fasts the ideals of social service, he weds with the latter the security of the Sabbath from all business.[4] So here Amos emphasises that the Sabbath is threatened by the same worldliness and love of money which tramples on the helpless. The interests of the Sabbath are the interests of the poor : the enemies of the Sabbath are the enemies of the poor. And all this illustrates our Saviour's saying, that *the Sabbath was made for man.*

[1] Or *price ;* Heb. *shekel.*

[2] This couplet is taken as an interpolation by most moderns because a mere echo of ii. 9, but, as Duhm says, it need not therefore be ungenuine.

[3] This line also most moderns regard as interpolated ; Duhm and A. R. Gordon put it after *and the Sabbath that we may open.*

[4] Isa. lviii. See the exposition of the passage in the writer's *Isaiah xl–lxvi,* pp. 417 ff.

But as in the rest of the book doom follows hard upon sin, the anger of the Lord, and its expression as in iv. 11 in a great convulsion of nature. The Pride or pride of Jacob is either Yahweh Himself, as that in which Jacob boasts, or Jacob's own haughtiness, in either case used ironically.

> 7. *Sworn hath Yahweh by the pride of Jacob*
> *I shall never forget all your* [1] *doings.*
> 8. *Shall not the earth be shaking for this,*
> *And her every inhabitant mourn ?*
> *She shall rise like the River in mass*
> *And* [2] *sink like the River of Egypt.* [3]

It is as before. The chief spring of the prophet's inspiration is his burning sense of the personal indignation of God against crimes so abominable. God is the God of the poor, and His anger rises, as we see the anger of Christ arise, heavy against their tyrants and oppressors. Such sins are intolerable to Him. But the feeling of their intolerableness is shared by the land itself, the very fabric of nature ; the earthquake is the proof of it.

To the earthquake is added the eclipse : one had happened in 803, and another in 763, the memory of which probably inspired the form of this passage.

> 9. *And it shall be in that day—*
> *Rede of Yahweh the Lord—* [4]

[1] So LXX ; Heb. *their.*

[2] Heb. adds *heave ;* LXX omits.

[3] Most moderns take ver. 8 as an interpolation, because most of it is found in ix. 5 ; but I agree with Harper that it is most natural here, forming one strophe with 7.

[4] This couplet may be editorial (Löhr) ; without it we have two stanzas of four lines each.

> *I shall bring down the sun at noon*
> *And cast darkness on earth in broad day ;* [1]

viii. 10. *I will turn your feasts to mourning,*
> *And all your songs to a dirge,*

> *Bring sack-cloth over all loins*
> *And baldness on every head,*
> *Make it* [2] *like mourning an only son*
> *And the end thereof as a bitter day.* [3]

The next verses to the end of the chapter fall, if ver. 13 be omitted (see below), into three regular stanzas of four lines each, which in itself forms a considerable reason for discarding the more drastic eliminations that have been proposed. [4] Besides the three stanzas yield a consistent and credible meaning which ver. 13 only disturbs : the threat of a famine of the Word of God to a people rushing in search of that Word from one of their discredited sanctuaries to another.

> **11.** *Behold the days come, Rede of Yahweh the Lord,*
> *When famine I send on the land,*
> *Not famine of bread nor drouth of water*
> *But of hearing the Word* [5] *of Yahweh.*

----

[1] Lit. *in the day of light.*

[2] So LXX ; Heb. *her* which Ewald takes to be Samaria.

[3] These two verses Marti takes as an interpolation for no adequate reason ; Guthe, Nowack, Wellhausen, Baumann, Harper, Moffatt as genuine ; the last two inserting ver. 3 between 9 and 10 or after 10*a*.

[4] Such as taking the first line of 11 as editorial (Guthe, Harper, etc.) ; or all vv. 11, 12 as a later interpolation (Gunning, *De Godspraken van Amos*, 1885, Wellhausen, König, *Einleitung*, p. 304, Nowack, Löhr, etc.), or such parts of 11 and 12 as indicate a famine of the Word (Guthe, Marti) ; or, while retaining 13, adding two lines to 14 and so constructing four stanzas of four lines each (A. R. Gordon, etc.).

[5] So LXX, Syr., Vulg. ; Heb. *Words.*

12. *And they wander from sea to sea*
    And wildly rush from the North to the Sunrise,
    To seek for the Word of Yahweh,
    But they shall not find it.

13. [*In that day the virgins shall swoon,*
    Fair women, strong youths with thirst.]

14. *Who swear by the Guilt (?)* [1] *of Samaria,*
    And say, As liveth thy God, O Dan !
    Or, as liveth the Way [2] *to Beer-sheba !—*
    They shall fall and rise no more.

Some part of these verses must go, because, as is
generally recognised, vv. 11, 12 speak of a famine of
the Word while the *thirst* of 13 is physical, affecting
the strength of youth, and if the latter verse is to be
retained the many critics are right who take as a later
interpolation either the whole of 11, 12 or such parts
of them as speak of a famine of the Divine Word.[3]
Yet 13 not only interrupts the regularity of the stanzas
but breaks the natural connection between 12 and 14.
For 14 surely follows 11 and 12 better than it follows
13, because the oaths by the Guilt (?) of Samaria, the
God of Dan and the Way to Beer-sheba cannot have
been cited as specially of the *fair maidens and strong*
youths of the nation, but are the oaths of the whole
nation *wandering from the dark North* [4] *to the Sunrise,*

---

[1] אשמה for which Stade, Oort, W. R. Smith, and Duhm propose
אשרה, Ashĕrah, and Guthe, Wellhausen, Cheyne, Marti, Gordon,
Moffatt substitute *God of Bethel*. The Heb. text is confirmed by the
LXX τοῦ ἱλασμοῦ Σαμαρείας. Samaria here, but not elsewhere in Amos,
is the name of the country.

[2] LXX *thy God, Beersheba*. So some propose to change Heb. דרך
way to דדך, *thy darling* or *patron-god*; cf. the Moabite Stone, l. 12.

[3] Above, p. 192, n. 4.

[4] The Heb. צפון is literally *dark region*, and therefore opposed here
to *Sunrise*.

from Dan to Beer-sheba, one end of the land to the other, to seek at the sanctuaries of their superstition for some Word from Yahweh. Moreover, the threat of a famine of the Word comes naturally after Amaṣiah's rejection at Bethel of God's Word through Amos. Therefore, with all respect to the many critics who hold the opposite opinion,[1] I feel a clear case for retaining vv. 11 and 12 and omitting 13 as a later addition. Note that this has an introductory formula of its own as if it were a separate oracle.

One of the superstitious oaths, *As liveth the Way to Beer-sheba*, is so curious that some doubt if the text be correct, or take *Way* to mean here *Practice* or *Ritual of*. But strange as it may appear to us to speak of the life of the lifeless, this often happens among the Semites. To-day Arabs ' swear *wa hyât*, " by the life of," even of things inanimate ; " By the life of this fire, or of this coffee." '[2] And as Amos here tells us that the Israelite pilgrims swore by the way to Beer-sheba, so do the Moslems affirm their oaths by the sacred way to Mecca.

Thus Amos returns to the chief target of his shafts, the corrupt worship of the national sanctuaries. And this time he tells Israel that, with all their running to and fro across the land, to shrine after shrine in search of the word, they shall suffer from a famine and drouth of it. This is perhaps the most effective contrast in which Amos has placed the stupid ritualism of his people. With so many things to swear by ; with so many holy places that once were the homes of Vision, Abraham's Beer-sheba, Jacob's Bethel, Joshua's Gilgal, nay, a whole land over which God's voice had broken in past ages, lavish as the rain ; with, too, all their

[1] Above p. 192, n. 4. [2] Doughty, *Arabia Deserta*, i. 269.

assiduity of sacrifice and prayer, they should never-theless starve and pant for that living word of the Lord, which they had silenced in His prophet.

Thus, men may be devoted to religion, may be loyal to their sacred traditions and institutions, may haunt the holy associations of the past and be assiduous with their ritual—and yet, because of their worldliness, pride, and disobedience, never feel that moral inspira-tion, that clear call to duty, that comfort in pain, that hope in adversity, that good conscience at all times, which spring up in a true heart like living water. Where these be not experienced, orthodoxy, zeal, lavish ritua are all in vain.

2. NEMESIS

Amos ix. 1–8*a*

There follows a Vision in Bethel, the opening of which, *I saw the Lord*, recalls the great inauguration of Isaiah. He also *saw the Lord ;* but how different the Attitude, how other the Word ! To the statesman-prophet the Lord is *enthroned*, surrounded by the court of heaven ; and though the temple rocks to the intolerable thunder of their praise, they bring to the contrite man beneath the consciousness of a life-long mission. But to Amos the Lord is *standing* and alone —to this lonely prophet God is always alone—and His message may be summed up in its initial word, *Smite*. There Government : hierarchies of service, embassies, clemencies, healings, and though at first devastation, thereafter the indestructible hope of a future. Here Judgement : that Figure of Fate which terror's fascinated eye ever sees alone ; one final blow and irreparable ruin. And so, as with Isaiah we saw how constructive prophecy may be, with Amos we behold only the preparatory havoc, the levelling and clearing of the ground of the future.

The passage (ix. 1–4) falls into five stanzas of four lines each.[1] In translation the lines of the first couplet may sound too short, but each has an emphasis of its own, and in the original each has three stresses like the rest ; in the first how strong and musical with its double stress is the Hebrew *Adonai, the Lord !*

ix. 1. *I have seen Adonai*
Standing over the altar,
He said, Smite [2] the capitals [3]
Till the thresholds be quaking.

Cut them down on the head of them all (?) [4]
And their last shall I slay with the sword.
Not a fugitive of them shall flee,
Not of them slip away a survivor.

2. *Although they should dig to Sheol,*
From there My Hand shall take them,
And though they should climb to the Heavens,
From there I shall bring them down.

3. *Though they hide on the top of Carmel,*
I [5] shall search them out and fetch them,

[1] Such an arrangement (which is also Duhm's) is preferable to Harper's division of vv. 1–4, 7, 8b, into four stanzas of six lines each.

[2] Some moderns read *I will smite ;* others following Volz *and He smote,* after removing *and He said* to the beginning of the next stanza.

[3] Heb. singular but apparently collective ; cf. the first *them* in the next stanza.

[4] This line is doubtful, the first *them* is the capitals, the second is the people. For בראש, *on the head of,* some would read ברעש, *by an earthquake,* which is attractive. Yet LXX confirms Heb.

[5] Here and twice below Heb. adds *from there,* which, however, seems to be only a scribe's wrong repetition of *from there* in the previous verse. It slightly overloads the metre, but is confirmed by LXX and retained by Baumann. See next page, n 2.

Though they screen them [1] upon the sea-floor,
I [2] shall charge the Dragon to bite them.

4. *Though they go into exile before their foes,*
   I [2] shall charge the sword and shall slay them,
   And shall set Mine Eyes upon them
   For evil and not for good.

The Vision seems subsequent to the prophet's visit to Bethel ; and it gathers under the roof of the temple there his whole attacks on the national worship into one decisive and irreparable blow. The shock is fundamental from roof-tree to threshold of the temple, of the national life. None of the people shall escape. Neither hell nor heaven, mountain-top nor sea-bottom, nor exile itself, to Israel of that time as terrible for distance from God's Face as Sheol itself, shall harbour one of them. Further, the passage is proof of God's omnipresence : a ruder parallel to the Hundred and Thirty-Ninth Psalm, but the Divine Pursuer is Nemesis, not Conscience.

There follows a perhaps interpolated ode, another of those doxologies, on which see the next chapter.

5. *And Yahweh of Hosts, the Lord,*
   Who toucheth the earth and it melts,
   And all its inhabitants mourn,
   (And it rises in mass like the Nile
   And sinks like the Nile of Egypt),
6. *Who hath built in the Heavens His Stories,*
   And His Dome on the Earth He hath founded,
   Who calleth the waters of the Sea,

---

[1] Heb. and LXX *before Mine eyes*, which overloads the line, and may have been inserted by a later scribe in whose time it was a well-used phrase. See Jeremiah. [2] See footnote 5 on opposite page.

198 THE TWELVE PROPHETS

And poureth them forth on the face of the Earth—
Yahweh [1] His Name !

Following naturally upon vv. 1–4, whether spoken
in immediate connection with them or at some other
time, is the famous ver. 7. Undoubtedly Amos himself
still speaks. Once more he emphasises the now familiar
truth (i, ii, etc.) that when it comes to judgement for
sin Israel is no more to their God, the God of righteousness, than any other people of His equal Providence.

ix. 7. *Are ye not to Me as the sons of the Kushites,[2]*
   O sons of Israel ?—Yahweh's Rede.
   Brought I not Israel up from the land of Egypt,
   And the Philistines from Kaphtor,[3]
   And Aram from Ḳîr [4] ?

Mark again the universal Providence which Amos
proclaims : it is the due concomitant of his universal
morality. Once for all the religion of Israel breaks
from the characteristic Semitic belief that gave a god
to every people, and limited his power and his interests
to that people's territory and fortunes. And if we
remember how everything spiritual in the religion of
Israel, everything in its significance for mankind, was
rendered possible only because at this date it broke
from and abjured the particularism in which it had
been born, we shall feel some of the Titanic force of
the prophet, in whom that break was achieved with an

---

[1] LXX adds *God of Hosts.*
[2] Probably the Ethiopians, though some suppose the N. Arabian tribe
of the same name (Cheyne, *Enc. Bibl.*).
[3] Most probably Crete (see my *Hist. Geog.*, p. 175) ; LXX *Cappadocia.*
[4] LXX ἐκ βόθρου *from a pit* reading קיר , Ḳîr as if it were from קור
to dig !

absoluteness that leaves nothing to be desired.   But
let us also emphasise, that it was by no mere method
of the intellect nor observation of history that Amos was
led to assert the unity of the Divine Providence.   The
inspiration of this was a moral one : Yahweh was ruler
and guide of all the families of mankind, because He
was exalted in righteousness ; and the field in which
that righteousness was proved and made manifest was
the life and the fate of Israel.   Therefore to this Amos
finally turns.

> 8a. *Lo the eyes of Lord Yahweh on the sinful kingdom,*
> *And I will destroy it from the face of the ground.*

In other words, Yahweh's sovereignty over the world
was not proved by Israel's conquest of the latter, but
by His unflinching application of the principles of
righteousness, at whatever cost, to Israel herself.

3. VOICES OF ANOTHER DAWN

Amos ix. 8b–15

Up to this point, then, the voice of Amos is unmistakable, uttering the doctrine, so original to him, that
in the judgement of God Israel shall not be specially
favoured, and the sentence, we have heard so often
from him, of her removal from her land.   Remember,
Amos has said hardly a word in mitigation of the
sentence : up to this point of his book it has been
presented as inexorable and final.   But now to a statement of it as absolute as any that has gone before,
there is suddenly added a qualification, 8b : *only that
I will not utterly destroy the house of Jacob—'tis the Rede
of Yahweh.*   And then there is added a new picture
of exile changed from doom to discipline, a process of

sifting by which only the evil in Israel, *all the sinners of My people*, shall perish, in their blind belief in their own security, but not a grain of the good.

> ix. 9. *For, behold, I am giving command,*
> *And Israel's House I will toss through all nations*
> *As corn* [1] *is tossed in a sieve,*
> *But never a kernel* [2] *shall fall to the earth*
> 10. *By the sword they shall die,*
> *All the sinners of My people,*
> *Who say : Nor shall reach nor prevent*
> *About us the evil.* [3]

Now as to these modifications of the hitherto almost unmitigated judgements of the book, it is to be noted that there is nothing in their language to lead us to deny them to Amos himself. On the contrary, the last clause describes what he has always called a characteristic sin of his day. Our only difficulties are that hitherto Amos has not qualified his sentences of doom, and that the change now appears so suddenly that the two halves of the verse in which it does so absolutely contradict each other. Read them again, ver. 8 : *Lo, the eyes of the Lord Yahweh are on the sinful nation, and*

---

[1] This word required by meaning and metre has clearly slipped out.

[2] The Heb. word צְרוֹר either means this, properly *knot* or *nodule*, or else, as in 2 Sam. xvii. 13, *little stone* or *pebble, pebbles* being used still in Syria for cleansing the winnowed corn, Preuschen, *Z.A.T.W.*, 1895, p. 24 ; cf. Hoffmann, *ibid.*, 1883, 125.

[3] The text here has been disturbed ; the verbs are in forms not possible to the sense. For תִּפּ֫שׁ read either תָּשׁ֫ית with Hitzig or תִּגַּשׁ with Wellhausen. תַּקְדִּים , Hiph., is not impossible in an intransitive sense, but probably Wellhausen is right in reading Pi. תְּקַדֵּם . The reading עָדֵ֫ינוּ which the Greek suggests and Hoffmann and Wellhausen adopt is not so appropriate to the preceding verb as בַּעֲדֵ֫ינוּ of the text.

I will destroy it from off the face of the ground—neverthe-
less destroying I shall not destroy the house of Jacob :
'tis the Rede of Yahweh.   Can we believe the same
prophet to have uttered at the same time these two
statements ?   And is it possible to see in that prophet
the hitherto unwavering, unqualifying Amos ?   Noting
these things, let us pass to the rest of the chapter.
We break from all shadows ; the verses are of pure
hope. The judgement on Israel is not averted ; but
having taken place her ruin is regarded as not irreparable.

The next piece of six lines [1] begins *in that day,* the
Day which Amos has threatened of overthrow and ruin !

11. *In that day I will raise the fallen hut of David,*
     Closing its [2] breaches and raising its [2] ruins,
     And build it again as in days of old,
12. *That they may possess the remnant of Edom,[3]*
     And all nations on whom My Name was called— [4]
     The Rede of Yahweh, the Doer of this.

The *fallen hut of David* undoubtedly means the fall
of the kingdom of Judah. It is not language Amos
uses, or, as it seems to me, could have used, of the fall
of the Northern Kingdom only.[5] Again, it is clear
that Amos contemplated the fall of Judah : this is

---

[1] But Marti divides ver. 11 into four, and 12 into three lines.

[2] So LXX, but Heb. *their breaches their ruins,* according to which
some read *huts* for hut of David (Hoffmann, *Z.A.T.W.*, 1883, 125 ;
Schwally, *ibid.*, 1890, 226, n. 1 ; Guthe). But LXX is right.

[3] LXX B, ὅπως ἐκζήτουσι οἱ κατάλοιποι τῶν ἀνθρώπων reading יִדְרְשׁוּ
for יִירְשׁוּ and Adam *man* for Edom ; and this is the reading quoted
in Acts xv. 17 : *that the residue of men may seek after—the Lord* being
added from LXX A.

[4] As that of their Possessor in David's time.

[5] This against Cornill, *Einleitung*, 176, and others, for the kingdom
was not Judah only but all Israel in David's day.

implicit in such a phrase as *the whole family that I brought up from Egypt*.[1] He saw then *the day* and *the ruins* of which ver. 11 speaks. The only question is, can we attribute to him the prediction of a restoration of these ruins ? And this is a question which must be answered because the rest of his book is hardly relieved by a gleam of hope, and his threat of the nation's destruction is final. Now it is significant that in face of those facts Cornill (though he changed his opinion) once believed that it was ' surely possible for Amos to include restoration in his prospect of ruin,' as (he might have added) other prophets undoubtedly do. I confess I cannot so readily get over the rest of the book and its gloom ; and I am the less inclined to be sure about these verses being Amos' own that it seems to have been not unusual for later generations, for whom the day-star was beginning to rise, to add their own inspired hopes to the unrelieved threats of their predecessors of the midnight. The mention of Edom does not help us ; if in the days of Amos after the partial conquest by Uzziah the promise of *the rest of Edom* was appropriate, yet on the other hand, what interest had so purely ethical a prophet in the mere addition of territory ? To this point we shall have to return for our final decision. We have still the closing oracle—a pleasant piece of music, as if the birds had come out after the thunderstorm, and the wet hills were glistening in the sun.

ix. 13. *Behold days are coming—Yahweh's Rede—*
When the ploughman catches up with the reaper
And the grape-treader him that strews the seed,
And the mountains shall drip with new wine,
And all the hills shall melt

[1] iii. 1.

with fertility, ripeness, and abundance. It is that
'happy contention of seasons' which Josephus [1] describes as the perpetual blessing of Galilee. So the
Septuagint renders : 'and the reaping shall overtake
the vintage, and the vine turn purple in the seed-time.'

> 14. *And I will restore the captivity [2] of Israel My
>   people ;*
>   *They shall build the waste cities and dwell therein,*
>   *And plant out vineyards and drink their wine,*
>   *And work up gardens and eat their fruits.*
> 15. *And themselves I shall plant upon their own soil.*
>   *Not again shall they ever be torn*
>   *From their soil I have given them.—*
>   *Spoken hath Yahweh thy God ! [3]*

Again we meet the difficulty. Does the voice that
speaks here speak with exile already realised, or is it
the voice of one who projects himself forward to a day
which by the Lord's own oath is certain to come ?

We have now surveyed the whole of this much-
doubted, much-defended passage. I have stated fully
the arguments on both sides. On the one hand, we
have the fact that nothing in the language of the verses,
and nothing in their historical allusions, precludes

---

[1] III, *Wars*, x. 8. With the above verses Lev. xxvi. 5 has been compared : *your threshing shall reach to the vintage and the vintage shall
reach to the sowing time.* There is no reason to suppose that either passage depends on the other ; both may be quoting a common saying.

[2] This is a more probable reading (Driver, Harper, Moffatt) *than turn
the fortune*, lit. *the turning*, of Israel My people (Ewald, Kuenen, Cheyne,
Marti) by deriving שבות from שוב, *to turn*, rather than from שבה,
to take captive. But even if the latter opinion be the right one the end is
the same, it is the exile that is meant.

[3] LXX read *God of Hosts*.

their being by Amos ; we have also to admit that, having threatened a day of ruin, it was possible for Amos to realise by his mind's eye its arrival, and standing at that point to see the sunshine flooding the ruins and to prophesy a restoration. In all this there is nothing impossible in itself or inconsistent with the rest of the book. On the other hand, we have the impressive and undeniable facts : *first*, that this change to hope comes suddenly, without preparation and without statement of reasons, at the very end of a book whose characteristics are not only a final and absolute sentence of ruin upon the people, and an outlook of unrelieved darkness, but scornful discouragement of every popular vision of a prosperous future ; and, *second*, that the prophetic books contain numerous signs that later generations wove their own brighter hopes into the abrupt and hopeless conclusions of earlier prophecies of judgement.

To this balance of evidence is there anything to add ? I think there is ; and that it decides the question. All these prospects of the future restoration of Israel are without a moral feature. They speak of return from exile, of political restoration, of supremacy over the Gentiles, and of a revived Nature, hanging with fruit, dripping with must. Such hopes are natural and legitimate to a people who were long separated from their devastated and neglected land, and whose punishment and penitence were accomplished. But they are not natural to a prophet like Amos. Imagine him predicting a future like this ! Imagine him describing the consummation of his people's history, without mentioning one of those moral triumphs to rally his people to which his whole passion and energy had been devoted. To me it is impossible to hear the voice that cried, *Let justice roll on like waters and right-*

eousness like a perennial stream, in a peroration which is content to tell of mountains dripping with must and of a people satisfied with vineyards and gardens. These are legitimate hopes; but they are the hopes of a generation of other conditions and of other deserts than the generation of Amos.

If then the gloom of this great book is turned into light, such a change is not due to Amos.[1]

---

[1] To this opinion, as expressed on pp. 188-195 of early editions of this volume, Marti (p. 224) refers with approval, and nearly all moderns agree.

CHAPTER XI

COMMON SENSE AND THE REIGN OF LAW

AMOS. III. 3–8 ; IV. 6–13 ; V. 8, 9 ; VI. 12 ; VIII. 8 ; IX. 5, 6

FOOLS, when they face facts, which is seldom, face them one by one, and, as a consequence, either in ignorant contempt or in panic. With this inordinate folly Amos charged the religion of his day. The superstitious people, careful of every point of ritual and greedy of omens, would not ponder facts nor set cause to effect. Amos recalled them to common life. *Does a bird fall upon a snare, except there be a loop on her ? Does the trap itself rise from the ground, except it be catching something*—something alive in it that struggles, and so lifts the trap ? *Shall the alarum be blown in a city, and the people not tremble ?* Life is impossible without putting two and two together. But this is what Israel will not do with the events of their time. To religion they will not add common sense.

For Amos himself, all things which happen are in sequence and in sympathy. He has seen this in the simple life of the desert ; he is sure of it throughout the tangle and hubbub of history. One thing explains another ; one makes another inevitable. When he has illustrated the truth in common life, Amos claims it for especially four of the great facts of the time. The sins of society, of which society is careless ; the physical

(206)

calamities, which it survives and forgets ; the approach of Assyria, which it ignores ; the word of the prophet, which it silences—all these belong to each other. Drought, Pestilence, Earthquake, Invasion conspire—and the Prophet holds their secret.

Now it is true that for the most part Amos describes this sequence of events as the action of the God of Israel. *Shall evil befall, and Yahweh not have done it ? . . . I have smitten you. . . . I will raise up against you a Nation. . . . Prepare to meet thy God, O Israel !* [1] Yet even where the personal impulse of the Deity is thus emphasised, we feel equal stress laid upon the order and inevitable certainty of the process. Amos nowhere uses Isaiah's great phrase : *a God of Mishpat, God of Order* or *Law*. But he means the same : God works by methods which irresistibly fulfil themselves. Nay more. Sometimes this sequence sweeps upon the prophet's mind with such force as to overwhelm his sense of the Personal within it. The Will and the Word of the God who causes the thing are merged in the ' Must Be ' of the thing itself. Take even the descriptions of those historical crises, which the prophet explicitly proclaims as the visitations of the Almighty. In some of the verses all thought of God Himself is lost in the roar and foam with which that tide of necessity bursts up through them. The fountains of the great deep break loose, and while the universe trembles to the shock, it seems that even the voice of the Deity is overwhelmed. In one passage, after describing Israel's ruin as due to the Word of their God, Amos asks how could it have happened otherwise :—

Shall horses run up a cliff, or oxen plough the sea ? that ye turn justice to poison, and the fruit of righteousness

[1] iii. 6*b* ; iv. 9 ; vi. 14 ; iv. 12*b*.

into wormwood.[1] A moral order exists, which it is as impossible to break without disaster as it would be to break the natural order by driving horses up a precipice. There is an inherent necessity in the sinners' doom. Again, he says of Israel's sin : *Shall not the Land tremble for this ? Yea, it shall rise up in mass like the Nile, and heave and sink like the Nile of Egypt.*[2] The crimes of Israel are so intolerable, that the natural frame of things revolts against them. In these great crises, therefore, as in the simple instances adduced from everyday life, Amos had a sense of what we call law, distinct from, and for moments even overwhelming, that sense of the personal purpose of God, admission to the secrets of which had marked his call to be a prophet.[3]

These instincts we must not exaggerate into a system. There is no philosophy in Amos, nor need we wish there were. More instructive is what we do find—a virgin sense of the sympathy of all things, the thrill rather than the theory of a universe. And this faith, which is not a philosophy, is especially instructive on two points : it springs from the moral sense ; and it embraces, not history only, but nature.

It springs from the moral sense. Other races have reached a conception of the universe along other lines : some by the observation of physical laws valid to the recesses of space ; some by logic and the unity of Reason. But Israel found the universe through the conscience. It is a fact that the Unity of God, the Unity of History and the Unity of the World, did, in this order, break upon Israel, through conviction and experience of the universal sovereignty of righteous-

---

[1] vi. 12. [2] viii. 8.

[3] iii. 7 : *Yahweh God doeth nothing, but He hath revealed His secret to His servants the prophets.*

ness. We see the beginnings of the process in Amos. To him the sequences which work themselves out through history and across nature are moral. Righteousness is the hinge on which the world swings; loosen it, and history and nature feel the shock. History punishes the sinful nation. But nature, too, groans beneath the guilt of man ; and in the Drought, the Pestilence, and the Earthquake provides his scourges. It is a belief which has stamped itself upon the language of mankind. What else is ' plague ' than ' blow ' or ' scourge ' ?

This brings us to the second point—our prophet's treatment of Nature.

Apart from the disputed passages (which we shall take afterwards) we have in the Book of Amos few glimpses of nature, and these under a moral light. There is not in any passage a landscape visible in its own beauty. Like all desert-dwellers, who when they would praise the works of God lift their eyes to the heavens, Amos gives us but the outlines of the earth— a mountain range,[1] or the crest of a forest,[2] or the bare back of the land, bent from sea to sea.[3] Nearly all his figures are drawn from the desert—the torrent, the wild beasts, the wormwood.[4] If he visits the meadows of the shepherds, it is with terror of the people's doom ; [5] if the vineyards or orchards, it is with mildew and locust ; [6] if the towns, it is with drought, eclipse, and earthquake.[7] To him, unlike his fellows, unlike especially Hosea, the land is one theatre of judgement, but a theatre trembling to its foundations with the drama enacted upon it. Nay, land and nature are themselves

---

[1] i. 2 ; ii. 9 ; ix. 3.   [2] ii. 9.   [3] viii. 12.
[4] v. 24 ; 19, 20, etc. ; 7 ; vi. 12.   [5] i. 2.
[6] iv. 9.   [7] iv. 6, 11 ; vi. 11 ; viii. 8 ff.

actors in the drama. Physical forces are inspired with moral purpose, and become the ministers of righteousness. This is the converse of Elijah's vision. To the older prophet the message came that God was not in the fire nor in the earthquake nor in the tempest, but only in the still small voice. But to Amos fire, earthquake, and tempest are in alliance with the Voice, and execute the doom which it utters. The difference will be appreciated by us, if we remember the respective problems set to prophecy in those two periods. To Elijah, prophet of the elements, wild worker by fire and water, by life and death, the spiritual had to be asserted and enforced by itself. Ecstatic as he was, Elijah had to learn that the Word is more Divine than all physical violence and terror. But Amos understood that for his age the question was different. Not only was the God of Israel dissociated in the popular feeling from the powers of nature, which were assigned by the popular mind to the various Ba'alim of the land, so that there was a divorce between His government of the people and the influences that fed the people's life ; but morality itself was conceived as provincial. It was narrowed to the national interests ; it was summed up in rules of police, and these were looked upon as not so important as the observances of the ritual. Therefore Amos was driven to show that nature and morality are one. Morality is not a set of conventions. ' Morality is the order of things.' Righteousness is on the scale of the universe. All things tremble to the shock of sin ; all things work together for good to them that fear God.

With this sense of law, of moral necessity, in Amos we must not fail to connect that absence of all appeal to miracle, which is also conspicuous in his book.

We come now to the three disputed passages :—

COMMON SENSE AND REIGN OF LAW **211**

iv. 13 :—*For, lo! He Who formed the hills,*[1] *and createth the wind,*[2] *and declareth to man what His*[3] *mind is ; Turning the dawn into darkness, and treading the heights of the earth—Yahweh, God of Hosts, is His Name.*

v. 8, 9 :—*Maker of the Pleiades and Orion,*[4] *turning to morning the murk, and day into night He darkeneth ; Who calleth for the waters of the sea, and poureth them forth on the face of the earth—Yahweh His Name ; Who flasheth ruin on the strong, and destruction comes down on the fortress.*[5]

ix. 5, 6 :—*And the Lord, Yahweh of the Hosts, Who toucheth the earth and it melts, and all that dwell on it mourn, and it rises in mass like the Nile, and sinks like the Nile of Egypt ; Who hath built in the heavens His Stories, and founded His Dome upon the earth ; Who calleth to the waters of the sea, and poureth them on the face of the earth—Yahweh*[6] *His Name.*

These sublime passages it is natural to take as the triple climax of the doctrine we have traced through the Book of Amos. Are they not the natural leap of the soul to the stars ? The same shepherd's eye which has marked sequence and effect unfailing on the desert soil, does it not now sweep the clear heavens above the desert, and find there also all things ordered and arrayed ? The same mind which traced the Divine processes down history, which foresaw the hosts of Assyria marshalled for Israel's punishment, which felt the overthrow of justice shock the nation to their ruin and read the disasters of the husbandman's year as the

---

[1] LXX *the thunder.* [2] Or *spirit.*
[3] *I.e.. God's ;* a more natural rendering than to take *his* (as Hitzig does) as meaning *man's.*
[4] See above, pp. 169 f.
[5] Text of last clause uncertain ; see above, p. 170.
[6] LXX *Yahweh of Hosts.*

vindication of a law higher than the physical—does it not now naturally rise beyond such instances of the Divine order, round which the dust of history rolls, to the lofty, undimmed outlines of the Universe as a whole, and, in consummation of its message, declare that ' all is Law,' and Law intelligible to man ?

But in the way of so attractive a conclusion the literary criticism of the book has interposed. It is maintained [1] that, while none of these sublime verses are indispensable to the argument of Amos, some of them actually interrupt it, so that when they are removed it becomes consistent ; that such ejaculations in praise of Yahweh's creative power are not elsewhere met with in Hebrew prophecy before the time of the Exile ; that they sound like echoes of the style of the Book of Job or of Second Isaiah, particularly in their accumulation of participles, more lavish than an English translation can reflect ; [2] and that in the Septuagint version of Hosea we actually find a similar doxology, wedged into the middle of an authentic verse of the prophet. [3] To these arguments against the genuineness of the three famous passages, other critics, not less able and not less free, like Robertson Smith and Kuenen, [4] have replied that such ejaculations at critical points of the prophet's discourse ' are not surprising under the general conditions of prophetic oratory ' ; and that, while one of the doxologies does appear to break the argument [5] of the context, they are all of them in the spirit and style of

---

[1] First in 1875 by Duhm, *Theol. der Proph.*, p. 119 ; and after him by Oort, *Theol. Tijdschrift*, 1880, pp. 116 f.; Wellhausen, *in locis;* Stade, *Gesch.*, I, 571 ; Cornill, *Einleitung*, 176 ; and other more recent critics.
[2] Cheyne, *Enc. Bibl.*, 153.   [3] Hosea xiii. 4.
[4] W. R. Smith, *Prophets of Israel*, p. 399 ; Kuenen, *Hist. Krit. Einl* (Germ; Ed.), II, 347.
[5] v. 8, 9.

Amos. To this point the discussion has been carried ;
it seems to need a closer examination.

We may at once dismiss the argument which is
drawn from that obvious intrusion into the Greek of
Hosea xiii. 4. Not only is this verse not so suited to
the doctrine of Hosea as the doxologies are to the
doctrine of Amos ; but while they are definite and
sublime, it is formal and flat—' Who made firm the
heavens and founded the earth, Whose hands founded
all the host of heaven, and He did not display them
that thou shouldest walk after them.' The passages
in Amos are vision ; this is a piece of catechism
crumbling into homily.

Again, an argument in favour of the authenticity
of these passages may be drawn from the character
of their subjects. We have seen the part which the
desert played in shaping the temper and the style of
Amos. But the works of the Creator, to which these
passages lift their praise, are just those most fondly
dwelt upon by the poetry of the desert. The Arabian
nomad, when he magnifies the power of God, finds his
subjects not on the bare earth about him, but in the
brilliant heavens and the heavenly processes.

Again, the critic who affirms that the passages in
Amos ' in every case sensibly disturb the connection,' [1]
exaggerates. In the case of the first, chap. iv. 13, the
disturbance is not at all ' sensible ' ; though it must be
admitted that the oracle closes impressively enough
without it. The last of them, chap. ix. 5, 6, which
repeats a clause already found in the book,[2] is as much
in sympathy with its context as most of the oracles
in the scattered discourse of that last section of the
book. The real difficulty is the second doxology,

---

[1] Cornill, *Einl.*, 176. [2] Cf. viii. 8.

chap. v. 8, 9, which does break the connection, and in a sudden and violent way. Remove it, and the argument is consistent. We cannot read chap. v without feeling that, whether Amos wrote these verses or not, they did not originally stand where they stand at present.

Now, taken with this dispensableness of two of the passages and this obvious intrusion of one of them, the following additional fact becomes ominous. *Yahweh is His Name* (which occurs in two of the passages),[1] or *Yahweh of Hosts is His Name* (which occurs at least in one),[2] is a construction which does not happen elsewhere in the book, except in a verse where it is awkward and where we have seen reason to doubt its genuineness.[3] But still more, the phrase does not occur in any other prophet, till we come down to the oracles in Isaiah xl–lxvi. Here it happens thrice—twice in passages dating from the Exile,[4] and once in a passage suspected by some to be of still later date.[5] In the Book of Jeremiah the phrase is found eight times but either in passages on other grounds judged by many critics to be later than Jeremiah,[6] or where by itself it is probably an intrusion into the text.[7] Now is it a mere coincidence that a phrase, which, outside the Book of Amos, occurs only in writing of the time of the Exile and in passages considered for other reasons

[1] v. 8 ; ix. 6, though here LXX read *Yahweh of Hosts is His Name.*
[2] iv. 13. See previous note.
[3] v. 27. See above, p. 178 ; cf. Hosea xii. 6 (Heb. ; but Eng. 5).
[4] xlvii. 4 and liv. 5.
[5] xlviii. 2 ; cf. Duhm, *in loco*, Cheyne, *Introduction to the Book of Isaiah*, 301, and the present writer's *Isaiah xl–lxvi, in loco*.
[6] x. 16 ; xxxi. 35 ; xxxii. 18 ; l. 34 (perhaps a quotation from Isa. xlvii. 4) ; li. 19, 57.
[7] xlvi. 18, where the words צבאות שמו fail in LXX ; xlviii. 15, where the clause in which it occurs is wanting in the LXX.

to be post-exilic insertions—is it a mere coincidence that within the Book of Amos it should again be found only in suspected verses ?

There appears to be in this more than a coincidence ; and the present writer cannot but feel a strong case against the traditional belief that these doxologies are original and integral portions of the Book of Amos. At the same time a case which has failed to convince critics like Robertson Smith and Kuenen cannot be considered conclusive, and we are so ignorant of many of the conditions of prophetic oratory at this period that dogmatism is impossible. For instance, the use by Amos of the Divine titles is a matter over which uncertainty still lingers ; and further argument on the subject must include a fuller discussion than space here allows of the distribution of those titles through the various sections of the book.[1]

---

[1] The titles for the God of Israel used in the Book of Amos are these : (1) *Thy God, O Israel,* אלהיך ישראל; (2) *Yahweh,* יהוה ; (3) *Lord Yahweh,* אדני יהוה; (4) *Lord Yahweh of Hosts,* אדני יהוה צבאות ; (5) *Yahweh God of Hosts* or *of the Hosts,* הצבאות or יהוה אלהי צבאות.

Now in the First Section, chs. i, ii, it is interesting that we find none of the variations which are compounded with *Hosts,* צבאות. By itself יהוה (especially in the phrase *Thus saith Yahweh,* כה אמר יהוה) is general ; and once only (i. 8) is *Lord Yahweh* employed. The phrase, *Rede of Yahweh,* נאם יהוה, is also rare ; it occurs only twice (ii. 11, 16),

and then only in the passage dealing with Israel, and not at all in the oracles against foreign nations.

In Sections II and III the simple יהוה is again most frequently used. But we find also *Lord Yahweh,* אדני יהוה (iii. 7, 8 ; iv. 2, 5 ; v. 3, with יהוה alone in the parallel ver. 4 ; vi. 8 ; vii. 1, 2, 4 *bis,* 5, 6 ; viii. 1, 3, 9, 11), used either indifferently with יהוה, or in verses where it seems more natural to emphasise the sovereignty of Yahweh than His simple Name (as, *e.g.,* where *He swears,* iv. 2, vi. 8, yet when the same phrase occurs in viii. 7 יהוה alone is used) ; or in the solemn Visions of the Third Section (but not in the Narrative) ; and sometimes we find in the Visions *Lord,* אדני, alone without יהוה (vii. 7, 8 ; ix. 1). The titles containing צבאות or אלהי צבאות occur *nine* times. Of these *five* are in passages which we have seen other reasons to suppose are

But if it be not given to us to prove this kind of authenticity—a question whose data are so obscure, yet whose answer fortunately is of little significance—let us welcome that greater Authenticity whose undeniable proofs these verses so splendidly exhibit. No one questions their right to the place which some great spirit gave them in this book, their suitableness to its grand and ordered theme, their pure vision and their eternal truth. That common sense, and that conscience, which, moving among the events of earth and all the tangled processes of history, find everywhere reason and righteousness at work, in these verses claim the Universe for the same powers, and see in stars and clouds and the procession of day and night the One Eternal God Who *declareth to man what His mind is.*

insertions : two of the Doxologies—iv. 13, יהוה אלהי צבאות , and ix. 5, אדני יהוה הצבאות (in addition the LXX read in ix. 6 יהוה צבאות), and in v. 14, 15 (see p. 168) and 27 (see p. 172), in all three יהוה אלהי צבאות . The *four* genuine passages are iii. 13, where we find יהוה אלהי הצבאות preceded by אדני ; v. 16, where we have יהוה אלהי צבאות followed by אדני ; vi. 8, יהוה אלהי צבאות, and vi. 14, יהוה אלהי צבאות . Throughout the last two sections of the book נאם is used with all these forms of the Divine title.

HOSEA

' For leal love have I desired and not sacrifice
And the knowledge of God rather than burnt-offerings.

CHAPTER XII

THE BOOK OF HOSEA

THE Book of Hosea consists of two unequal sections, chaps. i–iii and chaps. iv–xiv, which differ in the dates of their standpoints, to a large extent also in the details of their common subjects, but still more largely in their form and style.[1] The First Section is in the main narrative ; though the style rises to the pitch of passionate pleading and promise, it is fluent and equable. If one verse be omitted and three others transferred,[2] the argument is continuous. In the Second Section, on the contrary, we have a stream of addresses and reflections, appeals, upbraidings, sarcasms, recollections of earlier history, denunciations and promises, which, with little logical connection and almost no pauses or periods, start impulsively from each other, and for a large part are expressed in elliptic and ejaculatory phrases. In the restlessness of modern Biblical Criticism it would have been surprising if this difference of style had not prompted some to argue a difference of authorship. Grätz[3] distinguished two Hoseas, separated by a period of

[1] This division, generally accepted by moderns, ‘ does not recommend itself ’ to Marti, who regards ch. iii as an insertion of later date, and ii as impossible to separate from iv–xiv, ‘ with which it has much more in common than with i and iii.’ Cf. A. R. Gordon, p. 64, n.

[2] See below, pp. 221 f.

[3] *Geschichte*, II, pp. 93 ff., 214 ff., 439 f. ; cf. C. H. Toy, *J.B L.*, 1913, pp. 75 ff. who denies not only that i–iii are by the same author as iv–xiv, but the unity also of i–iii.

fifty years. But if, as we shall see, the First Section reflects the end of the reign of Jeroboam II, who died about 743, then the next few years, with their revolutionary changes in Israel, are enough to account for the altered outlook of the Second Section ; while the altered style is explained by difference of occasion and motive. In both Sections not only are the religious principles identical, and many of the characteristic expressions,[1] but there breathes throughout the same urgent and jealous temper, which renders Hosea's personality distinctive among the prophets. Within this unity, of course, we must not be surprised to find, as in the Book of Amos, verses which cannot well be authentic.

FIRST SECTION : HOSEA'S PROPHETIC LIFE

Chaps. i–iii

With the removal of some verses the argument becomes clear and consecutive. After the story of the wife and children (i. 2–9), who are symbols of the land and people of Israel in their apostasy from God (2, 4, 6, 9), the Divine voice calls on the living generation to plead with their mother lest destruction come (ii. 2–5, Eng. ; ii. 4–7, Heb.[2]), but then passes definite sentence of desolation on the land and of exile on the people (6–13, Eng. ; 8–15, Heb.), which, however, is not final doom, but discipline,[3] with the ultimate promise of the return of the nation's youth, their renewed betrothal to Yahweh and the restoration of nature (14–23). Then follows the story of the prophet's restoration of his wife, also with discipline (chap. iii).

---

[1] A list of the more obvious is given by Kuenen, p. 324.
[2] The first chapter in the Hebrew closes with ver. 9.
[3] Cf. this with Amos ; above, pp. 200 ff.

Notice that, although the story of the wife's fall has preceded the declaration of Israel's apostasy, it is Israel's restoration which precedes the wife's. The ethical significance of this order we shall illustrate in the next chapter.

In this section the most disturbing verses are i. 7 and the group of three—i. 10, 11, ii. 1 (Eng.; but ii. 1–3 Heb.). Chap. i. 7 introduces Judah as excepted from the curse passed upon Israel; it is so obviously intrusive in a prophecy dealing only with Israel, and so clearly reflects the deliverance of Judah from Sennacherib in 701, that we cannot hold it for anything but an insertion of a date subsequent to that deliverance, and introduced by a pious Jew to signalise Judah's fate in contrast with Israel's.[1]

The other three verses (i. 10, 11, ii. 1, Eng.; ii. 1-3, Heb.) introduce a promise of restoration before the sentence of doom is detailed, or any ethical conditions of restoration are stated. That is, they tangle an argument otherwise consistent and progressive from beginning to end of the Section. Every careful reader must feel them out of place where they lie. Their awkwardness has been so appreciated that, while in the Hebrew text they have been separated from chap. i, in the Greek and the English they have been distributed

---

[1] König's reasons (*Einleitung*, p. 309) for the possible genuineness of the verse are not convincing. He thinks it admissible because Judah had sinned less than Israel, the threat in vv. 4–6 is limited to Israel, the phrase *Yahweh their God* is so peculiar that it is difficult to assign it to a mere expander, and if a later writer interpolated the verse why did he not alter the judgements against Judah which occur further on? But practically all other critics take the verse as interpolated: Wellhausen, Stade (*Gesch.*, i. p. 577), Kuenen, Giesebrecht, Guthe, Cheyne (in W. R. Smith's *Prophets*, 2nd ed.), Marti along with 5 and last clause of 6, and so, too, Duhm; Cornill and Sellin (in their *Introductions to the O.T.*); Harper, Gordon, Moffatt. It is curious that LXX B omits the name Judah in this verse, though AQ have it; all three read *sons of* for *house of*.

between the two chapters. If they really belong to
the prophecy their proper place may be after the last
verse of Chap. ii ;[1] and this is actually the order in
which part of it and part of them are quoted by
St. Paul.[2] Yet even when so arranged they but repeat
somewhat awkwardly the language of ii. 23 (Heb. ii.
25), and scarcely form a climax to the chapter. Nothing
in their language would lead us to doubt that they
are Hosea's own, and i. 11 (Heb. ii. 2), has at least
the suggestion of being earlier than the captivity of
Northern Israel in 721. Yet most moderns take them
as exilic or post-exilic.[3]

In chap. ii the following verses have been marked by
several moderns [4] as later additions : in the English
order : 4, 6 f., 10 and, in part or whole, 13b–23 (Heb.
6, 8 f., 15b–25) because they picture the restoration of
Israel ; and so also iii. 5 for the same reason.[5] We
shall treat these passages along with others of their
kind in iv–xiv, on pages 233 f.

The text of the rest of the Section is pretty free from
obscurities. The Greek Version offers few variants, and
most of these are due to mistranslation ;[6] in iii. 1 for
beloved of a friend it reads *loving evil things*.

Apparently this section was written before the death
of Jeroboam II. The house of Jehu still reigns ; and

---

[1] So Kuenen, Cheyne, Moffatt; cf. Duhm. König agrees that they
have been removed from their proper place and the text corrupted.

[2] Rom. ix. 25, 26, which first give the end of Hosea ii. 23 (Heb. 25)
and then the end of i. 10 (Heb. ii. 1).

[3] Wellhausen, Nowack, Marti, Harper, etc.

[4] See Nowack, Marti, Harper.

[5] Cornill, Stärk, Oort, Volz, Marti, Harper ; but see Duhm. In iii.
some would eliminate *and David their King* (Stade), but if this be struck
out the verse is rendered awkward if not impossible by the immediate
repetition of the Divine Name, which would not have been required i
the absence of the suspected clause.

[6] ii. 7, 11, 14, 17 (Heb.). In i. 4 LXX B reads Ἰούδα for יהוא , while
codd. Qᵐᵍ have Ιηου.

as Hosea predicts its fall by war on the classic battle-ground of Jezreel the prophecy must have been written before the actual fall, which took the form of an internal revolt against Zechariah, the son of Jeroboam. With this agrees the tone of the section. There are the same evils in Israel which Amos exposed in the prosperous years of the same reign ; but Hosea appears to realise the threatened exile from a nearer standpoint. It may be also that part of the reason of his ability to see his way through the captivity to the people's restoration is due to a longer familiarity with the approach of captivity than Amos experienced before he wrote. But for Hosea's promise of restoration there were, as we shall see, greater reasons of a religious kind.[1]

SECOND SECTION

Chaps. iv–xiv

When we pass into these chapters we feel the times changed. The dynasty of Jehu has passed : kings are falling rapidly : Israel devours its rulers :[2] there is no

---

[1] In determining the date of the Book of Hosea the title in ch. i is of no use to us : *The Word of Yahweh which was to Hosea ben-Be'eri in the days of Uzziah, Jotham, Ahaz, Hezekiah, kings of Judah, and in the days of Jeroboam ben-Joash, king of Israel.* This is trebly suspicious. First : the given reigns of Judah and Israel do not correspond ; Jeroboam was dead before Uzziah. Second : there is no proof either in the First or Second Section of the book that Hosea prophesied after the reign of Jotham. Third : it is curious that by a prophet of Northern Israel kings of Judah should be stated first, and four be given while only one king of his own country is placed beside them. On these grounds critics are perhaps right who take the title as it stands to be the work of some Judæan scribe who sought to make it correspond to the titles of the Books of Isaiah and Micah. He may have been he who added ch. i. 7. The original form of the title probably was *The Word of Yahweh which was to Hosea son of Be'eri in the days of Jeroboam ben-Joash, king of Israel,* designed only for the First Section of the book, chs i–iii.

[2] vii. 7. There are also other passages which, while they may be referred, as they stand, to the whole succession of illegitimate dynasties

loyalty to the king ; he is suddenly cut off ;[1] all the princes are revolters.[2] Round so despised and unstable a throne the nation tosses in disorder. Conspiracies are rife. It is not only, as in Amos, the sins of the luxurious, which are exposed ; but also literal bloodshed : highway robbery with murder, abetted by priests ;[3] the thief breaks in and the robber-troop make a raid.[4] Amos looked out on foreign nations across a quiet Israel ; his views of the world are wide and clear ; but in the Book of Hosea the dust is up, and of what is happening beyond the frontier we get only glimpses. There is enough, however, to make visible another great change since the days of Jeroboam. Israel's self-reliance is gone. She is as fluttered as a startled bird : *They call unto Egypt, they go unto Assyria.*[5] Their wealth is carried as a gift to King ' Jareb,'[6] and they evidently intrigue with Egypt. But everything is hopeless : kings cannot save, for Ephraim is in the pangs of a fatal crisis.[7]

This broken description reflects—and the more faithfully because of its brokenness—the ten years which followed on the death of Jeroboam II about 743.[8] His son Zechariah, who succeeded him, was in six months assassinated by Shallum ben-Jabesh, who within a month more was himself cut down by Menahem

in Northern Israel from the beginning to the end of that kingdom, **more** probably reflect the same ten years of special anarchy and disorder **after** the death of Jeroboam II. See vii. 3 ff. ; viii. 4, where the illegitimate kingmaking is coupled with the idolatry of the Northern Kingdom ; xiii. 10, 11.

[1] x. 3, 7, 15.   [2] ix. 15.   [3] vi. 8, 9.   [4] vii. 1.
[5] vii. 11.   [6] x. 6.   [7] xiii. 12 f.

[8] The chronology of these years is uncertain. Jeroboam was dead about 743 ; in 738 Menahem gave tribute to Assyria ; in 734 Tiglath-Pileser had conquered Aram, Gilead and Galilee in response to King Ahaz, who had a year or two before been attacked by Rezin of Aram and Pekah of Israel.

ben-Gadi.[1] Menahem held the throne for six or seven years, but only by sending to the King of Assyria an enormous tribute which he exacted from the wealthy magnates of Israel.[2] Discontent must have followed these measures, such discontent with their rulers as Hosea describes. Pekahiah ben Menahem kept the throne for little over a year after his father's death, and was assassinated by his captain,[3] Pekah ben-Remaliah, with fifty Gileadites, and Pekah took the throne about 736. This second and bloody usurpation may be one of those on which Hosea dwells ; but if so it is the last historical allusion in his book. There is no reference to the war of Pekah and Rezin against Ahaz of Judah which Isaiah describes,[4] and to which Hosea must have alluded had he been still prophesying.[5] There is no allusion to its consequence in Tiglath-Pileser's conquest of Gilead and Galilee in 734–733. On the contrary, these provinces are still regarded as part of the body politic of Israel.[6] Nor is there any sign that Israel have broken with Assyria ; to the last

[1] 2 Kings xv. 8–16. It may be to this appearance of three kings within one month that there was originally an allusion in the now obscure verse of Hosea, v. 7, rendering *a month* for *the new-moon*.

[2] 2 Kings xv. 17-22.

[3] Or prince, שר ; cf. Hosea's denunciation of the שרים as rebels.

[4] Isa. vii ; 2 Kings xv. 37, 38.

[5] Some find a later allusion in x. 14 : *like unto the destruction* of (?) *Shalman* (of ?) *Beth'Arbe'l*. Pusey, p. 5*b*, and others refer this to a destruction of the Galilean Arbela, the modern Irbid, by Shalmaneser IV, who ascended the Assyrian throne in 727 and besieged Samaria in 724 ff. But since the construction of the phrase leaves it doubtful whether the name Shalman is that of the agent or object of the destruction, and whether, if the agent, he be one of the Assyrian Shalmanesers or a Moabite King Salman, *c.* 730 B.C., 't is impossible to use the verse in fixing the date of the Book of Hosea. See further, *in loco.* Wellhausen and others omit.

[6] v 1 ; vi. 8 ; xii. 11 (Heb. 12) ; cf. W. R. Smith, *Prophets*, p. 156.

the book represents them as fawning on the Northern Power.[1]

In all probability, then, the Book of Hosea was closed before 734 B.C. The Second Section dates from the years behind that and back to the death of Jeroboam II about 743, while the First Section, as we saw, reflects the period immediately before the latter.

We come now to the general style of chaps. iv-xiv. The period was one of the most broken in the history of Israel ; the political outlook, the temper of the people, were constantly changing. Hosea, who watched these kaleidoscopes, had himself a mobile and vibrant mind. There could be no greater contrast to that fixture of conscience which renders the Book of Amos so simple in argument, so firm in style.[2] It was a leaden plummet which Amos saw Yahweh setting to the structure of Israel's life.[3] But Hosea felt his own heart hanging at the end of the line ; and this was a heart that could never be still. Amos is the prophet of law ; he sees the Divine processes work themselves out, irrespective of the moods and intrigues of the people, to whom, after all, he did not belong. So each of his paragraphs moves steadily to a climax, and every climax is Doom—the captivity of the people to Assyria. You can divide his book by these things ;

---

[1] Cf. W. R. Smith, *l.c.*

[2] Cf. *ibid.*, p. 157 : Hosea's ' language and the movement of his thoughts are far removed from the simplicity and self-control which characterise the prophecy of Amos. Indignation and sorrow, tenderness and severity, faith in the sovereignty of Jehovah's love, and a despairing sense of Israel's infidelity are woven together in a sequence which has no logical plan, but is determined by the battle and alternate victory of contending emotions ; and the swift transitions, the fragmentary unbalanced utterance, the half-developed allusions, that make his prophecy so difficult to the commentator, express the agony of this inward conflict.'

[3] See above, p. 111.

it has its periods, strophes, and refrains. It marches like the hosts of the Lord of hosts. But Hosea had no such vision of great laws. He was too familiar with the rapid changes of his fickle people ; and his affection for them too anxious. His style has the restlessness and irritableness of hunger about it—the hunger of love. Hosea's eyes are never at rest. He seeks, he welcomes, for moments he dwells upon, every sign of his people's repentance. But a Divine jealousy succeeds, and he questions the motives of the change. You feel that his love has been overtaken and surprised by his knowledge ; and in fact his whole style might be described as a race between the two—a race uncertain to almost the end. The transitions are swift. You come upon a passage of exquisite tenderness : the prophet puts the people's penitence in his own words with a sympathy and poetry that are sublime and seem final. But suddenly he remembers how false they are, and another light is in his eyes. The lustre of their tears dies from his verses, like the dews of a summer morning in Ephraim ; and all is dry and hard again beneath the brazen sun of his amazement. *What shall I do unto thee, Ephraim ? What shall I do unto thee, Judah ?* Indeed, that figure of his own is insufficient to express the suddenness with which Hosea lights up some intrigue of the statesmen of the day, or some evil habit of the priests, or some hidden orgy of the common people. Rather than the sun it is the lightning—the lightning in pursuit of a serpent.

The elusiveness of the style is the greater that many passages do not seem to have been prepared for public delivery. They are more the play of the prophet's mind than his set speech. They are not formally addressed to an audience, and show no trace of oratorical art.

Hence the language of this Second Section of the Book of Hosea is impulsive and abrupt beyond all comparison. The rhythm is broken, there is almost no argument. Few metaphors are elaborated. Even the brief parallelism of Hebrew poetry seems too long for the quick spasms of the writer's heart. ' Osee,' said Jerome,[1] ' commaticus est, et quasi per sententias loquitur.' He speaks in little clauses, often broken off ; he is impatient even of copulas. And withal he uses a vocabulary full of strange words. which the paucity of parallelism makes the more difficult.

To this original brokenness and obscurity of the language are due, *first*, the corruption of the text ; *second*, the difficulty of dividing it ; *third*, the uncertainty of deciding its genuineness or authenticity.

1. The TEXT of Hosea is one of the most dilapidated in the Old Testament, and in parts beyond repair. It is probable that glosses were found necessary at an earlier period and to a larger extent than in other books : there are clear traces of some ; yet it is not always possible to disentangle them.[2] The value of the Greek version is curiously mixed. The authors had before them much the same difficulties as we have, and they made more for themselves. Some of their mistranslations are outrageous : they occur not only in obscure passages, where they may be pardoned ;[3] but even where there are parallel terms with which the translators show themselves familiar.[4] Sometimes they have translated word by word, without attempting to give the general sense ; and as a whole their version is devoid of beauty and compactness. Yet not infrequently they suggest a better reading than the

[1] *Præf. in Duod. Prophetas.*
[2] Especially in ch. vii.   [3] As in xi. 2*b*.
[4] This is especially the case in x. 11–13 ; xi. 4 ; xiv. 5.

Massoretic text. Occasionally they divide words properly which the latter misdivides.[1] They often give more correctly the easily confused pronominal suffixes;[2] and the copula.[3] And they help us to the true readings of other words.[4] Here and there an additional clause in the Greek is plethoric, perhaps copied by mistake from a similar verse in the context.[5] All these will be noticed separately as we reach them. But, even after such aids, we shall find that the text frequently remains impracticable.

2. As great as the difficulty of reaching a true text in this Second Section of the book is the difficulty of DIVIDING it. Here and there, it is true, the Greek helps us to improve upon the division into chapters and verses of the Hebrew text. Chap. vi. 1–4 ought to follow immediately the end of chap. v, with the connecting word *saying*. The last few words of chap. vi go with the first two of chap. vii, but both may be glosses. The openings of chaps. xi and xii are better arranged in the Hebrew than in the Greek. As for verses we shall have to make some rearrangements.[6] But beyond this more or less conventional division into chapters and verses our confidence ceases. It is

---

[1] *E.g.*, vi. 5*b*: M.T. משפטיך אור יצא , which is nonsense; LXX משפטי כאור , *My judgement shall go forth like light.* xi. 2: M.T. מְפְּנֵיהֶם ; LXX הֵם .

[2] iv. 4, עמי for עמך ; 13, צֵלָה for צֵלָה ; v. 2; vi. 2 (possibly); viii. 4, read יכרתנּ ; ix. 2; xi. 2, 3; xi. 5, where for לֹא read לוֹ ; xii. 9; xiv. 9*a*, לוֹ for לִי . On the other hand, they are either improbable or quite wrong, as in vii. 1*b*; xi. 1, 4; xii. 5; xiii. 14, 15 (ter.).

[3] v. 5 (so as to change the tense: *and Judah shall stumble*); xii. 2, etc.

[4] vi. 3; viii. 10, 13; ix. 2; x. 4, 13*b*, 15 (probably); xii. 2; xiii. 9; xiv. 3. Cf. also vi. 3.

[5] *E.g.*, viii. 13 (?), ix. 16.

[6] Cf. the Hebrew and Greek, of *e.g.*, iv. 10, 11, 12; vi. 9, 10; viii. 5, 6; ix. 8, 9.

impossible to separate all the Section, long as it is, into subsections, or into oracles, strophes, or periods.[1] The reason of this we have already seen, in the turbulence of the period reflected, in the divided interests and abrupt and emotional style of the author, and in the probability that part at least of the book was not prepared for public speaking. The periods and climaxes, the refrains, the catchwords by which we are helped to divide even the confused Second Section of the Book of Amos are hardly found in Hosea. Only twice does the exordium of a spoken address occur : at the beginning of the section (chap. iv. 1), and at what is now the opening of the next chapter (v. 1). The phrase *'tis the Rede of Yahweh*, which occurs periodically in Amos, and thrice in the second chapter of Hosea, is found only once in chaps. iv–xiv. Again, the obvious climaxes or perorations, of which we found many in Amos, are very few,[2] and even when they occur the next verses start impulsively from them, without a pause.

In spite of these difficulties, since the section is so long, attempts at division have been made. Ewald distinguished three parts in three different tempers : *First,* iv–vi. 11*a,* God's Plaint against His people ; *Second,* vi. 11*b*–ix. 9, Their Punishment ; *Third,* ix. 10 –xiv. 10, Retrospect of the earlier history, warning and consolation. Driver also divides into three subsections, but differently : *First,* iv–viii, in which Israel's Guilt predominates ; *Second,* ix–xi. 11, in which the prevailing thought is their Punishment ; *Third,* xi. 12–xiv. 10, in which both lines of thought are continued, but followed by a glance at the brighter

---

[1] Similarly Hitzig and Kuenen. For an opposite opinion see Harper (clxiii, n. 1), who allows, however, that the ' discourses uttered from time to time ' are ' put together without chronological or logical relationship.
[2] viii. 13 (14 must be omitted) ; ix. 17.

future.[1] What is common to these two arrangements
is the recognition of a certain progress from feelings
about Israel's guilt which prevail in the earlier chapters, to a clear vision of the political destruction await-
ing them ; and finally more hope of repentance in the
people, with a vision of the blessed future that must
follow. It is, however, more accurate to say that the
emphasis of Hosea's prophesying, instead of changing
from the Guilt to the Punishment of Israel, changes
about the middle of chap. vii from their Moral Decay
to their Political Decay, and that the description of
the latter is modified or interrupted by Two Visions
of better things : one of their God's early guidance of
the people, with a great outbreak of His Love upon
them, in chap. xi ; and one of their future Return to
Him and restoration in chap. xiv. It is on these
features that the division of the following Exposition is
arranged.[2]

3. It will be obvious that with a text so corrupt,
with a style so broken and incapable of logical division,
questions of AUTHENTICITY are raised to a pitch of
the greatest difficulty. Allusion has been made to the
number of glosses which must have been found necessary from even an early period, and of some of which
we can discern the proofs.[3] We will deal with these
as they occur.

But we may here discuss, as a whole, another class
of suspected passages—suspected for the same reason
that we saw a number in Amos to be, because of their
reference to Judah. In Hosea iv–xiv they are twelve

[1] *Introd.* 284.
[2] Harper distinguishes the discourses iv. 1–xiv. 1 into 'a group of
thirteen, presenting under varying circumstances the double thought of
guilt and inevitable punishment.'
[3] *E.g.*, iv. 15 (?) ; vi. 1 -vii. 1 (?) ; vii. 4 ; viii. 2 ; xii. 6.

Only one of them is favourable (iv. 15) : *Though Israel play the harlot, let not Judah sin.* Kuenen [1] argues that this is genuine, on the ground that the peculiar verb *to sin* or *take guilt to oneself* is used several other times in the book,[2] and that the wish expressed is in consonance with what he understands to be Hosea's favourable feeling towards Judah. Yet Hosea nowhere else makes any distinction between Ephraim and Judah in the matter of sin, but condemns both equally ; and as iv. 15 f. are to be suspected on other grounds as well, I cannot hold this reference to Judah to be beyond doubt.[3] Nor is the reference in viii. 14 genuine : *And Israel forgat his Maker and built temples, and Judah multiplied fenced cities, but I will send fire on his cities and it shall devour her palaces.* Kuenen [4] refuses to reject the reference to Judah, on the ground that without it the rhythm of the verse is spoiled ; but the whole verse is questionable, possibly a later quotation from Amos.[5] Nor can we be quite sure about v. 5 : *Israel and Ephraim shall stumble by their iniquities, and* (LXX) *stumble also shall Judah with them ;* or vi. 10, 11 : *In Bethel I have seen horrors : there playest thou the harlot, Ephraim ; there Israel defiles himself ; also Judah . . .* (the rest of the text is impracticable). In both these passages Judah is the awkward third of a parallelism, and is introduced by an *also,* as if an afterthought. Yet the afterthought may be the prophet's own ; for in other passages, to which no doubt attaches, he includes Judah in the sinfulness of Israel.[6] It is

---

[1] *Esnl.*, 323.   [2] אשם , v. 15 ; x. 2 ; xiii. 1 ; xiv. 1.

[3] So Stade, Wellhausen, Cornill, Nowack, and since I wrote the above, Marti and others. But see Harper, p. 262.

[4] P. 313.

[5] So Oort, Wellhausen, Nowack, Marti, Harper, Duhm, and Moffatt.

[6] Marti takes both passages as late ; Harper only the second. Duhm and Moffatt retain both.

difficult to believe that viii. 14 is original ; the verse
blunts a climax reached in the preceding one and its
reference to Judah has no apparent reason to be just
there ; most critics agree that it is a later addition.[1]
Cornill and others reject x. 11, *Judah must plough*, but
I cannot see on what grounds ; as Kuenen says, it has
no appearance of being an intrusion.[2] In xii. 3 (Eng.
xii. 2) Wellhausen reads *Israel* for *Judah*, but the latter
is justified if not rendered necessary by the reference to
Judah in ver. 1 (Eng., xi. 28), which Wellhausen admits.[3]
The other references form a group—v. 10, *The princes
of Judah are as removers of boundaries ;* 12, *I shall be
as the moth to Ephraim, and a worm to the house of
Judah ;* 13, *And Ephraim saw his disease, and Judah
his sore ;* 14, *For I am as a roaring lion to Ephraim,
and as a young lion to the house of Judah ;* vi. 4, *What
shall I do to thee, Ephraim ? what shall I do to thee,
Judah ?*—to which there are no insuperable objections.
It may be that v. 13 forms a climax which v. 14 only
weakens, and that its style is rather an echo of Amos
than Hosea's own. But there are no grounds for the
substitution through all the verses of Israel for Judah.[4]
And, as Kuenen, Harper, and Duhm say, it would have
been surprising if Hosea had made no reference to
Judah. His judgement of her is justified by that of
her own citizens, Isaiah and Micah.[5]

Another class of passages have also been doubted
by critics on the ground that like ii. 6 f., 10, 13*b*–23
(Heb. ii. 8 f., 12, 15*b*–25) and iii. 5 [6] they assume that

---

[1] Wellhausen, Cornill, Marti, Harper, Moffatt. [2] *Loc. cit.*
[3] Since then Marti takes xii. 1*b*, 3*a* as glosses, Harper only the former ;
Duhm accepts the references to Judah.
[4] Nowack, Kittel, Marti.
[5] On all the Judah passages see Cossmann, *Z.A.T.W.*, Beiheft 29,
p. 38 f.
[6] See above, p. 222.

Israel will repent and assure and describe a blessed future to the people. For example : v. 15–vi. 3 which has been held by one or two critics [1] to be inconsistent with the finality of v. 14, yet it is capable of quite another interpretation ; the clauses in xi. 8–11 [2] which revoke or mitigate that utterances of the Lord's wrath that the prophet elsewhere proclaims, and which foretell a return from exile ; and xiv. 1–8 (Heb. xiv. 2–9), a call to repent, with the assurance, if it is obeyed, of mercy, peace, and prosperity.[2]

We shall discuss such passages in both Sections of the Book as we come to them. But some general considerations may be stated here. Where, as in xi. 11 the Exile seems assumed as having already taken place, we cannot well hold that the passage is from Hosea or his time. But it is quite different where there is no reflection of the exile or other late circumstance of Israel, but all that is said is that Israel must or will return to their Lord and be restored after discipline and repentance or that peace will be the nation's lot on their own land quickened to its full fertility and beauty. In these cases we have to consider whether, after all, it was not possible for any prophet, however much he felt destruction inevitable for his own generation, to believe that the nation would cease to exist—that God would be without His Israel in the world ; and especially whether the impetuous heart of a prophet with all Hosea's love for his people and Hosea's joy in his country's beauty could not burst out with such verses of promise and of prospect as the verses in question. For those of us at least who accept chap. iii as Hosea's own the possibility for him sometimes of such a hope and rejoicing is indubitable.

[1] Marti, cf. Guthe ; to Nowack, Harper, Duhm the passage is genuine
[2] Marti and Harper.
[2] See Cossmann, *op. cit.*, Cornill. *Introd.*, pp. 324 f. (Eng. transl.).

Other phrases or passages of doubtful authenticity will be discussed as we come to them, but it cannot be too often emphasised that, in a book of such a style as this, certainty on the subject is impossible.

Finally, there may be given here the only notable addition which the Septuagint makes to the Book of Hosea. It occurs in xiii. 4, after *I am Yahweh thy God :* ' Who made fast the heavens and founded the earth, Whose hands founded all the host of the heaven, and I did not show them to thee that thou shouldest follow after them, and I led thee up '—*from the land of Egypt.*

At first this recalls those apostrophes to Yahweh's power which break forth in the Book of Amos ; and the resemblance has been taken to prove that they also are late intrusions. But this both obtrudes itself as they do not, and is manifestly of lower poetical value. See page 213.

We have now our material before us, and may proceed to the more welcome task of tracing our prophet's life, and expounding his teaching.

CHAPTER XIII

THE PROBLEM THAT AMOS LEFT

AMOS was a preacher of righteousness almost
wholly in its judicial and punitive offices. Ex-
posing the moral conditions of Israel in his day, emphasising on the one hand their obduracy and on the
other their intolerableness, he asserted that nothing
could avert the inevitable doom—neither Israel's
formal devotion to Yahweh nor His interest in Israel.
*You alone have I known of all the families of the ground :
therefore will I visit upon you all your iniquities.* The
visitation was to take place in war and in the captivity
of the people. This is practically the whole message
of the prophet Amos.

That he added to it the promise of restoration which
now closes his book, we have seen to be improbable.[1]
Yet even if that promise is his own, Amos does not tell
us how the restoration is to be brought about. With
wonderful insight and patience he has traced the
coming captivity of Israel to moral causes. But he
does not show what moral change in the exiles is to
justify their restoration, or by what means such a
change is to be effected. We are left to infer the
conditions and the means of redemption from the
principles which Amos enforced while there yet seemed
time to pray for the doomed people : *Seek the Lord and*

---

[1] See above, pp. 202 ff.

ye shall live.[1] According to this, the moral renewal of Israel must precede their restoration ; but the prophet seems to make no great effort to effect the renewal. In short Amos illustrates the easily-forgotten truth that a preacher to the conscience is not necessarily a preacher of repentance.

Of the great antitheses between which religion moves, Law and Love, Amos had therefore been the prophet of Law. But we must not imagine that the association of Love with the Deity was strange to him. This could not be to any Israelite who remembered the past of his people—the romance of their origins and early struggles for freedom. Israel had always felt the grace of their God ; and, unless we be wrong about the date of the great poem in the end of Deuteronomy, they had lately celebrated that grace in lines of exquisite beauty and tenderness :—

> *He found him in a desert land,*
>   *In a waste and a howling wilderness.*
> *He compassed him about, He cared for him,*
>   *Kept him as the apple of His eye.*
> *As an eagle stirs up his nest,*
>   *Flutters over his young,*
> *Spreads out his wings, and takes them,*
>   *Bears them up on his pinions—*
> *So Yahweh alone led him.*[2]

The patience of the Lord with their waywardness and obstinacy had been the ethical influence on Israel's life at a time when they had probably neither code of law nor system of doctrine. *Thy gentleness,* as an early

---

[1] v. 4.
[2] Deut. xxxii. 10–12 : a song probably earlier than the eighth century. But some put it later.

Psalmist says for his people, *Thy gentleness hath made
me great.*[1] Amos is not unaware of this ancient grace
of Yahweh. But he speaks of it in a fashion which
shows that he feels it to be exhausted and without
hope for his own generation. *I brought you up out of
the land of Egypt, and led you forty years in the wilderness, to possess the land of the Amorites. And I raised
of your sons for prophets and of your young men for
Nazirites.*[2] But this can now only fill the cup of the
nation's sin. *You alone have I known of all the families
of the earth : therefore will I visit upon you all your
iniquities.*[3] Yahweh's age-long Love but strengthens
now the justice and the impetus of His Law.

We perceive then, the problem which Amos left to
prophecy. It was not to discover Love in the Deity
whom he had so absolutely identified with Law. The
Love of God needed no discovery among a people with
the Deliverance, the Exodus, the Wilderness and the
Gift of the Land in their memories. But the problem
was to prove in God so great and new a mercy as was
capable of matching that Law, which the abuse of
His long-suffering gentleness now only the more fully
justified. There was needed a prophet with as keen
a conscience of Law as Amos himself, to affirm that
Love was greater still ; to admit that Israel were
doomed, and yet proclaim that their redemption was
possible by processes as reasonable and as ethical as
those by which the doom had been rendered inevitable.
The prophet of Conscience had to be followed by the
prophet of Repentance.

Such an one was found in Hosea, the son of Be'eri
a citizen and perhaps a priest of Northern Israel, whose
very name, *Salvation*, another form for Joshua and of

---

[1] Psalm xviii. 35.   [2] ii. 10 f.   [3] iii. 2.

Jesus, breathed the larger hope, which it was his glory
to bear to his people. Before we see how for this task
Hosea was equipped with the love and sympathy which
Amos lacked, let us do two things. Let us appreciate
the magnitude of the task itself, set to him first of
prophets ; and let us remind ourselves that, greatly as
he achieved it, the task was not one which could be
achieved even by him once for all, but that it presents
itself to religion again and again in the course of her
development.

For the first of these duties, it is enough to recall
how much all subsequent prophecy derives from Hosea.
We shall not exaggerate if we say that there is no
truth uttered by later prophets about the Divine Grace,
which we do not find in germ in him. Isaiah of Jerusalem was a greater statesman and a more powerful
writer, but he had not Hosea's tenderness and insight
into motive and character. Hosea's marvellous sympathy both with the people and with God is sufficient
to foreshadow every grief, every hope, every gospel,
which make the Books of Jeremiah and the great
Prophet of the Exile exhaustless in their spiritual value
for mankind. These others explored the kingdom of
God : it was Hosea who took it by storm.[1] He is the
first prophet of Grace, Israel's earliest Evangelist ; yet
with as keen a sense of law, and of the inevitableness of
ethical discipline, as Amos himself.

But the task which Hosea accomplished was not one
that could be accomplished once for all. The interest
of his book is not merely historical. For so often as
a generation is shocked out of its old religious ideals,
as Amos shocked Israel, by a realism and a discovery
of law, which have no respect for ideals, however ancient

[1] Matt xi 12

and however dear to the human heart, but work the
pitiless way to doom inevitable ; so often must th
Book of Hosea have a practical value for living mer
At such a crisis we stand to-day. The older Evar
gelical assurance, the older Evangelical ideals hav
been challenged and threatened by the realism to whic
the sciences, both physical and historical, have healthi
recalled us, and by their wonderful revelation of La
working through nature and society without respect t
our creeds and pious hopes. The question presses :
it still possible to believe in repentance and conversio
still possible to preach the power of God to sav
whether the individual or society, from the forces
heredity and of habit ? We can at least learn ho
Hosea mastered the similar problem which Amos le
to him, and how, with a moral realism no less ste
than his predecessor and a moral standard every wh
as high, he proclaimed Love to be the ultimate eleme
in religion ; not only because it moves man to a repe
tance and God to a redemption more sovereign tha
any law ; but because if neglected or abused, wheth
as love of man or love of God, it enforces a doom st
more inexorable than that required by violated tru
or by outraged justice. Love our Saviour, Love o
almighty and unfailing Father, but, just because
this, Love our most awful Judge—we turn to the li
and the preaching in which this eternal theme w
first unfolded

CHAPTER XIV

THE STORY OF THE PRODIGAL WIFE

HOSEA I–III

IT has often been remarked that, unlike the first Doomster of Israel, Israel's first Evangelist was one of themselves, a native and citizen, possibly a priest, of the land to which he was sent. This appears even in his treatment of the stage and soil of his ministry. Contrast him in this with Amos.

In the Book of Amos we have few glimpses of the scenery of Israel, and these always by flashes of the lightning of judgement : towns in drought or earthquake or siege ; vineyards and orchards under locusts or mildew ; Carmel itself desolate, or as a hiding-place from God's wrath.

But Hosea's love steals across his land like the dew, provoking every separate scent and colour, till Galilee and Ephraim lie before us, lustrous and fragrant as nowhere else outside the parables of Jesus. The Book of Amos, when it would praise God's works, looks to the stars. But the poetry of Hosea clings about his native soil like its trailing vines. If he appeals to the heavens, it is only that they may speak to the earth, and the earth to the corn and the wine, and the corn and the wine to Jezreel.[1] Even the wild beasts—and

---

[1] ii. 21 (Heb. 23).

Hosea tells us of their cruelty almost as much as Amos
—are not shut out of the hope of his love : *I will make
a covenant for them with the beasts of the field, and with
the fowls of heaven, and with the creeping things of the
ground.*[1] God's love-gifts to His people are corn and
wool, flax and oil ; while spiritual blessings are figured
in the joys of them who sow and reap. With Hosea
we feel the seasons of the Syrian year : early rain and
latter rain, the first flush of the young corn, the scent
of the vine blossom, the lavish vine, the *first ripe figs
of the fig-tree*, the bursting of the lily ; the wild vine
trailing on the hedge, the reeds in the water, the ever
green cypress ; the beauty of the olive in sunshine and
breeze ; the mists and dews of a summer morning in
Ephraim, the night winds laden with the air of the
mountains, *the scent of Lebanon.*[2] Or it is the dearer
human sights in valley and field : the smoke from the
chimney, the chaff from the threshing-floor, the dove
startled to their towers, the fowler and his net ; the
breaking up of the fallow ground, the harrowing of the
clods, the reapers, the heifer treading out the corn,
the team of draught oxen surmounting the steep road
and at the top the kindly driver setting in food to the
jaws.[3]

Where do we find anything like this save in the
parables of Jesus ? For the love of Hosea was as the
love of that greater Galilean : however high, or lonely
it soared, it was rooted in the common life below, and
fed with the grace of a thousand homely sources.

But just as the Love which first showed itself in the
sunny Parables of Galilee passed to Gethsemane and
the Cross, so the love of Hosea, that had wakened

---

[1] ii. 18 (Heb. 20) ; the last clause is doubtful.
[2] vi. 3, 4 ; ix. 10 ; x. 1 ; xiii. 3, 15 ; xiv. 5–8 (Heb. 6–9).
[3] vii. 11, 12 ; xi. 4 ; xiii. 3.

with the spring lilies and dewy summer mornings of the North, had also, ere his youth was spent, to meet its agony and shame. These came upon the prophet in his home, and in her in whom so loyal and tender a heart had hoped to find his chiefest sanctuary next to God. There are some of the ugliest facts of human life about this prophet's experience ; but the message is one suited to our own hearts and times. Let us read this story of the Prodigal Wife as we do that other Galilean tale of the Prodigal Son. There as well as here are harlots ; but here as well as there is the mirror of the Divine Love. For the Bible never shuns realism when it would expose the hatefulness of sin or magnify the power of God's love to redeem. To an age which so often treats infidelity either as a matter of comedy or as a problem of despair, the tale of Hosea and his wife may still become, what it proved to his own generation, a gospel of love and hope.

The story of his experience of marriage and how it led Hosea to understand God's experience of His relations with His unfaithful people is told partly in prose and partly in verse in the first three chapters of the Book, under a separate title,[1] i. 2a : —

THE BEGINNING OF YAHWEH'S SPEAKING BY HOSEA [2]

This Speaking opens, after the introductory formula, *And Yahweh said to Hosea* with an abrupt and startling verse of four lines :—

[1] So LXX, A.V., Guthe (3rd ed. of Kautzsch), Marti, Moffatt ; more probable than its connection in one sentence with what follows, as Syr., Vulg., R.V., Ewald, Wellhausen, Nowack. Others seek to connect it with what precedes it, but this also is unlikely.

[2] But the Heb. preposition may mean *in*, that is in the inner consciousness of the prophet (so LXX, Marti, etc.), or *through* or simply *with* (Ewald, Harper).

ii. 2b. *Go, take thee a wife of whoredoms*
And children of whoredoms,
For the land indeed goes a-whoring
From after Yahweh.

The meaning is clear and direct, but, as we shall see, this need not prevent us from believing that at the time the prophet was unaware of the character of his wife and only later came to know it ; the plural *whoredoms*—in which form alone the noun occurs in the Old Testament—is an abstract and intensive form ; and intensive also is the verb in the next couplet, literally *whoring goes a-whoring*. *From after* is a pregnant construction, equivalent to *in departing from.* The charge to marry, whether appreciated in its consequences or not by the prophet, was obeyed.

3. *So he went and took Gomer, the daughter of Diblaim,*[1] *and she conceived and bare him*[1] *a son.*

There is no reason to suppose that either of these names, which do not occur elsewhere, is symbolic, either of the sensual character of the woman or of the idolatry of the land. Both appear to be names of persons, unless the second be the name of the place from which Gomer came, instead of the name of her father, but this is uncertain.[2]

---

[1] Some Heb. and Gk. MSS. omit *him.*

[2] Gomer, Heb. גֹּמֶר, LXX Γομέρ ; Diblaim, Heb. דִּבְלָיִם, LXX B Δεβηλαιμ, A.Q. Δεβηλαειμ. These names have been interpreted allegorically in the interests of the theory discussed on pp. 246 f. Gomer has been taken to mean 'completion,' and translated in various phases of that meaning : 'the perfect one' (Jerome), 'fulfilment,' *i.e.*, of punishment (Raschi), 'consumptio' (Calvin), and so on. דבלים has been traced to דבלה, pl. דבלים, 'cakes of pressed figs,' as if a name had been sought to connect the woman at once with idol-worship and a rich sweetness ; or to an Arabic root *dabal* to press as if it referred either to the plumpness of the body (Ezek. xvi. 7 ; so Hitzig), or to the woman's habits. But these suggestions are far-fetched and unlikely. The

4. *And Yahweh said to him, Call his name Yizr'el*
(Jezreel), *for yet a little, and I shall visit the blood of
Yizr'el upon the House of Jehu, and will bring to an end
the kingdom of the House of Israel.* 5. *And it shall be
on that day that I will break the bow of Israel in the
Vale of Yizrē'el*—the classic battlefield of Northern
Israel,[1] on which the people of Yahweh had been
defeated by foreign foes, and would again be defeated,
the natural scene therefore for the certain overthrow
of the dynasty of Jehu and of the kingdom of Israel.
As it turned out, however, the dynasty fell through
a revolt of its own subjects, and the kingdom first
by the Assyrian invasion of Galilee and Gilead in 734,
and then in 721 by the taking of Samaria. Till the
birth of her first-born Gomer, it is implied, was faithful
to her husband,[2] but the name of her second child
reveals that by the time of its birth her guilt was clear.

6. *And she conceived again and bare a daughter; and
He said unto him, Call her name Lo-Ruhamah*—literally
she is Unloved,[3] or *Unpitied, Never-knew-a-Father's-
pity; for I will not again have pity*—such pity as a
father hath—*on the House of Israel that I should at all*

---

alternative suggests itself that דבלים is the name of Gomer's birthplace. But no such place-name occurs elsewhere in Israel; one can
hardly adduce Diblathaim in Moab (Num. xxxiii. 46 ff., Jer. xlviii. 2).

[1] *Hist. Geog.*, ch. xviii.

[2] So W. R. Smith, Kuenen, Wellhausen, Nowack; but Harper holds
that all three children were ' born in infidelity ' (p. 206). Cheyne held
that Hosea learned of this infidelity before the birth of the first (in W. R.
Smith's *Prophets*,[2] p. 112), but Marti not till after all three were born.

[3] רֻחָמָה most probably 3rd sing. fem. Pual (in Pause, cf. Prov.
xxviii. 13). The word means love as pity, *such pity as a father hath
unto his children* (Ps. ciii. 13) or God to a penitent (Ps cxvi. 5). The
Greek versions alternate between love and pity: LXX οὐκ ἠλεημένη διότι
οὐ μὴ προσθήσω ἔτι ἠλεῆσαι, for which the Complutensian has ἀγαπῆσαι, the
reading followed by Paul in Romans, ix. 25; cf. i. Pet. ii. 10.

forgive them. . . .[1] 8. *And she weaned Un-pitied and conceived and bare a son.*

9. *And He said, Call his name Lo-Ammi,* literally *Not-My-People, for ye are not My People and I—I am not for you,* so the received Hebrew text, but some codices of the LXX read *not your God,* which most moderns accept.[2]

We cannot wonder that very various interpretations have been put upon this tale.

1. In the first place many have taken it as an allegory or parable [3] invented by the prophet to illustrate through familiar human figures, what was at that period the difficult conception of the Love of God for sinful men. This theory is well-intentioned, being an effort to avoid imputing to the Deity a command so inconsistent with His Holiness and to the prophet such a violation of his lofty ethical ideals. But surely it is as derogatory to God and His prophet to describe this of them by parable as to impute it to them as actual fact.[4] There are also these insuperable objections to the theory. It implies that Hosea was first awakened to the relations of Yahweh and Israel—He faithful and full of affection, she unfaithful and thankless—and that then in order to illustrate these relations he had invented the story. To this we have an adequate

---

[1] Here ver. 7 is to be omitted as explained above, p. 221.

[2] *Not for you,* Heb. לא לכם, *not your God,* לא אלהיכם, so Wellhausen, Grätz, Nowack, Marti, Harper. The *I am,* אהיה, recalls the *I am* of Exodus iii 14.

[3] Rashi, Calvin, De Wette, Hitzig, Bleek, Reuss, König, etc. For a kindred theory, that the tale is only of a dream or trance, see Aben Ezra, Kimḥi, Hengstenberg, Keil, Wünsche.

[4] Cf. Harper, p. 208, and Leroy Waterman, *J.B.L.,* 1918, p. 193: ' The hypothesis, whether regarding the narrative as a vision or as pure allegory, has never been consistently worked out, and was posited primarily to avoid the natural and manifest force of the language, which is a suffi-cient comment upon it.'

reply. Even though it were possible it is very improbable that such a man should have invented such a tale about his wife, or, if he was unmarried, about himself. But again, he says expressly that his domestic experience was the *beginning of Yahweh's speaking by him*. He passed through it first, and only afterwards, with the sympathy and insight thus acquired, he came to understand and appreciate Yahweh's relation to Israel. And lastly, the style is clearly that of narrative rather than that of parable. Simple facts are told ; there is no elaboration nor effort to make the details symbolic. The names Gomer and Diblaim are apparently those of real persons (if Diblaim be not that of a place), and attempts to give them a symbolic value have failed ; [1] while the further details, that the second child was a daughter and that Gomer weaned her before the third was born are obviously intended as actual facts and would be useless in parable.

She was therefore no dream or fancy this woman, but flesh and blood : the sorrow, the despair, the sphinx of the prophet's life, yet a sphinx who in the end yielded her riddle to love.

2. Accordingly a large number of other interpreters, ancient and modern, have taken the story throughout as the literal account of actual facts. This is the theory of many Greek and Latin Fathers, [2] of some English Puritans like Matthew Henry, and last century of Dr. Pusey—in one of those agreements into which commentators of such opposite schools of theology are sometimes drawn by their common captivity to the letter of Scripture. This, however, cannot be said of several critics of this century who have revived the

---

[1] See above, p. 244, n. 2

[2] Ambrose, Augustine, Theodoret, Cyril Alex., and Theodore of Mopsuestia.

literal theory with no little acumen and force.[1] **To**
the question, How do you justify that first word of
God to Hosea [2] if you take it literally and believe that
He actually charged His prophet to marry a woman
of public shame, the older supporters of this literal
theory answered either that such a thing may be
justified by the express command of the Deity, or that
it was well-worth the end, the salvation of a lost soul.[3]
And indeed the tragedy would be invested with an
even greater horror if it meant that the human hero of
it consciously passed to a self-sacrifice so extreme and
incurred such a shame for such an end.

But there is really nothing in the story to compel
us to read it in this way, nothing as we have seen
either in Gomer's name or even in the epithet applied
to her, the abstract form of which instead of the usual
concrete name for *harlot*, means a woman of impure
tendencies rather than an actual practising harlot.[4]
Apart from these details the literal interpretation is
forbidden by the spirit of the story and the essence
of the analogy which it is made to serve.   Had not
Gomer been pure when Hosea took her to himself she
could not have served as a type of the people whose
innocency at the time of their union with their God
the prophet elsewhere emphasises ; as other prophets

---

[1] Volz (*Zeitschrift für wissenschaftliche Theologie*, xli. 321 ff.), C H
Toy (*J.B.L.*, 1913, 75 ff.), and G. M. P. Smith (*ibid.*, 94 ff.), this las
being the clearest and most detailed argument for the literal theory
Cf. Sellin, p. 159.

[2] Ch. i. 2.

[3] The former is Matthew Henry's view, the latter is implied by Pusey
The two interpretations are akin, but Pusey's has the more delicate tast
of his age.

[4] This against G. M. P. Smith, who takes אשת זנונים as equivalen
to זנה which it clearly is not (the texts he adduces are not paralle
in my opinion), and *daughter of Diblaim* as symbolic = daughter o
fig cakes, one ' whose person is held at low value.'

also do.[1] And this is confirmed by other features of the Book. Hosea had high ideals of marriage, and with the utmost scorn and indignation exposed the sexual immoralities of his generation ; therefore had he knowingly married, or without marriage consorted with, a harlot how ready and how just would have been their *tu quoque !* [2] Also if Gomer had been pure when he married her and continued faithful to him up to the birth of their first child, it is the more intelligible that he, remembering all this, and for the sake of all this, did not at first put her away when he became aware of her guilt, but for some years bore with her. And take also that sense of early goodness and early beauty passing away like morning mist which is so often and so pathetically expressed by Hosea that we cannot but catch in it the echo of his own experience. No ; the theory that he consciously married a harlot at the Divine command is contrary to the whole spirit of his story and to the essence of the analogy it is made to serve. As one has said to whom we owe more than to any other the exposition of the gospel in Hosea (W. R. Smith) : ' The struggle of Hosea's shame and grief, when he found his wife unfaithful, is altogether inconceivable unless his first love had been pure and full of trust in the purity of its object.' [3]

3. The same solid reasons are cogent against a recent modification of the literal theory. According to this

---

[1] Or as Waterman puts it (*J.B.L.*, 1918, 197) : ' If a wife who later becomes faithless truly represents Israel's relations to Yahweh, the prophet's conscious choice of an immoral consort does not truly illustrate the same thing, and in the latter case Hosea could not even excuse his conduct by saying that the land committed whoredom from Yahweh, let alone teach the nation a lesson. That is to say, the analogy taken realistically illustrates too much and logically would seem to eliminate the motive for the prophecy.'

[2] Waterman, *op. cit.*, p. 196.   [3] *Prophets of Israel*, p. 181.

Gomer was no common harlot, but simply a worshipper of the Baalim and therefore guilty of spiritual harlotry,[1] or even a priestess or devotee of that popular cult, who had sacrificed her physical as well as her spiritual chastity by her fanatic practice of it.[2] Hosea could not bring a charge of adultery against such a woman and have her put to death, for in the national view her position was honourable, and even sacred. So upon an ingenious interpretation of the text of iii. 2, or alternatively on as ingenious an emendation of it we are asked to read that what he did was to give Gomer what she had vowed, and owed, to the shrine to which she resorted, and then bring her home and isolate her. Not to speak of the doubtfulness of this textual emendation and exegesis, is it probable that such a prophet would have taken such a woman or indeed she him ? And, once more, how could such a woman serve as a type of the nation whom God had taken to Himself in the days of their innocency ?

4. We are therefore left with the only interpretation consistent with the character and teaching of Hosea and true to the analogy he draws between his own experience with Gomer and Yahweh's experience with Israel. Gomer was a pure woman when he married her, and continued pure till after the birth of her first child. This is the opinion that has recommended itself to most modern expositors.[3]

How then are we to reconcile with this the state-

---

[1] Riedel and others cited by Harper, p. 209.

[2] Leroy Waterman, *J.B.L.*, 1918, 199 ff.

W. R. Smith owns (*Prophets*, p. 410) his indebtedness for it to Ewald and Wellhausen. Others accepting it are Cheyne, Guthe, myself in the first edition of this work (1896), Budde, Marti, Harper, J. E. M'Fadyen, A. R. Gordon (who postpones Hosea's discovery of Gomer's guilt till after the birth of the third child), Smend, *A.T. Religionsgeschichte*, p. 205.

ment that God commanded His prophet to take such a woman ? In this way, and we owe the idea mainly to W. R. Smith. When some years after his marriage Hosea became aware of Gomer's character, and, while brooding over it, he by a natural anticipation of which other prophets also afford instances [1] pushed back his own knowledge of the providential purpose in his marriage to the date when that purpose began to be fulfilled, the date of his betrothal or wedding. This, though he was then unconscious of its fatal future, had been to Hosea the beginning of the word of the Lord. On that voyage he had sailed with sealed orders.

This is true to nature, and may be matched from our own experience. The beginning of God's word to any of us—where does it lie ? Does it lie in the first time the meaning of our life became articulate, and we were able to utter it to others ?

It lies far behind that, in facts and relationships, of the Divine meaning of which we were at the time unconscious, though now we know. How familiar this is in respect to the sorrows and adversities of life : dumb, deadening things that fall on us at the time with no more voice than clods falling on coffins of dead men, we have been able to read them afterwards as the call of God to our souls. But what we thus readily admit about the sorrows of life may be equally true of those relations which we enter with light, unawed hearts, conscious only of the novelty and the joy of them. It is most true of the love which meets a man as it met Hosea in his opening manhood.

[1] Two instances may be quoted : (1) Isaiah vi, where most agree that what is there stated as his inaugural vision is not only what happened at the beginning of his prophetic life, but this spelt out by his experience since. (See *Isaiah i–xxxix*) ; (2) Jer. xxxii. 8, where we are told by the prophet that the Lord had spoken to him on a certain occasion, only after a subsequent event proved this to be the case.

How long Hosea took to discover his shame he
indicates by a few hints which he suffers to break from
the delicate reserve of his story. He calls the first
child his own ; and the boy's name, though ominous of
the nation's fate, has no trace of shame upon it. Hosea's
Jezreel was as Isaiah's Shear-Jashub or Maher-shalal-
hash-baz. But Hosea does not claim the second child ;
and in the name of this lass, Lo-Ruhamah, *she-that-
never-knew-a-father's-love*, orphan not by death but by
her mother's sin, we find proof of the prophet's awakening to the tragedy of his home. Nor does he own the
third child, named *Not-my-people*, that could also mean
No-kin-of-mine. The three births must have taken
at least six years ; [1] and once at least, but probably
oftener, Hosea had forgiven the woman, and till the
sixth year she stayed in his house. Then either he
put her from him, or she went her own way. She
appears to have sold herself for money, and drifted,
like her class, into slavery. [2]

Such were the facts of Hosea's grief, and we have
now to attempt to understand how from that grief
was born his gospel.

While Hosea brooded on his pain one of the first
things he would remember would be the fact, which he
frequently illustrates, that the case of his home was
not singular, but characteristic of his day. Take the
evidence of his book, and there must have been in
Israel many such wives as his own. He describes their
sin as besetting the nation, and the plague of Israel's
life. But to lose your own sorrow in the vaster sense
of national trouble—that is the first consciousness of
a duty and a mission. In the analogous vice of intem-

[1] An Eastern woman seldom weans her child before the end of its
second year.
[2] iii. 2.

perance we have seen the same experience operating to the same effect. How many a man has joined the public warfare against intemperance, because he was roused to its national consequences by the ruin it had brought to his own home! And one remembers an illustrious instance, where a domestic grief of a different kind became not dissimilarly the opening of a career of service to the people :—

I was in Leamington, and Mr. Cobden called on me. I was then in the depths of grief—I may almost say of despair, for the light and sunshine of my house had been extinguished. All that was left on earth of my young wife, except the memory of a sainted life and a too brief happiness, was lying still and cold in the chamber above us. Mr. Cobden called on me as his friend, and addressed me, as you may suppose, with words of condolence. After a time he looked up and said : " There are thousands and thousands of homes in England at this moment where wives and mothers and children are dying of hunger. Now, when the first paroxysm of your grief is passed, I would advise you to come with me, and we will never rest until the Corn Laws are repealed." ' [1]

Not dissimilarly was Hosea's pain overwhelmed by the pain of his people. He remembered that there were in Israel thousands of homes like his own. Anguish gave way to sympathy. The mystery became the stimulus to a mission.

But, again, Hosea traces this sin of his day to the worship of strange gods. He tells the fathers of Israel, that they need not be surprised at the corruption of their wives and daughters when they themselves bring home from the heathen rites the infection of light views of love.[2] That is to say, the many sins against human love in Israel, the wrong done to his heart in his own home, Hosea connects with the wrong done to

---

[1] From a speech by John Bright.   [2] iv. 13, 14.

the Love of God, by His people's desertion of Him for
foreign and impure rites. Hosea's own sorrow thus
became a key to the sorrow of God. Had he loved this
woman, cherished and honoured her, borne with and
forgiven her, only to find at the last his love spurned
and hers turned to sinful men : so also had the Love
of God been treated by His chosen people, and they
had fallen to the loose worship of idols.

Hosea was the more naturally led to compare his
relations to his wife with Yahweh's to Israel, by
certain religious beliefs current among Semitic peoples.
It was common to the Semitic religions to express the
union of a god with his land or people by the figure
of marriage. The title which Hosea applies to the
heathen deities, Ba'al, meant originally not ' lord ' of
his worshippers, but ' possessor ' and endower of his
land, its husband and fertiliser. A fertile land was
' a land of Ba'al,' or ' Be'ulah,' that is, *possessed* or
blessed by a Ba'al.[1] Under the fertility was counted
not only the increase of field and flock, but the human
increase as well ; and thus a nation could speak of
themselves as the children of the Land, their mother,
and of her Ba'al, their father.[2] When Hosea then
called Yahweh the husband of Israel, it was not a
new symbol which he invented. Up to his time, however, the marriage of Heaven and Earth, of a god and
his people, seems to have been conceived in a physical
form which tended to become more gross ; and was
expressed, as Hosea points out, by rites of a sensual
and debasing nature, with disastrous effects on the
domestic morals of the people. By an inspiration,
whose ethical character is conspicuous, Hosea breaks

[1] Cf. the spiritual use of the term, Isa. lxii. 4.
[2] For proof and exposition of all this see Robertson Smith, *Religion of the Semites*, pp. 92 ff.

the physical connection altogether. Yahweh's Bride is not the Land, but the People, and His marriage with her is conceived as a moral relation. Not that He has no connection with the physical fruits of the land : corn, wine, oil, wool, and flax. But these are represented only as the signs and ornaments of the marriage, love-gifts from the husband to the wife.[1] The marriage itself is purely moral : *I will betroth her to Me in righteousness and justice, in leal love* [2] *and tender mercies*. From her in return are demanded faithfulness and growing knowledge of her Lord.

It is the re-creation of an Idea. Slain and made carrion by the heathen religions, the figure is restored to life by Hosea. And this is a life everlasting. Prophet and apostle, the Israel of Yahweh, the Church of Christ, have alike found in Hosea's figure significance and charm. Here we cannot trace the history of the figure ; but at least we ought to emphasise the creative power which its recovery to life proves to have been inherent in prophecy. This is one of those triumphs of which the God of Israel said : *Behold, I make all things new.* [3]

Having dug his figure from the mire and set it upon the rock, Hosea sends it on its way with all boldness. If her God be thus the husband of Israel, *her first husband, the husband of her youth*, then all her pursuit of the Ba'alim is unfaithfulness to her marriage vows. But she is worse than an adulteress ; she is a harlot. She has fallen for gifts. Here the historical facts wonderfully assisted the prophet's metaphor. It was

[1] ii. 8.
[2] So best is rendered חסד, hesedh, which means always not merely an affection, ' lovingkindness,' as our version puts it, but a relation loyally and lovingly observed.
[3] An expansion of this will be found in the present writer's *Isaiah xl-lxvi*, pp. 421–424.

a fact that Israel and Yahweh were wedded in **the** wilderness upon conditions, which by the circumstances of desert life could have little or no reference to the fertility of the earth, but were personal and moral. And it was also a fact that Israel's declension from her God came after her settlement in Canaan, and was due to her discovery of other deities, in possession of the soil and adored by the natives as the dispensers of its fertility. Israel fell under these superstitions, and, although she still formally acknowledged her bond to Yahweh, yet in order to get her fields blessed and her flocks made fertile, her orchards protected from blight and her fleeces from scab, she went after the local Ba'alim.[1] With scorn Hosea points out that there was no true love in this : it was the mercenariness of a harlot, selling herself for gifts.[2] And it had the usual results. The children whom Israel bore were not her husband's.[3] The new generation in Israel grew up in ignorance of their God, with characters and lives strange to His Spirit. They were Lo-Ruhamah : He could not feel towards them such pity as a father has.[4] They were Lo-Ammi : not at all His people. All was in exact parallel to Hosea's own experience with his wife ; and only the real pain of that experience could have made the man brave enough to use it as a figure of his God's treatment by Israel.

Following out the human analogy, the next step should have been for Yahweh to divorce His erring spouse. But He reveals to the prophet that this is not His way. For He is *God and not man, the Holy One in the midst of thee. How shall I give thee up, Ephraim ? How shall I surrender thee, O Israel ? My*

---

[1] ii. 13.   [2] ii. 5, 13.   [3] ii. 5.   [4] See above, p. 245

heart is turned within Me, My compassions are kindled together !

God will seek and bring back the wanderer. Yet the process shall not be easy. The gospel which Hosea here preaches is matched in its tenderness by a full recognition of the ethical requirements of the case. Israel may not be restored without repentance, and cannot repent without disillusion and chastisement. God will therefore show her that her lovers, the Ba'alim, are unable to assure the gifts for which she followed them. These are His corn, His wine, His wool, and His flax, and He will take them away for a time. Nay more, as if mere drought and blight might still be regarded as some Ba'al's work, He who has always manifested Himself by great historic deeds will do so again. He will remove herself from the land, and leave it waste and a desolation.

All that is set forth in chap. ii. 2–23 (Eng. ; 4–25 Heb.). As we have seen,[1] the authenticity of more or less of this fine passage has been doubted, and that its present state is partly due to the expansion of Hosea's own words by later writers is probable. Parts, too, may be out of their original and proper order. Yet its main argument and its spirit, even to the pitch of the high hopes to which it rises, are so consonant with the temper and teaching of the prophet [2] that we may well take it as a whole and in the order in which it now lies ; marking, of course, the portions of the text which are doubtfully Hosea's. Verses 2–13 (Eng. ; 4–15 Heb.) are, save for some additions, a unity, in clearly distinguishable metrical lines ; but it is uncertain whether these are so divisible into strophes as some

---

[1] See above, pp. 222, 233 f.
[2] *Ibid.*

suppose.[1]   The speaker is Yahweh Himself, those
addressed are the individual Israelites, called to argue
with their Mother, the Nation as a whole.   I number
the verses as in the English Version :—

> ii. 2. *Plead with your mother, plead,—*
> *For she is not My wife,[2]*
> *And I not her husband—*
> *That she put her harlotry from her,[3]*
> *And her adultery from between her breasts.*
>
> 3. *Lest I do strip her naked,*
> *And expose her as on the day she was born,*
> *Render her, too, as the desert*
> *And make her like waterless land,*
> *And bring her to death with thirst.*
>
> 4. *And her children I will not pity,*
> *For children of whoredom are they.[4]*
>
> 5. *For their mother has played the whore,*
> *Shameless is she who conceived them !*
> *For she said let me follow my lovers,*
> *That are giving my bread and my water,*
> *My wool and my flax, mine oil and my drinks.*

[1] Marti, omitting some lines, makes out twelve strophes of four lines
each ; Harper's scheme of four strophes of 8, 9, 8, 9 lines each is more
complicated, omitting more lines than Marti and bringing in 16, 17
(Eng. ; 18, 19 Heb.) after 11 (13).   But all this is very uncertain.

[2] Marti omits this line, Harper both it and the next one on the supposi-
tion that they interrupt the call to *plead* in the first line and the substance
of the pleading in the fourth and fifth.   But do they really do so ?   I
cannot but feel that these scholars make these omissions in the interest
of their respective schemes of strophes.   See above.

[3] Literally, *from her face.*   Kimchi, Hitzig, Guthe take the plural
harlotries as signs of harlotry, the paint or other marks of her trade on
her face, and in the next line the plural *adulteries* as the corresponding
jewels on her breast.   Both plurals are, of course, intensive, like that in
i. 2.

[4] Marti omits ; also Harper, along with the previous line.   But how
then, are the *their* and *them* of the next verse to be accounted for ?
Another instance of the sacrifice of sense to a theory of strophes.

6. *Therefore, I am to* [1] *hedge up*
   Her [2] *way with thorns,*
   And build against her a fence,
   That her paths she may not discover.
7. *So though she hunt for her lovers*
   She never shall reach them,
   And if she search for them
   She shall not find them. [3]

7b. *Then shall she say, Let me go and return to my first husband, for better for me was it then than now.* This sentence, though not wholly breaking the logical connection, somewhat does so, and not being in the metrical rhythm of its context, but in prose, may be a later intrusion. Indeed, some deny all vv. 6, 7 to Hosea, as breaking the connection between vv. 5 and 8, and out of harmony with iii. 3, [4] but this is groundless.

8. *But she, she had not known*
   It was I Who gave her
   The corn and the wine and the oil,
   And heaped on her silver and gold,
   [They made it into a Baal !] [5]

9. *Therefore I take back My corn in its time,*
   And My wine in its season,
   And withdraw My wool and My flax
   So as not to [6] *cover her nakedness.*

---

[1] The active participle, used by God of Himself in proclaiming His grace or doom has here (cf. ver. 14) and elsewhere, especially in Deuteronomy, the force of an immediate future.

[2] So LXX; Heb. *thy*.   [3] So LXX; Heb. omits *them*.

[4] Nowack, Volz, Harper.

[5] This may be a later addition; so Marti and others.

[6] So LXX.

ii. 10. *Yea, now I am baring her shame*
In the eyes of her lovers,[1]
And none from My hand shall save her.

11. *I will bring to an end all her joyaunce,*
Her feasts, her new-moons and her sabbaths,
[And all her solemn assemblies],[1]

12. *And destroy her vines and her fig-trees,*
Of which she has said :
My harlot's hire [2] *are those*
That my lovers have given me.
I shall turn them into jungle,
With beasts of the wild to devour them,[3]

13. *And visit upon her the days of the Baalim,*
In which she would offer [4] *to them,*
And decked with her rings and her jewels
Went after her lovers—
But Me she forgat—Rede of Yahweh.[5]

In short, Israel had deserted the religion that was
historical for the religion that was physical. But the
historical religion was also the physical. Yahweh,
Who had brought Israel to the land, was also the God
of the land and quickener of its fruits, and would
prove this by taking them away. By natural or by
political disasters ? Wellhausen thinks that only the
former are meant, but the *withdraw* or *snatch away* of
ver. 9, as well as others of the terms used, imply the
carrying away of the crops *in their season*, when they

---

[1] Kittel, Marti, and others omit these lines. Volz, Harper, etc., take
ver 11 after 12.
[2] So both Heb. and the LXX μισθώματά μου.
[3] LXX adds and *fowls of heaven and reptiles of earth.*
[4] Or *offer incense.*
[5] In his strophe-scheme Marti takes this line with the following three
in ver. 14 so as to form a quatrain, but logically the line belongs to what
precedes, not to what follows it.

had ripened, by invaders ; while the cessation of all worship and festival points to the removal of the people from their land, which, of course, is also implied in ver. 23*a*. Evidently, therefore, Hosea, writing about 745, had in view an imminent subjection of Israel by Assyria, subjection always followed up by the exile of the people subdued.

The rest of the chapter, vv. 14–23 (16–25 Heb.) are, all by some critics, or nearly all by others, denied to Hosea,[1] on the ground that while vv. 2–13 (4–15 Heb.) speak of a desolation of Israel's land, 14 describes a leading of the people into the wilderness and their subsequent return by God's grace to their country ; a difference which these critics regard as explicable only by supposing that a later writer interpreted Hosea's own words in 2–13 as a prediction of exile, and when *the* Exile actually happened added 14–23 as a promise of restoration from it. But, as we have seen on ver. 11, Hosea did foresee exile for the people, not the great Exile of 587 perhaps, but certainly that of Northern Israel in 734 and 721, and it cannot have been far from his heart to conceive also of its happening for the end of the penitence and restoration of the people whom he loved. See above [2] on the possibility of such high promises being from Hosea himself. In any case, these prophecies in 14–23 are after Hosea's own heart ; if from a later hand, they were certainly, as their place shows, due to his inspiration.

14. *Therefore, behold, I will woo* [3] *her*
    And bring her into the wilderness,
    And thence [4] *speak home to her heart.*

[1] Volz, Nowack, Marti, Harper. [2] Pp. 233 ff.
[3] Or *allure* or *persuade* ; sometimes used in a bad sense.
[4] To this line it is clear we must transfer the *thence* of the next line where its presence is difficult.

ii. 15. *And I will give her her vineyards,*
And Akhor's Vale [1] *a doorway of hope ;*
There shall she answer as in days of her youth,
As the day she came up from the land of Egypt.

To us the terms of this passage may seem formal
and theological. But to an Israelite some of these
terms must have brought back the days of his own
wooing. *I will speak home to her heart* is a forcible
expression, like the German ' an das Herz ' or the
sweet Scottish ' it cam' up roond my heart,' and was
used in Israel as from man to woman when he won
her.[2] But the other terms have an equal charm.
The writer, of course, does not mean that Israel shall
be literally taken back to the desert. But he describes
her coming (or as some think her actual) Exile under
that ancient figure, in order to surround her penitence
with the associations of her innocency and her youth.
By the grace of God, everything shall begin again as
at first. The old terms *wilderness, the giving of vine-*
yards, Valley of Akhor, are, as it were, the wedding
gifts restored.

As the result of all this—whether the words be by
Hosea or another [3]—

16. *It shall be in that day—Yahweh's Rede—*
She shall call Me, ' my Husband,'
And shall call Me no more ' Baalim.'

[1] Either because Akhor means trouble or because the Vale of that
name was the pass by which Israel first entered the hills of the land from
Jericho ; or more probably because of both.

[2] Cf. Isa. xl. 1 : which to the same exiled Israel is the fulfilment of
the promise here made. See *Isaiah xl–lxvi*, pp. 76 f.

[3] To Wellhausen, Volz, Nowack, Harper 16 (Heb. 18) is a gloss on 17
(19 Heb.) on the grounds that *my Husband* and *my Baal* are late terms
(but see next note), that 16, in part, is a repetition of 17 (which is not
clear), and that the metre differs from that of the context and ' is superfluous to the strophe structure ' (but see above, p. 258, n. 2).

17. *I will take from her mouth the Baalim's names,*
That no more they be mentioned by name.[1]

There follows, in 18–23, a picture of the ideal future in which—unlike the vision that now closes the Book of Amos—moral and spiritual beauty, the peace of the land and the restoration to righteousness of the people are mingled in a spirit worthy of Hosea's heart, though some deny that it is his.[2]   The real difficulty is the style, unlike the terse, clean, rapid utterance of his undoubted oracles.   If the passage started from himself it has been much expanded, yet to separate the later from the original elements in it is now impossible.   As it stands, little of it can be distinguished as metrical except through arbitrary elisions.

18. *And I will make them a covenant in that day*
with the beasts of the field and with the fowl of heaven,
and the reptiles of the ground.

> *And bow and sword and battle*
> *I will break from the earth,*
> *And make them* [3] *to dwell in safety*
> 19. *And I will betroth thee* [4] *to Me for ever,*
> *Yea, betroth thee to Me in right and in justice,*
> *And in leal love and tender mercies,*

---

[1] In 16 LXX reads καλέσει με Ὁ ἀνήρ μου, καὶ οὐ καλέσει με ἔτι βααλείμ; Guthe, Marti, and A. R. Gordon emend *she shall call to* or *on her husband, and call no more on the Baalim.*   Heb.: *thou shalt call Me ' My husband,' and shalt call Me no more, ' My Baal.'*

[2] Volz, Nowack, Marti (as we have seen) and Harper on the alleged grounds of its rhythmic structure, redundancy, and reflection of late ideas, *e.g.*, of universal peace.   Wellhausen, A. R. Gordon, and Moffatt retain the verses as Hosea's.   They may have been delivered at different times and put together, not in a logical order.

[3] LXX *thee,* some moderns *her.*

[4] This *thee* and the following two perhaps should be *her.*

ii. 20. *Yea, betroth thee to Me in faithfulness,*
And thou shalt know Yahweh.[1]

21. *In that day it shall be* [2]—*Yahweh's Rede*—[3]
I will call on [4] *the heavens,*
And they shall call on the earth,

22. *And the earth shall call on the corn, wine and oil,*
And they shall call on Yizre'el.

23. *And I will sow her* [5] *to Me in the land,*
And as a father pity Un-pitied,
And tell Not-My-People, My people thou art
And he shall say, My God! [6]

The circle is thus completed on the terms from which
we started. The three names which Hosea gave to
the children, omens of Israel's fate, are reversed and
the people restored to the love and favour of their God.

We might expect this to form the culmination of the
prophecy. What fuller prospect could be than that
we see in the close of the second chapter? But with
wonderful grace the prophecy turns back from this

[1] Some read *and in the knowledge of Yahweh.*

[2] Heb. inserts here *I will call on*, needless and wanting in LXX.

[3] The whole line may be an editorial formula, leaving to follow two
quatrains.

[4] The Heb. verb is the usual one for utterance in antiphon or dialogue,
and means both to *address* and to *answer;* here *call on, summon, challenge* or *bid speed.*

[5] So Heb., but we should probably read *him*, Yizre'el.

[6] It is at this point, if at any, that i. 10, 11, ii. 1 (Eng.; ii. 1-3 Heb.)
ought to come in. Even here, however, they are superfluous: *And the
number of the children of Israel shall be as the sand of the sea, which
cannot be measured nor counted; and it shall be in the place where it was
said to them, No People of Mine are ye! it shall be said to them, Sons of
the living God! And the children of Judah and the children of Israel
shall be gathered together, and they shall appoint themselves one head,
and shall go up from the land: for great is the day of Jezreel. Say
unto your brothers, My People, and to your sisters* (LXX *sister*), *She-is-
Pitied.* On the whole passage see above, p. 221.

vision of the restoration of the people as a whole, to pick up again the individual from whom it had started, and whose unclean rag of a life had fluttered out of sight before the national fortunes sweeping upon the scene. This was needed to crown the story.

iii. 1–5. *And Yahweh said unto me once more, Go love a woman, loved of*[1] *a paramour and an adulteress, as Yahweh loveth the children of Israel though they be turning to other gods and loving raisin-cakes,* some element in the feasts of the gods of the land, the reputed givers of the grape. *Then I bought her to me for fifteen pieces of silver and a homer of barley and a lethekh of wine.*[2] *And I said to her, For many days shalt thou abide for me* alone : *thou shalt not play the harlot, thou shalt not be for any husband ; and I for my part also shall be so towards thee. For the days are many that the children of Israel shall abide without a king and without a prince, without sacrifice and without massebah, and without ephod and teraphim.*[3] *Afterwards the children of Israel shall turn and seek Yahweh their God and David their king, and shall be in awe of Yahweh and towards His goodness in the end of the days.*[4]

---

[1] LXX and Syr. have *loving*. LXX *evil things* for *paramour*.

[2] So LXX for Heb. *of barley*. The homer was eight bushels. The lethekh is a measure not elsewhere mentioned.

[3] On these see above, Ch. III, pp. 35 f.

[4] The above translation and exposition take the woman described in ch. iii as Gomer, and what is described of her as the continuation of Hosea's dealings with her described in i. 2–9; so Ewald, Pusey, Cheyne, Wellhausen, Nowack, Cossmann (even ver. 5, as against Volz; he strikingly says : ' damit ist die Möglichkeit des Heilsgedanken bei Hosea gegeben. Sie wird noch durch xiv. 2 gestüzt'), Harper ; also Paton (*J.B.L.*, xv. 15). But other opinions have been offered and argued. On insufficient grounds Marti takes the whole chapter as a late story of a *second* marriage of Hosea (see Harper in answer to this). On a suggestion of Steuernagel (*Einleitung in das A.T.*, 605), G. M. P. Smith (*J.B.L.*, 1913, cited above, p. 248), takes the story as of the same woman Gomer, but as a version of Hosea's experience with her parallel to i. 2–9, and

Do not let us miss the fact that the story of the wife's restoration follows that of Israel's, although the story of the wife's unfaithfulness had come before that of Israel's apostasy. For this order means that, while the prophet's private pain preceded his sympathy with God's pain, it was not he who set God, but God who set him, the example of forgiveness. The man learned the God's sorrow out of his own sorrow ; but conversely he was taught to forgive and redeem his wife only by hearing God forgive and redeem the people. In other words, the Divine was suggested by the human pain ; yet the Divine Grace was not started by any previous human grace, but, on the contrary, was itself the precedent and origin of the latter. This is in harmony with all Hosea's teaching. God forgives because *He is God and not man*.[1] Our pain with those we love helps us to understand God's pain ; but it is not our love that leads us to believe in His love. On the contrary, all human grace is but the reflex of the Divine. So St. Paul : *Even as Christ forgave you, so also do ye.* So St. John : *We love Him,* and one another, *because He first loved us.*

But this return from the nation to the individual has another interest. Gomer's redemption is not the mere completion of the parallel between her and her people. It is, as the story says, an impulse of the Divine Love,

---

not the tale of Hosea's dealing with her subsequent to that. For Waterman's theory of the seclusion enforced by the prophet on his wife see above, p. 250. He ingeniously emends the difficult Heb. reading *and a lethekh of barley*, וַלְתֶךְ שְׂעֹרִים to וַתֵּלֶךְ שַׁעַר יָם *and she came to Sha'araîm* or *Sha'ar Yam*, which he suggests was Hosea's home in the Shephelah. But these hypotheses, though ingenious, are very precarious. Ver. 5 is regarded by most moderns as a late addition, both on account of its language and the Messianic hope expressed, though some limit their doubts of it to the phrase *and David their king*.

[1] xi. 9

recognised even then in Israel as seeking the individual. He Who followed Hagar into the wilderness, Who met Jacob at Bethel and forgat not Joseph in prison,[1] remembers also Hosea's wife. His love is not satisfied with His Nation-Bride : He remembers this single outcast. It is the Shepherd leaving the ninety-and-nine in the fold to seek the one lost sheep.

For Hosea himself his home could never be the same as it was at the first. *And I said to her, For many days shalt thou abide, as far as I am concerned, alone. Thou shalt not play the harlot. Thou shalt not be for a husband : and I on my side also shall be so towards thee.* Discipline was needed there ; and abroad the nation's troubles called the prophet to an anguish and a toil which left no room for the sweet love or hope of his youth. He steps at once to his hard warfare for his people ; and through the rest of his book we never again hear him speak of home, or of children, or of wife. So Arthur passed from Guinevere to his last battle for his land :—

> ' Lo ! I forgive thee, as Eternal God
> Forgives : do thou for thine own soul the rest.
> But how to take last leave of all I loved ?
>
> .   .   .   .
>
> I cannot touch thy lips, they are not mine ; . . .
> I cannot take thy hand ; that too is flesh,
> And in the flesh thou hast sinned ; and mine own flesh,
> Here looking down on thine polluted, cries
> " I loathe thee " ; yet not less, O Guinevere,
> For I was ever virgin save for thee,

[1] As the stories all written down before this had made familiar to Israel.

My love thro' flesh hath wrought into my life
So far, that my doom is, I love thee still.
Let no man dream but that I love thee still.
Perchance, and so thou purify thy soul,
And so thou lean on our fair father Christ,
Hereafter in that world where all are pure
We two may meet before high God, and thou
Wilt spring to me, and claim me thine, and know
I am thine husband, not a smaller soul. . . .
                                        Leave me that,
I charge thee, my last hope.   Now must I hence
Thro' the thick night I hear the trumpet blow.'

CHAPTER XV

THE THICK NIGHT OF ISRAEL

HOSEA IV–XIV

IT was indeed a 'thick night' into which this Arthur of Israel stepped from his shattered home. The mists drive across Hosea's long agony with his people, and what we see, we see blurred and broken. There is stumbling and clashing; crowds in drift; confused rallies; gangs of assassins breaking across the highways; doors opening upon lurid interiors of drunken riot. Voices, which other voices mock, cry for a dawn that never comes. God Himself is Laughter, Lightning, a Lion, a Gnawing Worm. Only one clear note breaks over the confusion—the trumpet summoning to war.

Take courage, great heart! Not thus shall it always be! There wait thee, before the end, of open Visions at least two—one of Memory and one of Hope, one of Childhood and one of Spring. Past this night, past the swamp and jungle of these fetid years, thou shalt see thy land in her beauty, and God shall look on the face of His Bride.

Chaps. iv–xiv are almost indivisible. The two Visions just mentioned, chaps. xi and xiv. 3–9, may be detached by virtue of contributing the only strains of gospel which rise victorious above the Lord's controversy with His people and the troubled story of

their sins The rest is the noise of a nation falling
to pieces, the crumbling of a splendid past. And as
decay has no climax and ruin no rhythm, so we may
understand why it is impossible to divide with any
certainty Hosea's record of Israel's fall.   Some arrangement we must attempt, but it is more or less artificial,
and to be undertaken for the sake of our own minds,
that cannot grasp so great a collapse all at once.
Chap. iv has a certain unity, and is followed by a
new exordium, but as it forms only the theme of which
the subsequent chapters are variations, we may take
it with them as far as chap. vii, ver. 7 ; after which
there is a slight transition from the moral signs of
Israel's dissolution to the political—although Hosea
still combines the religious offence of idolatry with
the anarchy of the land.   These form the chief interest
to the end of chap. x.   Then breaks the bright Vision
of the Past, chap. xi, the temporary victory of the
Gospel of the Prophet over his Curse.   In chaps. xii-
xiv. 2 we are plunged into the latter once more, and
reach in xiv. 3 ff. the second bright Vision, the Vision of
the Future.   To each of these phases of Israel's Thick
Night—we can hardly call them Sections—we may
devote a chapter of simple exposition, adding three
chapters more of detailed examination of the main
doctrines we shall have encountered on our way—the
Knowledge of God, Repentance, and the Sin against
Love.

CHAPTER XVI

A PEOPLE IN DECAY: I. MORALLY

HOSEA IV–VII. 7

PURSUING the plan laid down in the last chapter, we take the section of Hosea's discourse which lies between chap. iv. 1 and chap. vii. 7. Chap. iv is the only separable part of it ; but there are also slight breaks at v. 15 and vii. 2. So we may attempt a division into four periods : 1. Chap. iv, God's general charge against the people ; 2. Chap. v. 1–14, on the priests and princes ; 3. Chaps. v. 15–vii. 2, which abjures the people's attempts at repentance ; and 4. Chap. vii. 3–7, a lurid spectacle of the profligate court. All these give symptoms of the moral decay of the people,—the family destroyed by impurity, and society by theft and murder ; the corruption of the spiritual guides of the people ; the debauchery of the nobles ; the sympathy of the throne with evil,—with the despairing judgement that such a people are incapable even of repentance. The keynotes are these : *No troth, leal love, nor knowledge of God in the land. Priest and Prophet flounder. Ephraim and Judah flounder. I am as the moth to Ephraim. What can I make of thee, Ephraim ? When I would heal them, their guilt is only the more exposed.* Morally, Israel is rotten. The prophet cannot help adding signs of their political incoherence. But these he deals with more particularly in the discourse which follows chap. vii. 7.

1. The Lord's Quarrel with Israel

Hosea iv

By an order of words frequently different from that of prose and by a metrical distribution of accents or stresses the text of chap. iv (uncertain in parts as it is) falls into lines of verse, not so regular either in its lines or strophes as some moderns attempt to prove,[1] but, with all its irregularities, none the less unmistakable and none the less musical. Opening with four lines in something like the Ḳinah measure, and now and then harking back to the same, it consists mainly of lines longer than the Ḳinah's and approximately equal to each other.

iv. 1. *Hear ye the word of Yahweh,*
     Sons of Israel !
   For a quarrel [2] *there is to Yahweh*
   With the land's inhabitants :
   That troth there is none nor leal love
   Nor knowledge of God in the land.
2. *Perjury,*[3] *murder, theft and adultery* [4]
   Break out,[5] *and blood strikes upon blood.*

---

[1] Ewald, four strophes ; Marti, thirteen of four lines each, but this only by many arbitrary omissions ; Harper, five of twelve lines each, by more reasonable changes in the order.

[2] Or *contention :* Micah vi. 2, Jer. ii. 9.

[3] Literally, *swearing and falsehood.*

[4] Ninth, sixth, eighth, and seventh of the Decalogue.

[5] *They break out,* so Heb. text. By a slight change some read the noun *outbreak* or *brute force.*

3.   *Therefore the land is withering*
     And all its denizens languish,
     To the beasts of the field and the birds of heaven ;
     E'en the fish of the sea are swept off.

The stable, well-furnished life across which Amos hurled his alarm has broken up.   If there still be *ease in Sion* there is no more *security in Samaria*.[1]   The great Jeroboam is dead and society, so dependent in the East on the strong individual, is loosened and falling to pieces.   The sins exposed by Amos were those which lurked beneath a semblance of law and order, but Hosea adds outbreaks that set all order at defiance. Guthe and Marti omit ver. 3, but unreasonably, for like Amos and other early prophets Hosea feels the universal sickness of man and nature under man's sin.

Yet the guilt is that not of the people so much as of their religious guides.   Priest and prophet go staggering one after the other.   The priests are the most culpable, every jack-priest among them.   They have rejected knowledge so they shall be rejected by God.

4.   *Yet let none find fault and none upbraid,*
     For My people are but as their priestlings ! [2]

[1] Amos vi. 9.

[2] The text of vv. 4, 5 is very uncertain.   I render iv 4*b* according to the emendation of Beck (quoted by Wünsche, p. 142), who instead of וְעַמְּךָ כִּמְרִיב proposes וְעַמִּי כְּכֹּמְרִין, for the first word of which there is support in the LXX, ὁ λαός μου.   The second word, כֹּמֶר, is used for priest only in a bad sense, by Hosea himself, x. 5, in 2 Kings xxiii. 5 of the calf-worship and in Zeph. i. 4 of the Baal priesthood.   As Wellhausen says, this emendation restores sense to a passage that had none before.   ' Ver. 4 cannot be directed against the people, but must rather furnish the connection for ver. 5, and effect the transference from the reproof of the people (vv. 1–3) to the reproof of the priests (5 ff.).'   The letters יְכֹהֵן which are left over in ver. 4 by the emendation are then improved by Wellhausen (following Zunz) into the vocative הַכֹּהֵן, which, however, he leaves in ver. 4, while I take it with its natural neighbour *thou*

iv. 5. *O priest, thou hast floundered to-day,*
To-night the prophet shall flounder with thee, (?)
And I will destroy thy Mother. (?) [1]

6. *My people perish for lack of knowledge!*
Because thou hast rejected knowledge,
Thee I reject as priest to Me,
And hast forgotten thy God's instruction,
I will forget thy children, yea I.

7. *As many they be, they sin against Me,*
Their glory to shame I will turn. [2]

8. *On the sin of My people they feed*
And relish their guilt. [3]

The more the people sin, the more merrily thrive the priests by fines and sin-offerings. They live upon the vice of the day, and have a vested interest in its crimes. English Langland said the same thing of the friars of his time. The contention is obvious. The priests have given themselves wholly to ritual, and a ritual thoroughly immoral; they have forgotten that their office is an intellectual and moral one. We return to this when treating of Hosea's doctrine of knowledge and its responsibilities. Priesthood, let us remember, priesthood is an intellectual, as well as a moral, trust.

It is at first sight uncertain whether the next two verses, 9, 10, refer to priests or people. In previous

hast floundered in ver. 5; so too Harper. Duhm, and Marti would read *the people is like the priestling and the prophet like the priest*, which is not preferable to Beck's reading. Vv. 5, 6 are taken by Marti as a late intrusion. On iv. 4 f. see further, S. Feigin, *A.J.S.L.*, 1925, 64 ff.

[1] The application seems to swerve here. *Thy children* seems to imply that for this clause at least the whole people are addressed. But with W. R. Smith *thy mother* may be taken as equivalent, not to the nation, put to the priestly order.

[2] A reading current among Jewish writers and adopted by Geiger, *Urschrift*, 316, is *they have turned*: cf. Targ. and Syr.

[3] Lit., *lift up their appetite* or *their relish to their guilt*

editions I had thought the people, but Harper thinks the priests. Surely from the opening line we may consider that the two are combined, and this up to ver. 11, after which till the end of the chapter it is clear that the whole nation is meant. In vv. 9, 10 the sentences passed upon dishonest greed and harlotry are the natural ones—unsatisfied hunger and child-lessness.

> 9. *And it shall be like people like priest.*[1]
>   *I will visit upon him his* [2] *ways,*
>   *And his doings will bring back to him.*
> 10. *They shall eat and shall not be filled,*
>   *They shall whore* [3] *and shall not increase.* [4]
>   *[For Yahweh they left off to heed].* [5]
> 11. *Harlotry, wine and new wine*
>   *Capture the brains.*

The position of ver. 11 is doubtful; it is so general as to suit several points in the chapter, to which accordingly some moderns have variously removed it. [6] But as it stands it not unfitly precedes and explains the senseless consultation of stocks and staves described in the next verse. *The brains,* literally *the heart;* to the Hebrews the heart was the seat not only of the

---

[1] Except to fill up a supposed strophe of four lines I see no reason for Marti's expansion of this line to two : *like people like prophet, and like prophet like priest.*

[2] For *him, his* (Heb.) Syr. reads *them, their,* and so in the next line. Marti's rendering of the singular preposition accounts for it : *upon each his ways.*

[3] Reading זָנוּ for הִזְנוּ.   [4] LXX *find satisfaction.*

[5] It is difficult to see why this line should be just here. Gardner, bringing in the first word of the next line and altering its points, reads : they have left Yahweh to keep harlots.

[6] Harper after 12*ab*, Marti after 14*e*, so Moffatt.

affections but of the practical intellect.[1] In ver. 13
I have preferred *headlands* to *summits* (Heb. *heads*),
for on the latter no trees grow, and the altar seems to
have been built under a tree and near water on some
promontory from which too the flight of birds and
passage of the clouds might be observed.

  iv. 12. *My folk ! Of its stock it enquires,*
           And its staff reveals to it !
           For the spirit of whoredom has led it [2] *astray,*
           And [3] *they play the whore away from their God.*
     13. *On the headlands of hills they sacrifice*
           And on the heights burn [incense ?],
           Under an oak or poplar or terebinth,
           For good is its shade !
           Wherefore your [4] *daughters are given to whoredom,*
           And your brides to adultery.
     14. *On your daughters I will not visit their whoredom,*
           Nor on your brides their adultery,
           For the men *themselves go aside with harlots*
           And with kĕdēshôth [5] *do sacrifice.*
           So the people is witless and falls to ruin !

It was vain for the men to be impure and fancy that
their women would be chaste. In the third line *they*
or *themselves* stands alone, but *men*, or *fathers and sons*,
are implied by the masculine pronoun. There is some
doubt as to whether the next verse is original.

     15. *Though thou play the harlot, Israel,*
           Let not Judah bring guilt on himself!

[1] See below, Hos. vii. 7.   [2] Or *them*, cf. Targ. and Syr.
[3] *So that*, Wellhausen, Marti.   [4] Marti, *their*.
[5] The women set apart and devoted to impure practice at the shrines.
On the text of ver. 14, see W. H. Cobb, *J.B.L.*, 1917 ; also Gardner on
the last line.

> *And come not to Gilgal,*
> *Nor go up to Beth-'Aven.*
> *And take not your oath* at Beersheba,[1]
> *By the life of Yahweh!*
>
> 16. *Yea, like a wild cow Israel goes wild ;*
> *Can Yahweh now herd them,*
> *Like a lamb on broad meadows ?*

The only way to get sense out of the last two lines is to treat them as a question expecting a negative answer.[2] In the next verse the participle means *mated* or *leagued*. The corresponding noun is used of a wife as the *mate* of her husband,[3] and of an idolater as the *mate* of his idols.[4] The expression is doubly appropriate here since Hosea used marriage as the symbol of the relation of a deity to his people or land. Ephraim must go from bad to worse, leave him alone.

> 17. *Wedded to idols is Ephraim,*
> *Leave him alone !*
> 18. *Their orgies over,[5] a-whoring they go.*
> *They love, they love shame*
> *More than their pride,[6]*
> 19. *A wind has swept them up on its wings,*
> *They shall be shamed of their altars.[7]*

---

[1] Wellhausen naturally thinks this third place-name (cf. Amos **v. 5**) has dropped out, for Beersheba means Well-of-the-Oath.

[2] So all moderns since Hitzig.

[3] Mal. ii. 4.   [4] Isa. xliv. 11.

[5] סר סבאם , but Houtsma, followed by Marti, reads סוד = *an assembly of sots.*

[6] The verse is uncertain. Heb. *Her rulers dearly love shame.* LXX read a different and fuller text from *Ephraim* in the previous verse to *harlotry* in this : 'Ephraim hath set up for himself stumbling-blocks and chosen Canaanites.' The reading above is adapted from LXX, which for מגניה must have read מגאונם .

[7] So rightly LXX ; Heb. *their sacrifices.*

In spite of all their servile worship the Assyrian tempest shall sweep them away in its trail.

This brings the passage to such a climax as Amos loved. The opening of the next chapter offers a new exordium.

2. PRIESTS AND PRINCES FAIL

Hosea v. 1–14

The direction followed by this section—more or less regular lines of three accents or stresses each [1]—is almost parallel to that of chap. iv running out to a prospect of invasion. The charges are delivered mainly against the leaders, political and spiritual, of the people, anticipating the strictures of vii. 7 upon them ; those who have hitherto been the judges, this time shall be judged.

> v. 1. *Hear this, O ye priests,*
> *Pay heed, House of Israel,*
> *And the House of the King give ear.*
> *For on you is the sentence !*
> *A snare have ye been in Mispah,*
> *A net spread out upon Tabor,*
> 2. *And a pit ye made deep at Shittim,[2]*
> *But I am the scourge of you all.[3]*

[1] Marti by many omissions distinguishes twelve strophes of four lines each ; Harper, with more reasonable adherence to the text, marks four with twelve lines each. I am not sure that we can assume such regularity on the part of the prophet.

[2] The text of this line is impossible and has provoked a host of emendations ; of which the most satisfactory is that proposed by Wellhausen and adopted above ; so also Marti, Harper, Moffatt. On the place names see above, pp. 33 ff., and my *Hist. Geography*.

[3] So the Heb. (except that for its *them all* the LXX *you all* has been adopted). But Cheyne, Marti, Harper reading אֵין , *none*, for אֲנִי , achieve the rendering *there is no discipline* or *bettering for you all*.

3. *I, I know Ephraim,*
Israel is not hid from Me,—
How Ephraim now [1] has played the whore,
Defiled is Israel ! [2]

The worship on the high places, whether nominally of Yahweh or not was sheer service of Ba'alim. It was in the interest both of the priests and of the rulers to multiply these shrines, which were only traps for the people.

4. *Their doings will not allow them [3]*
To return to their God,
For a spirit of harlotry is in their midst,
And Yahweh they know not. [4]

5. *Yet Israel's pride attests to his face,*
Israel and Ephraim flounder in their guilt,
Flounders, too, Judah along with them. [5]

By *Israel's pride* some understand God. The term is used too opprobiously by Amos to allow us to agree to this. The phrase must mean that Israel's arrogance or confident prosperity, by the wounds it feels in this time of national decay, itself testifies against the people, a remarkable ethical symptom to which we shall return when treating of Repentance. Yet the line may be

---

[1] So Heb. עתה accepted by Marti and others. But Wellhausen, Nowack, Harper read אתה , *thou*.

[2] This couplet Wellhausen, Nowack, and Marti unreasonably take as a gloss.

[3] Wellhausen : *they will not leave their doings to return.*

[4] Wellhausen, Marti, and others take also this couplet as a gloss, but why ?

[5] Oort, Nowack, Marti regard this line as intruded ; ' but without sufficient reason '—so rightly Harper.

read in harmony with the context, *the pride of Israel shall be humbled to his face.*[1]

v. 6. *With their sheep and their cattle they hawk about,*
Yahweh to seek and shall not find Him.
He hath drawn away from them.
7. *Yahweh have they betrayed*
And begotten strange children.
Now may a month devour them and their portions !

By the national idolatry a generation has grown up who are not Yahweh's. They are ready for destruction. Any month[2] may bring the swift invader. Hark, the alarum of war ! How it reaches to the back of the land.

---

[1] *Note on the Pride of Israel.*—גָּאוֹן means *grandeur*, and is (1) so used of Yahweh's majesty (Micah v. 3 (Heb. ; Eng. 4) ; Isa. ii. 10, 19, 21 ; xxiv. 14), (2) of great human powers (Zech. x. 11 ; Ezek. xxxii. 12). In Psalm xlvii. 5 it is parallel to the land of Israel (cf. Nahum ii. 3). (3) In a grosser sense it is used of the rank vegetation of Jordan (A.V. wrongly *swelling*) (Jer. xii. 5 ; Zech. xi. 3 : cf. Job xxxviii. 11). It appears to be this sense of *rankness, arrogance,* in which Hosea vi. 8 takes it as parallel to *the palaces of Israel* which *Yahweh loathes and will destroy.* In Amos viii. 7 the phrase may be used in scorn ; yet some take it even there of God (Buhl, in his ed. of Gesenius' *Lexicon*). In Hosea it occurs twice in the phrase given above—וְעָנָה גְאוֹן יִשְׂרָאֵל בְּפָנָיו (v. 5, vii. 10). LXX, Targum, and Jewish exegetes take עָנָה as a ל״ה verb, *to be humbled,* and this suits both contexts. But בְּפָנָיו , *to his face,* almost compels us to take עָנָה as a ל״י verb, *to witness against* (cf. Job xvi. 8 ; Jer. xiv. 7). Hence Wellhausen renders ' With his arrogance Israel witnesses against himself,' and confirms the plaint of Yahweh—the arrogance being trust in ritual and feeling no need to turn from that and repent (cf. vii. 10). Orelli quotes Amos vi. 8 and Nahum ii. 3, and says injustice cleaves to all Israel's splendour, so it testifies against him. But the context, which in both cases speaks of Israel's decay, demands the interpretation that Israel's grandeur shows signs of breaking down. For the ethical development of this interpretation see Ch. XXII.

[2] For *month* חֹדֶשׁ some read חֶרֶשׁ *destruction*, cf. LXX ἐρυσίβη.
Marti : *now shall a destroyer destroy them.*

8. *Blow ye the horn in Gibeah,*
   The trumpet in Ramah,
   Rouse the slogan, Beth-Aven,[1]
   ' After thee Benjamin ! '

So the Hebrew text reads to the letter of the tribe's
ancient war-cry ;[2] but by a slight emendation some
render *Set Benjamin in a panic.*

9. *Ephraim becomes a waste*
   In the day of rebuke.
   Upon the tribes of Israel
   I make known what is sure.

At this point the discourse swerves from the religious to
the political leaders ; but as princes were included with
priests in the exordium we can hardly count this as a
fresh oracle.   He likens them to the lowest of cheats.

10. *The princes of Judah*[3] *become*
    Like removers of landmarks.
    Upon them I will pour
    Like water My wrath.
11. *Ephraim oppresses,*
    He breaks down right,[4]
    Israel [5] *has wilfully*
    Gone after vanity.[6]

---

[1] Wellhausen and others read *Bethel.*   [2] Judges v. 14.
[3] So Heb. and LXX, but most recent critics substitute *Israel ;* see
p. 233.
[4] In this couplet the verbs in Heb. are passive participles.   But LXX
is right in taking them as actives ; so most moderns.
[5] With others I take *Israel* to have dropped out of the Heb. text,
through the likeness of its letters to those of the predicate in this line,
which indeed is too short without *Israel.*
[6] For Heb. צַו read שָׁוְא or שְׁו ; so LXX.

v. 12. *But as the moth am I to Ephraim*
And like rot to the House of Judah.

Here again, and in the next verse, some would substitute *Israel* for *Judah*, but as it seems needlessly, for by this time Uzziah of Judah was dead and the weak politicians in charge whom Isaiah satirised.

13. *And Ephraim saw his sickness,*
And Judah his sore,
And Ephraim went to Asshûr,
And sent to King Yarib.

Many explanations of this name are given and emendations of it.[1] But I still think it a nickname for the Assyrian monarch, *King Combative, King Pick-Quarrel ;*[2] and if so the verse refers to the tribute sent by Menahem to the king of Assyria in 738, and Israel has drifted full five years into his ' thick night.' But if in the interests of parallelism we are (with Wellhausen) to introduce *Judah* before *sent* then the date of the verse is brought down to 734 in the reign of Ahaz.

But he is helpless to heal you
Or to dry your sore from off you.
14. *For I am as a lion to Ephraim,*
As the whelp of a lion to Judah's House.
I, I rend and I go My way,
I carry off with none to deliver.

It is the truth which Isaiah expressed with even greater grimness.[3] God is His people's sore ; and not all their

---
[1] For a full list see Harper *in loco*. Some read *the great King*.
[2] Similarly Guthe, *King Fighting-Cock ;* and A. R. Gordon. **Marti,** Moffatt, etc., *the great King*. LXX reads Ιαρειμ.
[3] See *Isaiah i-xxxix*, p. 249.

statecraft nor alliances can avert or heal what He inflicts. Priests and princes then have alike failed. A greater failure follows.

3. REPENTANCE FAILS

Hosea v. 15–vii. 2

Seeing that their leaders are helpless, and feeling their wounds, the people may themselves turn to God for healing, but that will be with repentance so shallow as also to be futile. They have no conviction of sin, nor sense of how deeply their evils have eaten.

This too facile repentance is expressed in a prayer which the Christian Church has paraphrased, but only by ethical additions,[1] into one of the most spiritual of its numerous hymns of conversion. Yet the introduction to this prayer, and the easy assurance of how soon God will heal the wounds He has made, as well as the impatience with which God receives it, oblige us to take the prayer in another sense than the hymn which has been derived from it.[2] It offers one more symptom of the optimism of this light-hearted people, whom no discipline and no judgement can impress with the reality of their incurable decay. They said of themselves, *The bricks are fallen, let us*

---

[1] *E.g.*, ' Come let us to the Lord our God *with contrite hearts* return '.

[2] Similarly Ewald, Wellhausen, Nowack, Harper. Others, thinking this view ' forced and artificial,' read the resolutions v. 1–3 as sincere, but because of the lateness which they allege in both the spirit and some of the phrases of the passage, and because the passage disturbs the connection between what precedes and what follows it, take it as an insertion dating from the Exile : so Cheyne with the addition of v. 15*a* and vi. 4 (Introd. to W. R. Smith's *Prophets*), Marti, with the addition of v. 15*a* and vi. 5*b*, and Volz (*Jahweprophetie*, p. 33). Their arguments are not convincing.

build with stones,[1] and now they say just as easily and airily of their God, *He hath torn* only *that He may heal:* we are fallen, but *He will raise us up again in a day or two.* At first it is still God who speaks.

v. 14e. *I go, I return to My Place,*[2]
    15. *Until they are startled*[3] *and seek My Face,*
        When trouble is theirs they soon will seek Me,
          Saying:[4]
vi. 1. *Come, and let us return to Yahweh,*
      For He hath rent, that He may heal us,
      And hath wounded,[5] *to bind us up.*
    2. *He will give us life in a couple of days,*
      On the third day raise us again,
      That we may live on before Him.
    3. *And let us know, follow up*[6] *to know, Yahweh;*
      As soon as we seek Him, find Him we shall.[7]
      And He will come like the winter-rain to us,
      As the spring-rain pours on the land!

But how is this fair prayer received by God? With incredulity, impatience.

    4. *What can I make of thee, Ephraim?*
      What can I make of thee, Judah?
      Since your love is like the morning mist,
      And like the early gone dew.

---

[1] Isa. ix. 10.   [2] Cf. Isa. xviii. 4.

[3] For Heb. יאשמו , *they feel,* or *own,* or *have borne, their guilt* read with Wellhausen and others, יֵשֹׁמּוּ , *they are startled* or *appalled;* cf. LXX ἀφανισθῶσιν, Vulg. *deficiatis.*

[4] So LXX, Syr. Targ.; Heb. omits.

[5] Read with Syr., Wellhausen, and most moderns וְיַחְבְּשֵׁנוּ .

[6] Lit. *hunt,* the same as used of Israel's pursuit of the Ba‘alim, ii. 9.

[7] So, by a rearrangement of consonants (כשחרנו כן נמצאהו) and the help of LXX (εὑρήσομεν αὐτόν), Giesebrecht (*Beiträge,* p. 208) proposes to read the clause, which in the traditional text runs, *like the morn His going forth shall be certain.*

Their shallow hearts need deepening. Have they not been deepened enough ?

> 5. *Wherefore I hewed by the prophets,*
> *I slew them by words of My Mouth,*
> *And My judgement goes forth like the lightning.*[1]
> 6. *For leal love has been My desire*
> *And not sacrifice,*
> *And the knowledge of God*
> *More than burnt-offerings.*

That the discourse comes back to the ritual is intelligible. For what could make repentance seem so easy as belief that forgiveness can be won by offering sacrifices ? Then the prophet leaps upon what each new year of that anarchy revealed afresh—the profound sinfulness of the people.

Hosea will now point out the places of their sin :

> 7. *But they in Adam (?)* [2] *have broken the covenant.*
> *There have betrayed* [3] *Me !*
> 8. *Gilead* [4] *is a city of doers of evil,*
> *Stamped with the footprints of blood.*
> 9. *Assassins,* [5] *marauders,*
> *A pack* [6] *of priests,*

---

[1] Read מִשְׁפָּטִי כָאוֹר יֵצֵא .

[2] A place-name seems here required parallel to *Gilead* in ver. 8, yet *Adam* as such is now unknown, but some read in Admah, cf. **xi. 8.** Heb. and Vulg. have *like Adam*, which some render *like men* (Harper), and some *like the heathen* (Guthe) ; Gardner, without cause, *in Shechem*.

[3] This verb = to be false to a contract, especially of marriage.

[4] For Gilead a city see Judges x. 17 ; uncertain whether Ramoth-Gilead, or Jabesh-Gilead, or Mispah the capital of Gilead.

[5] Read מְחַכֵּי אִישׁ lit. *that lie in wait for a man*.

[6] Or *gang,* חֶבֶר .

> *On the way to Shechem they murder,*
> *How they work villainy !* [1]

vi. 10. *In the house of Israel I have seen horrors,*
> *There Ephraim has played* [2] *the harlot,*
> *Defiled herself Israel !*

11. *[Judah, for thee too a harvest is set.]*

The first three lines of ver. 9 are uncertain in text and grammar. Following hints of the Septuagint many moderns read : *as marauders lie in wait for a man, the priests hide themselves on the road.*[3] Shechem was not only a city of priests and of refuge, and therefore of ways of pilgrims, but of all the centres on the Western Range it stood most open to approach from Eastern Palestine, by the fords of Jordan only eighteen miles away,[4] and thus *the way to Shechem* comes in here naturally after Gilead in the preceding verse. For *house of Israel* some [5] read *Bethel* because of *there* in the next line ; but this is unnecessary. The first line in ver. 11 is surely a gloss.[6]

The sinfulness of Israel is without end. Every effort to redeem them only discovers more of it.

11b. *When I would turn the fate of My people* (?),
vii. 1. *When Israel I would heal,*
> *Ephraim's guilt lays itself open*
> *And Samaria's evils—*

---

[1] In several O.T. verses the word equals *unchastity*. If that be accepted here the line connects logically with what follows, not with what precedes it.

[2] Read זָנָה (Oort) or זָנִיתָ (Wellhausen, etc.).

[3] So with variations most critics since Hitzig and Ewald ; reading with LXX ἔκρυψαν חבאו for חבר, and bringing in *on the way* from the next line.

[4] See my *Hist. Geog.*, pp. 119, 332.

[5] Since Wellhausen.   [6] So virtually all moderns.

How they exercise fraud,
And the thief steals into the house [1]
And crews of highwaymen foray. [2]

2. *And they never think in their hearts*
That I register all their evil ;
Their doings do now so beset them
That full in My face they are.

Evidently real repentance on the part of such a
people is impossible. As Hosea said before, *Their
deeds will not let them return.* [3]

4. WICKEDNESS IN HIGH PLACES

Hosea vii. 3–7

There follows another difficult passage. The text is
corrupt, and we have no means of determining what
events are intended. The drift of meaning, however,
is evident. The disorder and licentiousness of the
people are favoured in high places ; the throne is
guilty.

3. *With their evil they make a king* [4] *glad,* [5]
And with their falsehoods princes.

---

[1] Heb. omits *the house*, but LXX has πρὸς αὐτὸν, which is probably
a mistake for πρὸς οἶκον ; cf. Joel ii. 9, and N.T. *come as thief.*

[2] Lit. *marauders foray on the street* or *road* or *abroad.*

[3] v. 4.

[4] LXX *kings.*

[5] So Heb., old versions, the previous editions of this work, Cheyne,
and Moffatt, reading יִשְׂמְחוּ . But Wellhausen, Nowack, Oort, Marti,
and Harper read יִמְשְׁחוּ . *they anoint*, and understand the couplet as of
the frequent king-making of the time.

vii. 4. *All of them adulterers are*
Like an oven heated up by the baker

. . . . (?) [1]

5. *On the day of our king they were sick,*
The princes with fever of wine. [2]
He stretched out his hand to loose fellows, [3]

6. *Yea, they have fired* [4] *like an oven*
Their heart with their intrigues ;
All the night sleeps their anger, [5]
In the morning it blazes
A flaming fire.

7. *All of them glow like an oven*
And eat up their rulers.
All of their kings have fallen
None of them calls upon Me.

An obscure passage ; yet so lurid with the passion
of the people in the flagrant years 743–735 that we can
make out the crimes described. A king surrounded
by loose, unscrupulous nobles : adultery, drunkenness,
conspiracies, assassinations : every man striking for
himself ; none appealing in truth to God.

---

[1] The text is unsound. Heb.: ' like an oven kindled by the baker,
the stirrer (stoker or kneader ?) rests from kneading the dough until it
be leavened.' LXX : ὡς κλίβανος καιόμενος εἰς πέψιν κατακαύματος ἀπὸ
τῆς φλογός ἀπὸ φυράσεως στέατος ἕως τοῦ ξυμωθῆναι αὐτό—i.e., for ישבת
they read אש להבת . Oort emends Heb. to בוער הם אפהו , which
gets rid of the difficulty of a feminine participle with תנור . Wellhausen,
Marti, etc., omit the clause as a gloss on ver. 6. But if there be a gloss it
commences with ישבת .

[2] Marti emends the text to *they made our king sick and our princes*
with fever from wine ; understand by *our king* Ṣacharyah and the year
as 742 B.C.

[3] A gloss according to Marti and others.

[4] So LXX ; Heb. *they have made like.*

[5] אפהם . see Targ. and Syr.: Heb., with different points, אפהם ,
their baker.

From the court, then, downwards, by princes, priests, and prophets, to the common fathers of Israel and their households, immorality prevails. There is no redeeming feature, nor hope of better things. For repentance itself the capacity is gone.

In making so thorough an indictment of the moral condition of Israel, it would have been impossible for Hosea not to speak also of the political stupidity and restlessness which resulted from it. But he has largely reserved these for that part of his discourse which follows, and which we take in the next chapter.

CHAPTER XVII

A PEOPLE IN DECAY: II. POLITICALLY

HOSEA VII. 8–X

MORAL decay means political decay. Sins like those are the gangrene of nations. Part of Hosea's greatness is to have traced this, with the versatility which distinguishes him. The most spiritual of prophets, he is also one of the most political. We owe him an analysis of repentance to which the New Testament has little to add;[1] but he has also left us a criticism of society and of politics, unrivalled except by Isaiah. We owe him a conception of God,[2] which for the first time in Israel exploded idolatry; he also was the first to define Israel's position in the politics of Western Asia. With the simple courage of conscience Amos had said to the people: You are bad, therefore you perish. But Hosea had insight to follow the process by which sin brings death—to trace, for instance, the effects of impurity upon a nation's powers of reproduction, as well as upon its intellectual vigour.

So intimate are these two faculties of Hosea, that in chapters devoted to the sins of Israel we have seen him expose the disasters which follow. But from the point we have reached—vii. 8—the proportion is

[1] See below, Ch. XXII.   [2] See Ch. XXI.

reversed: he gives less of the sin and more of the social decay and political folly of his generation.

1. THE CONFUSION OF THE NATION

Hosea vii. 8–viii. 3

Hosea begins by summing up the public aspect of Israel in two epigrams, short but keenly apt :—

vii. 8. *Ephraim among the peoples*
Mixes himself up,[1]
Ephraim is become a cake
Not turned over.

It is a crisis for a nation to pass from the seclusion of its youth and become a factor in the history of the world. For Israel the crisis was trebly great. Their difference from other tribes had struck their neighbours on their entry to the land :[2] their earliest writers had emphasised their seclusion as their strength ;[3] and their first prophets deprecated overtures made by them to Egypt or Assyria. We feel the force of the prophets' warnings when we remember what happened to the Philistines. These were a people as strong and distinctive as Israel, with whom at one time they disputed possession of the land. But their position as traders on the line of traffic between Asia and Africa rendered the Philistines very open to foreign influence. They were now Egyptian vassals, now Assyrian victims ; and after the invasion of Alexander the Great their cities became centres of Hellenism, while the Jews upon their hills stubbornly held unmixed their race

---

[1] See p. 293, n. 1.   [2] Num. xxiii. 9b ; Josh. ii. 9.
[3] Deut. xxxiii. 28.

and their religion. This contrast, thus developed in later centuries, has justified the prophets of the eighth in their anxiety that Israel should not annul the advantages of her seclusion by trade or treaties with the Gentiles. But it was easier for Judah to take heed than for Ephraim. The latter lay as open and fertile as her sister-province was bare and aloof.[1] She had many gates into the world, and they led to many markets. Nobler opportunities there could not be for a nation in the maturity of its genius and loyal to its vocation :—

> Rejoice, O Zebulun, in thine outgoings :
> They shall call the nations to the mountain ;
> They shall suck of the abundance of the seas,
> And of the treasure stored in the sands.[2]

But in the time of his outgoings Ephraim was not sure of himself nor true to his God, the one secret of the national distinctiveness. So he met the world weak and unformed, and, instead of impressing it, was by it dissipated and confused. The tides of commerce scattered abroad the faculties of the people, and swept back upon their life alien fashions and tempers, to control which there was neither native strength nor definiteness of national purpose. This is what Hosea means by the first of his epigrams : *Ephraim—among the peoples he lets himself be poured out*, or *mixed up*. The form of the verb does not elsewhere occur ; but it is reflexive, and the meaning of the root is certain. *Balal* is to *pour out*, or *mingle*, as of oil in the sacrificial flour. Yet it is sometimes used of a mixing not sacred, but profane and hopeless. It is applied to the first confusion of mankind, to which a popular etymology

----

[1] *Hist. Geog.*, Chs. XIV-XVI.   [2] Deut. xxxiii. 18, 19.

has traced the name Babel, as if for Balbel.   Deriva-
tives of the stem bear the additional ideas of staining
and impurity.   The alternative readings proposed, *lets
himself be soaked*, or *scatters himself* abroad like wheat
among tares, or *fades away* are not so apt or probable,
yet hardly change the meaning.[1]   Ephraim wastes and
confuses himself among the Gentiles.   The nation's
character is so disguised that Hosea afterwards nick-
names him Canaan ;[2]   their religion so filled with
foreign influences that he calls the people the harlot of
the Ba'alim.

If the first of Hosea's epigrams satirises Israel's
foreign relations, the second, with equal brevity and
wit, hits off the temper and constitution of society at
home.   For the metaphor of this epigram Hosea has
gone to the baker.   Among all classes in the East,
especially under conditions requiring haste, there is in
demand a round flat scone, which is baked by being
laid on hot stones or attached to the wall of an oven.
The art of baking consists in turning the scone over at
the proper moment.   If this be mismanaged, one side
may be burnt to a cinder, while the other remains raw.[3]
Ephraim, says Hosea, *is an unturned cake.*

[1] יִתְבּוֹלָל from בלל , confirmed by LXX συνεμίγνυτο.   In Phœn. בלל
seems to have been used as in Israel of the sacrificial mingling of oil and
flour (cf. Robertson Smith, *Religion of Semites*, I. 203) ; in Arabic *ball*
is to weaken a strong liquid with water, while *balbal* is to be confused,
disordered.   The Syriac *balal* is to mix.   Some have taken Hosea's
יתבלל as if from בליל (Isa. xxx. 24 ; Job vi. 5), usually understood as
a mixed crop of wheat and inferior vegetables for fodder ; but there is
reason to believe בליל means rather fresh corn.   The derivation from
בלה or נבל , *to fade* or *grow old* (Ewald, Oettli, Marti), does not seem
probable.

[2] xii. 7 (Eng.; 8 Heb.).

[3] Marti quotes the rhyme of the children's game :—

> Your bannocks are burning
> And ready for turning.

By this he may mean one of several things, or all of them together, for they are infectious of each other. There was the social condition of the people. What can better be described as an unturned scone than a community one half of whose number are too rich, and the other too poor ? Or Hosea may refer to that unequal distribution of religion through life with which he elsewhere reproaches Israel. They keep their religion, as Amos more fully tells us, for their temples, and neglect its spirit in their daily business. Or he may refer to Israel's politics, which were equally in want of thoroughness. They rushed hotly at an enterprise, but having expended so much fire in the beginning of it, they let the end drop cold and dead. Or he may wish to satirise, like Amos, Israel's imperfect culture—the pretentious and overdone arts, stuck excrescencewise upon the unrefined bulk of the nation, just as in many German principalities of the eighteenth century society took on French fashions in rough and exaggerated forms, while at heart still brutal and coarse. Hosea may mean any of these, for the figure suits all, and all spring from the same defect. Want of thoroughness and equable effort was Israel's besetting sin, and it told on every side of their life. How better describe a half-fed people, a half-cultured society, a half-lived religion, a half-hearted policy, than by a half-baked bannock ?

We who are proud of our political bakers, we who scorn the rapid revolutions of our neighbours and complacently dwell upon our equable ovens, those slow and cautious centuries of political development which lie behind us—have we anything better than our neighbours, anything better than Israel, to show in our civilisation ? Hosea's epigram fits us to the letter. After all those ages of baking, society is still with us

an unturned scone : one side of the nation with the
strength burnt out of it by too much enjoyment of life,
the other with not enough of warmth to be quickened
into anything like adequate vitality.   No man can deny
this ; we are able to live only by shutting our hearts
to the fact.   Or is religion equably distributed through
the lives of the religious portion of our nation ?   Of
how many Christians is it true that they are but half-
baked—living a life one side of which reeks with the
smoke of sacrifice, while the other is never warmed by
one religious thought.   We may have too much religion if
we confine it to one day or one department of life : our
worship overdone, with the sap and the freshness burnt
out of it, cindery, dusty, unattractive, fit only for
crumbling ; our conduct cold, damp, and heavy, like
dough the fire has never reached.

Upon the theme of these two epigrams the other
verses of this chapter are variations.   Has Ephraim
mixed himself among the peoples ?   Senselessly con-
gratulating himself upon the increase of his trade and
wealth, he does not feel that these have sucked from
him his distinctive virtue as well as much of his money.
He makes his energy the measure of his life, as Isaiah
also marked,[1] but sees not that it all means waste and
decay.   Even when the national pride is cut to the
quick by humiliating overtures both to Egypt and to
Assyria, they seek not their own God.

vii.   9.   *Foreigners devour his strength*
            And he knows it not,
          Grey hairs, too, are sprinkled upon him
            And he knows it not.
     10.   *And the pride of Israel testifies to his face.*[2]

[1] ix. 9.
[2] See above, p. 280, and below, p. 364.   See also Harper, p. 303

Yet they turn not to Yahweh their God
Nor seek Him because of all this.[1]

With virtue and single-hearted faith have disappeared
intellect, expressed as before by *heart*, and the capacity
for affairs. The *silly pigeon* of a people flutters from
one refuge to another. But God will bring them down.

vii. 11. *And Ephraim is become like a dove,*
    Silly and senseless.[2]
    Unto Egypt they cry,
      They are off to Assyria.

12. *As soon as they are off*
    I fling o'er them My net,
    Like birds of the air bring them down,
      Scourge them by the fulness of their afflic-
      tions.(?) [3]

13. *Woe be to them that they strayed from Me,*
    Damnation be theirs, that from Me they revolted !
    And I, I would have redeemed them,
    But they, they spoke lies against Me.

[1] The tenses in this verse render the exact meaning uncertain. Harper
and others agree with the above in taking the clauses as co-ordinate.
But Ewald, Wellhausen, Nowack translate : *Israel's pride testifies to his
face and that they turn not*, etc. Marti and Moffatt dismiss the verse
as a gloss ; to the reasons Marti gives might be added the difference of
its metre from that of the context, though even this is not a conclusive
proof of unauthenticity.

[2] Heb. *without heart* or *brains ;* see p. 275 f.

[3] Heb. lit. *as the hearing of*, or *message to*, *their congregation*, proclaimed by their prophets. But this is doubtful, as the Versions show ;
LXX : Παιδεύσω αὐτοὺς ἐν τῇ ἀκοῇ τῆς Θλίψεως αὐτῶν, *in the hearing of
their affliction*, reading for צָרָתָם לַעֲדָתָם ; which some modify to
עַל רָעָתָם , *because of their wickedness* (Vollers, Oettli, Marti) ; but preferable is the reading בְּשֵׁבַע לְצָרָתָם (Gardner, Harper) adopted above.

Yet all is conjectural. Budde (*Zeitschrift für Assyriologie*, xxvi, 1911,
pp. 30 ff.) emends and renders thus : ' Sobald sie auffliegen, aus der Luft
hol' ich sie herunter, Putze sie fort, sobald man ihr Welschen hört '

14. *They cried not to Me with their hearts,*
    But keep howling upon their beds ; [1]
    For corn and new wine they gash them, [2]
    They rebel against Me.

No real repentance theirs, but fear of drought and
miscarriage of the harvests, a sensual and servile
sorrow in which they wallow. They seek God with
no appreciation of what He is, but use the senseless
means by which the heathen invoke their gods. The
next lines emphasise their fickle repentance ; conversion
for them is not Godward, but swerving on some impulse
of their ill-balanced natures.

15. *I, I trained,* [3] *I strengthened their arms,*
    But towards Me they keep thinking evil.
16. *They turn but not upwards* (?) [4]
    They are as a bow that swerves :
    Their princes must fall by the sword
    For the insolence [5] *of their tongues—*
    This their rebuff [6] *in the land of Egypt.*

For *insolence* we might have expected *falseness* or
duplicity ; the Septuagint has *want of culture* or *training.*
To the allusion in the last line we have no key. In the

---

[1] So Heb. and LXX, but Gardner and others propose *by their altars*

[2] For יִתְגּוֹרָרוּ read with LXX and some Heb. MSS. יִתְגּוֹדָדוּ .

[3] Omitted by some moderns.

[4] So literally the Heb. But LXX has εἰς οὐθέν, *to nothing,* which
suggests to some to emend the Heb. עַל לֹא , that is elliptic, to אֶל אַל
or to לַבַּעַל , *to Baal* (Marti, Harper, Moffatt).

[5] Or (as in previous editions of this work) *bitterness.* This word is
used only of God in the O.T. except in Jer. xv 17, where it is used of
men and so may be used here (this against Marti).

[6] Or *scorn ;* taken as a gloss by some (Marti, Harper), but unnecessarily.

negotiations with Egypt they had either been deceitful
or had overdone their case.   But the text is uncertain.

With so false a people nothing can be done.   Their
doom is inevitable, in spite of their appeal to their
God.

viii. 1. *To thy mouth* [1] *with the trump,* [1]
           For an eagle is down on the house of Yahweh.
           For they have transgressed My Covenant,
           And rebelled against My Law.
       2. *To Me they cry, My God,*
           We know Thee, we Israel.
       3. *Israel hath spurned the good,* [2]
           The foe must pursue him !

It is the same climax of inevitable war to which
Amos led up his periods ; and a new subject is now
introduced.

2. ARTIFICIAL KINGS AND ARTIFICIAL GODS

Hosea viii. 4–13

The curse of such a state of dissipation as that to
which Israel had fallen is that it produces no men.
Had the people had in them ' the root of the matter,'
had there been the stalk and the fibre of a national
consciousness and purpose, it would have blossomed to

---

[1] Wellhausen's objection, that one does not set a trumpet to one's
gums, which חֵךְ literally means, is beside the mark. חֵךְ is more than
once used of the mouth (Job xii. 11 ; Prov. v. 3).   The next line gives
the reason of the trumpet, the alarum trumpet.   Read כִּי נֶשֶׁר (so also
Wellhausen and Harper).

[2] Cf. Amos : *Seek Me = Seek the good ;* and Jesus : *Not every one
that saith unto Me, Lord, Lord ; but he that doeth the will of My Father
in heaven.*

a man.   Israel would have produced a leader, a heaven-
sent king, if the national spirit had not been squandered
on foreign trade and fashions.   But after the death of
Jeroboam every man who rose in Israel, rose, not on
the nation, but on the fevered and transient impulse of
some faction ; and through the broken years one party
monarch after another was lifted to the brief tenancy
of a blood-stained throne.   They were not from God,
these monarchs ; but man-made, and sooner or later
man-murdered.   Hosea likens these artificial kings to
the artificial gods, also the work of men's hands ; and
till near the close of his book the idols of the sanctuary
and the puppets of the throne form the twin targets of
his scorn.   But king after king, idol upon idol shall be
cut off.   All shall go to splinters.   They have sown
the wind and shall reap the whirlwind.   Clear, again,
is the note of Israel's dissipation of themselves among
foreigners.   This wilful roaming can only end in com-
pulsory exile, when all their unholy, artificial politics
and worship shall cease.

4. *Kings have they made but not from Me,*
   Princes have made and I knew it not ;
   With their silver and gold they made them idols—
   That they [1] *may be cut off !*
5. *Thy Calf I loathe,* [2] *O Samaria,*
   My wrath is kindled against it. [3]
   [How long shall they be incapable of cleanness ?] [4]

[1] So LXX, etc. ; Heb. *he* or *it*. Harper's reasons for taking the
whole line as a gloss, because it breaks the continuity and disturbs the
metre, are groundless.
[2] So since Oort most moderns ; Heb. *He loathes.*
[3] So since Oort most moderns ; Heb. *them.*
[4] Whether this interjected line is Hosea's or thrown in by a later
scribe (Marti, Harper, etc.) is a question ; probably the latter. Gardner
alters it to *how long shall they not be able to understand that it is from
Israel.*

viii. 6. *For it also* [1] *is out of Israel,*
A craftsman made it—God it is not. [2]
Splinters it shall become—
The Calf of Samaria !

The text of the rest of this chapter is very difficult ;
the following translation makes the most of it as it
stands, but with help from the Septuagint ; many are
the emendations naturally provoked by it.   Before the
whirlwind that he sees Israel's mad politics raising the
prophet's metaphors scatter like leaves.   The second
couplet, in rhyme, is probably a popular proverb.

7. *For wind are they sowing,*
And whirlwind shall reap.
Stock without shoot
Shall never yield fruit ; [3]
Perchance it did, strangers would swallow it. [4]

8. *Swallowed is Israel,*
Become now among the nations
Like a purposeless vessel.

9. *For they have gone up to Asshûr,*
Wild-ass [5] *running off by himself,*
Ephraim [5] *gives love-gifts.*

[1] A. B. Davidson, *Syntax*, § 136, Rem. 1.

[2] This couplet also Marti (almost alone) takes as a late insertion.

[3] Lit. *corn with no shoot* or *sprout to it shall never yield wheat* or
meal.   But the two lines rhyme : kamah 'en lô semach—b'lî ya'aseh
kemach.   For lô we should perhaps read lah.

[4] Marti takes this as a gloss, but ' without good reason ' (Harper).

[5] A play upon words P(h)ere, *wild-ass*, and *Ephraim*.   But for
P(h)ere Marti reads *Ephraim* (LXX has no trace of *P(h)ere*) and transfers
the line to be the second in ver. 8 ;   while for *Ephraim* some with Wellhausen read *Miṣraim, to Egypt gives love-gifts.*

> 10. *Yea as they give them away through the*
>   *nations (?)*
>   *Already I gather them in.*[1]
>   *And soon shall they cease to anoint*
>   *A king and princes.*[2]
> 11. *As Ephraim has multiplied altars*
>   *They have been to him altars to sin.*
> 12. *Should I write him My laws by the myriad.*[3]
>   *As a stranger's they would be accounted.*
> 13. *Sacrifice they love and they sacrifice,*
>   *Flesh and they eat it.*
>   *Yahweh in them hath no pleasure.*[4]
>   *Now must He* [5] *remember their guilt*
>   *And visit upon them their sins.*
>   *They shall return to Egypt . . .* [6]

Back to their ancient servitude must they go, as God
had formerly said He would withdraw them into the
wilderness.

3. THE EFFECTS OF EXILE

Hosea ix. 1–9

Hosea now turns to describe the effects of exile
upon the social and religious habits of the people. It
must break up at once the joy and the sacredness of
their lives. Every pleasure will be removed, every
taste offended. Indeed, even now, with their conscience

---

[1] Marti and Harper, perhaps rightly, take this couplet as a gloss.
[2] So LXX reads this couplet. Heb.: *they shall involve themselves
with tribute to the king of princes*, presumably the Assyrian monarch.
[3] After LXX.
[4] Some take this line as a gloss.   [5] Some read *I*.
[6] Ver. 14 is surely an addition; it is not in the style of Hosea but is
based on that of Amos. See above, p. 232.

of having deserted their God, they cannot pretend to enjoy the feasts of the Ba'alim in the same hearty way as the heathen with whom they mix. But, whether or no, the time is near when nature-feasts and all other religious ceremonies—all that makes life glad and regular and solemn—shall be impossible. Yahweh cannot be worshipped in any land but His own. In exile Israel shall be divorced from religion, unable to hold communion with their God.

ix. 1. *Rejoice not, Israel,*
       Nor exult [1] *like the peoples,*
       For thou hast a-whored from thy God. [2]
       It is harlot's hire thou hast loved,
       Upon every threshing-floor. [3]
    2. *Threshing-floor and vat shall not know* [4] *them*
       And the new wine shall play them [5] *false.*
    3. *They shall not abide in the land of Yahweh,*
       But Ephraim shall return to Egypt
       And in Assyria eat the unclean,
    4. *Nor pour out to Yahweh wine*
       Nor prepare [6] *Him their sacrifices.*
       Like the bread of mourning their bread [7] *shall be,*
       Whereof all who eat defile themselves.
       Yea, for their hunger their bread shall be,
       They shall not bring it [8] *to Yahweh's House.*

---

[1] So LXX ; Heb. *to* (the pitch of) *exultation like the peoples, i.e.,* the *heathen*, here for the first time in that sense (Wellhausen).

[2] Marti without reason takes this line as a gloss.

[3] On this couplet see below, Ch. XXII.

[4] So LXX and most moderns by change of one consonant from Heb. *shall not feed them.*

[5] So all the ancient versions ; Heb. *her.*

[6] For יערבו read with Kuenen יערכו (Gardner יעברו). With the whole passage compare iii. 4 f.

[7] לחם for לחמם.   [8] Read יָבִיאוּ.

> 5. *What shall ye do for the days* [1] *of Assembly,*
>   *Or for the day of Yahweh's feast ?*
> 6. *For lo, they are gone to Assyria,* [2]
>   *Egypt shall gather them,*
>   *Memphis bury them.*
>   *Nettles shall own their silver shrines (?)*
>   *With thorns in their homes.*

The threat of exile still wavers between Assyria and Egypt. And in Egypt Memphis is chosen as the destined grave of Israel ; for even then her Pyramids and mausoleums were ancient and renowned, her vaults and sepulchres spacious and countless.

But what need is there to look to the future for Israel's doom, when already this is spiritually evident by their hostile, contemptuous attitude to their own prophets, perhaps Amos, perhaps Hosea himself, calling these *fools* and *mad*, and plotting their destruction.

> 7. *Come are the days of visitation,*
>   *Come are the days of requital,*
>   *Israel know* them already :
>   *' A fool is the prophet,*
>   *A madman the man of the spirit.'* [3]
>   *It is for the mass of thy guilt*
>   *And thy* [4] *multiplied treachery !*

[1] Plural : so LXX.

[2] So most moderns ; Heb. *have gone from destruction.* This is the prophetic perfect realising the future.

[3] This couplet can only be some outburst of the people against the prophet ; who replies in the next one.

[4] So LXX.

ix. 8. *Ephraim's watcher from* [1] *my God is the prophet :*
     But the fowler's snare is on all his ways,
     Enmity throughout the House [2] *of his God :*
    9. *They make deep his destruction* (?)
       As in Gibeah's days,
       Their guilt is remembered,
       Visitation is made on their sins.

So with as little emendation as possible I render what
is a pretty hopeless text.[3]   But the drift is clear.   With
a broken-up home behind him the prophet had to face
the deep, the insidious hostility of the nation.

These then were the symptoms of the political decay
which followed on Israel's immorality.   The national
spirit and unity of the people had disappeared.   Society
was half of it raw, half of it *fired* to a cinder.   The
nation, broken into factions, produced no man to lead,
no king with the stamp of God upon him.   Anarchy
prevailed ; monarchs were made and murdered.   There
was no prestige abroad, nothing but contempt among
the Gentiles for a people whom they had exhausted.
Judgement was inevitable by exile, nay, it was already
required by the contemptuous hostility of the people to
their prophet.

Hosea turns to probe a deeper corruption still.

---

[1] Reading מעם for עם ; the letter *mim* having probably been dropped
out through immediately following itself at the end of the previous word.

[2] That is, of course, not *temple* but *land*.

[3] For a drastic but precarious rearrangement of the text see Marti ;
also the considerable emendations of Wellhausen, Nowack, Harper,
Duhm, and Gardner.   Marti takes the last but Harper the last three lines
of ver. 9 as a later addition.

4. 'THE CORRUPTION THAT IS THROUGH LUST'

Hosea ix. 10–17: cf. iv. 11–14

Those who at present foster among us the revival of Paganism—without the Pagan conscience—and exalt licentiousness to an art, forget how frequently the human race has attempted their experiment, with more sincerity than they can put into it, and how invariably the result has been recorded by history to be weariness, decay, and death. On this occasion we have the story told to us by one who to the experience of the statesman adds the vision of the prophet.

Hosea's generation practised a periodical unchastity under the alleged sanction of religion. And, although their prophet told them that they could never do so with the abandon of the Pagans, for they carried the conscience of a higher faith, it appears that even the fathers of Israel resorted without shame to the licentious rites of the popular sanctuaries. In an earlier passage Hosea insists that all this must damage the people's intellect. *Harlotry takes away the brains.*[1] He has shown also how it confuses the family, and exposed the delusion that men may be impure and keep their womankind chaste.[2] But now he diagnoses another of the results of this sin. After tracing the sin, and the theory of life which permitted it, to their historical beginnings at the entry of the people into Canaan, he describes how the long practice of it leads to the decay of the national vigour, to barrenness, and a diminishing population.

[1] iv. 11.   [2] iv. 13, 14.

ix. 10. *Like grapes in the wilderness*
I found Israel,
Like firstlings on the fig-tree [1]
I looked on your fathers.
They, they came to Ba'al-Peor,
And gave themselves up to Ba'al, [2]
And became abominations
Like the thing of their love.

11. *Ephraim are like birds,*
Fluttering off is their glory
No more birth, no more motherhood,
No more conception !

[3] **16** *Smitten is Ephraim,*
Withered their root,
Fruit they shall never produce.
Even though they were bearing
To death would I do the darlings of their womb.

12. *Even if their children they reared*
To a man I would bereave them.
Yea also woe to themselves
When I turn from them ! [4]

13. *Ephraim, as I have seen,(?)*
For prey [5] *are his sons destined,* [6]
Ephraim to bring forth
His own sons to the slaughter.

---

[1] Heb. adds *in its first season ;* but this is superfluous both to sense and to metre. Syr. omits and so most moderns.

[2] Heb. *bôsheth, shame,* but this is the usual substitution by later scribes for the name it was unlawful to utter. See Driver on 2 Sam. iv. 4.

[3] Wellhausen, Nowack, Oettli, and Harper transfer here this verse as I did in my first edition ; Marti only the last couplet. Where it stands in the text it disturbs the connection.

[4] This couplet, which Marti takes as a gloss, Harper and Moffatt transfer to the end of 15.

[5] For לָצוֹר , which is unintelligible, read, with LXX, εἰς θηραν, לָצַיד

For further emendations see Marti and Harper.

[6] After the LXX.

The prophet then breaks out in his own person :—

> 14. *Give them, O Yahweh,*
> *What wilt Thou give ?*
> *Give them mis-carrying wombs* [1]
> *And shrivelling breasts !*

In the next verse we have again the Voice of the
Lord :—

> 15. *Their wickedness all is in Gilgal,*
> *There have I learned to hate them ;*
> *Because of the evil of their doings*
> *Out of My House* [2] *I will drive them,*
> *No more will I love them,*
> *All their nobles are rebels.* [3]

And finally once more the prophet :—

> 17. *My God will cast them away.*
> *For they hearkened not to Him,*
> *And they shall be vagabonds thorough the nations.*

Some of the warnings which Hosea enforces upon
this sin have been instinctively felt by mankind since
the beginnings of civilisation, and are found expressed
among the proverbs of many languages. [4] But I am

---

[1] Heb. singular but collective.   [2] Again meaning *the Land.*
[3] Assonant for so is the original, *sārĕhem sôrerîm.*
[4] Cf., *e.g.*, the *Proverbs of Ptah-Hotep* the Egyptian, *circa* 2500 B.C.
' There is no prudence in taking part in it, and thousands of men destroy
themselves in order to enjoy a moment, brief as a dream, while they
gain death so as to know it. It is a villainous . . . that of a man who
excites himself (?) ; if he goes on to carry it out, his mind abandons
him. For as for him who is without repugnance for such an [act], there
is no good sense at all in him.'—From the translation in *Records of the
Past*, Second Series, vol. iii, p. 24.

unaware of any earlier moralist who traced the effects
of national licentiousness in a diminishing population,
or who exposed the delusion of libertine men that they
may resort to vice, yet keep their womankind chaste.
Hosea appears to have been the first to do this.   History in many periods has confirmed the justice of his
observations, and by one strong voice after another
enforced his warnings.   The experience of ancient
Persia and Egypt ;   the languor of the Greek cities ;
the ' deep weariness and sated lust ' which in Imperial
Rome ' made human life a hell ' ;   the decay which
overtook Italy after the renascence of Paganism without
the Pagan virtues ;   the strife and anarchy that rent
every court where, as in the case of Henri Quatre, the
king set the example of licentiousness ;   the incom-
petence, poltroonery, and treachery that have corrupted
every camp where, as in French Metz in 1870, soldiers
and officers gave way to open vice ;   the checks suffered
by modern civilisation in face of barbarism because its
pioneers mingled in vice with the races they were subduing ;   the number of statesmen falling by their
passion, and in their fall frustrating national hopes ;
the great families worn out by indulgence ;   the homes
broken up by infidelities ;   the tainting of the blood of
a new generation by the poisonous practices of the old,
—have not all these things been in every age, and do
they not still happen near enough to ourselves to give
us a dread of the sin which causes them ?   How slow
men are to listen and to lay to heart !   Can we gild by
the names of frivolity and piquancy habits the wages
of which are death ?   Is it possible to enjoy comedies
which make such things their jest ?   We have with us
some who find their business in the theatre, or in some
of our periodical literature, in writing, speaking, or
exhibiting as closely as they dare to the limits of

decency. When will they learn that it is not on the easy edge of mere conventions they caper, but upon the brink of those eternal laws whose further side is death and hell—that it is not the tolerance of their fellows they are testing, but the patience of God Himself ? As for those loud few who claim licence in the name of art, let us not shrink from them as if they were strong or their high words true. They are not strong, but only reckless ; their claims are lies. All history, the poets and the prophets, Christian or Pagan, are against them. They are traitors alike to art, to love, and to other high interests of mankind.

It may be said that part of the art of the day, which freely deals with these subjects, is exercised by ambition to expose that decay which Hosea affirms. This is true. Some of our ablest writers have pictured the facts, which Hosea describes, with so sober a realism that we cannot but judge them inspired to confirm his warnings, and excite a disgust of vice in a generation which otherwise treats vice so lightly. But if so, their ministry is narrow, and it is by their side that we best estimate the greatness of the ancient prophet. Their transcript of life may be true to the facts it selects, but we find in it no trace of facts greater and more essential to humanity. They have nothing to tell us of forgiveness and repentance, yet these are as real as the things they describe. Their pessimism is unrelieved. They see the *corruption that is in the world through lust ;* they forget that there is an *escape* from it.[1] Hosea's greatness is that, while he felt the vices of his day with thoroughness, he never allowed them to be inevitable or ultimate, but preached repentance and pardon, with the possibility of holiness even for his depraved

---

[1] 2 Peter i.

generation. It is the littleness of much of the art of our day that it forgets these great facts. When it remembers them again, the greatness of its past will return.

5. Once More : Puppet-Kings and Puppet-Gods

Hosea x

In the tenth chapter the prophet returns to the twin targets of his scorn : the idols and the puppet-kings. Observe the reiterated connection between the fertility of the land and the idolatry of the people. The uncertain text needs many notes.

> x. 1. *A wanton vine is Israel,*
> *His fruit he lavishes ;* [1]
> *The more his fruit has increased*
> *The more he has made his altars,*
> *The goodlier grew his land,*
> *The goodlier he made* his *pillars.* [2]
>
> 2. *Slippery* [3] *is their heart,*
> *Now must they pay for it.* [4]

---

[1] Doubtful. The Heb. text gives an inappropriate if not impossible clause, even if יְשַׁוֶּה be taken from a root שָׁוָה, to *set* or *produce* (Barth, *Etym. Stud.*, 66). LXX : ὁ καρπὸς εὐθηνῶν αὐτῆς (A.Q. αὐτῆς εὐθηνῶν), ' her [the vine's] fruit flourishing '. Some parallel is required to בקק of the first clause ; and it is possible that it may have been from a root שׁחח or שִׁיחַ, corresponding to Arabic sâh, to wander in the sense of scattering or being scattered. Marti reads נָאוָה, *lovely, beautiful.*

[2] Heb. *maṣṣēboth ;* the verb with it implies that they were artificial Heb. *they made.*

[3] Or *divided*, i.e., between Yahweh and Baal.

[4] LXX, *be destroyed* or *disappear*, as in v. 15.

> *Himself shall break the neck of their altars,*
> *He shall ruin their pillars.*

3. *For now they are saying,*
   No king is ours
   For Yahweh we have not feared (?),[1]
   And the king, what can he do for us?

4. *Speaking of words, swearing of falsehood,*
   Making of treaties,
   And law-suits (?) break out like weeds
   In the field's furrows.

5. *For the Calf [2] of Beth-Aven shall tremble*
   Samaria's dwellers,[3]
   Yea, his people shall mourn upon him
   And his priestlings howl [4] because of him.[5]

6. *Himself they shall pack to [6] Assyria,*
   To King Yareib as tribute.
   Disgrace shall Ephraim take
   And Israel be shamed of his counsel.[7]

7. *Undone is Samaria's king,*
   Like a chip [8] on the face of the waters,

---

[1] This confession, if that of Hosea's contemporaries, is surprising, unless it is his scorn for them that imagines it, which is possible. And is the judgement described in vv. 3, 4 consistent with that in 5-8? Because of these doubts Nowack, Marti, and Harper take 3, 4 as a later addition. *Lawsuits* is a questionable rendering for *mishpaṭ, judgement* or *right* or *law*. If we are to take it in any of these senses it is ironical. Some propose to read *mispaḥ, bloodshed.*

[2] So LXX; Heb. *calves* (feminine).

[3] So LXX; Heb. *dweller.*

[4] So with Wellhausen most moderns read: others *writhe;* Heb. the impossible *rejoice.*

[5] The text adds *for his glory that is exiled from him;* most take this as a gloss.

[6] So LXX; wanting in Heb.

[7] I agree with Harper that Wellhausen's reading *idols* is needless.

[8] קצף: compare Arabic qṣf, 'to break'; but there is also the assonant Arabic qṣb, 'reed.' The Rabbis translate *foam:* cf. the other meaning of קצף = outbreak of anger, which suggests *bubble.*

x. 8. *Ruined are Israel's shrines.*[1]
  Thistles and thorns are up on their altars.
  And they say to the mountains, Cover us,
  And to the hills, Fall upon us !

It cannot be too often repeated : these handmade gods, these chips of kings, shall be swept away.

Once more the prophet returns to the ancient origins of Israel's sins, and to their shirking of the discipline necessary for spiritual results, but only that he may lead up as before to the inevitable doom.

So much is clear in a text even more disordered than usual. With the least possible emendation it may be read :—

  9. *From*[2] *the days of Gibeah*[3] *thou hast sinned,*
    Israel,[4]
   There stood against Me the sons of iniquity,[5]
   Did not war overtake them[6] *in Gibeah ?*
  10. *When I will*[7] *to chastise them I shall,*

---

[1] Removing with most moderns the words *idolatry* and *sin* (so Heb.) as later additions.

[2] Or *more than in* (Rosenmüller and others).

[3] Not the days of the beginning of the monarchy (Wellhausen), for with this Hosea has no quarrel, but either the idolatry of Micah (Judges xvii. 3 ff.) or more probably the crime of Benjamin (xix. 22).

[4] Wellhausen, Nowack, Harper read *is the sin of Israel.*

[5] This and the next line are uncertain. With Ruben, Nowack, and Harper I have transferred *against the sons of iniquity* from the end of the verse ; and for עַל , *against*, read עָלָי , *against Me*. Other emendations have been proposed. For *stood* Wellhausen reads *betrayed*, Halévy, *said*, Gardner, *transgressed*. For the impossible עַלְוָה read with many MSS. עַוְלָה , *iniquity*.

[6] Reading הִשִּׂיגֵם for תַּשִּׂיגֵם (cf. Gardner). But some retain the latter *shall not war overtake them* in *Gibeah ?* even as far south as that (Harper).

[7] LXX, *I am come* ; Syr. *in My wrath*

And peoples [1] be gathered [2] against them
To chastise them for their double guilt.

This can scarcely be the two calves at Bethel and Dan. More probably it is still the idols and man-made kings. Now Hosea turns to the ambition of the people for religious results, without spiritual discipline. It is all very well for the young unmuzzled [3] beast to love the threshing-floor, but before this can be heaped with sheaves come the hard labours of ploughing and harrowing.

> 11. *Ephraim a young heifer trained,* [4]
> *Loving the threshing ;*
> *But I come upon [5] her fair neck,*
> *I will yoke [6] Ephraim,*
> *Judah [7] must plough,*
> *Jacob harrow for himself.*

> [8] 12. *Sow for you righteousness,*
> *Reap the fruit [9] of leal love,*

[1] Some take this as proof of lateness of the passage ; *peoples* being a frequent post-exilic term, while the early prophets always name Israel's foes ; but this is uncertain.

[2] Some read *I will gather*.

[3] Deut. xxv. 4 ; 1 Cor. ix. 9 ; 1 Tim. v. 18.

[4] Wellhausen, Nowack, Harper, etc., omit *trained* as a gloss.

[5] Harper and others render *spared*, lit. *passed over*. Marti and Duhm, *caused the yoke to pass upon*.

[6] Lit. *make to ride*, but in a secondary sense *to yoke* or *draw*.

[7] On *Judah* see above, p. 233. Some would read *Israel*.

[8] This verse is possibly late (Marti, Duhm) ; some of its grammar, the preposition *to* for the accusative, sounds so ; and two of its phrases may be echoes of Jeremiah and Second Isaiah ; while ver. 13 naturally follows on 11. Yet all is uncertain, and several moderns take it as Hosea's (*e.g.*, Harper and Moffatt).

[9] After the LXX which reads *fruit of life ;* Heb. *reap in proportion to leal love.*

x. 12b. *Fallow up your fallow-ground,*[1]
There is time[2] *to seek Yahweh,*
Till He come and rain righting[3] *upon you.*

13. *Ye have ploughed in wickedness,*
Injustice have reaped,
Ye have eaten the fruit of lies.

Because thou dost trust in thy chariots,[4]
In the mass of thy warriors,

14. *War-tumult shall rise in thy tribes*[5]
And thy forts all be ruined,
As Shalman ruined Beth-Arbel.[6]
In the day of war shall the mother
Be broken upon the children.[7]

15. *Thus shall I do to you, House of Israel ;*[8]
Because of your utter wickedness
Soon undone shall be Israel's king.

The political decay of Israel, so deeply figured in these chapters, must end in collapse. Let us sum up

---

[1] Heb. *niru lakhem nir ;* also in English verb and noun are the same, *to fallow* or *fallow up = break* or *plough up* (Oxford Dictionary). Jer. iv. 3 also has this phrase. It is impossible to say that he quotes it from here or that it is here quoted from him ; it probably was a current saying.

[2] For Heb. וְעֵת, Oort, etc., read דַּעַת, *knowledge*, LXX, γνώσεως.

[3] צֶדֶק, *righteousness*, but here in the sense in which it frequently occurs in the Second Isaiah of *righting* or *salvation ;* see *Isaiah xl–lx*, pp. 237, 243, etc. But Harper after LXX, γενήματα, reads פְּרִי, *fruit*, for וְיוֹרֶה, *and rain*, and renders *that the fruit of righteousness may come to you.* On this passage see further Ch. XXII.

[4] So LXX. Wellhausen and others suspect the whole clause.

[5] Wellhausen proposes בְּעָרֶךָ, *in thy cities*, for בְּעַמֶּיךָ, but there is no need.

[6] See above, p. 225, n. 5.

[7] *Mother =* the country, *children =* the cities.

[8] LXX ; Heb. *Beth-el.*

the features of this decay : the substance of the people scattered abroad ; the national spirit dissipated ; their prestige humbled ; the kings mere puppets ; the prophets corrupted ; the national vigour sapped by impurity ; idolatry conscious of its impotence.

CHAPTER XVIII

THE FATHERHOOD AND HUMANITY OF GOD

HOSEA XI

FROM the jungle of Hosea's travail the eleventh
chapter breaks a high and open mound. The
prophet enjoys the first of his two clear visions—that
of the Past.[1] Judgement continues to descend. Israel's
Sun is near setting, but before he sinks—

> ' A lingering light he fondly throws
> On the dear hills, whence first he rose.'

Across the confused and vicious years, through which
he has made his way, Hosea sees the romance of the
early history of his people. And although he must
strike the old despairing note—that, by the insincerity
of the present generation, the ancient guidance of their
God must end in this !—yet for moments the blessed
memory shines by itself, and God's mercy appears
to triumph over Israel's ingratitude. Surely their sun
will not set ; Love must prevail. To which assurance
a later voice from the Exile has added, in vv. 10 and
11, a confirmation suitable to its own circumstances.

xi. 1. *When Israel was young I came to love him*
And from Egypt I called him to be My son.

[1] See above. p 269.

The early history of Israel was a romance. Before
the Most High there spread an array of kingdoms and
peoples. At their head were three strong princes,
sons of God, if all the heritage of the past, the power of
the present, and the promise of the future be tokens.
Egypt, wrapt in the jewelled web of centuries, basked
by Nile and Pyramid, the wonder of the world's art
in his dreamy eyes. Opposite him Assyria, with barer
but more massive limbs, stood upon his highlands,
grasping the promise of the world's power. Between
the two, and using both, yet with his eyes westward
on an empire of which neither dreamed, the Phœnician
on his sea-coast built storehouses and sped navies, the
promise of the world's wealth. It remains the supreme
wonder of history that the true son of God, bearer of
His love and righteousness to mankind, should be found,
not only outside this powerful trinity, but in the puny
and despised captive of one of them, a people without
a country, without a history, and, if appearances be
true, still devoid of the rudiments of civilisation—a
child people and a slave.

That was the Romance, and Hosea shows the Grace
which made it. *When Israel was young I loved him.*
The verb is a distinct impulse : *I began, I learned,
to love him.* God's eyes, passing the princes of the
world, fell upon this slave boy, and He loved him
and gave him a career : *from Egypt I called* him *to be
My son.*

The persuasion of this made Israel. Their distinctiveness and character, their progress from a level with
other nomads to the rank of the religious teachers of
humanity, started from the memory of these facts—
that God loved them, and that God called them. This
was an unfailing conscience—the obligation that they
were not their own, the motive to repentance in their

backsliding, the hope of a destiny in their days of defeat and scattering.

Some may cavil at the narrow, national scale on which such a belief was held, but let them remember that it was held in trust for mankind. To snarl that Israel felt their sonship to God only for themselves, is to forget that it is they who have persuaded humanity that sonship as a trust is the only kind of sonship worth claiming. Almost every other nation of antiquity imagined a filial relation to the deity, but either through fabulous physical descent, often confined to kings and heroes, or by mystical mingling of the Divine with the human, which was just as gross and sensuous. Israel alone defined the connection as historical and moral. *The sons of God are begotten not of blood, nor of the will of the flesh, nor of the will of man, but of God.*[1] Sonship to God is not physical, but moral and historical, into which men are carried by awakening to the Divine love and authority. Israel, it is true, felt this only for the nation as a whole ;[2] but their conception of it embraced those moral contents which form the glory of Christ's doctrine of the Divine sonship of the individual. The belief that God is our Father does not come to us with our carnal birth—except in possibility : the persuasion of it is not conferred by our baptism except in so far as that is Christ's seal to the fact that God loves us and has marked us for His own. To us sonship is a becoming, not a being—the awakening of our minds to the surprise of a Father's undeserved mercy, the constraint of His authority and the assurance of the destiny He has for us. It is conferred by love, and confirmed by duty. Neither has power brought it,

[1] St. John's Gospel, i. 12, 13.
[2] Or occasionally for the king as the nation's representative.

nor wisdom, nor wealth, but it has come with the wonder that God loves us, and has always loved us, as well as in the sense of a vocation to serve Him. Sonship less than this is no sonship at all. But so much is possible to every man through Jesus Christ. His constant message is that the Father loves every one of us, and that if we *know*[1] that love, we are God's sons indeed. To them who feel it, adoption into the number of the sons of God comes with the wonder and romance which glorified God's choice of Israel. *Behold, what manner of love the Father hath bestowed upon us, that we should be called the sons of God.*[2]

But we cannot be loved by God and left where we are. Beyond the grace there lie the discipline and the destiny. We are called to freedom, from the world to God—each to run a course, and do a work, which can be done by no others. That Israel did not perceive this was God's sorrow with them.

> **xi. 2.** *The more*[3] *I called to them*
> *The further they went from Me.*[4]
> *They to the Ba'alim kept sacrificing,*
> *And burning incense to idols.*

But God persevered with grace, and the story is at first continued in the figure of Fatherhood with which it commenced ; then it changes to the metaphor of a humane man's goodness to his beasts.

---

[1] See below, pp. 347 ff.
[2] 1 John iii. 1.
[3] So rightly the LXX.
[4] LXX, rightly separating מִפְּנֵיהֶם into מִפְּנֵי and הֵם, which latter is the nominative to the next clause.

xi. 3. *But I, Myself, taught Ephraim to walk,*
  Taking them up on Mine [1] *arms,*
  Yet they knew not I healed [2] *them.*

This presumably was when they fell and hurt them
selves.   Or may we translate *nursed ?*

 4 *.With cords of a man I would draw them,*
  With bands of love.
  And be as one lifting the yoke [3] *from their jaws,*
  And gently [4] *would give them to eat.*

It is the picture of a team of bullocks, in charge of
kind driver.   Israel are no longer the wanton youn
cattle of the previous chapter, which need the yok
firmly fastened on their neck,[5] but a team of toilin
oxen mounting some steep road.   There is no nee
now for the rough ropes, by which frisky animals ar
kept to their work ; but the driver, coming to hi
beasts' heads, by the gentle touch of his hand at thei
mouths and by words of sympathy *draws* them afte
him.   *I would draw them with cords of a man, with band
of love.*   Yet yoke is there, and it would seem tha
certain forms of this, when beasts were working up
wards, as we should say ' against the collar,' presse
and rubbed upon them, so that the humane drive

---

[1] So again rightly the LXX.

[2] Nowack, *reared ;* Graetz, *redeemed.*

[3] LXX and Targ. omit *yoke ;* and indeed the line as it stands is to
long.

[4] ואט, but some would point ואט, *and I inclined to him* (LXX
καὶ ἐπιβλέψομαι πρὸς αὐτόν).   If this is done then the לא, *not,* begi
ning the next verse must be read with LXX לו, *to him,* and broug
into this verse.

[5] x. 11.

when he came to their heads, eased the yoke with his hands. *I would be as one lifting the yoke off their jaws ;* [1] and then, when they got to the top of the hill, he would rest and feed them. That is the picture, and uncertain as we may feel about some of its details, it is obviously a passage—Ewald says ' the earliest of all passages,'— in which ' human means precisely the same as love.' It ought to be taken along with that other in the great Prophecy of the Exile, where God is described as He that *led them through the deep, as an horse in the wilderness, that they should not stumble : as a beast goeth down into the valley, the Spirit of the Lord gave him rest.* [2]

Thus the figure of the fatherliness of God changes into that of His gentleness or humanity. Do not let us think that this is either a descent of the poetry or a want of connection between the two figures. The change is true, not only to Israel's, but to our own experience. Men are either the eager children of happy, irresponsible days, or the bounden, plodding draught-cattle of life's burdens and charges. Hosea's double figure reflects human life in its whole range. Which of us has not known this fatherliness of the Most High, exercised upon us, as upon Israel, throughout our years of carelessness and disregard ? It was God Himself who taught and trained us then :—

' When through the slippery paths of youth
   With heedless steps I ran,
Thine arm unseen conveyed me safe,
   And led me up to man '

Those speedy recoveries from the blunders of early wilfulness, those redemptions from the sins of youth—

---

[1] Or *lifting it forward* from the neck *to the jaws.*
[2] Isa. lxiii. 13, 14.

happy were we if we knew that it was *He who healed us*. But a time comes when men pass from leading-strings to harness—when we feel faith less and duty more—when our work touches us more closely than our God. Death must be a strange transformer of the spirit, yet surely not more strange than life, which out of the eager buoyant child makes in time the slow bondsman of duty. Such a stage the fourth of these verses suits, when we look up, not so much for the fatherliness as for the gentleness and humanity of our God. A man has a mystic power upon the animals over whom he is placed. On any of our roads we may see it, when a kind carter gets down at a hill, and throwing the reins on his beast's back, comes to its head and touches it with his hands, and speaks to it as to his fellow ; till the deep eyes fill with light, and out of these things, so much weaker than itself, a touch a glance, a word, there comes new strength to pull onward the stranded waggon. The man is a god to the beast, coming down to help it, and it almost makes the beast human that he does so. Not otherwise does Hosea feel the help which God gives to His own on the hills of life. We need not discipline, for work is discipline enough, and the cares we carry keep us straight and steady. But we need sympathy and gentleness—this humanity which the prophet attributes to our God. God takes us by the head ; through the mystic power which is above us, but which makes us like itself, we are lifted to our task. Let no one judge this incredible. The incredible would be that our God should prove less to us than the merciful man is to his beast. But we are saved from argument by experience. When we remember how, as life has grown steep and our strength is exhausted, there has visited us a thought which sharpened to a word, a word which warmed to a touch, and we have drawn ourselves together and leapt up new men, can we feel that God was any less in these things, than in the voice of conscience or the message of forgiveness, or the restraints of His discipline ? Nay, though the reins be no longer felt, God is at our head, that we should not stumble nor stand still.

Upon this gracious passage there follows one of those swift revulsions of feeling, which we have learned to expect in Hosea. His insight again overtakes his love. The people will not respond to the goodness of their God ; it is impossible to work upon minds so fickle. Discipline is what they need, it is still uncertain whether in Egypt or Assyria.

> **xi. 5.** *Ephraim* [1] *shall return to Egypt,*
> *Or Asshûr shall be his king ;*
> *For they refuse to turn to Me.*
>
> **6.** [*And the sword shall whirl in his towns,*
> *And consume his branches,*
> *And devour them in their forts.*] [2]
>
> **7.** *My people have a bias* [3] *from Me,*
> *Though they are calling them upwards,*
> *Not one can lift them.* [4]

Not one of the prophets is able to raise a people, sunk in sin and ignorance.

Yet God is God, and though prophecy fail He will

---

[1] So LXX ; Heb. *he shall not return.*

[2] Ver. 6 has a corrupt text, and, weakening the climax of ver. 5, may be an insertion ; with Marti read *forts* for Heb. *counsels.*

[3] *Are hung* or *swung towards turning away from Me.*

[4] This verse is also uncertain ; for other readings and renderings of it, see Harper, pp. 367 f., also Speiser in *J.B.L.*, xliv, 1925, 189 f.

attempt His Love once more. There follows the
greatest passage in Hosea—deepest if not highest of
his book—the breaking forth of that exhaustless
mercy of the Most High which no sin of man can bar
or wear out.

xi. 8. *How am I to give thee up, Ephraim ?*
How can I let thee go, Israel ?
How am I to give thee up ?
Am I to make thee like Admah, like Ṣeboim ? [1]
My heart is turned upon Me,
All My compassions are boiling.
9. *I will not perform the heat of Mine anger,*
I will not turn to destroy Ephraim ;
For God am I and not man,
The Holy One in thy midst,
Yet I come not to consume. [2]

Such a love has been the secret of Hosea's persistence
with so faithless a people, and now, when he has failed,
it takes voice and makes this last appeal. Once more
before the end let Israel hear God in the utterness of
His Love !

The verses are a climax, and obviously to be succeeded by a pause. On the brink of his doom, will
Israel turn to such a God, at such a call ? The next
verses, 10 and 11, though dependent for their promise

[1] Or this couplet may be thus arranged :—

How am I to give thee up like Admah,
And make thee like to Ṣeboim ?

[2] For בעיר , which makes nonsense, read לבעור , *to consume*, or
with Wellhausen emend further so as to render, *I am not willing to
consume.*

on this same exhaustless Love, are from different circumstances, and cannot have been put by Hosea here.[1]

[1] 10. *They will follow Yahweh ; like a lion He will roar, yea He roars, and they hurry sons from the west.*

11. *Like birds they hurry from Egypt, and like doves from the land of Asshûr. and I will bring them **back** to their homes—the Rede of Yahweh.*

Not only do these verses contain expressions unusual to Hosea, and a strange metaphor, but they are not connected historically or logically with the previous verse. This deals with the people before God has scattered them—offers them one more chance before exile comes on them. But in vv. 10, 11 they are already scattered, and about to be brought back. It is such a promise as in language and metaphor was common to prophets of the Exile. In LXX the verse is taken from ch. xi and put with xii.

CHAPTER XIX

THE FINAL ARGUMENT

HOSEA XII–XIII

THE call with which last chapter closed was **not** assurance of salvation : *How am I to give thee up, Ephraim ? how let thee go, Israel ?* It was the anguish of Love, hovering over its own on the brink of the destruction to which their wilfulness has led them, and before relinquishing them it would seek some last way to redeem them. Surely that fatal morrow and the people's mad leap into it are not inevitable ! Before they take the leap, let the prophet go back upon the moral situation of to-day, go back once more upon the past of the people, and see if he can find anything to explain that bias to apostasy[1] which has brought them to this fatal brink—which may move them to repentance even there. So in chaps. xii and xiii Hosea turns upon the now familiar trail of his argument, full of the Divine jealousy, determined to give the people one other chance to turn ; but if they will not, he will justify God's relinquishment of them. The chapters throw an even clearer light upon the temper and habits of that generation. They again explore Israel's ancient history for causes of the present decline ; and, in especial, they cite the spiritual experience of the Father of the nation.

[1] xi. 7.

(326)

as if to show that what repentance was possible for him is possible for his posterity. But once more hope is seen vain ; and Hosea's last travail with his obstinate people closes in a doom even more awful than its predecessors.

While chap. xiii is ordered and clear, the arrangement, and partly the meaning, of chap. xii are obscure.

1. THE PEOPLE AND THEIR FATHER JACOB

Hosea xi. 12–xii

In no part even of the Book of Hosea does the text bristle with more problems. It may be doubted whether the verses lie in their proper order, or, if so, whether we have them as they came from the prophet, for the connection is not always perceptible.[1] We cannot believe, however, that the chapter is a bundle of isolated oracles, for the analogy between Jacob and his living posterity runs through the whole of it,[2] and the refrain that God must requite upon the nation their deeds is found both near the beginning and at the end of the chapter.[3] One is tempted to take the two fragments about the Patriarch (vv. 3, 4, and 12) by themselves, and the more so that ver. 7 would follow suitably on either ver. 1 or 2. But this clue is insufficient ; and till a more evident is discovered, it is perhaps best to keep to the extant arrangement, and to note the later passages as we come to them.[4]

---

[1] This is especially true of vv. 11 and 12.

[2] Even in the most detachable portion, vv. 8-10 (Heb.), where the אוֹן of ver. 9 seems to refer to the בָּאוֹנִי of ver. 4 (Heb.).

[3] *Viz.*, in vv. 2 and 14 (Eng. ; 3, 15, Heb.).

[4] Beer indeed, at the close of an analysis of the chapter (*Z.A.T.W.*, 1893, pp. 281 ff.), claims to have proved that it contains ' eine wohl-gegliederte Rede des Propheten ' (p. 292). But he reaches this conclusion only by forced and precarious arguments. Especially unsound

As before, the argument starts from the falseness of Israel, which is illustrated in the faithlessness of their foreign relations.

[1] xi. 12. *Ephraim has compassed Me with lies,*
And the House of Israel with deceit.
And Judah. . . .

.   .   .   .   **(?)** [2]

xii. 1. *Ephraim is herding* [3] *the wind,*
And ever a-hunting the east wind.
They heap up falsehood and fraud. [4]
They strike a treaty with Asshûr
And carry oil into Egypt. [5]

2. *Yahweh hath a quarrel with Judah* [6] *(?)*
To visit on Jacob his ways,
After his doings He will requite him.

are his pleas that in 8*b* לְעָשֵׁק is a play upon the root-meaning of כְּנַעַן , *lowly ;* that כְּנַעַן , in analogy to בְּבֶטֶן of ver. 4 (Eng. 3), is the crude original, the raw material, of the Ephraim of ver. 9 ; and that כִּימֵי מוֹעֵד is *the determined time* of the coming judgement on Israel.

[1] Heb. xii. 1.

[2] Something is written about Judah, but the text is too obscure for translation. The theory that it has been altered by a later Judæan writer in favour of his own people may be correct : A.V. translates in favour of Judah ; so too Guthe. But an adverse statement is required by the parallel clauses, and the Hebrew text allows this : *Judah is still wayward with God, and with the Holy One who is faithful.* So virtually Ewald, Hitzig, Wünsche, Nowack, Cheyne, and Moffatt. But Cornill and Wellhausen read the second line as עַם־קְדֵשִׁים נִצְמָד , *profanes himself with ḳedeshim (Z.A.T.W., 1887, pp. 286 ff.).* Marti and Harper after LXX : *And Judah is still known with God and with the Holy One faithful.*

[3] Why should not Hosea, the master of many forced phrases, have also uttered this one ? This in answer to Wellhausen, Marti, and others.

[4] So LXX, reading שָׁוְא for שֹׁד .

[5] Cf. Isa. xxx. 6.

[6] So Heb., but some read Israel as required by the next verse, which is a play upon the two names Israel and Jacob. Marti takes the line as a gloss.

3. *In the womb he grasped at his brother,*
   And in his man's strength wrestled with God.[1]
4. *Yea wrestled with an angel, and prevailed,*
   Wept and besought of Him mercy.
   At Beth-el he found Him,
   And there He spake with ourselves.[2]
5. *[And Yahweh, is God of the hosts,*
   Yahweh His Name!] [3]
6. *So thou by thy God* [4] *shouldest return,*
   Leal love and justice to keep,
   And constantly wait on thy God. [5]

To this verse we shall return when treating of Hosea's doctrine of Repentance.

The discourse, in characteristic fashion, now swerves from the ideal, to the real, moral estate of the people, nick-naming the mercenary generation a very *Canaan.* [6]

7. *A Canaan, in his hand false balances,*
   He loves to defraud.
8. *Ephraim has said, I grow rich,*
   I have found myself wealth, [7]
   None of my labours hit me
   With guilt which is sin. (?) [8]

---

[1] Heb. *'aḳab, took by the heel*, the presumable root of the name *Ya'aḳôb* (Jacob), as in the next line *wrestled with God* is *sarah eth-'elôhim*, the presumable origin of the name *Yisra'el* (Israel).

[2] So Heb., *i.e., to us* in the person of our father ; LXX, *to them.*

[3] This couplet is, as generally recognised, a pious later addition. See above, p. 231, n. 3.

[4] This is the natural rendering of the Heb. and not *to thy God* (Beer) ; Hitzig, ' durch deinen Gott.'

[5] Some take these three lines as addressed by God to the patriarch.

[6] So nearly all moderns. Hitzig aptly quotes Polybius, *De Virtute*, L. ix : διὰ τὴν ἔμφυτον Φοίνιξι πλεονεξίαν. One might refer also to the Odyssey xiv. 288 f., and to the Roman opinion of the ' Punica fides.'

[7] Or *full man's strength ;* cf. ver. 3 (Heb. 4).

[8] But LXX has, *all his gair shall not be found of him* because *of the iniquity which he has sinned ;* and this Wellhausen emends to, *all his gain suffices not for the guilt it has incurred.*

But God can destroy that commercial civilisation of Israel and reduce them to their ancient level of life in tents as in the time of their gathering at Horeb.

> xii. 9. *But I am Yahweh, thy God*
> *From the land of Egypt,*
> *Again I could plant thee in tents*
> *As in the days of the Tryst.*[1]
>
> 10. *And I spake to the prophets*
> *And I multiplied vision,*
> *And by the hand of the prophets gave parables.*
>
> 11. *In Gilead they worked idolatry, vanity ;*[2]
> *In Gilgal sacrificed to demons,*[3]
> *Their altars shall be but stone-heaps*[4]
> *Among the field's furrows.*
>
> 12. *And Jacob fled to the country*[5] *of Aram,*
> *And Israel served for a wife,*
> *For a wife he herded.*
>
> 13. *By a prophet Yahweh brought Israel from Egypt,*
> *And by a prophet was he herded.*
>
> 14. *Ephraim has bitterly provoked Me*
> *But left him his blood-guilt shall be,*
> *And his reproach his Lord shall return to him.*

[1] Or *Diet*, or *solemn assembly*.

[2] The text of this line is uncertain ; with most moderns I read *In* for Heb. *If*, and *worked* for Heb. *were*.

[3] Heb. has שְׁוָרִים, *bullocks*, LXX ἄρχοντες, *princes*, reading שָׂרִים; it is but a slight change to read לַשֵּׁדִים , *to demons*, the initial letter ל having slipped out as following the final ל of the preceding word. So after Hitzig most moderns.

[4] Heb. *gallîm*, doubtless, with *Gilgal*, a play upon words.

[5] Heb. *field*, but in the sense of territory ; see below, p. 355, also *Hist. Geog.*, pp. 79 f.

Such are the verses. As they stand in the text, it is not possible to trace a continuous argument through them. We cannot wonder that some have transposed them,[1] and others regarded a number of them as additions or glosses to the original.[2] Their climax, however, is clear—again the doom of Israel.

2. THE LAST JUDGEMENT

Hosea xiii

The crisis draws on. On the one hand Israel's sin, accumulating, bulks ripe for judgement. On the other the times grow more fatal, or the prophet feels them to be so. He will gather again the old truths on the old lines—the early past when Yahweh was God alone, the descent to Baalim or idols and the mushroom monarchs of to-day ; the people, who once were strong, but now are sapped by luxury, forgetful, stupid, not to be roused. The discourse has marks of being Hosea's latest. There is clearness and definiteness beyond anything since chap. iv. There are ease and lightness of treatment, a playful sarcasm, as if the themes were now familiar both to the prophet and his audience. But chiefly there is the passion of how different it all might have been, if to this crisis Israel had come with store of strength instead of guilt. How these years, with their opening into the history of the world, might have meant a birth for the nation, which instead was lying upon them like a dying child in the mouth of the womb ! A fatality God Himself cannot help ! Death and Hell remain. Let them, then, have

---

[1] *E.g.*, Harper (taking the Heb. numbers of the verses), 1–4, 13, 5–11, 14, 15, 12.

[2] *E.g.*, Marti, 1*b*, 3*a*, 5–7, 9*b*–11, 13, 14

their way !   Samaria must expiate her guilt in the
worst horrors of war.

Instead of with one definite event, this last effort of
Hosea opens naturally with a summary of Ephraim's
previous history.   The tribe had been first in Israel
till they took to idols.

xiii. 1. *When Ephraim would speak there was trembling.*[1]
       Prince[2] *in Israel was he,*
       But he fell into guilt through the Ba'al,
       And he died.

    2. *Even now they continue to sin,*
       And have made themselves molten gods ;
       Idols out of their silver, after their model,[3]—
       Smiths' work the whole of it is !
       To those they are speaking,[4]
       Sacrificing men a-kissing of calves !

    3. *Therefore shall they be like the morning cloud*
       And the dew that vanishes early,
       Like chaff whirling off the threshing-floor,
       And like smoke from a window.

    4. *But I Yahweh have been thy God*[5]
       From the land of Egypt,
       And god save Myself thou knowest not,
       Nor saviour besides Me.

    5. *I, I in the desert did shepherd*[6] *thee.*
       In the land of droughts.

---

[1] Other renderings or reading are unsatisfactory ; those which take
trembling adverbially of Ephraim himself and those which for trembling
read with LXX read *judgements* or the like.

[2] For נָשָׂא read נָשִׂיא .

[3] With Ewald and others read כתבנתם .

[4] Some suggest *are saying*, O God.

[5] Here LXX brings in the insertion noted above, pp. 212 f.

[6] So LXX and Syr. ; Heb. *knew.*

But then they came to the fertile Canaan with its many gods, and once there they gave way to its pleasures and to pride, and forgot their own God.

6. *As they got pasture [1] they filled themselves full,*
   They were filled and their heart was uplifted,
   Therefore Me they forgat.
7. *So I must be [2] like a lion towards them,*
   Like a leopard on the way I must leap,[3]
8. *Strike them like a bear bereaved of its young,*
   Tear up the caul of their heart,
   Devour them there like a lion,[4]
   Wild beasts shall rend them.

9. *When I have [5] destroyed thee, Israel,*
   Who then may help thee ? [6]
10. *Where is thy king now, that he may deliver thee,*
    And all thy princes that they may rule thee ? [7]
    Of whom thou didst say, Give unto me
    A king and princes.
11. *I give thee kings in Mine anger,*
    And take them away in My wrath.

---

[1] Some read *as they fed*, כְּרְעוֹתָם .

[2] Or *shall be ;* with LXX read וְאֶהְיֶה .

[3] אַשּׁוּר , 'ashur, usually taken as 1st pers. future of שׁוּר , shûr, *to lurk*. But in Arabic there is a root *sar*, ' to spring suddenly,' of wine to the head, or of a lion on its prey ; and *sawâr*, ' springer,' is one of the names for the lion. LXX, Syr., and Vulg., however, all read אַשּׁוּר , *to Assyria*, and this is accepted by Hitzig, Wellhausen, and others.

[4] LXX, καὶ καταφάγονται αὐτοὺς ἐκεῖ σκύμνοι δρυμόν, which is a good parallel to the following line.

[5] So Syr. ; Heb., *thou hast destroyed thyself.*

[6] After the LXX.

[7] Read with Houtsma and others after the LXX, וכל שריך וישפטוך . The Heb. text is meaningless.

That is a fit summary of the short and bloody reigns of these last years in North Israel.

The nation pregnant with guilt is in the throes of a cruel birth ; then with all Hosea's abruptness the figure changes to that of the child that will not come to the birth, or is still-born.

> xiii. 12. *Gathered is Ephraim's guilt,*
> *Stored is his sin.*
> 13. *Birth-pangs are coming upon **him**,*
> *An unwise son is he.[1]*
> *This is no time to stay*
> *In the mouth of the womb.[2]*

The years that might have been the nation's birth are by their own folly to prove their death. Israel lies in the way of its own redemption—how truly this has been forced home upon them in one chapter after another ! Shall God then step in and work a deliverance on the brink of death ? Nay, let Death and Sheol have their way. Here with them !

> 14. *From the hand of Sheol shall I save them ?*
> *Shall I redeem them from Death ?*
> *Where [3] are thy plagues, O Death,*
> *Where [3] thy destruction, Sheol ?—*
> *Repentance is hid from Mine eyes.*

This great verse has been variously rendered. Some take it as a promise : *I will deliver . . . I will redeem*

---

[1] So literally the Heb., *impracticable, abortive,* a name for children whose birth was difficult, who could not find their way forth.

[2] Lit. *for it is time he should not stand in the place of the breaking forth of children.*

[3] Reading with LXX איה for אהי of the text. Marti renders *here with thy plagues . . . here with thy destruction* or *pestilence.*

. . . So the Septuagint translated, and St. Paul borrowed, not the whole Greek verse, but its spirit and one or two of its terms, for his triumphant challenge to death in the power of the Resurrection of Christ.[1] As it stands in Hosea, however, the verse must be a call for death to devour. The last clause unambiguously abjures mercy, and the statement that His people will not be saved, for God cannot save them, is one in harmony with Hosea's teaching.[2]

An appendix follows with illustration of the form which doom shall take. As frequently with Hosea, it opens with a play upon the people's name, which at the same time echoes the opening of the chapter—*Ephraim yaphri'*.

15. *Though he among his brothers be the Fruitful,*[3]
   An east wind shall come, Yahweh's own blast,

---

[1] The LXX reads : Ποῦ ἡ δίκη σου, θάνατε ; ποῦ τὸ κέντρον σου, ᾅδη ; But Paul says : Ποῦ σου, θάνατε, τὸ νῖκος ; ποῦ σου, θάνατε, τὸ κέντρον ; 1 Cor. xv. 55 (Westcott and Hort's Ed.).

[2] The following is a list of the interpretations of verse 14 :—

A. Taken as a threat. 1. ' It is I who redeemed you from the grip of the grave, and who delivered you from death—but now I will call up the words (*sic*) of death against you ; for repentance is hid from My eyes.' So Raschi. 2. ' I would have redeemed them from the grip of Sheol, etc., if they had been wise, but being foolish I will bring on them the plagues of death.' So Kimchi, Eichhorn, Simson, etc. 3. ' Should I ' or ' shall I deliver them from the hand of Sheol, redeem them from death ? ' etc., as above. So Wünsche, Wellhausen, Guthe, Marti, Harper, Moffatt, A. R. Gordon, and others.

B. Taken as a promise. ' From the hand of Sheol I will deliver them, from death redeem them,' etc. So Umbreit, Ewald, Hitzig, A.V. and R.V. In this case repentance in the last clause must be taken as *resentment* (Ewald). But, as Ewald sees, the whole verse must then be put in a parenthesis, as an ejaculation of promise in the midst of a context that only threatens. Some without change of word render : ' I will be thy plagues, O death ? I will be thy destruction, O grave ! ' So A.V. and R.V.'s note.

[3] So they called him from the beginning. There is no need to change, as most do, to *like the grass-reed in the waters*, a forced and doubtful simile.

xiii. 15*b*. *Mounting up from the desert,*
    And shall dry off [1] *his fountain,*
    And parch his spring,
    And strip the treasury of every jewel. [2]
[3] 16. *Samaria must bear her guilt,* [4]
    For against her God she rebelled.
    By the sword they shall fall,
    Their infants be dashed to pieces,
    And their women with child ripped up.

To this simple issue has the impenitence of the people finally reduced the many possibilities of those momentous years ; and their prophet leaves them looking forward to the crash which came some dozen years later in the invasion and captivity of the land. Horrible are the details, but at that period certain to follow every defeat in war.

[1] So LXX : Heb. takes these verbs in the passive.
[2] Marti and others take this line as a gloss, but wrongly, as I agree with Harper. Assyria is the parching wind from the east and her policy would be to strip the land of its treasures.
[3] Heb. xiv. 1.
[4] Calvin, Pusey, and A.V. read *become desolate* or *be laid waste.*

CHAPTER XX

'I WILL BE AS THE DEW'

Hosea xiv

LIKE the Book of Amos, the Book of Hosea, after proclaiming the people's inevitable doom, turns to a prospect of their restoration. It will be remembered that we decided against the authenticity of such an epilogue in the Book of Amos ; and it may be asked, how can we come to any other conclusion as to the similar peroration in the Book of Hosea ? For the following reasons.

We decided against the genuineness of the closing verses of Amos, because their sanguine temper is opposed to the temper of the rest of the book, and because they neither propose ethical conditions for the attainment of the blessed future, nor in their picture of this do they emphasise one trace of the justice, or purity, or social kindliness, on which Amos has insisted as the ideal relations of Israel to Yahweh. It seemed impossible that Amos could imagine the restoration of his people in terms only of requickened nature, and say nothing about righteousness, truth, and mercy to the poor. The prospect which now closes his book is psychologically alien to him, and, being painted in the terms of later prophecy, may be judged to have been added by some prophet of the Exile, speaking from the standpoint, and with the legitimate desires, of his own day.

But the case is different for this epilogue in Hosea. First, Hosea has not only preached repentance, and been, from his affectionate temper of mind, unable to believe repentance impossible ; but he has predicted the restoration of his people on certain ethical conditions. In chap. ii he has drawn in detail the prospect of God's successful treatment of his erring spouse. Israel should be weaned from their sensuousness and accompanying trust in idols by severe discipline, which the prophet describes in terms of their ancient wanderings in the wilderness. They should be reduced, as at the beginning of their history, to moral converse with their God ; and abjuring the Ba'alim (later chapters imply also their foreign allies and foolish kings and princes) should return to Yahweh, when He, having proved that the Ba'alim could not give them the fruits of the land, should Himself quicken the course of nature to bless them with fertility of the soil and the friendliness even of the wild beasts.

In the epilogue and its prospect of Israel's repentance we find no feature, physical or moral, which has not already been furnished by those promises of the book. All their ethical conditions are provided ; nothing but what they have conceived of blessing is again conceived. Israel is to abjure senseless sacrifice and come to God, with rational, contrite confession.[1] She is to abjure her foreign alliances,[2] to trust in the fatherly love of her God.[3] He is to heal her,[4] and His anger is to turn away.[5] He is to restore nature, just as described in chap. ii, and the scenery of the restoration is that of Hosea's own Galilee. There is, in short,

[1] Cf. vi. 1-6.   [2] Cf. xii. 1, etc.   [3] Cf. i. 6; ii. 23.
[4] Cf. xi. 3.   [5] Cf. xi. 8, 9.

no phrase or allusion of which we can say that it is
alien to the prophet's style or environment, while the
keynotes of his book—*return, backsliding, idols the work
of our hands, such pity as a father hath*, and perhaps
even the *answer* or *converse* of ver. 9—are all struck
once more.

The epilogue then is different from the epilogue to
the Book of Amos, nor can the present expositor
conceive of a stronger case for the genuineness of any
passage of Scripture. The sole difficulty is the place
in which we find it—where its contradiction to the
preceding sentence of doom is brought out into relief.
We need not suppose, however, that it was uttered by
Hosea in proximity to the latter, nor even that it
formed his last word to Israel. But granting only
(as the above evidence obliges us) that it is the prophet's
own, this fourteenth chapter may have been a discourse
addressed by him at one of those many points when,
as we know, he had hope of the people's return. I
think it likely that Hosea's ministry closed with that
final, hopeless proclamation in chap. xiii : no other
conclusion was possible so near the fall of Samaria,
and the destruction of the Northern Kingdom. But
Hosea had already in chap. ii painted the opposite
issue as a possible ideal for his people ; and during
some break in those years when their insincerity was
less obtrusive, and their doom still uncertain, the
prophet's heart swung to its natural pole in the exhaustless love of God, and he uttered his unstinted
gospel. That either himself or the editor of his prophecies should have placed this at the very end of his
book is not less than what we might have expected.
For if the book were to have validity beyond the circumstances of its origin, beyond the judgement which
was near and inevitable, was it not right to let some-

340 THE TWELVE PROPHETS

thing else than the proclamation of the latter be its last word to men? was it not right to put as the conclusion of the whole matter the ideal eternally valid for Israel—the gospel which is ever God's last word to His people? [1]

At some point or other, then, in the course of his ministry, there was granted to Hosea an open vision like his vision recounted in the second chapter. He called on the people to repent. For once, and in the power of that Love to which he had already said all things are possible, it seemed to him as if repentance came. The tangle and intrigue of his generation, the

---

[1] Professor Cheyne, in his introduction to W. R. Smith's *The Prophets of Israel* (p. xix), reaches with regard to Hosea xiv conclusions opposite to those reached above. He denies the passage to Hosea on the grounds that it is akin in language, imagery, and ideas to writings of the age which begins with Jeremiah, and among other works includes the Song of Songs. But, as has been shown above, the 'language, imagery, and ideas' are akin to what he admits to be genuine prophecies of Hosea; and the likeness to them of, *e.g.*, Jer. xxxi. 10–20 may be explained, like much else in Jeremiah, by the influence of Hosea. The allusion in ver. 3 suits Hosea's day more than Jeremiah's. He says that ' to understand Hosea aright we must omit it' (*i.e.*, the whole epilogue). But after the argument I have given above it will be plain that if we ' understand Hosea aright' we have every reason *not* ' to omit it.' His last contention, that ' to have added anything to the stern warning in xiii. 16 would have robbed it of half its force,' is met by the considerations stated above on p. 339. Guthe (3rd Ed.), Marti, Duhm, and Harper agree with Cheyne. Cornill, Budde, A. R. Gordon, Sellin, and Moffatt accept the passage as Hosea's. Volz and Nowack admit a Hosean basis worked over by later hands. I feel grateful to Professor Budde (*Der Schluss des Buches Hosea*), who calls my argument for the authenticity a ' mannhafte Verteidigung ' and who defends the genuineness of the passage, when subjected to certain emendations (noted below) with equal common sense and ingenuity. The whole piece,' he says, ' is as Hoseanic as possible since it straight-forwardly contains the programme of Hosea.' One of the many good points that he makes is that the repeated *Ephraim* as the name of the people of Yahweh could hardly have been given them after the time of Jeremiah. But Budde does not agree with me that the epilogue is not Hosea's final prophecy, and his argument that it is in its proper place is well worthy of consideration.

reeking sacrifices and the vain show of worship, all fell away. The people, turned from their idols and puppet-kings, from Assyria and from Egypt, would with contrite hearts come to God Himself, who, healing and loving, opens to them the gates of the future. It is not strange that down this spiritual vista the prophet should see the same scenery as daily filled his bodily vision. Throughout Galilee Lebanon [1] dominates the landscape. You cannot raise your eyes from any spot of Northern Israel without resting them upon the vast mountain. From the unhealthy jungles of the Upper Jordan, the pilgrim lifts his heart to the cool hill air above, to the ever-green cedars and firs, to the streams and waterfalls that drop like silver chains off the great breastplate of snow. From Esdraelon and every plain the peasants look to Lebanon to store the clouds and scatter the rain ; it is not from heaven but from Hermon that they expect the dew,[2] their only hope in the long drought of summer. Across Galilee and in Northern Ephraim, across Bashan and in Northern Gilead, across Hauran and on the borders of the desert, the mountain casts its spell of power, its lavish promise of life.[3] Lebanon is everywhere the summit of the land, and there are points from which it is as dominant as heaven.

No wonder then that our northern prophet painted the blessed future in the poetry of the Mountain—its

---

[1] By Lebanon in the fourteenth chapter and almost always in the Old Testament we must understand not the western range now called Lebanon, for that makes no impression on the Holy Land, its bulk lying too far north, but Hermon, the southmost and highest summits of Anti-Lebanon. See *Hist. Geog.*, pp. 417 f.

[2] Psalm cxxxiii. 3.

[3] Full sixty miles off, in the Jebel Druze, the ancient Greek amphitheatres were so arranged that Hermon might fill the horizon of the spectators.

air, its dew, and its trees. Other seers were to behold, in the same latter days, the Mountain of the Lord above the tops of the mountains ; the ordered city, her stead-fast walls salvation, and her open gates praise ; the wealth of the Gentiles flowing into her, profusion of flocks for sacrifice, profusion of pilgrims ; the Temple and its solemn services ; and *the glory of Lebanon shall come unto thee, fir-tree and pine and box-tree together, to beautify the place of My Sanctuary.*[1] But, with his home in the north, and weary of sacrifice and ritual, weary of everything artificial whether idols or puppet-kings, Hosea turns to the *glory of Lebanon* as it lies, untouched by human tool or art, fresh and full of peace from God's own hand. Like that other seer of Galilee, Hosea in his vision of the future *saw no temple therein.*[2] His sacraments are the open air, the mountain breeze, the dew, the vine, the lilies, the pines ; and what God asks of men are not rites nor sacrifices, but life and health, fragrance and fruitfulness, beneath the shadow and the Dew of His Presence.

[3] xiv. 1. *Return, Israel, unto Yahweh thy God,*
For by thy guilt thou hast floundered.

2. *Take with you words,*[4]
And return [5] *to Yahweh,*
Say unto Him, Wholly [6]
Lift away guilt,

[1] Isa. lx. 13.   [2] Revelation of St. John xxi. 22.
[3] In Heb. and LXX this verse is xiv. 2.
[4] On this exhortation see below, p. 369. Budde, for metrical reasons, would read *good words*, and to *Yahweh* in the next line would add from LXX *your God ;* but unnecessarily for lines as brief as these are frequent in Hosea's style.
[5] To avoid the repetition of *return* in previous verse Budde reads *come*.
[6] Heb. כל , for which LXX (ὅπως μή) read בל , which Budde emends to אֲבָל , *surely*.

> *Take it well* [1] *(?) that we render*
> *The fruit* [2] *of our lips.*

Confessions, vows, these are the offerings pleasing to God ; which vows are now registered :—

> 3. *Asshûr shall not save us,*
> *We will ride not on horses,*
> *Nor again say, Our God*
> *To the work of our hands.*
> *For in Thee the fatherless finds a father's pity.* [3]

Alien help, whether the protection of Assyria, or the horses sent by Egypt in return for Israel's homage ; and alien gods, our own work, we abjure, for we remember how Thou didst promise to show a father's pity to the people whom Thou hadst named for their mother's guilt Lo-Ruhamah, *Unpitied.*

To these promises God replies :—

> 4. *I will heal their backsliding,*
> *I will love them freely,*
> *For Mine anger is turned away from them.* [4]
> 5. *I will be as the dew to Israel,*
> *He* [5] *shall blossom as the lily,*
> *And strike out his roots like Lebánon.* [6]

[1] For קח טוב Oort, Oettli, Marti read נקחה טוב , *let us receive good, i.e.,* at Thy hand.

[2] So LXX reading פרי for Heb. פרים , *calves.*

[3] To Marti this line is a gloss ; but is more reasonably removed by Harper and Moffatt to the end of ver. 2. For ירחם Budde would read נרחם , *we find mercy,* and out of יתום , *fatherless,* and the third line of ver. 4 he suggests a line מִי יִתֵּן יָשֻׁב אֶפְרַיִם , *Would that Ephraim would return.*

[4] Marti, etc., take this line as a gloss ; for other treatment of it see the previous note.

[5] Budde proposes *Ephraim shall blossom.*

[6] Some emend to *like the Libneh, the poplar.* Others omit the line.

xiv. 6.

His branches shall spread,[1]
His beauty shall be as the olive
And his scent as Lebánon[2]—

the fresh air of the mountain and the scent of its pines.

The figure in the end of ver. 5 seems forced to some critics, who have proposed various emendations, such as ' like the fast-rooted trees of Lebanon,'[3] but any one who has seen how the mountain himself rises from vast roots, cast out across the land like those of some giant oak, will not feel it needful to mitigate the metaphor.

The prophet now speaks :—

7.

They shall return and dwell in His shadow,
They shall live as a garden, well-watered (?)
And shall flourish like the vine,
And be fragrant like the wine of Lebánon.[4]

---

[1] Wellhausen would add *like the vine*.

[2] Budde proposes *as lebonah*, frankincense.

[3] So Guthe ; but others, *like the poplar* or *the cedar ;* Wellhausen, for וילכו‎ , reads ויך‎.

[4] Ver. 7 (Heb. 8) needs emendation. The text contains one question-able construction, and gives no sense : ' They that dwell in his shadow shall turn, and revive corn and flourish like the vine, and his fame,' etc To cultivate corn and be themselves like a vine is mixed. LXX reads : ἐπιστρέψουσιν καὶ καθιοῦνται ὑπὸ τὴν σκέπην αὐτοῦ, ζήσονται καὶ μεθυσθήσονται σίτῳ· καὶ ἐξανθέσει ἄμπελος μνημόσυνην αὐτοῦ ὡς οἶνος Λιβάνου. This removes the grammatical difficulty from line 1, which then reads יָשֻׁבוּ וְיָשְׁבוּ בְּצֵלּוֹ‎ ; the supplied *vau* may easily have dropped after the final *vau* of the previous word. In the second line LXX takes יחיו‎ as intransitive, which is better suited to the other verbs, and adds καὶ μεθυσθήσονται, ורוין‎ (a form that may have slipped from the text, through its likeness to the preceding ויהיו‎). *And they shall be well-watered.* After this it is probable that דגן‎ should read כַּגָּן‎ . In the third line the Heb. text may stand. In the fourth זכר‎ may not, as many propose, be taken for זכרם‎ and translated *their perfume ;* but the parallelism makes it probable that we have a verb here ; and if זכר‎ in the Hiph. has the sense *to make a perfume* (cf. Isa. lxvi. 3), there is no

God speaks :—

> 8. *Ephraim, what has he*[1] *to do more with idols !*
> *I respond to him, and look after him.*
> *I am like an ever-green cypress ;*
> *From Me is thy fruit found.*

This version is not without difficulties ; but the alternative that God is addressed and Ephraim is the speaker—*Ephraim says, What have I to do more with idols ? I answer and look to Him : I am like an ever-green cypress ; from me is Thy fruit found*—has even greater difficulties,[2] although it avoids the unusual comparison of the Deity with a tree. The difficulties of both interpretations might be overcome by dividing the verse between God and the people :—

> *Ephraim ! what has he to do more with idols !*
> *I respond to him, and look after him.*

In this case *respond* would be intended in the same sense as the *respond* in chap. ii to the heavens and earth, that they might *speak* to the *corn and wine*.[3]

---

reason against the Kal being used in the intransitive sense. Harper accepts my emendation here. So Moffatt. Budde : *his sons shall return . . . revive corn and bring the vine to sprouting.* In the LXX for μεθυσθήσονται Q. reads στηριχθήσονται.

[1] So LXX, and most moderns ; Heb. *I.*

[2] This alternative, which Robertson Smith adopted, though not without hesitation (*Prophets*, p. 413) is that which follows the Heb. text, reading in the first line לִי , and not, like LXX, לֹ . But it does not account for the emphasis laid in the second line on the first personal pronoun, and implies that God, whose name has not for several verses been mentioned, is meant by the mere personal suffix, ' I will look to Him.' Wellhausen suggests changing the second line to *I am his Anat and his Aschera ;* Marti for וַאֲשׁוּרֶנּוּ reads וְאֲשִׁיבֶנּוּ , *I give him dwelling ;* Gardner, וַאֲשִׁיבֶנּוּ , *I bring him back ;* Budde, *I respond to thee with new wine and corn.*

[3] ענה , ii. 23 (Heb. ; Eng. 21).

Then Ephraim replies :—

> *I am like an ever-green cypress ;*
> *From me is Thy [1] fruit found.*

But the division appears artificial, and the text does not suggest that the two *I*'s belong to different speakers. The first version therefore is the preferable.

Some one has added a summons to later generations to lay this book to heart in face of their own problems and sins.   May we do so for ourselves !

xiv. 9. *Who is wise, that he understands these things ?*
Intelligent, that he knows them ?
For, straight are the ways of Yahweh,
And the righteous shall walk therein,
But sinners shall flounder upon them.

[1] LXX *his*.

CHAPTER XXI

THE KNOWLEDGE OF GOD

HOSEA *passim*

WE have finished the translation and exposition of Hosea's prophecies. We have followed his examination of his people's character, his
criticism of his fickle generation's attempts to repent,
and his presentation of religion in contrast to their
shallow optimism and sensual superstitions. We have
felt an inwardness and spirituality of the highest kind
—a love not only warm and mobile, but nobly jealous,
and in its jealousy assisted by extraordinary insight
and expertness in character. Why Hosea should be
distinguished among prophets for spirituality must
by this time be clear to us. From his remote watch-
fulness, Amos had seen the nations move across the
world as the stars cross heaven ; had seen, within
Israel, class distinct from class, and had given types of
all : rich and poor ; king, priest, merchant, and judge ;
the panic-stricken, the bully ; the fraudulent and the
unclean. The observatory of Amos was the world
and the nation. But Hosea's was the home ; there
he had watched a soul decay through every stage from
innocence to corruption. It was a husband's study of
a wife which made Hosea the most inward of the
prophets. This was *the beginning of God's word by him.*[1]

[1] i. 2.

Among the subjects, in the treatment of which Hosea's service to religion is original and conspicuous, there are three that deserve a more detailed treatment than we have given them. These are the Knowledge of God, Repentance, and the Sin against Love. We may devote a chapter to each, beginning with the most fundamental truth Hosea gave to religion—the Knowledge of God.[1]

If to the heart there be one pain keener than another, it is the pain of not being understood. This prevents argument : how can you reason with one who will not come to quarters with your real self ? It paralyses influence : how can you do your best with one who is blind to your best ? It stifles Love ; for how dare she speak when she is mistaken for something else ? Here as elsewhere ' against stupidity the gods themselves fight in vain.'

This anguish was Hosea's. As closely as two souls may live, he had lived with Gomer. Yet she had never wakened to his worth. She was a woman with a power of love, or such a heart had hardly wooed her. He was a man of deep tenderness and exquisite powers of expression. His tact, delicacy, and enthusiasm are sensible throughout his book. Gomer must have tasted them before Israel did. Yet she never knew him. It was her curse that, being married, she was not roused to the meaning of marriage, and, being married to Hosea, she never appreciated the tenderness and patience which were deemed by God not unworthy of becoming a parable of His own.

We do not go wrong if we conclude that it was this

[1] To this new edition I would add a reference to what Marti, p. 39, has finely said on the subject.

experience of a soul who loved, but had neither conscience nor ideal in her love, which made Hosea lay frequent and pathetic emphasis upon Israel's *ignorance* of their God. To have his character ignored, his purposes baffled, his gifts unappreciated, his patience mistaken—this was what drew Hosea into that sympathy with the heart of God towards Israel which comes out in passionate words : *My people perish for lack of knowledge.*[1] *There is no troth, nor leal love, nor knowledge of God in the land.*[2] *They have not known Yahweh.*[3] *She knew not I gave her corn and wine.*[4] *They knew not I nursed them.*[5] *For now, because thou hast rejected knowledge, I will reject thee.*[6] *I will have leal love and not sacrifice, and the knowledge of God rather than burnt-offerings.*[7] Repentance consists in change of knowledge. And the climax of the new life which follows is again knowledge : *I will betroth thee to Me, and thou shalt know the Lord.*[8]

To understand what Hosea meant by knowledge we must examine the supple word which his language lent him to express it. The Hebrew root ' Yadh'a,'[9] almost always rendered in the Old Testament by the English verb ' to know,' is employed of the many processes of knowledge, for which richer languages have separate terms. It is by turns to perceive, be aware of, recognise, understand or conceive, experience and be expert in.[10] But there are besides nearly always a practical effectiveness, and in connection with religious objects a moral consciousness.

The barest meaning is to be aware that something is present or has happened, and perhaps the root meant

---

[1] iv. 6.   [2] iv. 1.   [3] v. 4.   [4] ii. 8 (Heb. 10).
[5] xi. 3.   [6] iv. 6.   [7] vi. 6.   [8] ii. 20 (Heb. 22).   [9] ידע.
[10] The Latin *videre, scire, noscere, cognoscere, intelligere, sapere* and *peritus esse.*

simply to see.[1] But it was the frequent duty of the
prophets to mark the difference between perceiving
a thing and laying it to heart. Isaiah speaks of the
people *seeing*, but not so as *to know* or *perceive ;*[2] and
Deuteronomy renders the latter sense by adding *with
the heart*, which to the Hebrews was the seat, not of
the feeling, but of the practical intellect :[3] *And thou
knowest with thy heart that as a man chastiseth his son,
so Yahweh thy God chastiseth thee.*[4] Usually, however,
the word *know* suffices by itself. This practical vigour
developed in such directions as *intimacy, conviction,
experience,* and *wisdom.* Job calls his familiars *my
knowers ;*[5] of a strong conviction he says, *I know that
my Redeemer liveth,*[6] and referring to wisdom, *We are
of yesterday and know not ;*[7] while Ecclesiastes says,
Whoso keepeth the commandment shall know—that is,
experience—*no evil.*[8] But the verb rises into a practical
sense—to the knowledge that leads a man to regard or
care for its object. Job uses the verb *know* when he
means, *I do not care for my life ;*[9] and in the description of the sons of Eli, that *they were sons of Belial, and
did not know God*, it is that they did not have regard
for Him.[10] Finally, there is a moral use of the word
in which it reaches the meaning of conscience : *Their
eyes were opened, and they knew they were naked.*[11] They
were aware of this before, but felt it now with a new

---

[1] Cf. the Greek οἶδα from εἰδειν.   [2] vi. 9.

[3] See above, pp. 275 f., 296 ; and below, p. 352.

[4] viii. 5 : cf. xxix. 3 (Eng. 4), *Yahweh did not give you a heart to know.*

[5] Job xix. 13 : still closer of the intimacy between the sexes for which
the verb is often used in the Old Testament.

[6] xix. 25 ; cf. Gen. xx. 6.   [7] viii. 9.

[8] viii. 5 ; cf. Hosea ix. 7.   [9] ix. 21.

[10] 1 Sam. ii. 12. A similar meaning is to be attached to the word in
Gen. xxxix. 6 : Potiphar *had no thought* or *care for anything* in Joseph's
hand. Cf. Prov. ix. 13 ; xxvii. 23 ; Job xxxv. 15.

[11] Gen. iii. 7.

sense. Also it is the mark of the awakened and the fullgrown to *know*, or feel, the difference between good and evil.[1]

Here, then, we have a word for *knowing*, the utterance of which almost invariably starts a moral echo, whose very sound is haunted by sympathy and by duty. It is knowledge, not as an effort of, so much as an effect upon, the mind. It is not *to know* so as to see the fact of, but *to know* so as to feel the force of ; knowledge, not as acquisition but as impression. To quote Paul's distinction, it is not so much the apprehending as the being apprehended. It leads to a vivid result—either warm appreciation or change of mind or practical effort. It is sometimes the talent conceived as the trust, sometimes the enlistment of all the affections. It is knowledge that is followed by shame, or by love, or by reverence, or by the sense of a duty. One sees how near it is to the meaning of our ' conscience,' and how easily there was developed from it the evangelical name for repentance, Metanoia—change of mind under a new impression of facts.

Three writers thus use knowledge as the key to the divine life—in the Old Testament Hosea and the author of Deuteronomy, in the New St. John. We likened Amos to St. John the Baptist : it is not only upon his similar temperament, but far more upon his use of the word *knowledge* for spiritual purposes, that we may compare Hosea to St. John the Evangelist.

Hosea's chief charge against the people is one of stupidity. High and low they are *a people without intelligence*.[2] Once he defines this as want of political

---

[1] Gen. iii. 5 ; Isa. vii. 15, etc.

[2] iv. 14, עַם לֹא־יָבִין : if the original meaning of בִּין be to *get between*, *see through* or *into*, so *discriminate*, *understand*, then intelligence is its etymological equivalent.

wisdom : *Ephraim is a silly pigeon without heart*, **or**, as we say, *without brains ;* [1] and again, as insensibility to ominous fact : *Strangers have devoured his strength, and he knows it not ; yea, grey hairs are scattered upon him, and he knows it not,*[2] or *lays it not to heart.*

But Israel's most fatal ignorance is of God Himself. This is the sign and the cause of all their defects. *No troth, nor leal love, nor knowledge of God in the land.*[3] *They have not known Yahweh.*[4] *They have not known Me.*

With the causes of this ignorance the prophet deals explicitly in the fourth chapter.[5] They are two : the people's own vice and the negligence of their priests. Habitual vice destroys a people's brains. *Harlotry, wine and new wine take away the heart* or *brains of My people.*[6] Lust blinds them to the domestic consequences of their indulgence in the heathen worship, *and so the stupid people come to their end.*[7] Again, their want of political wisdom is due to their impurity, drunkenness, and greed to be rich.[8] Let those take heed who among ourselves assert that art is independent of moral conditions—that wit and genius may break every law of decency. They lie : such licence corrupts the natural intelligence of a people, and robs them of insight and imagination.

Yet Hosea sees that all the fault does not lie with the people. Their teachers are to blame, priest and prophet alike, for both *stumble* or *flounder*, and it is true that a people shall be like its priests.[9] *The priests have rejected knowledge and forgotten the Torah of their*

---

[1] vii. 11. See above, p. 350, n. 2.
[2] vii. 9. [3] iv. 1. [4] v. 4.
[5] For exposition of this chapter see above, pp. 272 ff.
[6] iv. 11, 12. [7] iv. 14. See above, p. 276.
[8] vii, *passim*. [9] iv. 4–9. Above, pp. 273 f.

God ; they think only of the ritual of sacrifice and the fines by which they fill their mouths. This was, as we have seen, *the* sin of Israel's religion in the eighth century. To the priests religion was a mass of ceremonies which satisfied the people's superstitions and kept themselves in bread. To the professional prophets it was an equally sensuous, an equally mercenary ecstasy. But to Hosea religion is above all a thing of the intellect and conscience : that *knowing* which is at once common-sense, plain morality and the recognition by a pure heart of what God has done and is doing in history. Of such a knowledge the priests and prophets are the stewards, and because they have ignored their trust the people have been provided with no antidote to the vices which corrupt their intelligence and make them incapable of seeing God.

In contrast to such ignorance Hosea describes the essential temper and contents of a true understanding of God. Using the word *knowledge* in the passive sense characteristic of his language, as not so much the acquisition as the impression of facts, an impression which masters not only a man's thoughts but his heart and will, Hosea describes the *knowledge of God* as feeling, character, and conscience. He makes it parallel to loyalty, repentance, love, and service. He emphasises that it comes from God Himself. It is not something which men reach by their own endeavours, or by a mere turn of their fickle hearts. It requires God Himself to speak, and discipline to chasten. The only passage in which the knowledge of God is described as the prize of man's own pursuit is that prayer of the people on whose facile religiousness Hosea pours his scorn.[1] *Let us know, let us follow up to know the Lord,*

---

[1] vi. 1 ff. See above, pp. 283 ff.

he heard them say, and promise themselves, *As soon as we seek Him we shall find Him.* But God replies that He can make nothing of such ambitions; they pass off like morning clouds and the early dew.[1] This discarded prayer, then, is the one passage in the book in which the knowledge of God is described as man's acquisition. Elsewhere, in conformity to the temper of the Hebrew word *to know,* Hosea presents the knowledge of the Most High, not as something man finds for himself, but something which comes down on him from above.

The means which God took to impress Himself upon the heart of His people were, according to Hosea, the events of their history. Hosea, indeed, also points to another means. *The Torah of thy God,* which once [2] he makes parallel to *knowledge,* is the body of instruction, judicial, ceremonial, and social, which has come down by the tradition of the priests so far as God Himself had given it to them. This was not all oral; part at least was already codified in the form we know as the Book of the Covenant.[3] But Hosea treats of the Torah only in connection with the priests. And the more frequent and direct means by which God has sought to reveal Himself to the people are the great events of their past. These Hosea never tires of recalling. More than other prophets, he recites the deeds done by God in the making of Israel. So numerous are his references that from them alone we

---

[1] vi. 4.   [2] iv. 6. See above, p. 274.

[3] See above, pp. 33, 97. On viii. 12—literally *I write multitudes of My Torah, as a stranger they have reckoned it*—no argument can be built; for even if (as above, p. 301) we take the first clause as conditional and render, *Though I wrote multitudes of My Torôth, yet as those of a stranger they would regard them,* this would not necessarily mean that no Torôth of Yahweh were yet written, but, on the contrary, might equally imply that some at least had been written.

could almost rebuild the early history. Let us gather them. The nation's father Jacob *in the womb grasped at his brother, and in his manhood wrestled with God ; yea, he wrestled with an Angel and overcame,*[1] *he wept and supplicated Him ; at Bethel he found Him, and there He spake with us—Yahweh God of Hosts, Yahweh is His name.*[2] . . . *And Jacob fled to the country*[3] *of Aram, and Israel served for a wife, for a wife he herded. By a prophet Yahweh brought Israel up out of Egypt, and by a prophet he was herded.*[4] *When Israel was young,*[5] *then I came to love him, and out of Egypt I called My son.*[6] *The more I called to them, the further did they go from Me :*[7] *they to the Ba'alim kept sacrificing, and to images offering incense. But I taught Ephraim to walk, taking him upon Mine*[8] *arms, and they did not know that I nursed them.*[9] . . . *Like grapes in the wilderness I found Israel, like firstlings on the fig-tree I looked on* your *fathers ; but* they *went to Ba'al-Peor, and consecrated themselves to Ba'al.*[10] . . . *But I am Yahweh thy God from the land of Egypt, and god save Myself thou knowest not, and Saviour there is none but Me. I shepherded thee in the wilderness, in the land of burning heats. But the more pasture they had, the more they fed them-*

---

[1] Or *was overcome.*

[2] xii. 3–6. See above, p. 329. LXX reads *they supplicated Me . . . they found Me . . . He spoke with them.* Many propose to read the last clause *with him.* The passage is obscure. Note the order—the wrestling at Peniel, the revelation at Bethel, then the flight to Aram. This however does not prove that in Hosea's information the last happened after the two first.

[3] שָׂדֶה , *field,* here used in its political sense : cf. *Hist. Geog.,* p. 79. Our word *country,* now meaning territory and now the rural as opposed to the urban districts, is analogous to the Hebrew *field.*

[4] xii. 12, 13 (Heb. 13, 14).   [5] *A youth.*

[6] xi. 1 ; LXX, followed by many critics, *his sons.* But *My son* is a better parallel to *young* in the preceding clause. Or trans. : *to be My son.*

[7] So LXX. See p. 319.   [8] So rightly LXX ; see p. 320.

[9] xi. 3 f.   [10] ix. 10.

*selves full ; as they fed themselves full their heart was
lifted up : therefore they forgat Me.*[1] *. . . I Yahweh thy
God from the land cf Egypt.*[2] And the revelation of
God was not only in that marvellous history, but in
the yearly gifts of nature and even in the success of
the people's commerce : *She knew not that it is I who
have given her the corn and the wine and the oil, and
silver have I multiplied to her.*[3]

This, then, is how God gave Israel knowledge of
Himself. *First* it broke upon the Individual, the
Nation's Father. And to him it had not come by
miracle, but in the fashion in which it has broken
upon men from then until now. He woke to find God
no tradition, but an experience. Amid the strife with
others of which life largely consists, Jacob became
aware that God also has to be reckoned with, and that,
hard as is the struggle for bread and love and justice
with one's fellow-men, with the Esaus and the Labans,
a more inevitable wrestle awaits the soul when left
alone in the darkness with the Unseen. This is our
sympathy with those patriarchs, not that they saw
the sea dry up before them or the bush ablaze, but
that upon some lonely battle-field of the heart they
endured those moments of agony, which imply a more
real Foe than is ever met in flesh and blood, and which
leave upon us marks deeper than heavy toil or the
rivalry of the world can inflict. So the Father of the
Nation came to *find* God at Bethel, and there, adds
Hosea, God *spake with us* [4] in the person of our ancestor.

The *second* stage of the knowledge of God was when
the Nation awoke to His leading, and *through a prophet,*
Moses, were *brought up out of Egypt.* Again no miracle

---

[1] xiii. 4–6.

[2] xii. 9 (Heb. 10). Other references to the ancient history are the story
of Gibeah and the Valley of Akhor.

[3] ii. 8 (Heb. 10).   [4] See above, p. 329, n. 2.

is adduced by Hosea. but with full heart he appeals to the grace and tenderness of the story. To him it is a wonder, a romance. Passing by the empires of earth, the Almighty chose for Himself this people that was no people, this tribe that were slaves. And the choice was of love only : *When Israel was young I came to love him, and out of Egypt I called My son.* It was the adoption of a slave-boy, adoption by the heart ; and the fatherly figures continues, *I taught Ephraim to walk, taking him upon Mine arms.* The charm is the same when Hosea hears God say that He *found Israel like grapes in the wilderness, like the first-lings on a fig-tree I looked on your fathers.*

Now these may seem imperfect figures, and the ideas they present may start more questions than their poetry can soothe to rest : as, for instance, why Israel alone was chosen—why this of all tribes was given such an opportunity to know the Most High. With these problems prophecy does not deal, and for Israel's sake had no need to deal. What alone Hosea is concerned with is the Character discernible in the origin and the liberation of his people. He hears that Character speak for Itself ; and It speaks of a love and of a joy, to find figures for which It goes to childhood and to spring—to the love a man feels for a child, to the joy a man shows at the sight of the firstfruits of the year. As the human heart feels in those two great dawns, when nothing is yet impossible, but all is full of hope and promise, so humanly, tenderly, joyfully had God felt towards Israel. The God of Israel is Love and Springtime to His people. Grace, patience, pure joy of hope and possibility—these are the Divine elements which this spiritual man, Hosea, sees in the early history of his nation, and not the miraculous, about which, from end to end his book is silent.

It is ignorance, then, of such a Character, so evident in these facts of their history, with which Hosea charges his people—not ignorance of the facts themselves, nor want of devotion to the memory of these, for they are a people who crowd the sacred scenes of the past, at Bethel at Gilgal at Beersheba, but ignorance of the Character which shines through the facts. Hosea also calls it forgetfulness, for the people once had knowledge.[1] The cause of their losing this has been their prosperity in Canaan : *As their pastures were increased they grew satisfied ; as they grew satisfied their heart was lifted up, and therefore they forgat Me.*[2]

Equally instructive is the method by which Hosea seeks to rouse Israel from this oblivion and bring them to a true knowledge of God. He insists that their recovery can only be the work of God Himself—the living God working to-day as He did in the past of the nation. To those past deeds it is useless for this generation to go back, and seek again the memory of which they have disinherited themselves. Let them rather realise that the same God still lives. The knowledge of Him may be recovered by appreciating His deeds in their own life. And these deeds must first be violence and terror, to rouse them from their sensuous sloth. The last verse we have quoted, about Israel's complacency and pride, is followed by these : *I shall be* [3] *to them like a lion, like a leopard I shall leap* [4] *upon the way, strike them as a bear bereft* of her cubs, *tear the caul of their heart, devour them there like a lion : wild beasts shall rend them.*[5] This means that into Israel's insensibility God must break with facts, with wounds

---

[1] iv. 6. [2] xiii. 6.

[3] With Wellhausen read אֶהְיֶה for וָאֱהִי .

[4] See above, p. 333, n. 3. [5] xiii. 7 f.

and horrors they cannot evade. Till He so acts, their own efforts, *then shall we know if we hunt up to know*,[1] and their protest, *My God, we do know Thee*,[2] are vain. Hosea did not speak for nothing. Events were about to happen as momentous as the Exodus and the Conquest of the Land. By 734 the Assyrians depopulated Gilead and Galilee; in 725 Samaria was invested, and by 721 the whole nation carried into captivity. God made Himself known.

We are already aware that Hosea did not count this as God's final revelation to His people. Doom is not doom to him, as to Amos, but discipline; and God withdraws His people from their fascinating land only that He may have them to Himself. He will bring His Bride into the wilderness again, the wilderness where they first met, and there, when her soul is tender and her stupid heart broken, He will plant in her again the seeds of His knowledge and His love. The passages which describe this are among the most beautiful of the book. They tell us of no arbitrary conquest of Israel by Yahweh, of no magic and sudden transformation. They describe a process as natural and gentle as a human wooing; they use the very terms of this: *I will woo her, bring her into the wilderness, and speak home to her heart. . . . And it shall be in that day that thou shalt call Me, My husband, . . . and I will betroth thee to Me for ever in righteousness and in justice, and in leal love and in mercies and in faithfulness; and thou shalt know Yahweh.*[3]

---

[1] vi. 3.　　　[2] viii. 2.　　　[3] ii. 14, 16, 19 f. (Heb. 16, 18, 21 f.).

CHAPTER XXII

REPENTANCE

HOSEA *passim*

IF we keep in mind what Hosea meant by knowledge —a new impression of facts implying a change both of temper and of conduct—we shall feel how natural it is to pass at once from his doctrine of knowledge to his doctrine of repentance. Hosea may be styled the first preacher of repentance, yet so thoroughly did he deal with this subject of eternal interest to the human heart, that between him and ourselves almost no teacher has increased the insight with which it has been examined, or the passion with which it ought to be enforced.

One thing we must hold clear. To us repentance is intelligible only in the individual. There is no motion of the heart which more clearly derives its validity from its personal character. Repentance is the conscience, the feeling, the resolution of a man by himself and for himself—' *I* will arise and go to my Father.' Yet it is not to the individual that Hosea directs his passionate appeals. For him and his age the religious unit was not the Israelite but Israel. God had called and covenanted with the nation as a whole ; He had revealed Himself through their historical fortunes and institutions. His grace was shown in the succour and guidance of them as a people ; His final judgement was threatened in their destruction as a state. Similarly, when by Hosea God calls to repentance, it is the nation whom He addresses.

At the same time we must remember those qualifications which we adduced with regard to Hosea's doctrine of the nation's knowledge of God.[1] They affect also his doctrine of the national repentance. Hosea's experience of Israel had been preceded by his experience of an Israelite. For years the prophet had carried on his anxious heart a single human character— lived with her, travailed for her, pardoned and redeemed her. As we felt that this long cure of a soul must have helped Hosea to his spiritual sense of the knowledge of God, so now we may assume that the same cannot have been without effect upon his personal teaching about repentance. But with his experience of Gomer, there conspired also his intense love for Israel. A warm patriotism necessarily personifies its object. To the passionate lover of his people, their figure rises up one and individual—his mother, his lover, his wife. Now no man ever loved his people more intimately or tenderly than Hosea loved Israel. The people were not only dear to him, because he was their son, but dear and vivid also for their loneliness and distinction among the peoples, and for their long experience as the intimate of the God of grace. God had chosen this Israel as His Bride ; and the remembrance of the unique endowment and destiny stimulated Hosea's imagination in personifying and individualising his people. He treats Israel with the tender particularity with which the Shepherd, leaving the ninety and nine, seeks the one lost lamb. Hosea's analysis of his fickle generation's

[1] See the previous chapter.

efforts to repent, of their motives in turning to God, and of their failures, is as inward and definite as if it were a single heart he were dissecting. Centuries have passed ; the individual has displaced the nation ; the experience of the human heart has been infinitely increased, and prophecy and preaching have grown more and more personal. Yet it has scarcely ever been found either necessary to add to the terms which Hosea used for repentance, or possible to go deeper in analysing the processes which these denote.

Hosea's simplest definition of repentance is that *of returning unto God.* For *turning* and *re-turning* the Hebrew language has one verb—shûbh. In the Book of Hosea there are instances in which it is employed in the former sense ; [1] but, even apart from its use for repentance, the verb usually means to return. Thus the wandering wife in the second chapter says, *I will return to my former husband ;* [2] and in the threat of judgement it is said, *Ephraim shall return to Egypt.* [3] Similar is the sense in the phrases *His deeds will I turn back upon him* [4] and *I will not turn back to destroy Ephraim.* [5] The usual meaning of the verb is, therefore, not merely to turn or change, but to turn right round, to turn back or home. [6] This is obviously the

[1] vii. 16, *They turn, but not upward* (*?*) ; xiv. 4, *Mine anger is turned away.*

[2] ii. 7 (Heb. 9).

[3] viii. 13 ; ix. 3 ; xi. 5.

[4] iv. 9 ; cf. xii. 2, 14 (Heb. 3, 15).

[5] xi. 9 ; cf. ii. 9 (Heb. 11).

[6] This may be further seen in the very common phrase שבות שוב עמי , *to turn again the fate of My people* (Hosea vi. 11) ; or in the use of שוב in xiv. 8 (Heb.), where it has the force, auxiliary to the other verb in the clause, of repeating or coming back to do a thing. But the text here needs emendation : cf. above on xiv. 7. Cf. Amos' use of the Hiphil form to *draw back, withdraw,* i. 3, 6, 9, 11, 13,; ii. 1, 4, 6.

force of its employment to express repentance. For this purpose Hosea seldom uses it alone.[1] He generally adds either the name by which God had always been known, Yahweh,[2] or the designation of Him, as *their own God*.[3]

We must emphasise this if we would appreciate the thoroughness of our prophet's doctrine, and its harmony with the New Testament. To Hosea repentance is no mere change in the direction of one's life. Repentance is a turning back upon one's self, a retracing of one's footsteps, a confession of what one has abandoned. It is a coming back and a coming home to God, as Jesus Himself describes in the Parable of the Prodigal. Hosea affirms that the Return to God, like the New Testament Metanoia, is the effect of new knowledge ; but the new knowledge is not of new facts —it is of facts which have been present for long and which ought to have been appreciated before.

Of these facts Hosea describes three kinds : the nation's misery, the grace of their God, and their guilt in turning from Him. Again it is as with the prodigal : his hunger, his father, and his cry, ' I have sinned against heaven and in thy sight.'

We have felt the pathos of those passages in which Hosea describes the decay and misery of Israel, the unprofitableness and shame of their traffic with other gods and alien empires. The state is rotten ; [4] anarchy, prevails.[5] The national vitality is lessened : *Ephraim hath grey hairs*.[6] Power of birth and begetting have gone ; the general unchastity bereaves the population :

---

[1] Cf. xi. 5, *they refuse to return.*

[2] vi. 1, *Come and let us return to Yahweh ;* vii. 10, *They did not return to Yahweh ;* xiv. 1, 2, *Return, O Israel, to Yahweh.*

[3] iii. 5, *They shall return and seek Yahweh their God ;* v. 4, *Their doings do not allow them to return to their God.*

[4] v. 12, etc.   [5] iv. 2 ff. : vi. 7 ff., etc.   [6] vii. 9

their glory flutters off like a bird.[1] The presents to
Egypt,[2] the tribute to Assyria, drain the wealth of the
people : *strangers devour his strength.*[3] The prodigal
Israel has his far-off country where he spends his
substance. In this connection we must take the
repeated verse : *the pride of Israel testifies to his face.*[4]
We have seen [5] the impossibility of the usual exegesis,
that by *the Pride of Israel* Hosea means Yahweh ; the
word ' pride ' is to be taken in the sense in which
Amos employs it of the exuberance and arrogance of
Israel's civilisation. If we are right, Hosea describes
a subtle symptom of the moral awakening whether of
the individual or of a community. The conscience of
many a man, of many a kingdom, has been reached
only through their pride. Pride is the last nerve which
comfort and habit leave quick ; and when summons to
a man's better nature fail, it is possible to touch his
pride with proofs of his decadence. This is what
Hosea means. Israel's prestige suffers. The civilisation of which they are proud has its open wounds.
Their politicians are the derision of Egypt ; [6] their
wealth, the gold of their Temple, is lifted by Assyria.[7]
The nerve of pride was also touched in the prodigal :
' How many hired servants of my father have enough
and to spare, while I perish with hunger.' Yet, unlike
him, this prodigal son of God will not therefore return.[8]
Though there are grey hairs upon him, though strangers
devour his strength, *he knoweth it not ;* of him it cannot
be said, ' he has come to himself.' And that is why
the prophet threatens the further discipline of exile
from the land and its fruits,[9] of bitter bread [10] and

[1] ix. 11 ff. [2] xii. 1 (Heb. 2). [3] vii. 9. [4] v. 5 ; vii. 10.
[5] See above, p. 279. [6] vii. 16. [7] x. 6. [8] vii. 10.
[9] ii. 14 (Heb. 16), etc. ; ix. 3 ff., etc. [10] ix. 4.

poverty [1] on an unclean soil. Israel also must eat husks and feed with swine before he arises and *returns to his God*.

But misery alone never led either man or nation to repentance : the sorrow of this world worketh only death. Repentance is the return to God ; and it is the awakening to truth about God, to facts of His nature and His grace, which alone makes repentance possible. No man's doctrine of repentance is intelligible without his doctrine of God ; and it is because Hosea's doctrine of God is so rich and tender, that his doctrine of repentance is so full and gracious. Here we see the difference between him and Amos. Amos had also used the phrase with frequency ; he also had appealed to the people to seek God and return to God.[2] But from Amos this went forth only as a pursuing voice. Hosea lets loose behind it a heart, plies the people with gracious thoughts of God, and brings about them, not the voices only, but the atmosphere, of love. *I will be as the dew unto Israel*, promises the Most High ; but He is before His promise. The prophecies of Hosea are drenched with the dew of God's mercy, of which no drop falls on those of Amos, but there God is rather the roar as of a lion, the flash as of lightning. Both prophets bid Israel turn to God ; but Amos means by that, to justice, truth, and purity, while Hosea describes a husband, a father, long-suffering and full of mercy. ' I bid you come back,' cries Amos. But Hosea pleads, ' If only you were aware of what God is, you would come back.' ' Come back to God and live,' cries Amos ; but Hosea, ' Come back to God, for He is Love.' Amos calls, ' Come back at once, for there is little time left till God visit you in judgement.' ;

---

[1] xii. 9 (Heb. 10).   [2] iv. 6, 8, 9, 10, 11.

but Hosea, ' Come back at once, for God has loved
you so long and so kindly.' Amos cries, ' Turn, for in
front of you is destruction ' ; but Hosea adds, ' Turn,
for behind you is God.' And that is why Hosea's
preaching of repentance is so evangelical. ' I will arise
and go *to my Father.*'

But the *third* element of the new knowledge which
means repentance is the conscience of guilt. *My
Father, I have sinned.* On this point it might be
averred that the teaching of Hosea is less spiritual than
that of later prophets, and that here he comes short
of the inwardness of the New Testament. There is
truth in this opinion ; and here we feel the defects of
his standpoint, as one who appeals, not to the individual,
but to the nation. But, at least, he is not satisfied to
exhaust his sense of Israel's guilt by his exposure of
the social sins of his day, and their terrible results.
He, too, understands what is meant by a conscience of
sin. He has called Israel's iniquity harlotry, unfaithfulness to God ; and in a passage of equal insight and
beauty he points out that in the service of the Ba'alim
God's people can never feel ought but a harlot's shame
and bitter memories of their better past.

*Rejoice not, Israel, to the pitch of rapture like the
peoples : for thou hast played the harlot from thine own
God ; 'tis hire thou hast loved on all threshing-floors.
Floor and vat shall not own them ; the new wine shall
play them false.*[1] Mere children of nature may abandon
themselves to the riotous joy of harvest and vintage,
for they have never known other gods than are worshipped by these orgies. But Israel has a past—
memory of a holier God, conscience of deserting Him
for material gifts. With such a conscience she can

[1] ix. 1. See above, p. 392.

never enjoy the latter; as Hosea puts it, they will not *own* or *take to* [1] her. Here is instinct the truth, that even in the fulness of life conscience is punishment; the sense of guilt is judgement.

Hosea does not attack the service of strange gods only because it is unfaithfulness to Yahweh, but also because, as the worship of images, it is senseless stupidity, inconsistent with that spiritual discernment of which repentance so largely consists. And with the worship of heathen idols Hosea equally condemns the worship of Yahweh under the form of images.

Hosea was first in Israel to attack the idols. Elijah had assailed the worship of a foreign god, but neither he nor Elisha nor Amos condemned the worship of Israel's God in the form of a calf. Indeed Amos, except in one doubtful passage,[2] never attacks idols or false gods. The reason is obvious. Amos and Elijah were concerned with the proclamation of God as justice and purity: and to the moral aspects of religion the question of idolatry is not relevant; the two things do not come directly into collision. But Hosea had deeper views of God, with which idolatry conflicted at a hundred points. We know what Hosea's *knowledge of God* was—how spiritual, how extensive—and we appreciate how incongruous idolatry must have shown against it. We are prepared to find him treating the images, whether of Ba'alim or of Yahweh, with that scorn which a passionate monotheism, conscious of its intellectual superiority, has ever passed upon the idolatry even of civilisations in other respects higher than its own. To Hosea the idol is an *'eseb*, *a made thing*,[3] made of the silver and gold with which Yahweh

---

[1] See above, p. 302, n. 4.   [2] v. 26.

[3] עֶצֶב from עָצַב, which in Job x. 8 is parallel to עָשָׂה.

Himself had endowed the people.[1] It is made only *to be cut off*[2] by the invader ! Chiefly, however, Hosea's scorn falls upon the image under which Yahweh Himself was worshipped. *Thy Calf, O Samaria !*[3] he calls it. *From Israel is it also*, as much as the Ba'alim. *A workman made it, and no god is it : chips shall the Calf of Samaria become !* In another place he mimics the *anxiety of Samaria for their Calf ; his people mourn for him, and his priestlings howl for his glory*, why ?— *because it is going into exile :*[4] the gold that covers him shall be stripped for the tribute to Assyria. Once more : *They continue to sin ; they make them a smelting of their silver, idols after their own model, smith's work all of it. To these things they speak ! Sacrificing men a-kissing of calves !*[5] All this is in the vein of satire which we find brilliant in the Prophet of the Exile.[6] Hosea was the first in whom it sparkled ; and it was due to his conception of *the knowledge of God*. Its relevancy to his doctrine of repentance is this, that so spiritual an apprehension of God as repentance implies, so complete a *metanoia* or *change of mind*, is intellectually incompatible with idolatry. He could not speak of repentance to men who *kiss calves* and worship blocks of wood. Hence he says : *Ephraim is wedded to idols : leave him alone.*[7]

More than idolatry, however, was in the way of Israel's repentance. The national worship was an obstacle. Its formalism and easy, mechanical methods of *turning to God* disguised the need of discipline and change of heart, without which no repentance is genuine. Amos contrasted the ritualism of the time with the duty of justice and service of the poor :[8]

[6] ii. 8 (Heb. 10).   [2] viii. 4.   [3] viii. 5.   [4] x. 5.
[1] xiii. 2.   [6] Isa. xli ff.   [7] iv. 17.   [8] Amos v.

Hosea opposes to it love and the knowledge of God. *I will have leal love and not sacrifice, and the knowledge of God rather than burnt-offerings.*[1] It is characteristic of Hosea to class sacrifices with idolatry. Both are senseless and incapable of expressing or answering the feelings of the heart. True repentance is rational, articulate, definite. *Take with you words,* says Hosea, *and* so *return to Yahweh.*[2]

To us who, after centuries of talk, know how words may be abused, it is strange to find them enforced as tokens of sincerity. But consider against what the prophet enforces them : *kissing of calves* and such mummery—worship of images that neither hear nor speak. Let us realise the inarticulateness of so much ritualism, how it stifles rather than utters the feelings of the heart. Imagine the dead routine of the legal sacrifices, their original symbolism worn bare, bringing to the young hearts of new generations no interpretation of their ancient, distorted details, reducing those who perform them to irrational machines. Then remember how our Reformers had to grapple with the same mechanical worship of their time, and how they bade the heart of every worshipper *speak*—speak for itself to God with rational, sincere words. So in place of the frozen ritualism of the Church there broke forth from all lands of the Reformation, as though it were birds in spring, a burst of hymns and prayers, with clear notes of the Gospel in the common tongue. So intolerable was the memory of what had been, that it was enacted that no sacrament should be dispensed

---

[1] vi. 6.

[2] xiv. 2. Perhaps the curious expression at the close of the verse, *so will we render the calves of our lips,* or (as a variant reading gives) *fruit of our lips,* has the same intention. Articulate confession or vows are the sacrifices, *the calves,* acceptable to God.

without the Word being given to the people along with it. If we keep these things in mind, we shall know what Hosea means when he says to Israel in their penitence, *Take with you words*.

No one, however, was more conscious of the danger of words. Upon the lips of the people Hosea has placed a confession of repentance, which, so far as the words go, is both musical and pathetic.[1] In some Christian languages it has been paraphrased into a confessional hymn. But Hosea describes it as rejected. The words are too easy ; the thoughts of God and of His power to save too facile. Repentance, it is true, starts from faith in the mercy of God, for without this there were only despair. Nevertheless in true penitence there is despair. Genuine sorrow for sin includes a feeling of the irreparableness of the past, and the penitent as he casts himself upon God does not dare to feel that he can be the same again. *I am no more worthy to be called Thy son : make me as one of Thy hired servants.* Such necessary thoughts as these Israel does not mingle with her prayer. *Come and let us return to Yahweh, for He hath torn* only *that He may heal, and smitten* only *that He may bind up. He will revive us again in a couple of days, on the third day raise us up, that we may live before Him. Then shall we know if we hunt up to know Yahweh. As soon as we seek Him we shall find Him : and He shall come upon us like winter-rain, and like the spring-rain pouring on the land.* This is too facile, too shallow. No wonder that God despairs of such a people. *What am I to make of thee, Ephraim ?* [2]

Another familiar passage, the Parable of the Heifer, describes the same ambition to reach spiritual results

---

[1] vi. 1–4.
[2] For the reasons for this interpretation see above, pp. 283 ff.

without spiritual processes. *Ephraim is a trained heifer—one that loves to tread* out the corn. *But I will pass upon her goodly neck. I will give Ephraim a yoke. Judah must plough. Jacob must harrow for himself.*[1] Cattle, being unmuzzled by law[2] when treading the corn loved this best of their year's work. Yet to reach it they must first go through the harder trials of ploughing and harrowing. So Israel would spring at the rewards of penitence, the peaceable fruits of righteousness, without going through the discipline which alone yields them. Repentance is no mere turning or even re-turning. It is a deep ethical process—the breaking up of fallow ground, the labour and long expectation of the sower, the seeking and waiting for God till Himself send the rain. *Sow to yourselves in righteousness ; reap love* (the love you have sown), *break up your fallow ground : for it is time to seek Yahweh, until He come and rain righting upon us.*[3]

A repentance so thorough cannot but result in a clear and steadfast living. Truly it is a returning not by oneself, but *a returning by God,* and it leads to the *keeping of leal love and justice, and constant waiting upon God.*[4]

[1] x. 11. [3] See above, p. 313.
[2] x. 12. [4] xii. 6 (Heb. 7).

CHAPTER XXIII

THE SIN AGAINST LOVE

HOSEA I–III; IV. 11 ff; IX. 10 ff; XI. 8 f

THE Love of God is a terrible thing—that is the last lesson of the Book of Hosea. *My God will cast them away.*[1]

My God—let us recall the right which Hosea had to use these words. Of all prophets he was the first to break into the full aspect of the Divine Mercy—to learn and to proclaim that God is Love. But he was worthy to do so, by the patient love of his own heart towards another who for years had outraged his trust and tenderness. He had loved, believed, and been betrayed; pardoned, waited and yearned, and sorrowed and pardoned again. It is in such long-suffering that his breast beats upon the breast of God with the cry *My God*. As he had loved Gomer, so had God loved Israel, past hope, against hate, through ingratitude and apostasy. Quivering with his own pain, Hosea has exhausted human care and affection for figures to express the Divine tenderness, and he declares God's love to be deeper than all the passion of men, and broader than all their patience: *How can I give thee up, Ephraim? How can I let thee go, Israel? I will not execute the fierceness of Mine anger. For I am God, and not man.*[2] And yet, like human affection,

[1] ix. 17.　　　　[2] xi. 8, 9.

this Love of God, too, confesses its failure—*My God shall cast them away*.[1] It is God's sentence of relinquishment upon those who sin against His Love, but the human lips which deliver it quiver with an agony of their own, and here, as more explicitly in other passages of the book, declare it to be equally the doom of those who outrage the love of their fellow men and women.

It has been said : ' The lives of men are never the same after they have loved ; if they are not better they must be worse.' ' Be afraid of the love that loves you : it is either your heaven or your hell.' ' The discipline of men springs from their love—if they take it not so, then their sorrow shall spring from the same source.' ' There is a depth of sorrow, which can be known only to a soul that has loved the most perfect thing and beholds itself fallen.' These things are true of the Love both of our brother and of our God. And the eternal interest of the life of Hosea is that he learned how, for strength and weakness, for better for worse, our human and our Divine loves are inseparably joined.

I

Most men learn that love is inseparable from pain where Hosea learned it—at home. There when love is strongest she feels her weakness most. For the anguish which love must bear is the contradiction at her heart between the largeness of her wishes and the littleness of her power to realise them. A mother feels this, bending over her child, when its body is racked with pain or its breath spent with coughing. So great is

[1] ix. 17.

the impulse of her love to do something, that she will feel herself cruel because nothing can be done. If the sick-bed become the beach of death, she must feel the helplessness and the anguish still more as the dear life is now plucked from her and now tossed back, and then drawn slowly out to sea upon the ebb from which there is no returning.

But the pain which disease and death cause to love is nothing to the agony which Sin inflicts when he takes the game into his hands. We know what pain love brings, if our love be a fair face and fresh body on which Death brands his sores while we stand by, as if bound. But what if our love be a childlike heart, and a frank expression and honest eyes, and a clean, clever mind! Our powerlessness is just as great and infinitely more tormented when Sin casts his shadow over these. That is Love's greatest torment when her children, who have run from her to the bosom of sin, look back and their eyes are changed. That is the greatest torment of Love—to pour herself without avail into one of those careless natures which seem capacious and receptive, yet never fill with love, for there is a crack and a leak at the bottom of them. The fields where Love suffers her sorest defeats are not the sick-bed and not death's margin, not the cold lips and sealed eyes kissed without response ; but the changed eyes of children, and the breaking of ' the full-orbed face,' and the darkening look of growing sons and daughters, and the home the first time the unclean laugh breaks across it. To watch, though unable to soothe, a dear body racked with pain, is peace beside the awful vigil of watching a soul shrink and blacken, and your love unable to redeem it.

Such a clinical study Hosea endured for years. The prophet of God, we are told, brought a dead child to life by taking him in his arms and kissing him. But Hosea with all his love could not make Gomer a true wife again. Love had no power on this woman. Hosea, who had once placed hope in tenderness, had to admit that Love's moral power is not absolute. Love may retire defeated from the highest issues of life. Sin may conquer Love.

Yet it is in this his triumph that Sin must feel the ultimate revenge. When a man has conquered this weak thing and beaten her down beneath his feet, God speaks the sentence of abandonment.

There is enough of the whipped dog in us to make us dread penalty when we come into conflict with the strong things of life. But it takes us long to learn that there is far more condemnation to them who offend the weak things of life, and particularly the weakest of all, its love. It was on sins against the weak that Christ passed His sternest judgements : *Woe unto him that offends one of these little ones ; it were better for him that he had never been born.* God's little ones are not only children, but all things which, like children, have only love for their strength. They are pure and loving men and women—men with no weapon but their love, women with no shield but their trust. They are the innocent affections of our own hearts, the memories of our childhood, the ideals of our youth, the prayers of our parents, the faith in us of our friends. These are the little ones of whom Christ spake, that he who sins against them had better never have been born. Often may the dear solicitudes of home, a father's counsels, a mother's prayers seem foolish against the challenges of a world, calling us to play the man and do as it does ; often may the vows and enthusiasms of boyhood seem impertinent against the temptations which are necessary to manhood : yet let us be true to the weak, for if we betray them, we betray our own souls. We may sin against law and maim or mutilate ourselves, but to sin against love is to be cast out of life. He who violates the purity of the love with which God has filled his heart, he who abuses the love God has sent to meet him in his opening manhood, he who slights any of the affections, whether of man or woman, of young or of old, which God lays upon us as the most powerful redemptive forces of our life, next to that of His Son—he sinneth against his own soul, and it is of such that Hosea spake : *My God will cast them away.*

We talk of breaking law : we can only break ourselves against it. But if we sin against Love, we destroy her ; we take from her the power to redeem and sanctify us. Though in their youth men think Love a quick and careless thing—a servant always at their side, a winged messenger easy of despatch—let them know that every time they send her on an evil errand she returns with heavier feet and broken wings. When they make her a pander they kill her outright. When she is no more they waken to that which Gomer came to know, that love abused is love lost, and love lost means Hell.

II

This, however, is only the margin from which Hosea beholds an abandonment still deeper. All that has been said of human love and the penalty of outraging it is equally true of the Divine love and the sin against that.

The love of God has the same weakness which we have seen in the love of man. It, too, may fail to redeem ; it, too, has been defeated on some of the

highest moral battle-fields of life. God Himself has
suffered anguish from His rejection by men. 'Herein,'
says a theologian, ' is the mystery of this love, . . . that
God can never by His Almighty Power compel that
which is the very highest gift in the life of His creatures
—love to Himself, but that He receives it as the free
gift of His creatures, and that He is only able to allow
men to give it to Him in a free act of their own will.'
So Hosea tells us how God does not compel, but allures
or *woos* the sinful back to Himself. And it is the
deepest anguish of the prophet's heart, that this free
grace of God may fail through man's apathy or insincerity. The anguish appears in those frequent antitheses in which his torn heart reflects herself in the
style of his discourse. *I, I would have redeemed them
—but they, they spoke lies against Me.*[1] *I found Israel
like grapes in the wilderness—they went to Ba'al-Peor.*[2]
*When Israel was a child, then I loved him . . . but they
sacrificed to the Ba'alim.*[3] *I taught Ephraim to walk,
but they knew not that I nursed them.*[4] *How can I give
thee up, Ephraim ? how can I let thee go, O Israel ? . . .
Ephraim compasses Me with lies, and the house of Israel
with deceit.*[5]

We fear to apply all that we know of the weakness
of human love to the love of God. Yet, though God
and not man, as man He commended His love to us.
He came nearest us, not in the thunders of Sinai,
but in Him Who presented Himself to the world as a
little child ; Who met men with no majesty or aureole,
but Whom when they saw they found nothing that *they*
should desire Him, His visage was marred more than
any man, and His form than the sons of men ; Who
came to His own and His own received Him not ; Who,

[1] vii. 13.   [2] ix. 10.   [3] xi. 1, 2.
[4] xi. 3.   [5] xi. 8, 12 (Heb. xii. 1).

having loved His own that were in the world, loved them up to the end, and yet at the end was by them deserted and betrayed,—it is of Him that Hosea prophetically says : *I drew them with cords of a man and with bands of love.*

We are not bound to God by any unbreakable chain. The strands which draw us up to God, to holiness, and everlasting life, have the weakness of those which bind us to the earthly souls we love. It is possible for us to break them. We love Christ, not because He has compelled us by any magic, irresistible influence to do so ; but, as John in his great simplicity says, *We love Him because He first loved us.*

Now this is surely the awfulness of God's love—that it can be resisted ; that even as it is manifest in Jesus Christ we men have the power, not only to remain, as so many do, outside its scope, feeling it far-off and vague, but having tasted it to fall away from it, having realised it to refuse it, having allowed it to begin its moral purposes in our lives to baffle and nullify these ; to make the glory of Heaven ineffectual in our own characters ; and to give our Saviour the anguish of rejection.

Give Him the anguish, yet pass upon ourselves the doom ! For, as I read the New Testament, the one unpardonable sin is the sin against our Blessed Redeemer's Love as this is brought home to the heart by the Holy Spirit. Every other sin is forgiven to men but to crucify afresh Him who loved us and gave Himself for us. The most terrible of His judgements is ' the wail of a heart wounded because its love has been despised ' : *Jerusalem, Jerusalem ! how often would I have gathered thy children as a hen gathereth her chickens, and ye would not. Behold, your house is left unto you desolate !*

Men say they cannot believe in hell, because they cannot conceive how God may sentence men to misery for the breaking of laws which they were born without power to keep. And one would agree with the inference, if God had done any such thing. But for them which are under the law and the sentence of death, Christ died once for all that He might redeem them. Yet this does not make a hell less believable. When we see how Almighty was that Love of God in Christ Jesus, lifting mankind and sending them forward with a freedom and a power of growth which nothing else in history has won for them ; when we prove again how weak that Love is, so that it is possible for characters which have felt it to refuse its enduring influence for the sake of some base and transient passion ; nay when *I myself* know this power and this weakness of Christ's love, so that one day being loyal I am raised beyond the reach of fear and of doubt, beyond the desire of sin and the habit of evil, and the next day finds me capable of putting it aside in preference for some enjoyment or ambition—then I know the peril and the terror of this love, that it may be to a man either Heaven or Hell.

MICAH

' But I am full of power by the Spirit of Yanweh
To declare to Jacob his transgressions, and to Israel his sin.

CHAPTER XXIV

THE BOOK OF MICAH

THE Book of Micah lies sixth of the Twelve Prophets in the Hebrew Canon, but in the order of the Septuagint third, following Amos and Hosea. The latter arrangement was doubtless directed by the sizes of the books; [1] in the case of Micah it has coincided with the prophet's proper chronological position. Though his exact date be not certain, he appears to have been a younger contemporary of Hosea, as Hosea was of Amos.

The book is not two-thirds the size of that of Amos, and about half that of Hosea. It has been arranged in seven chapters, which follow, more or less, a natural method of division.[2] They are usually grouped in three sections, distinguishable by their subject-matter, by their temper and standpoint, and to a less degree by their literary form. They are A. Chaps. i–iii; B. Chaps. iv, v; C. Chaps. vi, vii.

There is no book of the Bible, as to the date of whose different parts there has been more discussion,

[1] See above, pp. 6 f.
[2] Note that the Hebrew and English divisions do not coincide between chs. iv and v. In the Hebrew ch. iv includes a fourteenth verse, which in English stands as the first verse of ch. v. In this the English agrees with the Septuagint.

especially within recent years. The history of this is
shortly as follows :—

Tradition and the criticism of the early nineteenth century
accepted the statement of the title, that the Book was composed
in the reigns of Jotham, Ahaz, and Hezekiah—that is, between
740 and 700 B.C. It was agreed that there were in it traces
only of the first two reigns, but that the whole was put together
before the fall of Samaria in 721.[1] Then Hitzig and Steiner
dated chaps. iii–vi after 721 ; and Ewald denied that Micah
could have written chaps. vi, vii, and placed them under
Manasseh, *circa* 690–640. Next Wellhausen [2] sought to prove
that vii. 7–20 must be post-exilic. Stade [3] took a further step,
and, on the ground that Micah could not have blunted his
sharp pronouncements of doom, by the promises in chaps. iv
and v, he withdrew these from the prophet and assigned
them to the Exile.[4] The sufficiency of this argument was
denied by Vatke [5] ; and Kuenen [6] refused to believe that Micah
could have been content with the announcement of the fall of
Jerusalem as his last word, that therefore much of chaps. iv and
v is probably from himself, but since their argument is broken
and confused, we must look in them for interpolations, and
he found such in iv. 6–8, 11–13, and the working up of v. 9–14.
The famous passage in iv. 1–4 may have been Micah's, but
was probably added by another. Chaps vi and vii. 1–6 were
written under Manasseh by persecuted adherents of the prophetic school, but vii. 7–20 is from the Exile.

We may next notice two critics who adopted an extremely

---

[1] Caspari.

[2] In the fourth edition of Bleek's *Introduction*. In *Die Kleinen
Propheten* (1892) Wellhausen, while admitting that parts of iv, v might
be Micah's or from his time, took the rest as post-exilic (see below),
vi. 1–8 as from Manasseh's time, vi. 9–16 as yielding no proof of its date,
and vii. 1–6 as probably post-exilic.

[3] *Z.A.T.W.*, vols. I, III, IV.

[4] See also Cornill, *Einleitung*, 183 f. Stade takes iv. 1–4, iv. 11–v. 3,
v. 6–14, as originally one prophecy (distinguished by certain catchwords and an outlook similar to that of Ezekiel and the great Prophet
of the Exile), in which the two pieces iv. 5–10 and v. 4, 5, were afterwards
inserted by the author of ii. 12, 13.

[5] *Einleitung in das A.T.*, pp. 690 ff.   [6] *Einleitung*.

conservative position. Ryssel,[1] as the result of a thorough examination, declared that all the chapters were Micah's, even the much doubted ii. 12, 13, which have been placed by an editor of the book in the wrong position, and chap. vii. 7-20, which he agrees with Ewald can only date from the reign of Manasseh, Micah having lived long enough into that reign to write them. Another analysis by Elhorst[2] also reached the conclusion that the bulk of the book was authentic, but for his proof of this Elhorst requires a radical rearrangement of the verses on grounds which do not always commend themselves. He holds chap. iv. 9-14 [v. 1] and v. 8 [9] for post-exilic insertions. Driver[3] contributes a careful review of the book, and reaches the conclusions that ii. 12, 13, though in their wrong place, need not be denied to Micah; that the difficulties of ascribing chaps. iv, v to the prophet are not insuperable, nor is it necessary to suppose in them interpolations. He agrees with Ewald as to the date of vi-vii. 6, and, while holding it possible for Micah to have written them, thinks they are probably due to another, though no confident conclusion can be achieved. As to vii. 7-20, he judges Wellhausen's inferences to be unnecessary. A prophet in Micah's or Manasseh's time may have thought destruction nearer than it proved to be, and, imagining it as arrived, may have put into the mouth of the people a confession suited to its circumstance. Wildeboer[4] goes further than Driver. He replies in detail to the arguments of Stade and Cornill, denies that the reasons for withdrawing so much from Micah are conclusive, and assigns to the prophet the whole book, with the exception of several interpolations.

So far had criticism of the Book developed up to the date of the writing of this volume in 1896. Since then fresh analyses have been made.

In 1897 Volz regarded as Micah's the bulk of i-iii (but certainly not ii. 12 f.), and parts of iv, v with additions from later editors. In *Enc. Bibl.*, 'Micah (Book)' 1902 is a composite article by W. R. Smith and Cheyne. Smith seems

[1] *Untersuchungen über die Textgestalt u. die Echtheit des Buches Micha*, 1887.
[2] *De Profetie van Micha*, 1891, which I have not seen. It is summarised in Wildeboer's *Litteratur des A.T.*, 1895.
[3] *Introduction*, 1892.
[4] *Litteratur des A.T.*, pp. 148 ff.

responsible for the opinion that i–v form a single well-con-
nected Book of Micah from the eighth century with interpolations ii. 12 f., iv. 10, 11–13, and uncertainly iv. 1–4 ; chap. vi.
suits the time of Manasseh, so too vii. 1–6 ; vii. 7–20 is from
the Exile.   Cheyne holds that i–iii are mostly genuine, but that
in no part of iv–vii can we detect the hand of Micah.   Marti
finds oracles of Micah only in i–iii (with many interpolations)
to which the earliest additions were iv. 1–4, vi. 6–8, which harmonise with his teaching ; all the other additions, of which Marti
discerns very many, come from later centuries.   Budde (1906)
finds in i–iii the only passages which may be safely assigned
to Micah, but these chapters, especially the two first, have
suffered badly in tradition ; while iv–vii are a series of oracles
from many sources of which vi. 9 ff. may be pre-exilic, but
the most of the rest are of later date.   Further details of all
these opinions from Volz to Budde, as well as the opinions of
Duhm (1910), J. M. P. Smith (in his full commentary of 1911),
and others will be given in the following pages and footnotes
as we reach the successive passages of the Book.

We see, then, that critics are agreed as to the presence
of interpolations in the text, as well as to the occurrence
of some verses out of their proper order.   This indeed
must be obvious to every careful reader as he notes the
frequent breaks in the logical sequence, especially of
chaps. iv and v.   All critics, too, admit the authenticity
of chaps. i–iii, with the possible exception of ii. 12, 13,
and other verses ; while a number hold that chaps.
vi and vii, whether by Micah or not, must be assigned
to the reign of Manasseh ; but others relegate vi, vii
in part or whole to the Exile or to post-exilic times.
On the authenticity of chaps. iv and v—*minus* interpolations—and of chaps. vi and vii, opinion is most
divided ; but we ought not to overlook the fact that
some who have written very full monographs on
Micah [1] incline to believe in the genuineness of the

[1] Wildeboer (*De Profet Micha*), Ryssel and Elhorst

book as a whole. Before we enter upon the discussion of the Sections, let us note how much of the controversy turns upon the question, whether after decisively predicting the overthrow of Jerusalem it was possible for Micah to add prophecies of her restoration. We have had to discuss this point with regard both to Amos and Hosea. In the case of the former we decided against the authenticity of visions of a blessed future which now close his book ; in the case of the latter we decided for the authenticity. Our reasons for this difference were, that the closing vision of the Book of Amos is not in harmony with the ethical spirit of his authentic prophecies ; while the closing vision of the Book of Hosea is not only in language and in ethical temper consonant to the chapters which precede it, but in some details has been anticipated by these. Hosea, therefore, furnishes us with the case of a prophet who, though he predicted the ruin of his impenitent people (and this was verified by events), also spoke of the possibility of their restoration upon conditions conformable to his reasons for the inevitableness of their fall. And we saw, too, that the hopeful visions of the future, though placed last in the collection of his prophecies, need not necessarily have been spoken last by the prophet, but stand where they do because they had a lasting validity for the remnant of Israel.[1] What was possible for Hosea is possible for Micah. That promises come in his book, and closely after the threats which he gave of the fall of Jerusalem, does not imply that originally he uttered them all in close proximity. This indeed would have been impossible. But considering how often the political prospect in Israel changed during Micah's time, and

---

[1] See above, p. 339 ; and below, pp. 391 f. and 429 ff.

how far the city was in his day from her destruction
—more than a century distant—it seems improbable
that he should not (in whatever order) have uttered
both threat and promise. And naturally, when his
prophecies were arranged in their present order, the
promises would be placed after the threats.[1]

First Section : Chaps. i–iii

No critic doubts the authenticity of much of these
chapters. The main question is the date or the dates
of them. Only chap. ii. 12, 13 are generally regarded
as out of place.

Chap. i trembles with the destruction of both
Northern Israel and Judah—a destruction either imminent or actually happening. The verses which deal
with Samaria, 6 ff., do not simply announce her inevitable ruin. They throb with the sense either that
this is immediate or is going on, or has just been accomplished. The verbs suit each of these alternatives
And I shall set, or *am setting*, or *have set*, *Samaria for a
ruin of the field*, and so on. We may assign them to
any time between 725 B.C., the beginning of the siege
of Samaria by Shalmaneser, and a year or two after
its destruction by Sargon in 721. Their intense feeling
precludes the possibility of their having been written
in the years to which some assign them, 705–700, or
twenty years after Samaria was overthrown.

In the next verses the prophet mourns the fact
that the affliction of Samaria reaches even to the gate
of Jerusalem, and he singles out as partakers in the

---

[1] Wildeboer seems to have good grounds for his reply to Stade's
assertion that the occurrence of promises after the threats only blunts
and nullifies the latter. ' These objections,' he says, ' arise only against
the spoken, not against the written word.' See, too, the remarks he
quotes from De Goeje.

danger of Jerusalem a number of towns, which lie not between Jerusalem and Samaria, but at the other corner of Judah, in the Shephelah, or out upon the Philistine plain.[1] This was the region which Sennacherib invaded in 701, simultaneously with his detachment of a corps to attack the capital ; and accordingly we might have to conclude that this end of chap. i dates from that invasion, were no other explanation of the place-names possible. But another is possible. Micah belonged to one of these Shephelah towns, Moresheth-Gath, and it is natural that, anticipating the invasion of Judah, after the fall of Samaria (as Isaiah [2] also did), he should single out for mourning, his own district of the country. This appears to be the probable solution of a doubtful problem, and we may date the whole of chap. i between 725 and 720 or 718 ; for in 719 Sargon marched past this district of the Shephelah in his campaign against Egypt, whom he defeated at Raphia.[3]

Our conclusion is supported by chap. ii. Judah, though Yahweh plan evil against her, is in the full course of her social activities. The rich absorb the lands of the poor (vv. i, ff.) : note the phrase *upon their beds ;* it signifies a time of security. The enemies of Israel are internal (8). The public peace is broken by the lords of the land ; men and women, disposed to live quietly, are robbed (8 ff.). The false prophets have sufficient signs of the times in their favour to

[1] See below, pp. 408 ff.   [2] x. 28–32.

[3] Smend assigns the prophecy of the destruction of Jerusalem in iii. 14, along with Isa. xxviii–xxxii, to 704–701, and suggests that the end of ch. i refers to Sennacherib's campaign in Philistia in 701 (*A.T. Religionsgeschichte*, p. 225, n.). The former is possible, but the latter passage, following closely on i. 6, which implies the fall of Samaria as recent, if not actual, is more suitably placed in the time of Sargon's campaign over the same ground.

regard Micah's threats as calumnies (6). And although he sees destruction as inevitable, it is not to be to-day ; but *in that day* (4), some indefinite date in the future, the blow will fall and the nation's elegy be sung. On this chapter, then, there is no shadow of a foreign invader. We might assign it to the years of Jotham and Ahaz (under whose reigns the title of the Book places part of the prophesying of Micah), but since there is no sense of a double kingdom, no distinction between Judah and Israel it belongs probably to the years when immediate danger from Assyria had passed away, between Sargon's withdrawal from Raphia in 719 and his invasion of Ashdod in 710, or between the latter date and Sennacherib's accession in 705.

Chap. iii contains three separate oracles, which exhibit a similar state of affairs : the abuse of the people by their chiefs and rulers, who are implied to be in full power and security. They have time to aggravate their doings (4) ; their doom is still future —*then, at that time* (*ib.*). The bulk of the prophets determine their oracles by the amount men give them (5), another sign of security. Their doom also is future (6 f.). In the third of the oracles the authorities of the land are in the exercise of their offices (9 f.), and the priests and prophets of their oracles (11), and all these persons practise for bribes. Jerusalem is still being built and embellished (10). But the prophet, not because political omens point to this, but simply in the force of his indignation at the sins of the upper classes, prophesies the destruction of the capital (12). The oracles of chap iii may be later than those of the previous chapters.[1]

---

[1] See above on this page.

SECOND SECTION : CHAPS. IV, V.

This Section of the Book opens with two passages, iv, 1–5 and 6, 7, which there are serious objections against assigning to Micah.

1. The first of these, 1–4, is the prophecy of the Mountain of the Lord's House, repeated in Isaiah ii, 2–5. Probably the Book of Micah presents this in the more original form.[1] The alternatives are four : Micah was the author, and Isaiah borrowed from him ; or both borrowed from an earlier source ;[2] or the oracle is original in Micah, and has been inserted by an editor in Isaiah ; or it is late and has been inserted by editors in both Micah and Isaiah.

The last of these conclusions is required by the arguments of Stade and Hackmann, elaborated by Cheyne. Hackmann, marking the want of connection with the previous chapter, alleges the keynotes of the passage to be three : that it is not the arbitration of Yahweh,[3] but His sovereignty over foreign nations, and their adoption of His law, which the passage predicts ; that it is the Temple whose future supremacy is affirmed ; and that there is a strong feeling against war. These, Cheyne contends, are the doctrines of a later age than Micah's ; he holds the passage to be the work of a post-exilic imitator of the prophets, which was first intruded into the Book of Micah and afterwards borrowed from this by an editor of Isaiah's prophecies. It is just here, however, that the theory of these critics loses strength. Agreeing as I do that the genuine writings of early prophets have received

---

[1] So Hitzig (' ohne Zweifel '), and Cheyne, *Introduction to the Book of Isaiah ;* Ryssel, *op. cit.*, pp. 218 f. Hackmann (*Die Zukunftserwartung des Jesaia*, 127–8, n.) prefers the Greek of Micah. Ewald is doubtful. Duhm inclines to authorship by Isaiah, and would assign it to his old age.

[2] Hitzig ; Ewald.   [3] As against Duhm.

some, and perhaps considerable, additions from the Exile and later periods, it seems to me improbable that the same post-exilic insertion should find its way into *two* books.   And in fact the gentle temper shown by the passage towards foreign nations, contrasts strongly with the temper of many exilic and post-exilic prophecies ; [1] while the position which it demands for Yahweh and His religion is consistent with the principles of earlier prophecy.   The passage claims no more than the influence of Yahweh over the heathen, with the result that their war with Israel and one another shall cease ; not that they shall become, as the great prophecy of the Exile demands, tributaries and servitors.   Such a claim was no more than the natural deduction from the early prophets' belief in Yahweh's supremacy in righteousness.   And although Amos had not driven the principle so far as to promise the cessation of war, he also had recognised in unmistakable fashion the responsibility of the Gentiles to Yahweh, and His supreme arbitrament upon them.[2]   And Isaiah himself, in his prophecy on Tyre, promised a still more complete subjection of the life of the heathen to the service of Yahweh.[3]   Moreover, the fifth verse of the passage in Micah (though its connection with the previous four is not apparent) is more in harmony with pre-exilic than with post-exilic prophecy : *All the nations shall walk each in the name of his god, and we will walk in the name of Yahweh our God for ever and aye.*   This is consistent with more than one prophetic utterance before the Exile,[4] but not consistent with the beliefs of Judaism after the Exile.   Finally, the triumph achieved for Jerusalem in 701 is sufficient to have

[1] So rightly Duhm on Isa. ii. 2–4.
[2] Amos i and ii.   See above, pp. 122, 133.
[3] Isa. xxiii. 17 f.   [4] Jer. ii. 11.

prompted the feelings expressed by this passage for the *mountain of the house of the Lord ;* though if we are to bring it down to a date subsequent to 701, we must rearrange our views with regard to the date and meaning of the second chapter of Isaiah. In Micah the passage is devoid of connection, not only with the previous chapter, but with the subsequent verses of chap. iv. The possibility of a date in the eighth or beginning of the seventh century is all we can determine ; the other questions must remain in obscurity.[1]

2. Verses 6, 7 may refer to the Captivity of Northern Israel, the prophet adding that when it shall be restored the united kingdom shall be governed from Mount Sion ; but a date either on the eve of or during the Exile is more probable.

3. Verses 8–13 contain a series of small pictures of Jerusalem in siege, yielding different issues from the siege and possibly not the utterances of the same prophet nor concerning the same siege (see below, pp. 439 ff.). The words *thou shalt go to Babylon* may be, but are not necessarily, a gloss. If not, this particular

---

[1] More recent criticism tends to support Stade. Marti admits that iv. 1–4, breathing a genuinely humane and ethical spirit, makes an excellently suitable appendage, along with vi. 6–8, to Micah's oracles in i–iii ; but denies that it is the work of Isaiah or of Micah or of an earlier prophet, because its ideas are those of Ezekiel, Second Isaiah, and later prophets, *e.g.*, that Sion and her temple have a meaning for all peoples, that the Torah is to serve all mankind, and that there will be universal peace with other details. But against this, see above, p. 392. Budde (*Gesch.*, 86) and Duhm (*op. cit.*, 1910) follow Stade, of whose arguments J. M. P. Smith says that they ' seem irrefutable.' Edghill (pp. 182 ff.) thinks both the rhythm and ideas of iv i–4 are not Micah's, but sees ' no valid cause for assigning the fragment to a post-exilic date.' But A. R. Gordon (p. 94) thinks ' thought and language alike point to a date soon after the Restoration.' But see below, pp. 430 f. ; we must not forget how Ewald and the older generation of critics were satisfied that iv. 1–4, whether by Micah or not, was an early pre-exilic prophecy.

oracle cannot be earlier that 600 B.C. But it is possible
that in this series of oracles there are genuine words of
Micah worked over by later hands.

4. Chap. v. 1–9 (Eng. ; iv. 14–v. 8 Heb.) again pictures
a siege of Jerusalem, but promises a Deliverer out of
Bethlehem, the city of David.[1] Sufficient heroes will
be raised with him to drive the Assyrians (?) from
the land, and what is left of Israel after these disasters
shall prove a sovereign influence upon the peoples.
These verses were probably not uttered at the same
time (see below, pp. 442 ff.).

5. Verses 10–15 (Eng. ; 9–14 Heb.).—In prospect of
such a deliverance the prophet returns to what chap. i
has already described and Isaiah frequently emphasises
as the sin of Judah—her armaments and fortresses,
her magic and idolatries, the things she trusted instead
of trusting in her own God. They will no more be
necessary, and disappear. The nations that serve not
Yahweh will feel His wrath.

In these oracles there is little inconsistent with
authorship in the eighth century : there is much
suitable to this date. Everything they threaten or
promise is threatened or promised by Hosea and Isaiah,
except the destruction (in ver. 13) of the Masseboth
or sacred pillars, against which we find no sentence
from Yahweh before the Book of Deuteronomy, while
perhaps Isaiah promises the erection of a Massebah to
Yahweh in the land of Egypt.[2] But waiving for the
present the possibility of a date for Deuteronomy, or for
part of it, in the reign of Hezekiah, we must remember

---

[1] Roorda, reasoning from the Greek text, takes *House of Ephratha*
as the original reading, with Bethlehem added later ; and Hitzig reads
Ephrath, giving its final letter to the next word which improves the
grammar, thus : אפרת הצעיר.

[2] Isa. xix. 19 ; see *Isaiah i–xxxix*, p. 294.

the destruction, which took place under this king, of idolatrous sanctuaries in Judah, and feel also that, in spite of such a reform, it was possible for Isaiah to introduce a Maṣṣebah into his vision of the worship of Yahweh in Egypt. For has he not also dared to say that the *harlot's hire* of the Phœnician commerce shall one day be consecrated to Israel's God ? [1]

THIRD SECTION : CHAPS. VI, VII

The style changes. We have had a series of oracles, as if delivered orally. These are succeeded by a series of conferences or arguments, by several speakers. Ewald doubtfully accounts for the change by supposing that the latter date from a time of persecution, when the prophet, unable to speak in public, uttered himself in literature. But chap. i is also dramatic.

1. Chap. vi. 1–8.—An argument in which the prophet calls on the hills to listen to Yahweh's case against the people (1, 2). Yahweh Himself appeals to the latter, and in a style similar to Hosea's cites His deeds in their history as evidence of what He seeks from them (3–5). The people, presumably penitent, ask how they shall come before God (6, 7). And the prophet tells them what He has declared (8). Opening like Micah's first oracle (chap. i. 1), this argument contains nothing strange either to Micah or the eighth century. Exception has been taken to the reference in ver. 7 to the sacrifice of the first-born, which appears to have become more common from the age of Manasseh onwards, and which, therefore, led Ewald to date chaps. vi and vii from that king's reign. But, as Wellhausen admits, child-sacrifice is stated simply as a possibility, and—occurring at the climax of the sentence—as an

[1] *Idem*, ch. xviii.

extreme possibility. Of those who place it under
Manasseh, some, like Driver, still reserve it to Micah,
whom they suppose to have survived Hezekiah and
seen the evil days which followed. On the other hand,
it is claimed that the humble tone of the people's
enquiry is foreign to the tone of chaps. i–iii, and that
such expressions as *God of the Height* and *humbly walk*
are not found in pre-exilic writings, and that the closing
appeal not to the Jewish nation but to *man*, the individual, points to a time after Jeremiah, say the
fifth century.[1] These are somewhat weighty reasons
against assigning the passage to either the eighth or the
seventh century ; but are they conclusive ? In previous
editions I have said, ' I see no necessity to deny the
piece to Micah or the reign of Hezekiah,' and Duhm
remarks : ' Why the address to *man* should point to
a later time is not clear to me ; prophets who do not
hold sacrifice as necessary but substitute for it ethical
demands thereby betake themselves to the universal
human.' Similarly A. R. Gordon. Whatever be its
date the passage superbly sums up the teaching of the
prophets, and the question of its literary, is immaterial
in face of its manifest spiritual, authenticity.

2. Verses 9–16.—Many expositors [2] take these verses
along with the previous eight, as well as with the six
which follow in chap. vii. But there is no connection
between vv. 8 and 9 ; and 9–16 are better taken by
themselves. The prophet heralds, as before, the speech
of Yahweh to *tribe and city council* (9). Addressing
Jerusalem, God asks how He can forgive such fraud and
violence as those by which her wealth has been gathered
(10–12). Then addressing the people (note the change
in the second personal pronouns) He tells them He

[1] So virtually Nowack, Marti, J. M. P. Smith.
[2] *E.g.*, Ewald and Driver ; but not more recent ones.

must smite ; they shall not enjoy the fruit of their
labours (13–15). They have sinned the sins of Omri
and the house of Ahab (query—should it not be of
Ahab and the house of Omri ?), so that they must bear
the reproach upon the whole people [1] (16). In this
section three or four words have been marked as of
late Hebrew.[2] But this is uncertain, and the inference
from it precarious. The deeds of Omri and Ahab's
house have been understood as the persecution of the
adherents of Yahweh, and the passage has been assigned
by Ewald and others to the reign of the tyrant Manasseh.
But such habits of persecution could hardly be imputed
to the City or People as a whole ; and we may conclude
that the passage means others of that dynasty's sins.
Among these it is possible to make a large selection—
the favouring of idolatry, or the absorption by the rich
of the land of the poor (as in Naboth's case), a sin which
Micah has marked as that of his age. The whole treatment of the subject whether under the head of the
sin or of its punishment, resembles the style and
temper of Amos. It is, therefore, not impossible for
this passage also to have been by Micah, and we leave
the question of its date undecided. We are not shut
up, as the many suppose, to a date under Manasseh
or Amon, or later.[3]

3. Chap. vii. 1–6.—These verses are spoken by the
prophet in his own name or in that of the people. The

---

[1] For עַמִּי the LXX read עַמִּים.

[2] Wellhausen states four. But תּוּשִׁיָּה of ver. 9 is uncertain and
occurs in a parenthesis. רְמִיָּה is found in Hosea vii. 16, though the
text of this, it is true, is corrupt. זָכָה in another verbal form is found in
Isa. i. 16. There only remains מַטֶּה , but again it is uncertain whether
this in the sense of tribe was only late.

[3] ' The utterance might belong to any period . . . subsequent to the
reign of Ahab ' (J. M. P. Smith) ; Duhm and others assign it to Micah,
Marti to after the Exile.

land is devastated ; the righteous have disappeared !
everybody is ready to take his neighbour unawares.
There is no justice : the great of the land are free to
do what they like ; they have bribed the authorities.
Informers have crept in. Men must be silent, for
members of their families are their foes. Some of these
sins have been marked by Micah as those of his age
(chap. ii), but others point to a time of persecution such
as under Manasseh. Wellhausen remarks the simi-
larity to the state of affairs described in Mal. iii. 24
and in some Psalms. We cannot fix the date.[1]

4. Verses 7–20.—This passage starts from a different
temper of prophecy, and presumably from different
circumstances. Israel, as a whole, speaks in penitence.
She has sinned, and bows herself to the consequences,
but in hope. A day shall come when her exiles shall
return and the heathen acknowledge her God. The
passage, and with it the Book of Micah, concludes by
apostrophising Yahweh as the God of forgiveness and
grace to His people. Ewald and Driver assign the
passage, with those which precede, to the times of
Manasseh, in which of course it is possible that Micah
was still active, though Ewald supposes a younger and
anonymous prophet as the author. Wellhausen [2] goes
further, and, while recognising that the situation and
temper of the passage resemble those of Isaiah xl ff., is
inclined to bring it down to post-exilic times, because
of the wide extent of the Diaspora. Driver objects
to these inferences, and maintains that a prophet in
the time of Manasseh, thinking the destruction of

---

[1] J. M. P. Smith says that the general condition of depravity pictured
here and especially the faithlessness so widely prevalent are more easily
accounted for in the post-exilic period than at any previous time. This
is doubtful.

[2] Also Giesebrecht, *Beiträge*, p. 217.

Jerusalem to be nearer than it was, may have pictured it as having taken place, and put an ideal confession in the mouth of the people. It seems to me that some have failed to appreciate a piece of evidence stronger than any they have insisted on in their argument for a late date. This is, that the passage speaks of a restoration of the people only to Bashan and Gilead, the provinces overrun by Tiglath-Pileser III in 734. It is not possible to explain such a limitation either by the circumstances of Manasseh's time or by those of the Exile. In the former Samaria would have been included ; in the latter Sion and Judah would have been emphasised before any other region. It would be easy for the defenders of a post-exilic date to account for a longing after Bashan and Gilead, though they also would have to meet the objection that Samaria or Ephraim is not mentioned. But it would be natural for a prophet writing soon after the captivity by Tiglath-Pileser III to make this precise selection. And although there remain difficulties (in the temper and language of the passage) against assigning all of it to Micah or his contemporaries, I feel that on the geographical allusions much can be said for the origin of this part of the passage in their age, or even in an earlier,[1] that of the Syrian wars in the end of the ninth century, with which there is nothing inconsistent either in the spirit or the language of vv. 14–17. I am sure that if the defenders of a late date had found a selection of districts as suitable to the post-exilic circumstances of Israel as the selection of Bashan and Gilead is to the circumstances of the eighth century, they would

---

[1] See, however, J. M. P. Smith : ' the days when Bashan and Gilead were occupied (eighth century, B.C.) are " days of old." This indicates a time after the return movement under Ezra and Nehemiah and the accompanying development of particularism.'

have emphasised it as a conclusive confirmation of
their theory. On the other hand, ver. 11 can date
only from the Exile, or the following years, before
Jerusalem was rebuilt. Verses 18–20 appear to stand
by themselves.

It seems, therefore, that vii. 7–20 is a Psalm composed of pieces from various dates, which, combined,
give us a picture of the secular sorrows of Israel, and
of the conscience she ultimately felt in these, and conclude by a doxology to the mercies of her God.

CHAPTER XXV

MICAH THE MORASHTITE

MICAH

SOME time in the reign of Hezekiah, when the kingdom of Judah was still inviolate, but shivering to the shock of the fall of Samaria, and probably while Sargon the destroyer was pushing his way past Judah to meet Egypt at Raphia, a Judæan prophet of the name of Micah, standing in sight of the Assyrian march, attacked the sins of his people and prophesied their speedy overthrow beneath the same flood of war. If we be correct in our surmise, the exact year was 720–719 B.C. Amos had been silent thirty years, Hosea hardly fifteen; Isaiah was in the midway of his career. The title of Micah's book asserts that he had previously prophesied under Jotham and Ahaz, and though we have seen it to be possible, it is by no means proved, that certain passages of the book date from these reigns.

Micah is called the Morashtite.[1] For this designation there appears to be no other meaning than that of a native of Moresheth-Gath, a village mentioned by himself.[2] It signifies *Property* or *Territory* of Gath, and after the fall of the latter, which from this time no

[1] Micah i; Jer. xxvi. 18. But Budde (*Gesch.*, 85) points the name *Marishtî*, the Mareshite (as Luther read it), *i.e.*, from Mareshah.

[2] i. 14.

more appears in history, Moresheth may have been used alone. Compare the analogous cases of Helkath (*portion of*—), Galilee, Ataroth, Chesulloth, and Iim.[1]

In our ignorance of Gath's position, we should be equally at fault about Moresheth, for the name has vanished, were it not for one or two plausible pieces of evidence. Belonging to Gath, Moresheth must have lain near the Philistine border : the towns among which Micah includes it are situate in that region ; and Jerome declares that the name—though the form, Morasthi, in which he cites it is suspicious—was in his time still extant in a small village to the east of Eleutheropolis or Beit-Jibrin. Jerome cites Morasthi as distinct from the neighbouring Mareshah, which is also quoted by Micah beside Moresheth-Gath.[2]

Moresheth was, therefore, a place in the Shephelah, or range of low hills which lie between the hill-country of Judah and the Philistine plain. It is the opposite exposure from the wilderness of Tekoa,[3] some seventeen miles away across the watershed. As the home of Amos is bare and desert, so the home of Micah is fair and fertile. The irregular chalk hills are separated by broad glens, in which the soil is alluvial and red, with room for cornfields on either side of

---

[1] Ataroth (Num. xxxii. 3) is Atroth-Shophan (*ib.* 35) ; Chesulloth (Josh. xix. 18) is Chisloth-Tabor (*ib.* 12) ; Iim (Num. xxxiii. 45) is Iye-Abarim (*ib.* 44).

[2] ' Michæam de Morasthi qui usque hodie juxta Eleutheropolim haud grandis est viculus.'—Jerome, Preface to Micha. ' Morasthi, unde fuit Micheas propheta, est autem vicus contra orientem Eleutheropoleos.'—*Onomasticon*, which also gives ' Maresa, in tribu Juda ; cuius nunc tantummodo sunt ruinæ in secundo lapide Eleutheropoleos.' See too, the *Epitaphium S. Paulæ* : ' Videam Morasthim sepulchrum quondam Michææ, nunc ecclesiam, et ex latere derelinquam Choræos, et Gitthæos et Maresam.' The occurrence of a place bearing the name Property-of-Gath so close to Beit-Jibrin seems to strengthen the claims of the latter to be Gath. See *Hist. Geog.*, p. 196.

[3] See above, pp. 72 f

the perennial or almost perennial streams. The olive
groves on the braes are finer than either those of
the plain below or of the Judæan tableland above.
There is herbage for cattle. Bees murmur everywhere, larks are singing, and although to-day you
may wander in the maze of hills for hours without
meeting a man or seeing a house, you are never out
of sight of the traces of ancient habitation, and seldom
beyond sound of the human voice—shepherds and
ploughmen calling to their flocks and to each other
across the glens. There are none of the conditions or
of the occasions of a large town. But, like much of the
south of England, the country is one of villages and
homesteads, breeding good yeomen—men satisfied and
in love with their soil, yet borderers with a far outlook
and a keen vigilance and sensibility. The Shephelah
is sufficiently detached from the capital and body of the
land to beget in her sons an independence of mind and
feeling, but so much upon the edge of the open world
as to endue them with that sense of the responsibilities
of warfare, which the national statesmen, aloof and at
ease in Sion, could hardly have shared.

Upon one of the westmost terraces of this Shephelah,
nearly a thousand feet above the sea, lay Moresheth
itself. There is a great view across the undulating
plain with its towns and forts, Lachish, Eglon, Shaphir,
and others, beyond which runs the coast road, the
famous war-path between Asia and Africa. Ashdod
and Gaza are hardly discernible against the glitter of
the sea, twenty-two miles away. Behind roll the
bush-covered hills of the Shephelah, with David's hold
at Adullam,[1] the field where he fought Goliath, and
many another scene of border warfare ; while over

---

[1] For the situation of Adullam in the Shephelah see *Hist. Geog.*, p. 229.

them rises the high wall of the Judæan plateau, with the defiles breaking through it to Hebron and Bethlehem.

The valley-mouth near which Moresheth stands has always formed the south-western gateway of Judæa, the Philistine or Egyptian gate, as it might be called, with its outpost at Lachish, twelve miles across the plain. Roads converge upon this valley-mouth from all points of the compass. Beit-Jibrin, which lies in it, is midway between Jerusalem and Gaza, about twenty-five miles from either, nineteen miles from Bethlehem and thirteen from Hebron. Visit the place at any point of the history of Palestine, and you find it either full of passengers or a centre of campaign. Asa defeated the Ethiopians here. The Maccabees and John Hyrcanus contested Mareshah, two miles off, with the Idumeans. Gabinius fortified Mareshah. Vespasian and Saladin both deemed the occupation of the valley necessary before they marched upon Jerusalem. Septimius Severus made Beit-Jibrin the capital of the Shephelah, and laid out military roads, whose pavements still radiate from it in all directions. The *Onomasticon* measures distances in the Shephelah from Beit-Jibrin. Most of the early pilgrims from Jerusalem by Gaza to Sinai or Egypt passed through it, and it was a centre of Crusading operations whether against Egypt during the Latin kingdom or against Jerusalem during the Third Crusade. Not different was the place in the time of Micah. Micah must have seen pass his door the embassies which Isaiah tells us went down to Egypt from Hezekiah's court, and seen return those Egyptian subsidies in which a foolish people put their trust instead of in their God.

In touch, then, with the capital, feeling every throb of its follies and its panics, but standing on that border which must, as he believed, bear the brunt of the invasion that its crimes were attracting, Micah lifted up his voice. They were days of excitement. The words of Amos and Hosea had been fulfilled upon Northern Israel. Should Judah escape, whose injustice and impurity were as flagrant as her sister's? It were vain to think so. The Assyrians had come up to her northern border. Isaiah was expecting their assault upon Mount Ṣion.[1] The Lord's Controversy was not closed. Micah will summon the earth to hear the old indictment and unexhausted sentence

The prophet speaks :—

i. 2. *Hear ye, O peoples [2] all ;*
   Hearken, O Earth, and her fulness !
   That Yahweh may be for a witness among [3] you,
   The Lord from His Holy Temple ! [4]

   3. *Yahweh behold, going forth from His Place,*
   To come down and to march [5] on the heights of the earth.

---

[1] Isa. x. 28 ff. This makes it conceivable that Micah i. 9, *it has struck right up to the gate of Jerusalem*, was composed immediately after the fall of Samaria, and not, as Smend supposes, during the campaign of Sennacherib. Against the latter date is the objection that by then the fall of Samaria, which Micah i. 6 describes as imminent or present, was already nearly twenty years past.

[2] The address is either to the tribes, in which case we must substitute *land* for *earth* in the next line ; or more probably to the Gentile *nations*, but in this case we cannot translate (as most do) in the third line that the Lord will be a witness *against* them, for the charge is only against Israel. They are summoned in the same sense as Amos summons a few of the nations in ch. iii. 9 ff.—The opening words of Micah are original to this passage, and interpolated in the exordium of the other Micah, 1 Kings xxii. 28. Stade and Marti deny 2–4 to Micah but on insufficient grounds.

[3] Not *against* as most translate ; see preceding note.

[4] Yahweh's Temple or Place is not as in Judges v. 4, Deut. xxxiii. 2, but Heaven, as in Isa. xviii. 4, Ps. xxix. 9.

[5] LXX and some moderns omit ; others omit *to come down*.

i. 4. *And the mountains are molten beneath Him.*
And the valleys burst open,
Like wax in face of the fire,
Like waters shot over a fall.[1]

5. *All this for Jacob's transgression,*
For the sin of the House of Judah.[2]
What is the transgression of Jacob ?
Samaria is it not ?
And what is the sin [3] *of Judah ?*
Is it not Jerusalem ?

6. *So I will turn to a field* [4] *Samaria,*
To vineyard terraces,
And pour down her stones to the glen,
Laying bare her foundations.

7 *Her images all shall be shattered,*
And all her ashērim (?) [5] *be burned*
In the fire, and the whole of her idols
I shall lay waste.
For from a harlot's hire were they gathered,
And to a harlot's hire shall return [6]

The last couplet can only mean that as all the wealth which produced this costly idolatry was regarded by Israel as paid to her by the Ba'alim in return for devotion to them as lords of the soil, so when it fell into the hands of the invaders it would be regarded by these idolaters as their god's rewards to them or be

---

[1] Ver. 4 is needlessly denied to Micah by some.

[2] Heb. *of Israel*, but *Judah* is required by the third line further on.

[3] So Syr. ; LXX, Targ., Jerome, *sin of the house of Judah :* Heb. *high places*.

[4] Heb. *ruin* (?) *of the field*. Objections to this phrase are arbitrary. So Samaria lies to-day. *Terraces* lit. *planting-places*.

[5] So Wellhausen suggests. Heb. *her harlot hires*.

[6] Some (*e.g.*, Marti, J. M. P. Smith, A. R. Gordon) take ver. 7 as an interpolation, but, I feel, on insufficient grounds.

used in unchaste rites. If the verbs in vv. 6, 7 are to
be rendered in the future as above, the passage will
date just before the fall of Samaria in 721 ; but just
after if the verbs are taken in the present tense.

8. *For this let me mourn, let me wail,*
   Let me go about barefoot and stripped,
   Make lamentation like jackals,
   And mourning as the daughters of the desert.[1]
9. *For desperate is her stroke.*[2]
   Yea, it is come on to Judah,
   Has struck right up to the gate of my people,
   Right up to Jerusalem.

Within the capital Isaiah also was predicting the
advance of the Assyrian invasion to its walls, but in
a different temper.[3] He was full of assurance that,
although at the very gate, the Assyrian could not
harm the city of Yahweh, but must fall when he lifted
his hand against it. Micah has no such hope : he is
overwhelmed with the sense of Jerusalem's danger.
Provincial though he be, and wrathful at the danger
into which the politicians of Jerusalem had dragged
the country, he mourns the peril of *the gate of my
people*, as he fondly calls her. Therefore we must
not exaggerate the frequently drawn contrast between
Isaiah and himself.[4] To Micah also Jerusalem was
dear, and his subsequent prediction of her overthrow [5]
ought to be read with the accent of this previous
mourning for her peril. Yet his heart clings most
to his home, and while Isaiah pictures the Assyrian

---

[1] בנות יענה, that is, the ostriches : Arab. wa'ana, ' white, barren
ground.' Arabs call the ostrich ' father of the desert : abu sahârâ.'
[2] LXX. [3] Isa. x. 28 ff.
[4] It is well put in W. R. Smith's *Prophets* [2], pp. 289 ff.
[5] iii. 12.

entering Judah from the north by Migron, Michmash, and Nob, Micah anticipates invasion by the opposite gateway of the land, at the mouth of the avenue to his own village. His elegy sweeps across the landscape so dear to him. This was even more than Jerusalem, the world of his heart. It gives us a living interest in the man that the fate of these small villages, many of them vanished, should excite in him more passion than the fortunes of Ṣion. In such a passion we can incarnate his spirit. Micah is no longer a book, or an oration, but flesh and blood upon a home and a countryside of his own. We see him on his housetop pouring forth his words before the hills and the far-stretching heathen land. In the names of villages within sight he reads symbols of the curse coming upon his country, and of the sins that have earned the curse. So poets have caught their music from the nameless brooklets of their boyhood's fields; and many a prophet has learned to read the tragedy of man and God's verdict upon sin in his experience of village life. But there was more than feeling in Micah's choice of his own country as the scene of the Assyrian invasion. He had better reasons for his vision than Isaiah, who imagined the approach of the Assyrian from the north. For it is remarkable how invaders of Judæa, from Sennacherib to Vespasian and from Vespasian to Saladin and Richard, have shunned the northern approach to Jerusalem and endeavoured to reach her by the gateway at which Micah stood mourning. He had, too, this greater motive for his fear, that Sargon, as we have seen, was actually in the neighbourhood, marching to the defeat of Judah's chosen patron, Egypt.[1] Was it

---

[1] This seems more probable than to take as the cause of the alarm Sennacherib's invasion of southern Palestine in 701, as do Wellhausen, Cornill, Marti, and J. M. P. Smith.

not probable that, when the latter was overthrown, Sargon would turn back upon Judah by Lachish and Mareshah ? If we keep this in mind we shall appreciate, not only the anxiety, but the foresight that inspires the following passage, which is to our Western taste strangely cast in a series of plays upon place-names.[1] The disappearance of some of these names, and our ignorance of the transactions to which the verses allude, often render both text and meaning uncertain. Micah begins with the well-known play upon the name of Gath ; the name of the place which he couples with it is illegible. It cannot be Akka as some suppose, but must be a Philistine town, called either Bokîm or Bekaîm, or it may be Yabneh, if with the LXX we alter the verb, and so the line forms with the previous one an intelligible couplet : *Tell it not in Tell-town ; Weep ye in Weep-town ; or build not again He-buildeth.* The following Beth-le-'Aphrah, *House of Dust*, must be taken with them, for in the phrase *roll ye* there is a play upon the name ' Philistine.' So, too, Shaphîr, or Beauteous, the modern Suafîr, lay in the Philistine region. Sa'anan, Beth-esel, and Maroth are unknown ; but if Micah, as is probable, begins his list far off on the western horizon and comes gradually inland, they also are to be sought for on the maritime plain.[2] Then he draws nearer by Lachish, on the first hills and in the leading pass towards Judah, to Moresheth-Gath, Achzib, Mareshah, and Adullam, which all lie within Judah's territory and about the prophet's own home. We understand the allusion, at least, to Lachish in ver. 13. As the last Judæan outpost towards Egypt, and on a main road thither,

---

[1] With J. M. P. Smith (p. 42) I agree that Marti's rejection of the passage because of its play upon place-names is unfounded.

[2] On the above place-names, see notes on next page.

Lachish would receive the Egyptian subsidies of horses and chariots, in which the politicians put their trust instead of in their God.   Thus she *was the beginning of sin to the daughter of Şion.*   And if we can trust the text of ver. 14, Lachish would pass on the Egyptian ambassadors to Moresheth-Gath, the next stage of their approach to Jerusalem.   But this is uncertain.   With Moresheth-Gath is coupled Achzib, a town at some distance from Jerome's site for the former, to the neighbourhood of which, Mareshah, we are brought back again in ver. 15.   Adullam, with which the list closes, lies some eight or ten miles to the north-east of Mareshah.

The prophet speaks :—

i. 10.   *Tell it not in Gath,*[1]
           In . . .(?) weep ye ![2]
           In Beth-'Aphrah[3] *roll ye*[4] *in dust,*
11.   *Pass along, dwellers*[5] *in Shaphîr,*[6]

---

[1] Some take this as a later addition, quoted from 2 Sam. i. 20.

[2] Heb. *weeping weep not* בכו אל־תבכו, *i.e., weep not at all,* but a place-name is required and is found in LXX, ἐν Ἀκείμ; so some emend בכו to בעכו *in Akko* or *Akka ;* yet not only is the loss of the initial ע of the name unlikely, but *Akka* lies too far north from the other towns mentioned to be natural here.   Some propose בבכים *in Bokîm* or *Bekaîm* (Vollers, Nowack, Wellhausen) and also delete אל , *not,* as a dittography from the אל of the preceding line ; yet LXX has *not,* and the whole line in LXX, ἐν Ἀκείμ μὴ ἀνοικοδομεῖτε, suggests another reading which is a play on the name of a Philistine town, יבנה אל־תבנו *rebuild not Yabneh,* which name means *He builds.*   This would solve the difficulty, but all is uncertain.

[3] This cannot be Ophrah of Benjamin ; the name, however, may not be from '*aphar, dust,* but from '*opher, a gazelle ;* and S. of Beit-Jibrin is Wady el-Ghufr the corresponding Arabic word.   But as stated above the name should be that of a Philistine town.

[4] LXX ; Heb. *I have rolled myself.*

[5] Heb. *inhabitress* here and in following lines ; but the feminine is a collective one (Driver on 1 Sam. xvii. 21).

[6] ' Beauty-town,' usually taken as the modern Suafîr on the Philistine plain, 4½ miles S.E. of Ashdod, identifiable with Sapheir of the *Onomasti-*

In nakedness, shame. (?) [1]
The dwellers in Ṣaanan [2] *march not forth,*
The lament of Beth-'esel [3] *from you takes its blow. (?)* [4]

12. *How anxiously hope for good*
The dwellers in Maroth !
For evil comes down from Yahweh
To the gate of Jerusalem.

13. *Harness the car to the horse,*
O dwellers of Lakhish, [5]
Beginning of sin to the daughter of Ṣion,
In thee are found the transgressions of Israel,

14. *Therefore thou givest ambassadors* [6] *(?)*
Unto Moresheth-Gath. [7]
The houses of Akhzib [8] *are for a lie*
To Israel's kings.

15. *Again the Possessor I bring you,*
Dwellers of Mareshah. [9]

---

con, ' between Eleutheropolis and Ascalon,' except that Sapheir is also described as ' in the hill-country.' Guérin found the name Safar a little N. of Beit-Jibrin (*Judée,* ii. 317).

[1] The fate of captives ; but LXX omits *shame* and the line has provoked several emendations.

[2] ' March-out-town,' perhaps Ṣenan of Josh. xv. 37, not known.

[3] Beth-'esel and Maroth *bitternesses,* are also unknown.

[4] Syr.; LXX, πληγὴν ὀδύνης (? αυτης, see Kittel's note); Heb. *its standing :* J. M. P. Smith reads *Beth-eṣel is taken from its site.*

[5] Tell-el-Hesy. *Lakhish* rhymes with *rekhesh, horse.*

[6] Or *letters of dismissal* (?).

[7] See above, p. 402.

[8] Lit. *Lie-town ;* Josh. xv. 44 ; mentioned with Keilah and Mareshah ; perhaps the present 'Ain Kezbeh, 8 miles N.N.E. of Beit-Jibrin.

[9] מָרְשָׁה, but in Josh. xv. 44 מראשה, which is identical in spelling with the present name of a ruin 1 mile S. of Beit-Jibrin. Μαρεσα is placed by Eusebius (*Onom.*) 2 Roman miles S. of Eleutheropolis (= Beit-Jibrin). Another play on names *ha-yoresh* (Possessor) *Mareshah.*

> *Unto Adullam* [1] *shall come*
> *Israel's glory.*

i. 16. *Make thyself bald and shave*
For thy darling sons,
Broaden thy baldness like to the vulture,
For they go into exile from off thee.

This was the fate which the Assyrian kept for the peoples whom he fought. Others raided, burned, and slew: he carried whole populations to exile.

Having thus pictured the doom which threatened his people, Micah turns to declare the sins for which it has been sent upon them.

---

[1] Six miles N.E. of Beit-Jibrin.

CHAPTER XXVI

THE PROPHET OF THE POOR

MICAH II, III

WE have proved Micah's love for his countryside
in the effusion of his heart upon her villages,
with a grief for their danger greater than his grief for
Jerusalem. Now in his treatment of the sins, which give
that danger its fatal significance, he is inspired by the
same affection for the fields and folk about him. While
Isaiah satirises the fashions of the town and intrigues
of the court, Micah scourges the avarice of the land-
owner and the injustice which oppresses the peasant.
He could not help sharing Isaiah's indignation at the
fatal politics of the capital, any more than Isaiah could
help sharing his sense of the economic dangers of the
provinces ;[1] but it is the latter with which Micah is
familiar and on which he spends his wrath. These so
engross him that he says almost nothing about the
idolatry, luxury, or vice, which, according to Amos
and Hosea, were corrupting the nation.

Social wrongs are felt most acutely, not in the town,
but in the country. So in the days of Rome, whose
earliest social revolts were agrarian.[2] So in the Middle

[1] Isa. v. 8.
[2] Congreve, in his Essay on Slavery in his edition of Aristotle's *Politics*,
p. 496, points out that all the servile wars from which Rome suffered arose,
not in the capital, but in the provinces, notably in Sicily.

Ages : the fourteenth century saw both the Jacquerie in France and the Peasants' Rising in England ; Langland, who was equally familiar with town and country, expends nearly all his sympathy upon the poverty of the latter, ' the poure folk in cotes.' So after the Reformation, under the new spirit of which the first social revolt was the Peasants' War in Germany. So at the French Revolution, which began with the march of the starving peasants into Paris. And so still, for our new era of social legislation was forced open, not by the poor of London and the large cities, but by the peasantry of Ireland and the crofters of the Scottish Highlands. Political and religious discontent start among manufacturing centres, but the springs of the social revolt are nearly always found among rural populations.

Why the country should begin to feel social wrong before the town is obvious. In the town there are mitigations and escapes. If the conditions of one trade become oppressive, it is easier to pass to another. The workers are better educated and organised ; there is a middle class, and a tyrant dare not bring matters to such a crisis. The power of the wealthy is divided ; the poor man's employer is seldom his landlord But in the country power easily gathers into the hands of the few. The labourer's opportunities and means of work, his home, his standing-ground, are often the property of one man. In the country the rich have almost the power of life and death, and are less hampered by competition with each other and by public opinion. One man cannot hold a town in fee, but one man can affect for evil or for good almost as large a population as that of some towns, when it is scattered across a countryside.

This is the state of wrong which Micah attacks.

The social changes of the eighth century in Israel were
favourable to its growth.[1] The increase of money
which had been produced by the trade of Uzziah's reign
threatened to overwhelm the simple economy under
which every family had its croft.   As in many another
land and period, the social problem was the descent
of wealthy men, land-hungry, upon the rural districts.
They made the poor their debtors, and bought out the
peasant proprietors.   They absorbed into their power
numbers of homes, and had at their disposal the lives
and happiness of thousands of their countrymen.
Isaiah had cried, *Woe upon them that join house to
house, that lay field to field, till there be no room* for the
common people.[2]   Micah pictures the recklessness of
those plutocrats—the fatal ease with which their wealth
enabled them to dispossess the yeomen of Judah.

The prophet speaks :—

ii. 1.   *Woe to them that plan mischief,*
    And on their beds work evil ! [3]
    As morning breaks they carry it out,
    For it lies to the power of their hands !
  2.   *They covet fields and—seize them,*
    Houses and—lift them up.
    So they crush a good man and his home,
    A man and his heritage.

This is the evil, the ease with which wrong is done
in the country !   *It lies to the power of their hands :
they covet and seize.*   And what they get so easily is
not merely so much land and stone and lime, but

---

[1] See above, pp. 30 ff.   [2] Isa. v. 8.
[3] Most moderns omit *work evil*, I think unnecessarily : by leaving the
words four regular lines are obtained.   Budde: *plan mischief on their
beds, and work evil.*

human life, with all that makes up personal independence, and the security of the home and the family. That these should be at the mercy of the passion or the caprice of one man, is what stirs the prophet's indignation.   We shall see how the tyranny of wealth was aided by the bribed judges of the country ; and how, growing reckless, the rich betook themselves, as the lords of the feudal system in Europe did, to the basest assaults upon the persons of peaceful men and women.   But meantime Micah feels that by themselves the economic wrongs explain and justify the doom impending on the nation.   When this doom falls, by the Divine irony of God it shall take the form of a conquest of the land by the heathen, and the disposal of those great estates to the foreigner.

The prophet speaks :—

ii. 3. *Therefore thus saith Yahweh :*
       Behold, I plan evil against this race,[1]
       From which ye cannot withdraw your necks,
       Nor be able to walk erect—
       So evil a time it will be ! [2]

   4. *In that day they shall raise a rune* [3] *about you,*
       And wailing a wail [4] *shall say :*
       Measured off [5] *is my people's Portion,*
       How they despoil me ! [6]

[1] Marti, J. M. P. Smith, and Budde omit *against this race.*

[2] Cf. Amos v. 13, from which some regard the line as a late addition here.   I agree with J. M. P. Smith that there is no reason for this opinion.

[3] Heb. *mashal, rhyme, verse,* also *parable.*

[4] With most moderns (after LXX and Targ.) omit נהיה , a dittography on the words preceding it.   But should we read ונהה ינהה ואמר ?

[5] So LXX, and adds *with the measuring rope.*

[6] But LXX and most moderns *there is none to restore to me.*

To traitors [1] *our fields are allotted,* [2]
We be utterly undone. [3]

The next, hardly metrical, verse seems, as most
now agree, to be an interpolation.

5. *So thou shalt have none to cast the line by lot*
   In the congregation of Yahweh.

No restoration at time of Jubilee for lands taken away
in this fashion !   There will be no congregation of the
Lord left !

At this point the prophet's pessimist discourse, which
must have galled the rich, is interrupted by their
clamour to him to stop.

The rich speak :—

6. *Prate* [4] *not (they are prating)*
   Let none prate of such things. [5]
   Never cease will revilings !
7. *Is the House of Jacob accursed,* [6]
   Is the temper of Yahweh too short,
   Or could such be His doings ?

---

[1] After Stade most read *our captor.*   *Traitors = apostates, i.e.,* the unjust.

[2] After the LXX ; Heb. *he allots* or *divides.*

[3] With most I bring this line from the beginning to the end of the verse.

[4] Lit. *drop* in tiresome reiteration.   Heb. and LXX have this verb in
the plural, but Ruben naturally suggests the singular since it is Micah
who is being answered.

[5] J. M. P. Smith takes this line as dittography on the preceding one
but without reason.

[6] Heb. הָאָמוּר is unlikely, though Ewald and Guthe make the best
of it by rendering *what a saying!*   From LXX ὁ λέγων some would
read הָאֹמֵר, *O that sayest.*   But on the whole it is better to read, with
Richter quoted by Budde, הָאָרוּר, *Is accursed ?* or with Budde himself
הָאֻמְלָל, *Is decayed* or *withered ? the house of Jacob.*

ii. 7b *Shall not His [1] words mean well*
       To an honest people.[2]

So the rich, in their immoral confidence in themselves
and their God, tell the prophet that his sentence upon
the nation, and especially on themselves, is absurd,
impossible. They cry the constant cry of Respecta-
bility : ' God can mean no harm to the like of us !
His words are good to them that are honest—and we
are conscious of being such. What you, prophet,
have charged us with are nothing but natural transactions.' The Lord Himself has His answer ready.
Honest indeed ! They have been unprovoked plun-
derers !

God speaks :—

8. *But ye [3] are as foes to My people,*
   Suddenly starting [4] on peaceful men,[5]
   Ye strip from confiding passers by
   Booty [6] of war.

---

[1] So LXX ; Heb. *My.*

[2] Heb. confirmed by LXX, *with him that walks honestly ;* but *that
walks* is doubted by most moderns, and עִם , *with*, is read עַם , *people ;*
while some propose *His people Israel.* But all is conjectural.

[3] For וְאֶתְמוּל read לְ אַתֶּם ; so in previous editions I followed
W. R. Smith, *Prophets*, p. 127, and so now practically all critics, however
variously they read what follows.

[4] For יְקֹמֵם , *is risen up*, read either תְּקֹומֵמוּ , *ye rise up*, or better וְקָמִים ,
and rising up. But (as against some) we must retain מִמּוּל or read it
לְמוּל , *in front of*, for this adds to the *rising up* the sense of suddenness
and forms a good parallel to the next line. These robbers surprise the
simple, confiding poor by their startling exactions.

[5] Heb. has שַׂלְמָה , *robe*, followed by אֶדֶר , *garment.* But on the
hint of the LXX τῆς εἰρήνης we must read שֹׁלְמִים (שְׁלֵמִים) , *the
peaceful*, and take אדר as a gloss ; so most moderns. For another
reading of this line see Budde.

[6] Reading with most שֶׁבִי for שׁוּבֵי , *averse to.*

9. *The women of My people ye tear*
   Out of their [1] *happy homes,* [2]
   From their [1] *children ye take away*
   My glory for ever.

10. *Rise and get you gone,*
    For this is no rest for you.
    Because of uncleanness ye shall be destroyed
    With sickening destruction (?) [3]

Of outrages on the goods of honest men, and on
the persons of women and children, possible in times
of peace, when the rich are oppressive and abetted by
mercenary judges and prophets, we have an illustration
analogous to Micah's in the complaint of Peace in
Langland's vision of English society in the fourteenth
century. The parallel to our prophet's words is
striking :—

' And thanne come Pees into parlement · and put forth a bille,
How Wronge ageines his wille · had his wyf taken.
" Both my gees and my grys [4] · his gadelynges [5] feccheth ;
I dar noughte for fere of hym · fyghte ne chyde.
He borwed of me bayard [6] · he broughte hym home nevre,
Ne no ferthynge ther-fore · for naughte I couthe plede.

[1] So after LXX ; Heb. *her.*
[2] For בית , *home,* Wellhausen reads בני , *children,* unnecessarily.
[3] The text of this couplet is very uncertain, but for תְּחַבֵּל וְחֶבֶל
we may with LXX read תְּחֻבְּלוּ חֶבֶל as above.   But Budde, partly
following Ehrlich, and taking not חבל = *destroy,* but another חבל =
pledge, reads the couplet thus :—

בַּעֲבוּר מְעַט מְאוּמָה
תַחְבְּלוּ חֶבֶל נִמְרָץ

For the sake of any trifle, Ye decree distraint pitilessly.   But if this be
the original, is it not out of place just here ?
[4] Little pigs.   [5] Fellows.   [6] A horse.

He meyneteneth his men · to morther myne hewen,[1]
Forstalleth my feyres [2] · and fighteth ın my chepynge,
And breketh up my bernes dore · and bereth aweye my whete,
And taketh me but a taile [3] · for ten quarteres of otes,
And yet he bet me ther-to · and lytħ bi my Mayde,
I nam [4] noughte hardy for hym · uneth [5] to loke." '

They pride themselves that all is stable and God is
with them. How can such a state of affairs be stable !
They feel at ease, yet injustice can never mean rest.
God has spoken the final sentence, but with a rare
sarcasm the prophet adds his comment on the scene.
These rich men had been flattered into their religious
security by hireling prophets, who had opposed himself.
As they leave the presence of God, having heard their
sentence, Micah looks after them and muses.

ii. 11. *If a man were to come,*[6]
Were with wind and falsehood to cozen :
*' Let me preach [7] unto thee of wine and strong
drink,'*
Then might he be such a people's preacher.[8]

At this point there have somehow slipped into
the text two verses (12, 13), which all agree do not
belong to it, and for which we must find another
place.[9] They speak of return from the Exile, and in-

---

[1] Servants.   [2] Fairs, markets.
[3] A tally.   [4] Am not.   [5] Scarcely.
[6] For הֹלֵךְ read הָלַךְ , cf. 1 Sam. xiv. 30.

[7] Or *prattle*, lit. *let drop.*
[8] This verse seems more appropriate after ver. 6.
[9] *I will gather, gather thee, Jacob, in mass,*
I will bring, bring together the Remnant of Israel !
I will set them together like sheep in a fold,
Like a flock in the midst of the pasture (?)
They shall hum with men !
The breach-breaker has gone up before them ı

terrupt the connection between ver. 11 and the first
verse of chap. iii.

With the latter Micah begins a series of three oracles,
which give the substance of his own prophesying in
contrast to that of the false prophets whom he has
just been satirising. He has told us what they say,
and now begins the first of his own oracles with, *But I
said*.[1] It is an attack upon the authorities of the
nation, whom the false prophets flatter. Micah speaks
plainly to them. Their business is to know justice,
yet they love wrong. They flay the people with their
exactions ; they cut up the people like meat.

The prophet speaks : *But I said,*

iii. 1. *Hear ye now this,*[2] *O chiefs of Jacob,*
    And rulers of Israel's House :
    Is it not yours to look after [3] *justice,*
  2. *O haters of good and lovers of evil ?* [4]
  3. *Who devour the flesh of my people,*
    And their skin have flayed off them

> *They have broken the breach, and passed on by the gate*
> *And gone forth by it,*
> *And their king hath passed on before them,*
> *And Yahweh at the head of them.*

In the first line read after LXX כֻּלוֹ for כְּלָךְ ; *in a fold,* LXX
ἐν Θλίψει, *in trouble.*

[1] Now generally taken as a marginal note. But, as Budde says,
as such it would be meaningless, and he makes the interesting conjecture
that something has gone lost between ii. 11 and iii. 1, which might be
Micah's account of how upon the climax of his charges in iii. 11 he was
like Amos and Jeremiah attacked by his opponents, and only its final
phrase, *But I said*, in answer to them has been left (*Z.A.T.W.*, 1919, 20
pp. 16 ff.).

[2] So LXX and Syr. ; and LXX and Targ. read *Jacob's House*. Heb.
is without either.

[3] Heb. *know*, but see above, p. 350, n. 10.

[4] The rest of ver. 2 is rightly omitted by most as a mere redundancy on
ver. 3   Marti transfers it to after the first couplet of ver 4.

iii. 3b. *And laid bare* [1] *their bones.*
           And served up (?) [2] *as if in a pot,*
           Like meat from the thick of the caldron !
      4. *Then shall they cry unto Yahweh,*
           And He will not answer them ;
           But will hide His face from them, [3]
           Because they have worsened their doings.

Micah's words are terribly strong, but there have
been other ages and civilisations of which they have
been no more than true. ' They crop us,' said a French
peasant of the lords of the great Louis' time, ' as the
sheep crops grass.' ' They treat us like their food,'
said another on the eve of the Revolution.

Is there nothing of the same with ourselves ? While
Micah spoke he had wasted lives and bent backs before
him. Pinched peasant-faces peer between his words
and fill the ellipses. Among the poor to-day are there
not starved and bitten faces—bodies with the blood
sucked from them, with the Divine image crushed out ?
We cannot explain all of these by vice. Drunkenness
and unthrift account for much ; but how much more
only the following facts ! Men among us live in fashion-
able streets and keep their families comfortable by
paying their employés a wage on which it is impossible
for men to be strong or women to be virtuous. Are
those not using these as their food ? They say that if
they gave higher wages they must close their business,
and cease paying wages at all ; and they are right if

---

[1] Usually rendered *cleft* or *broken* (as in previous editions of this work).
Heb. *piṣṣiḥu*. But as Bevan, quoted by Marti, points out, this verb
corresponds to Arab. paṣaḥ, ' to bare,' and not to paṣah, ' break up '.

[2] So Heb. פרשׂו , but some read פרסו , *chopped up*. Marti and
others take the couplet as a gloss.

[3] Heb. adds *at that time* which, destroying the metre, may be a gloss.

they continue to live on the scale they do. As long
as any families are maintained in comfort by the profits of businesses in which some or all of the employés
work for less than they can nourish their bodies upon,
the fact is that the one set are feeding upon the other.
It may be inevitable, it may be the fault of the system
and not of the individual, it may be that to break up the
system would mean to make things worse—but the
truth is clear that some families of the middle class,
and some of the wealthiest of the land, are nourished
by the waste of the lives of the poor. Now and again
the fact is acknowledged with as much shamelessness
as by any tyrant in the days of Micah. To a large
employer of labour, who complained that his employés,
by refusing to live at the low scale of Belgian workmen,
were driving trade from this country, the present writer
once said : ' Would it not meet your wishes if, instead
of your workmen being levelled down, the Belgians
were levelled up ? This would make the competition
fair between you and the Belgian employers.' His
answer was, ' I care not so long as I get my profits.'
He was a religious man, a liberal giver to his Church,
and he died leaving more than a hundred thousand
pounds.

Micah's tyrants, too, had religion to support them.
Hireling prophets, whom both Amos and Hosea attack,
gave their blessing to this system, which crushed the
poor, for they shared its gains. They lived on the
alms of the rich, and flattered as they were fed. To
them Micah devotes the second oracle of chap. iii, and
his words confirm the principle we laid down, that
in that age the difference between the false and the
true prophet was what it has been in every age—
an ethical difference ; and not a difference of dogma,
or tradition, or ecclesiastical note. The false prophet

spoke, consciously or unconsciously, for himself and his living. He sided with the rich ; he shut his eyes to the condition of the people ; he did not attack the sins of the day. This made him *false*, robbed him of insight and the power of prediction. But the true prophet exposed the sins of his people. Ethical insight and courage, indignation at wrong, vision of the facts of the day—this was what God's Spirit put into him, what Micah felt to be inspiration.

The prophet speaks :—

iii. 5. *Thus sayeth Yahweh against the prophets*
Who are leading my people astray :

While they have ought between their teeth
Then they preach peace,[1]
But upon him who lays not to their mouths
They sanctify war.

6. *Therefore shall night be yours without vision,*
And darkness yours without divination.
The sun shall go down on the prophets,
And the day grow dark about them,

7. *And the seers* [2] *shall be ashamed*
And the diviners abashed ;
All of them cover their lips,
For there is no answer from God.[3]

---

[1] J. M. P. Smith refers to similar charges against venal prophets in Æschylus, *Agamemnon*, 1168, and Sophocles, *Antigone*, 1036.

[2] LXX *seers of dreams* or *visions* which better fills the line.

[3] LXX omitting *God*, probably read *they shall have none to answer them ;* so Budde.

8. *But I am filled with power by the spirit of Yahweh,*[1]
   With right and with might,
   To declare unto Jacob his crime
   And to Israel his sin.

In the third oracle of this chapter (9–12), rulers and
prophets are combined—how close is the conspiracy
between them! We note that, in harmony with
Isaiah, Micah speaks no word against the king. But
evidently Hezekiah had no power to restrain the
nobles and the rich. When this oracle was uttered
there was peace, and the lavish building, which we
have seen to be characteristic of Israel in the eighth
century,[2] was in process. Jerusalem was larger and
finer than ever. Ah, it was a building of God's own
city *in blood!* Judges, priests, and prophets were
alike mercenary, and the poor were oppressed for a
reward. No walls, however sacred, could stand on
such foundations. Did they say that they built her
so grandly for Yahweh's sake? Did they believe her
inviolate because He was in her? They should see.
Ṣion—yes, Ṣion—should be ploughed like a field, and
the Mountain of the Lord's Temple become desolate.

The prophet speaks :—

9. *Hear ye now this, O chiefs of Jacob,*
   Rulers of Israel's House,
   Ye who are spurning justice
   And twisting all that is straight,

---

[1] This line is too long for the metre. Most regard *by the spirit of
Yahweh* as a pious note ; but if anything must be omitted I agree with
Giesebrecht and Budde it is *power* which is not required before *might* in
the next line.

[2] For sing. בֹּנֶה in ver. 10 read pl. בֹּנֵי with LXX, Targ., Syr.

iii. 10. *Building up Ṣion in blood*
     And in crime Jerusalem.

    11. *Her chiefs give judgement for bribes,*
        And her priests utter redes for hire,

        Her prophets divine for money
        And lean upon Yahweh and say,
        Is not Yahweh within our midst ?
        Never can ill befall us !

    12. *Therefore on your account* [1]
        Ṣion shall be ploughed as a field
        And heaps shall Jerusalem become,
        And the Mount of the House a mound [2] *in a*
             jungle.

It is difficult to place ourselves in a society in which
bribery is prevalent, and the fingers of justice and of
religion are gilded by their suitors. But such corruption has always been common in the East. ' An
Oriental State can never altogether prevent the abuse
by which officials, small and great, enrich themselves
in illicit ways.' [3] A strong government takes the
bribery for granted, and periodically prunes the rank
fortunes of its greater officials. A weak government
lets them alone. But in either case the poor suffer
from unjust taxation and from laggard or perverted
justice. Bribery has been found, even in the primitive and puritan forms of Semitic life. Mr. Doughty
has borne testimony to this among the austere Waha-
bees of Central Arabia. ' When I asked if there

---

[1] Budde proposes to add from the quotation of this saying in Jer. xxvi.
18, *thus saith Yahweh of Hosts.*

[2] Or *high-place*, so LXX ; Heb. *mounds.*

[3] Nöldeke, *Sketches from Eastern History*, translated by Black, pp. 134 f.

were no handling of bribes at Hâyil by those who are
nigh the prince's ear, it was answered, Nay. The
Byzantine corruption cannot enter into the eternal and
noble simplicity of this people's (airy) life, in the poor
nomad country ; but (we have seen) the art is not
unknown to the subtle-headed Shammar princes, who
thereby help themselves with the neighbour Turkish
governments.' [1]   The bribes of the ruler of Hâyil 'are,
according to the shifting weather of the world, to great
Ottoman government men ; and now on account of
Kheybar, he was gilding some of their crooked fingers
in Medina.' [2]   Nothing marks the difference of modern
government in the West more than the absence of this,
especially from our courts of justice.   Yet the improvement has only come within comparatively recent centuries.   What large space does Langland give to the
arraigning of ' Mede,' the corrupter of authorities and
influences in the society of his day !   Let us quote his
words, for again they provide a parallel to Micah's,
and enable us to realise a state of life so contrary to
the present.   It is Conscience who arraigns Mede before
the King :—

' By ihesus with here jeweles · youre justices she shendeth,[3]
And lith [4] agein the lawe · and letteth hym the gate,
That feith may noughte have his forth [5] · here floreines go so
    thikke,
She ledeth the lawe as hire list · and lovedays maketh,
And doth men lese thorw hire love · that law myghte wynne,
The mase [6] for a mene man · though he mote [7] hir eure.

[1] *Arabia Deserta*, I, 607.
[2] *Idem.*, II, 20.
[3] Ruins.
[4] Lieth.
[5] Course.
[6] Confusion.
[7] Summon.

Law is so lordeliche · and loth to make ende,
Withoute presentz or pens ¹ · she pleseth wel fewe.

*   *   *   *   *   *   *   *

For pore men mowe ² have no powere · to pleyne ³ hem though
  thei smerte ;
Suche a maistre is Mede · amonge men of gode.⁴ ’

¹ Pence.   ² May.
³ Complain.   ⁴ Substance or property

CHAPTER XXVII

ON TIME'S HORIZON

MICAH IV 1-7

THE prospect of Sion's desolation which closes chap. iii is followed in chap. iv by an ideal picture of her exaltation *in the issue of the days*. We cannot doubt that this arrangement has been made of purpose, nor deny that it is natural. Whether it be due to Micah himself, or whether he wrote the second passage, are questions we have already discussed.[1] Like many others of their kind, they cannot be answered with certainty. But I repeat, I see no conclusive reason for denying either to the circumstances of Micah's times or to the principles of their prophecy the possibility of such a hope as inspires chap. iv. 1–4. Remember how the prophets of the eighth century identified Yahweh with supreme and universal righteousness ; how Amos condemned the aggravations of war and slavery among the heathen as sins against Him, how Amos heard His voice come forth from Jerusalem, and Isaiah counted upon the inviolateness of His shrine and city,—and you will not think it impossible for a third Judæan prophet of that age, whether Micah or another, to have drawn the prospect of Jerusalem which now opens before us.

---

[1] See above, pp. 391 ff.

It is the far-off horizon of time, which, like the spatial horizon, always seems a fixed and eternal line, but as constantly shifts with the shifting of our standpoint or elevation. Every prophet has his own vision of *the latter days ;* seldom is that the same. Determined by the circumstances of the seer, by the desires these prompt or only partly fulfil, it changes from age to age. The ideal is ever shaped by the real, and in this vision of the eighth century there is no exception. This is not any of the ideals of later ages, when the evil was the oppression of the Lord's people by alien governors or their scattering in exile ; it is not, in contrast, the spectacle of the armies of the Lord of Hosts imbrued in the blood of the heathen, or of the columns of returning exiles filling the narrow roads to Jerusalem, *like streams in the south ;* nor, again, is it a nation of priests gathering about a rebuilt temple and a restored ritual. But because the pain of the greatest minds of the eighth century was the contradiction between faith in the God of Sion as Universal Righteousness and the experience that, nevertheless, Sion had no influence upon surrounding nations, this vision shows a day when Sion's influence will be as great as her right, and from far and wide the nations whom Amos has condemned for their transgressions against God will acknowledge His law, and be drawn to Jerusalem to learn of Him. Observe that nothing is said of Israel going forth to teach the nations the law of the Lord. That is the ideal of a later age, when Jews were scattered across the world. Here, in conformity with the experience of a still un-travelled people, we see the Gentiles drawing in upon the Mountain of the House of the Lord. With the same lofty impartiality which distinguishes the oracles of Amos on the heathen, the prophet takes no account of their enmity to Israel; nor is there any talk—such as later generations were almost forced by the hostility of neighbouring tribes to indulge in—of politically subduing them to the king in Șion. Yahweh will arbitrate between them, and the result shall be the institution of a great peace, with no political privilege to Israel. But among the heathen there will be a resting from war: the factions and ferocities of that wild Semitic world, which Amos so vividly characterised,[1] shall cease. In all this there is nothing beyond the possibility of suggestion by the circumstances of the eighth century or by the spirit of its prophecy.

A prophet speaks :—

iv. 1. *It shall come to pass in the issue of the days,*[2]
    That the Mount of the House [3] *of Yahweh shall be*
    Established on the tops [4] *of the mountains,*
    And lifted it shall be above the hills.
    And peoples shall flow to it,[5]
  2. *And many nations shall go and shall say :*
    Come, let us up to the Mount of Yahweh,
    And to the House of the God of Jacob,

---

[1] See above, ch. vii.

[2] אחרית is the hindmost, furthest, ultimate, whether of space (Ps. cxxxix. 9 : *the uttermost part of the sea*), or of time (Deut. xi. 12 : *the end of the year*). It is the end as compared with the beginning, the sequel with the start, the future with the present (Job xlii. 12). In Proverbs it is chiefly used in the moral sense of issue or result. But it chiefly occurs in the phrase used here, אחרית הימים, not *the latter days*, as A.V., not ultimate days (so even Marti), for in these phrases lurks the idea of time having an end, but the *after-days* (Cheyne, and my version of Isa. ii. 2), or, better still, the *issue of the days.*

[3] LXX omits *of the House.* So Marti, who would bring into this line *established* and add to the next *the House of our God.*

[4] So LXX ; Heb. sing.

[5] For עליו read אליו with Isa. ii. 2, which runs, *all the nations shall stream to it and many peoples,* etc.

iv. 2b. *That of His ways He may teach us,*
  And we may walk in His paths.
  For from Sion goes forth instruction,
  And the word of Yahweh from out of Jerusalem!
 3. *And He shall judge between many peoples,*
  And decide [1] *for strong nations afar;*
  They shall hammer their swords into ploughshares
  And their spears into pruning-knives.
  They shall not lift, nation to nation, a sword,
  And shall not learn war any more.
 4. *Every man shall dwell under his vine*
  And under his fig-tree, with none to alarm. [2]
  For the mouth of Yahweh of Hosts has spoken. [3]

There is no ground for separating this verse from the oracle, but what connection is intended between them is not wholly clear. The verse may mean that every family among the Gentiles shall dwell in peace; or, as suggested above, that with the voluntary disarming of the surrounding heathen, Israel herself shall dwell secure, in no fear of raids and slave-hunting expeditions, with which especially Micah's Shephelah and other borderlands were familiar. The verse does not occur in Isaiah's quotation of the three which precede it. We can scarcely suppose, fain though we may be to do so, that the verse was added in order to exhibit the future correction of the evils deplored in chap. iii: the insecurity of the householder in Israel before the land-grabbing of the wealthy. Such are

[1] Or *arbitrate*.
[2] J. M. P. Smith's reasons for detaching this couplet from the preceding oracle are rather reasons for taking it as a natural part of the oracle, the peace between nations made perfect by peace between individuals and their security (so Guthe and Marti).
[3] Marti and others take this line as an editorial addition.

not the evils from which this passage prophesies redemption. It deals only, like the first oracles of Amos,
with the relentlessness and ferocity of the heathen :
under the arbitrament of the God of Sion these shall
be at peace, and whether among themselves or in Israel,
hitherto so exposed to their raids, men shall dwell
in unalarmed possession of their houses and fields.
Security from war, not from social tyranny, is promised.

The next verse can hardly be by the same hand
as the foregoing oracle but seems to have come
from a later writer to whose generation the blessed
future promised by the oracle has not arrived, but
the nations still follow their own gods, and who therefore falls back on his own and his contemporaries'
duty in such circumstances—to follow and obey
Yahweh.

5. *But all the peoples are walking*
   Each in the name of its god ;
   So we, let us walk in Yahweh's Name,
   Our God for ever and aye.

The next oracle, uttered by God Himself, returns to
the blessed future, *in that day*, but promises other
things in it than did vv. 1-4 ; to peace among men
shall be added the restoration of the banished and the
gathering in of the halt or the weary. These objects
of the verbs *gather, bring in, and set* are in the feminine
singular, to be taken either in the collective sense
(for which we have already found the feminine singular
used [1]), or else as figuring the nation Israel. The date
of the oracle must be either just before the Exile or
during the Exile :—

[1] See above, pp. 410 f.

iv. 6. *In that day—is the Rede of Yahweh—*
I will gather the halt,
And the banished bring in,
And whom I afflicted.

7. *I will set the halt for a remnant,*[1]
And the far removed [2] *for a powerful nation.*
And over them Yahweh shall reign
On Mount Ṣion [3] *from now on for ever.*

Whatever be the origins of the separate oracles which compose this passage (iv. 1–7), they form as they stand a beautiful whole, rising from Obedience to God through Peace and Freedom to Love. See how the Divine spiral ascends. We have, first, Religion the centre and origin of all, compelling the attention of men by its historical evidence of justice and righteousness. We have the world's willingness to learn of it. We have the results in the widening brotherhood of nations, in universal Peace, in Labour freed from War, and with none of her resources absorbed by the conscriptions and armaments which are still deemed necessary for enforcing peace. We have the diffusion and security of Property, the prosperity and safety of the humblest home. And, finally, we have this free strength and wealth inspired by the example of God Himself to nourish the broken and to gather in the forwandered.

Are we nearer the Vision to-day, or does it still hang upon time's horizon, that line which seems so

[1] Which shall be the stock of the nation's future.
[2] This passive participle is not found elsewhere ; some read instead *the wearied* and some *the sick ;* LXX *the cast off.*
[3] Marti omits *on Mount Ṣion* unnecessarily.

stable from the seer's point of view, but which moves from the generations as fast as they travel to it ?

There is much in the Vision that is not only nearer to us than to the Hebrew prophets, and not only abreast of us, but achieved and behind us, as we live and strive still onward. Yes, actually behind us ! History has in part fulfilled the promised influence of religion upon the nations. The Unity of God has been owned, and the civilised peoples bow to the standards of justice and of mercy first revealed from Mount Sion. *Many nations* and *powerful nations* acknowledge the arbitrament of the God of the Bible. We have had revealed that High Fatherhood of which every family in heaven and earth is named ; and wherever that is believed the brotherhood of men is confessed. We have seen Sin, that profound discord in man and estrangement from God, of which all human hatreds are the fruit, atoned for and the hatreds reconciled by a Sacrifice in face of which human pride and passion stand abashed. The first part of the Vision is fulfilled. *The nations stream to the God of Jerusalem and His Christ.* And though to-day our Peace be but a paradox, and the ' Christian ' nations stand still from war less in love, than in fear of one another, there are in every nation an increasing number of men and women, with growing influence, who, without being fanatics for peace, or blind to the fact that war may be a people's duty in its own defence or in relief of the enslaved, do yet keep themselves from foolish forms of patriotism, and by their recognition of each other across all national differences make sudden and unconsidered war less and less possible.

I wrote the above in 1895 under the sound of a call to stand upon arms which broke like thunder upon our Christmas peace ; but, amid the ignoble jealousies

and hot rashness which prevailed, how the air, burned
clean by that first electric discharge, became filled with
the determination that war should not happen in the
interests of mere wealth or at the caprice of a tyrant !

I added then the following sentences : God help us
to use this peace for the last ideals of His prophet !
May we see, not that of which our modern peace has
been far too full, mere freedom for the wealth of the
few to increase at the expense of the mass of mankind.
May our Peace mean the gradual disarmament of the
nations, the increase of labour, the diffusion of property,
and, above all, the redemption of the waste of the people
and the recovery of our outcasts. Without this, peace
is no peace ; and better were war to burn out by its
fires those evil humours of our secure comfort, which
render us insensible to the needy and the fallen at
our side. Without the redemptive forces which Christ
brought to earth, peace is no peace ; and the cruelties
of war, that slay and mutilate so many, are as nothing
to the cruelties of a peace which leaves us insensible
to the outcasts and the perishing, of whom there are
so many even in our civilisation.

Since these sentences were written in 1895 we have
had more than one great war, the last the greatest in
which nations were ever engaged. The peace which
has followed does indeed seem more potential for the
effects, international and civic, which the prophets
promised for *the issue of the days*. The civilised peoples
are more afraid of war than ever before in history ;
they have organised themselves to prevent it if possible ;
there has been a partial disarmament ; and some efforts
to reduce social injustice and suffering. But in spite
of this the prophets' ideals and warnings are not less
needed. May we as a people lay them to heart and
strive more and more to fulfil them !

CHAPTER XXVIII

THE KING TO COME

MICAH IV 8-v

WHEN a people has to be purged of long injustice, when some high aim of liberty or
of order has to be won, it is remarkable how often
the drama of revolution passes through three acts.
There is first the period of criticism and of vision,
in which men feel discontent, dream of new things,
and put their hopes into systems : it seems then as
if the future were to come of itself. But often a
catastrophe, relevant or irrelevant, ensues : the visions
pale before a vast conflagration, and poet, philosopher,
and prophet disappear under the feet of a mob of
wreckers. Yet this may be the greatest period of
all, for somewhere in it a strong character is forming,
and men, by the very anarchy, are being taught, in
preparation for him, the indispensableness of obedience
and loyalty. With their chastened minds he achieves
the third act, and fulfils all of the early vision that
God's ordeal by fire has proved worthy to survive.
Thus history, when distraught, rallies again upon the
Man.

To this law the prophets of Israel only gradually
gave expression. We find no trace of it among the
earliest of them ; and in the essential faith of all there

was much which predisposed them against the conviction of its necessity. For, on the one hand, the seers were so filled with the inherent truth and inevitableness of their visions, that they described these as if already realised; there was no room for a great figure to rise before the future, for with a rush the future was upon them. On the other hand, it was a principle of prophecy that God is able to dispense with human aid. ' In presence of the Divine omnipotence all secondary causes, all interposition on the part of the creature, fall away.' [1] The more striking is it that before long the prophets should have begun, not only to look for a Man, but to paint him as the central figure of their hopes. In Hosea, who has no such promise, we already see the instinct at work. The age of revolution which he describes is cursed by the want of men : there is no leader of the people sent from God ; those who come to the front are the creatures of faction and party ; there is no king from God.[2] How different it had been in the days of old, when God had ever worked for Israel through some man—a Moses, a Gideon, a Samuel, but especially a David. Thus memory equally with the present dearth of personalities prompted to a great desire, and Israel learned to wait for a Man. The hope of the mother for her firstborn, the pride of the father in his son, the eagerness of the woman for her lover, the devotion of the slave to his liberator, the enthusiasm of soldiers for their captain—unite these noblest affections of the human heart and you shall yet fail to reach the passion with which prophecy looked for the King to Come. Each age, of course, expected him in

[1] Schultz, *A. T. Theol.*, p. 722.
[2] See above, pp. 288, 299, 311, 314, 333.

the qualities of power and character needed for its own troubles, and the ideal changed from glory unto glory. From valour and victory in war, it became peace and good government, care for the poor and the oppressed, sympathy with the sufferings of the whole people, but especially of the righteous among them, with fidelity to the truth delivered unto the fathers, and, finally, a conscience for the people's sin, a bearing of their punishment and a travail for their spiritual redemption. But all these qualities and functions were gathered upon an individual—a Victor, a King, a Prophet, a Martyr, a Servant of the Lord.

We saw how clearly, if how variously, Isaiah focussed the hope of his people on a coming Redeemer and Ruler possessing the qualities just described.[1] Did Micah also predict Him? In the Book of Micah there is the prediction of such a Personage, v. 2 ff. (Eng. ; v. 1 ff. Heb.), but whether from Micah himself is uncertain and is not unreasonably doubted by many.[2] It is preceded by a number of detached oracles, iv. 8– v. 1 (Eng. ; iv. 8-14 Heb.), all of them reflecting sieges, but sieges with different duties for the nation and different issues ; these oracles have no clear connection with each other or with the passage predicting Him. In iv. 8 Jerusalem is addressed in terms which imply that she is reduced to narrow limits, isolated and the solitary defence of her people, *Tower of the Flock*.[3] This suits her position during her siege by

---

[1] *Isaiah i–xxxix*, pp. 129 ff. Of course those who deny these Messianic prophecies to Isaiah are not likely to attribute anything similar to Micah.

[2] *E.g.*, Wellhausen, Stade, Cornill, Marti, Budde, Duhm, J. M. P. Smith.

[3] Wellhausen indeed thinks that ver 8 presupposes a Jerusalem devastated. This is not correct. All that can be inferred from the verse is that the country is overrun by the foe, Jerusalem alone standing as a told for the flock of God. (Cf. the similar figures in Isa. i.) Consequently

Sennacherib in 701, and the confident promise to her
of the return of her sovereignty over Israel was surely
as possible to Micah, if he was still living in 701, as
were Isaiah's promises to his fellow-citizens in that
same siege. The address to her in verse 9 follows
naturally as rallying her patience under the same
pressure. But verse 10 gives another prospect; she
must capitulate and go forth to the field, yea even
unto Babylon; which of course is not in the temper
of Isaiah nor what was required of the City by him
in 701, but is in the temper of Jeremiah and his predictions, during the siege by Nebuchadrezzar, of the
Babylonian Exile. Verses 11-13 also reflect a siege
but again rally Jerusalem to beat down her foes, with
an additional call, v. 1 (Eng.; iv. 14 Heb.), which
best explains itself as from the time of Micah.[1] It
is on this last that the promise of the Deliverer immediately follows.

> iv. 8. *But thou, O Tower of the Flock,*[2]
>   *'Ophel of the daughter of Ṣion,*
>   *Unto thee shall arrive the former rule*
>   *And the kingdom of Israel come* back,[3]
>   9. *Now why dost thou cry so loud ?*
>   *Is there no king in thee,*

the contradiction which Wellhausen and others feel between ver. 8 and
vv. 9, 10 does not exist. He grants that the latter may belong to the time
of Sennacherib's invasion—unless it be *a vaticinium post eventum*.

[1] As even Wellhausen frankly admits. Nowack leaves it to Micah.

[2] See above, p. 439, n. 3. It is doubtful whether *Migdal-'Eder, Tower* of
the flock is to be taken here figuratively or was an actual early name for
Jerusalem; but in either case the effect is the same. On this name and
'Ophel = mound or *swelling* see the present writer's *Jerusalem*, vol. i,
pp. 152, 287.

[3] So I read with most moderns; Heb. *and the kingdom come to the
daughter of Jerusalem ;* so LXX, curiously adding *out of Babylon.*

Is thy counsellor perished ? [1]
That throes have seized thee. [2]

10. *Writhe and thrust,* [3] *O daughter of Ṣion,*
     Like a bearing woman,
     For now must thou forth from the city
     And camp in the field.
     Yea thou shalt come even to [4] *Babel,*
     There to be rescued,
     There shall Yahweh [5] *redeem thee*
     From the hand of thy foes

11. *Even now are gathered against thee*
     Nations many, that say:
     Be she defiled, that we may gloat
     With our eyes over Ṣion.

12. *But they, they never have known*
     The thoughts of Yahweh,
     Nor have understood His purpose,
     To gather them in like sheaves on the floor.

13. *Rise and thresh, O daughter of Ṣion !*
     For thy horns I turn to iron
     And thy hoofs I turn to bronze ;
     Thou shalt beat down many peoples
     And devote to Yahweh their spoil,
     Their wealth to the Lord of all the earth.

[1] With this couplet compare Jer. viii. 19. Those who assign it to the Exile understand Yahweh as *King* and *Counsellor*.

[2] Heb. adds *like a child-bearing woman*, probably a gloss suggested by the next oracle ; but if genuine it was the motive of attaching the latter to this one.

[3] Or *labour ;* Heb. נֹחִי ; but some would read הֹגִי, *moan,* and some הֵאָנְחִי, *groan*. LXX B. adds a third verb, καὶ ἐγγίζε.

[4] Heb. the emphatic עַד , *up to, as far as.*

[5] LXX adds *thy God*.

v. 1. *Now gash thyself, gash thyself,*[1]
A siege they [2] *have laid about us,*
With a ruler [3] *they smite on the cheek*
The Ruler [3] *of Israel !*

[4]**2.** *But thou, O Beth-Ephrathah,*[5]
The smallest of Judah's thousands,[6]
From thee shall come forth for Me
The Ruler to be in Israel,
Whose goings forth are of old
From the days of long ago. . . .[7]

3. *He shall stand* [8] *and herd* [9] *in Yahweh's strength*
In the Name Sublime of Yahweh his God,
And they shall abide for now is He great
Up to the ends of the earth.[10]

Bethlehem was the birthplace of David, but when
Micah says that the Deliverer shall emerge from her

---

[1] For the text תתגדדי בת־גדוד , *gash* or *press thyself*, or *gather in troops, daughter of troops* (?) or *of pressure*, read rather התגדד תתגדדי , *gashing gash thyself :* sign of excessive grief.

[2] So Syr., Targ., Vulg. ; Heb. *he.*

[3] A play on words שבט , *rod*, and שפט , *judge* or *ruler*.

[4] Heb. v. 1.

[5] The name Bethlehem is a later insertion. I read with Roorda, Hitzig, and others אפרת הצעיר or אפרתה , and omit להיות , which is ungrammatical here and probably copied by mistake from the next line. On Bethlehem Ephratha see *Hist. Geog.*, pp. 318 f. The two names seem synonymous in Ruth iv. 11, but B. was the name of the township. E. of the district.

[6] Smallest form of district : cf. English *hundreds.*

[7] All efforts to bring ver. 3 (2 Heb.) into logical or rhythmical connection with its context have failed. It seems an intrusion based on Isaiah's prediction of Immanuel, ch. vii.

[8] LXX adds a verb here καὶ ὄψεται (?) shall *appear* or *watch*. It lends an extra line of the metre.

[9] LXX adds *his flock*, this at least is implied, note *they* in the second next line.

[10] Whether this short emphatic line goes with the preceding or with what follows is doubtful.

district, Ephrathah, he may not mean what Isaiah affirms by his promise of a scion from the stock of Jesse, that the King to Come shall spring from the one great dynasty in Judah. Micah seems rather to emphasise the rural and popular origin of the Messiah, in the *smallest among the thousands of Judah.* David, the son of Jesse the Bethlehemite, was a dearer figure than Solomon son of David the King. He impressed the people's imagination, because he had sprung from themselves, and in his lifetime had been the popular rival of an unlovable despot. Micah himself (if he be the author of these lines) was the prophet of the country as distinct from the capital, of the peasants as against their rich oppressors. When, therefore, he fixed upon Bethlehem as the Messiah's birthplace, he doubtless desired, without departing from the national hope in the Davidic dynasty, to throw round its representative those associations which had endeared to the people their father-monarch. The shepherds of Judah, strong source of undefiled life from which the fortunes of the state and prophecy itself had been recuperated, should again send forth salvation. Had not Micah already declared that, after the overthrow of the capital and the rulers, the glory of Israel should come to Adullam, where of old David had gathered its soiled and scattered fragments ? [1]

We conceive how such a promise would have affected the peasants for whom Micah wrote. A

[1] Recent critics (it is fair to say) mostly deny the prophecy to Micah; Nowack, ' either exilic or post-exilic '; Marti, about 500, both on the alleged ground that to the writer David is already very ancient and that no Davidic prince is reigning ; Budde (*Gesch.*, p. 87), neither this nor any of the accompanying passages is from Micah ; J. M. P. Smith, ' the date cannot be decisively settled,' but ' the period of Haggai and Zechariah,' with its Messianic hopes, ' furnishes the kind of background necessary to such an utterance as this.'

Saviour, who was one of themselves, not born up in the capital, foster-brother of the nobles who oppressed them, but born among the people, sharer of their toils and of their wrongs !—this would bring hope to every heart among the disinherited poor of Israel. In any case, be it observed, this was a promise, not for the peasants only, but for the whole people. In the present danger of the nation class disputes are forgotten, and the hopes of Israel gather upon their Hero for a common deliverance from the foreign foe. He is *to stand and shepherd His flock*, conspicuous and watchful. The country-folk knew what such a figure meant to themselves for security and weal on the land of their fathers. Heretofore their rulers had not been shepherds, but thieves and robbers.

We can imagine the contrast which such a vision offered to the fancies of the false prophets. What were they beside this ? Deity descending in fire and thunder, with other features of the ancient Theophanies that had become so much cant in the mouths of mercenary traditionalists. Beside those, how sane was this, how footed upon earth, how practical, how popular in the best sense !

We see, then, the value of such a prophecy for the prophet's day. Has it any value for ours—especially in that aspect which must have appealed to the hearts of those for whom chiefly the prophet wrote ? ' Is it wise to paint the Messiah, to paint Christ, so much as a working-man ? Is it not more to our purpose to remember the general fact of His humanity, by which He is able to be Priest and Brother to all classes, high and low, rich and poor, noble and peasant alike ? Is not the Man of Sorrows a wider name than the Man of Labour ? '

The value of such a prophecy of Christ lies in the

correctives which it supplies to the Christian apocalypse
and theology. Both have raised Christ to a throne
too far above the circumstance of His earthly ministry
and the theatre of His eternal sympathies. Whether
enthroned in the praises of heaven, or by scholasticism
relegated to an ideal and abstract humanity, Christ
is lifted out of touch with the common people. But
His lowly origin was a fact. He sprang from the most
democratic of peoples. His ancestor was a shepherd,
His mother a peasant girl. Himself was a carpenter:
at home, as His parables show, in the fields, the folds,
and the barns of His country; with the servants of
great houses, with unemployed in the market; with
the woman seeking one piece of silver, with the shepherd seeking the lost sheep. *The poor had the gospel
preached to them; and the common people heard Him
gladly*. As the peasants of Judæa must have listened
to the promise of His origin among themselves with
new hope and patience, so in the Roman empire
the religion of Jesus Christ was welcomed chiefly, as
Apostles and Fathers bear witness, by the lowly and
labouring of every nation. In the persecution which
bears his name, the Emperor Domitian heard of two
living relatives of this Jesus whom so many acknowledged as their King, and he sent for them to put
them to death. But when they came, he asked them
to hold up their hands, and seeing these brown and
chapped with toil, he dismissed the men, saying,
' From such slaves we have nothing to fear.' Yes,
but it was just the horny hands of this religion that
he and his gods had to fear! Any cynic or satirist
of his literature from Celsus onwards could have told
him that it was by men who worked with their hands
for their bread, by domestics, artisans, and all manner
of slaves, that the power of this King should spread.

which meant destruction to him and his empire!
From little Bethlehem came forth the Ruler, and *now He is great to the ends of the earth.*

There follows upon this prophecy of the Shepherd a curious fragment which divides His office among a number of His order, though the grammar returns towards the end to One. The mention of Assyria encourages us to ascribe this oracle also to the eighth century, whether it be by Micah or not.[1] Mark the refrain which opens and closes it. But a number of recent critics, on the grounds that the name Asshûr or Assyria is used in late, post-exilic passages of the Old Testament for Babylon, Persia, and the Seleucid kingdom,[2] and that the numbers *seven* and *eight* stated in it betray the influence of the later Apocalyptic literature,[3] place it very late; some even referring these numbers to the Maccabean and Hasmonean leaders of the Jews.[4]

[5] v. 5. *And this [6] shall be peace—*
    When Asshûr comes into our land,
    When he marches upon our soil,[7]
    Then shall we raise seven shepherds against him,
    Yea eight princes of men.

    6. *And they shall herd Asshûr with the sword*
    And Nimrod's land with her own bare blades,[8]

[1] So Volz, and the previous editions of this volume.
[2] Babylon in Lam. v. 6; Persia, Ezr. vi. 22; Syria, Ps. lxxxiii. 8 (?).
[3] Wellhausen, Nowack; and see J. M. P. Smith on the passage.
[4] Guthe and Marti.
[5] In the Heb. arrangement v. 4.
[6] Or *this one*, referring to the shepherd of the preceding verses.
[7] So LXX and Syr., reading בְּאַדְמָתֵנוּ for the בְּאַרְמְנוֹתֵינוּ, *our palaces*, of the Heb. text. Wellhausen reads *our borders*, as in the next verse.
[8] Reading בִּפְתִחוֹתֶיהָ, *with her drawn swords*, for בִּפְתָחֶיהָ, *in her entrances* or *passes* into the land.

> *And he shall save from Asshûr,*
> *When into our land he comes*
> *And marches upon our borders.*

An oracle follows that bears no evidence of being from Micah or from his times ; but if it carries any proof of a date this is a late one.   Whether the figure means the infinite numbers of Israel among the peoples, or a power of blessing to these, is uncertain.

> 7. *But the remnant of Jacob shall be* [1]
> *Amidst many peoples,*
> *Like to the dew from Yahweh,*
> *As showers upon the grass,*
> *Which do not wait for man*
> *Nor tarry for the children of men.*

> 8. *And the remnant of Jacob shall be 'mong the*
> *nations,*
> *And amidst many peoples,*
> *Like a lion among the beasts of the jungle,*
> *Like a lion cub among flocks of sheep,*
> *Who when he comes by tramples down*
> *And tears with none to deliver.*

> 9. *Let thy hand be* [2] *high on thine adversaries*
> *And all thy foes be cut off !*

Finally in this Section is an oracle with many of the notes sounded by Micah in the first two chapters of the Book (cf. Micah ii and Isaiah ii).   The older critics left the oracle with Micah [3] ; of the more recent

---

[1] LXX adds *among the nations.*
[2] So Heb. ; but some read *shall be.*
[3] So Ewald and others.

some said that it might, except for (15), well be his ;[1]
others are doubtful ;[2] others take it as later than the
publication of Deuteronomy by Josiah.[3]

> v. 10. *And it shall be in that day*
> *—The Rede of Yahweh—*
> *That thy horses I cut from thy midst*
> *And destroy thy chariots,*
>
> 11. *Cut off the towns of thy land,*
> *And tear down all thy fortresses,*
>
> 12. *Cut off from thy hands*[4] *enchantments,*
> *Soothsayers no more shalt thou have.*
>
> 13. *And I shall cut off thine images*
> *And thy pillars from out of thy midst.*
> *No more shalt thou bow thee down*
> *To the works*[5] *of thy hands.*
>
> 14. *I will uproot from thy midst thine Asherim*
> *And destroy thine idols.*[6]
>
> 15. *I shall work in anger and wrath,*
> *Vengeance on nations who have not hearkened.*[7]

[1] Wellhausen and Nowack.
[2] J. M. P. Smith except 14, 15 which he denies to Micah.
[3] Marti.
[4] So LXX ; Heb. *thy hand*, but probably collective.
[5] Heb. sing., but again probably collective.
[6] Read עצביך for the עריך *thy cities*, of the text, and of LXX.
Cf. 2 Chron. xxiv. 18. J. M. P. Smith doubts the connection of this
couplet with the preceding, but needlessly.
[7] This couplet has no natural connection with the preceding.

CHAPTER XXIX

THE REASONABLENESS OF TRUE RELIGION

MICAH VI. 1–8

WE have reached a passage from which obscurities of date and authorship [1] disappear before the transparence and splendour of its contents. ' These few verses,' says a great critic, ' in which Micah sets forth the true essence of religion, may raise a well-founded title to be counted as the most important in the prophetic literature. Like almost no others, they afford us insight into the innermost nature of the religion of Israel, as delivered by the prophets.'

Usually it is only the last of the verses upon which the admiration of the reader is bestowed : *What doth the Lord require of thee, O man, but to do justice and love mercy and walk humbly with thy God ?* But the rest of the passage differs not in glory ; its wonder lies no more in its peroration than in its argument as a whole.

The passage is cast in the same form as the opening chapter of the Book—that of an Argument or Debate between the God of Israel and His people, upon the theatre of Nature. The heart must be dull that does not leap to the Presences before which the trial is enacted.

[1] See above, pp. 395 ff.

The prophet speaks the Word given him by Yahweh᾽

vi. 1. *Hear, I pray ye, the Word*
Which Yahweh the Lord hath spoken [1] *:*
Arise, plead unto [2] *the mountains,*
And the hills let them hear thy voice.

2. *O mountains, hearken to Yahweh's Plea,*
And give ear [3] *ye foundations of earth,*
For Yahweh hath a suit with His people
And with Israel cometh to argue.

This is not mere scenery. In moral questions between God and man, the prophets feel that Nature is involved. Either she is called as a witness to the history of their relations, or as sharing God's feeling of the intolerableness of the evil which men have heaped upon her, or by her droughts, floods, and earthquakes as the executioner of their doom. [4] It is in the first of these capacities that the prophet here appeals to the mountains and foundations of earth. They are called, not because they are the biggest of beings, but because they are the most full of memories and associations with both parties to the Trial.

The main idea of the passage, however, is the Trial itself. We have seen more than once that the forms of religion which the prophets had to combat were those which expressed it mechanically in ritual and

---

[1] So this couplet should run according to LXX; the Heb. text has dropped *the Word* and *the Lord*, and reads *is speaking* or *about to speak.*

[2] So LXX; Heb. has the sign of the accusative.

[3] With Wellhausen and most moderns read וְהַאֲזִינוּ for the Heb. text's וְהָאֵתָנִי, *and the eternal.*

[4] See *Isaiah i-xxxix*, pp. 16 f., and, indeed, the whole of the chapter, ' The Argument of the Lord,' which concludes with that passage.

sacrifice, and those which expressed it in sheer enthusiasm and ecstasy. Between such extremes the prophets insisted that religion was knowledge and conduct—rational intercourse and loving duty between God and man. This is what they figure in their favourite scene of a Debate which is now before us.

> *Yahweh hath a suit with His people,*
> *And with Israel He cometh to argue.*

To us, accustomed to communion with the Godhead as with a Father, this may seem formal and legal. But to regard it so is to do it injustice. This form sprang by revolt against mechanical and sensational ideas of religion. It emphasised religion as rational and moral, and preserved at once the reasonableness of God and the freedom of man. God spake with the people whom He had educated : He pled with them, listened to their statements and questions, and produced His own evidences and reasons. Religion, such a passage as this asserts, is not a thing of authority or of ceremonial or of mere feeling, but of argument, reasonable presentation, and debate. Reason is not put out of court : man's freedom is respected ; and he is not taken by surprise through his fears or his feelings. This sublime and generous conception of religion, which we owe to the prophets in their contest with superstitious and slothful theories of religion that unhappily survive among us, was carried to its climax in the Old Testament by another class of writers. We find it elaborated with power and beauty in the Books of Wisdom. In these the Divine Reason emerges from the legal forms now before us, and becomes the Associate and Friend of Man. The Prologue to the Book of Proverbs tells how Wisdom, fellow of God from the

foundation of the world, descends to dwell among men.
She comes into their streets and markets, she argues
and pleads with an urgency equal to the urgency of
temptation itself. But it is not till the earthly ministry
of the Son of God, His arguments with the doctors,
His parables to the common people, His gentle and
patient education of His disciples, that we see the
reasonableness of religion in its full strength and
beauty.

In that free court of reason in which the prophets
saw God and man plead together, the subjects were
such as became them both. For God unfolds no
mysteries, and pleads no power, but the debate proceeds upon the facts and evidences of life : the appearance of Character in history ; whether the past be
not full of the efforts of Love ; whether God had not, as
human wilfulness permitted Him, achieved the liberation
and progress of His people.

God speaks :—

vi. 3. *My people, what have I done thee ?*
   And how have I wearied thee—answer Me !

   4. *For I brought thee up from the land of Egypt,*
   And from the house of bondage redeemed thee.
   And I did send before thee Moses,
   Aaron and Miriam.[1]

   5. *My people, remember what Balak planned*
   And what Balaam answered him,
   From Shittim even to Gilgal,
   So that thou know the righteous deeds of Yahweh.

[1] This couplet is taken as a gloss by some. Others take *from Shittim
up to Gilgal* as such. The passage has certainly had additions made to
it ; Heb. adds *King of Moab* after Balak and *son of Beor* after *Balaam*,
both of which disturb the metre. J. M. P. Smith and Moffatt transfer
remember to before *from Shittim*. Duhm takes vv. 4*b* and 5 as a prosaic
addition.

Always the prophets go back to Egypt or the wilderness. There God made the people, there He redeemed them. In lawbook as in prophecy, it is the fact of redemption which forms the main ground of His appeal. Redeemed by Him, the people are not their own, but His. Treated with that wonderful love and patience, like patience and love they are called to bestow upon the weak and miserable beneath them. One of the interpreters of the prophets to our own age, Frederick Denison Maurice, has said upon this passage : ' We do not know God till we recognise him as a Deliverer ; we do not understand our own work in the world till we believe we are sent into it to carry out His designs for the deliverance of ourselves and the race. The bondage I groan under is a bondage of the will. God is emphatically the Redeemer of the will. It is in that character He reveals Himself to us. We could not think of God at all as the God, the living God, if we did not regard Him as such a Redeemer. But if of my will, then of all wills : sooner or later I am convinced He will be manifested as the Restorer, Regenerator—not of something else, but of this—of the fallen spirit that is within us.'

In most of the controversies which the prophets open between God and man, the subject on the side of the latter is his sin. But that is not so here. In the controversy which opens the Book of Micah the argument falls upon the transgressions of the people, but here upon their sincere though mistaken methods of approaching God. There God deals with dull consciences, but here with darkened and imploring hearts. In that case we had rebels forsaking the true God for idols, but here are earnest seekers after God, who have lost their way and are weary. Accordingly, as indignation prevailed there, here prevails pity ; and though

formally this be a controversy under the same legal
form as before, the passage breathes tenderness from
first to last. By this as well as by the recollections
of the ancient history of Israel we are reminded of the
style of Hosea. But there is no expostulation, as in
his book, with the people's continued devotion to
ritual. All that is past, and a new temper prevails.
Israel have at last come to feel the vanity of the zeal
with which Amos pictures them exceeding the legal
requirements of sacrifice ; [1] and in a despair, evident
from the superlatives which they use, they confess the
futility of the whole system, even in the most lavish
forms of sacrifice. What then remains for them to
do ?   The prophet answers with words that express
an ideal of religion to which no subsequent century
has been able to add either grandeur or tenderness.[2]

The people speak :—

vi. 6. *Wherewithal shall I come before Yahweh,*
Shall I bow me to God [3] the Most High ? [4]
Shall I come before Him with burnt-offerings,
With calves of one year ?

7. *Will Yahweh be pleased with thousands of rams,*
With myriads of rivers of oil ?
Shall I give my firstborn for my trespass,
The fruit of my body for the sin of my soul ?

The prophet answers :—

8. *He hath shown [5] thee, O man, what is good ;*
And what doth Yahweh require of thee—

[1] See above, p. 161.
[2] On the date of the passage, see above, pp. 395 f.
[3] LXX, *my God.*
[4] So LXX ; Heb. *God of the Height* or *on high*, synonymous with the
late phrase *God of Heaven.*
[5] LXX, *It hath been shown* or *declared to*, which many moderns adopt

But to do justice and to love mercy,
And humbly [1] *to walk with thy God ?*

These four lines sum up the preaching of the Prophets, as Christ summed up the teaching of the Law : *Thou shalt love Yahweh thy God and thy neighbour as thyself.*

[1] This word הַצְנֵעַ is only once used again, in Prov. xi. 2, in another grammatical form, where also it might mean *humbly*. But the root-meaning is evidently *in secret*, or *secretly* (cf. the Aram. צְנַע, to be hidden ; צָנִיעַ, one who lives noiselessly, humble, pious ; in the feminine of a bride who is modest) ; and it is uncertain whether we should not take that sense here.

CHAPTER XXX

THE SIN OF THE SCANT MEASURE

MICAH VI. 9–VII. 6

THE text of Micah vi. 9–vii. 6 is difficult, yielding in parts neither reason nor rhythm and provocative of emendations which at best are uncertain. But, as in similar cases, the general meaning is clear and forcible. The passage falls into two portions which may not have been originally connected, but reflect the same social disorders with judgement impending. In the first, vi. 9–16, the prophet calls for attention to the Voice of God, which describes the fraudulent life of Jerusalem and the evils He is bringing upon her. In the second, vii. 1–6, Jerusalem bemoans her condition but perhaps we hear her only in verse 1, and thereafter the prophet, whoever he may be.[1]

The prophet speaks :—

vi. 9. *Hark ! Yahweh calls to the city . . .*[2]

---

[1] See above, pp. 396 ff. ; but also Gunkel, *What Remains of the O.T.*, IV.

[2] Here some pious hand has added a line to the text : *and wisdom or success it is to fear Thy Name.* The word תּוּשִׁיָה occurs but once in the prophets, Isa. xxviii. 29, but is common in the Wisdom literature, *e.g.*, Prov. ii. 7, iii. 21, xviii. 1 ; Job v. 12, xi. 6, xii. 6, xxvi. 3, sometimes as *wisdom*, sometimes as the *success* wisdom brings. For *Thy* LXX reads *His.*

(456)

God speaks :—

> *Hear ye, O tribe and council of the city !* [1]
> 10. *Can I forget (?)* [2] *the hoards in the house of*
>   *the wicked.*
>   *And the scant measure accursed ?*
>
> 11. *Can I acquit her* [3] *of the fraudulent balance*
>   *And of the bag of false weights ?—*
> 12. *Whose rich men are rife with violence,*
>   *And her habitants utter falsehoods* [4]—
>   *Their tongue is deceit in their mouth.* [5]
>
> 13. *But I on My part begin* [6] *to smite thee,*
>   *To lay thee in ruin because of thy sins.*
> 14b. *Should ought* [7] *in thy midst be set aside*
>   *Thou shalt never secure it,*

[1] Wellhausen and most moderns reading with help of LXX (πολιν) ומועד העיר for the senseless ומי יעדה עוד; the next line relieved of an unusual formation of עוד with a following negative האש. Yet see Gen. xix. 12.

[2] Heb. האש , *is it not ?* which LXX reads האש, *not the fire ?* Something seems to have slipped out; which Wellhausen supplies by reading האשה, *can I forget* or *overlook ?*, Duhm, האשא, *can I bear ?*; Oort takes in the next word ההשבית, which, however, does not agree with the general sense. For אצרות LXX read אצרת אצרות which raises the question whether in the letters האשבית there was not originally another feminine participle, both participles describing the city.

[3] For האזכה read האזבה, after Vulg. ' numquid justificabo '; LXX has δικαιωθήσεται = התזכה.

[4] The singular feminine suffix, twice, is clear in this couplet.

[5] Some take this line as a later addition because of the plural suffix.

[6] So all the ancient versions ; Heb. *have made thee sick.*

[7] Heb. וישחך is untranslatable unless one were to read וירחשך, *and thy emptiness,* cf. Arab. waḥash, which in Form V means ' inani ventre fuit præ fame ' (Freytag); in colloquial Arabic waḥasha means *longing.* Read either וישׁ לך or as above eliminate ה and ך, the latter in its form of כ as a dittography of the following ב

Or whatever thou mayest secure
To the sword I will give.

vi. 14a. *Thou shalt eat but never feel filled,*[1]
15. *Thou shalt sow but shalt not reap,*
Tread olives but never anoint with oil,
And must but never drink wine.

16. *Thou keepest*[2] *the statutes of Omri,*
Every habit of Ahab's house,
And ye walk in their counsels,[3]
That I may give thee to ruin,
And for a jest thy dwellers—
Yea, ye shall bear the reproach of My people ![4]

vii. 1. *Woe unto me for I am become*
Like sweepings of summer,[5] *gleanings of vintage*
There is not a cluster to eat,
Not a fig that any[6] *would long for.*

2. *Lost are the leal from the land,*
Among men there is none that is upright,
All of them lurking for blood,
They hunt each his brother with a net.[7]

---

[1] This line is more in place here than as the first of ver. 14.

[2] So LXX, Syr., Vulg. ; Heb. *are kept*.

[3] Because of the change to the plural *ye* this is taken by some as a late addition.

[4] Observe the return to the plural. For *My people* LXX reads *peoples ;* Marti and others take this line as a gloss.

[5] Or *summer-fruit*.

[6] So Marti after LXX ; Heb. *my soul*.

[7] Heb. חֵרֶם for which some would read חִנָּם, *for nothing*.

3. *With both hands on evil to carry it through,[1]*
   The prince demands [and the judge][2] a bribe,
   And the great man utters the greed of his soul,
   ' Let it be ! '(?)—so together they weave it (?).[3]

4. *Their best are but briars,*
   Their straightest[4] a hedge of thorn,
   Woe, Woe ![5]—their visitation is come,
   Now be their havoc ![6]

5. *Trust not in a friend,*
   Rely on no confident,
   From her who lies in thy bosom
   Guard the gates of thy mouth !

6. *For the son makes a fool of the father,*
   The daughter withstands her mother,

[1] So Heb. literally ; but after LXX and Vulg. some would read *to do evil their hands they make ready.*

[2] Some omit *and the judge*, which comes in awkwardly.

[3] This line is quite uncertain ; so are all emendations upon it. For the two words נַפְשׁוֹ הוּא, *his soul he*, Marti proposes הַמִּשְׁפָּט, *justice.*

J. M. P. Smith suggests that a verb has fallen out after הוּא, *he ;* but may not הוּא itself be the remains of a verb, יְהוּא, *let it be*, the dictate of the great man ; this form is found in Eccl. xi 3. Instead of the unusual verb *weave it*, וַיְעַבְּתוּהָ, Wellhausen and others would read וַיְעַוְּתֻהוּ, *and pervert it.*

[4] By adding מ from the following word *so* as to correspond with *their best.*

[5] So LXX ; Heb. *the day of.* In the same line Heb. has *thy visitation* and before it *of thy watchmen* or *spies*, which some rightly regard as a gloss ; it overloads the metre

[6] Roorda, by rearranging the letters and clauses of vv. 3, 4 (some of them after LXX), and by changing points, gets a reading which may be rendered : *For evil are their hands ! To do good the prince demands a bribe, and the judge, for the reward of the great, speaks what he desires. And they entangle the good more than thorns, and the righteous more than a thorn hedge.* With *their havoc* cf. Isa. xxii. 5.

vii. 6b. *The bride her mother-in-law,*
    The foes of a man are the men of his house.

Micah, prophet of the country and stern critic of
its life, had characterised Jerusalem as the centre of
the nation's sins.   He did not refer to idolatry alone,
but also to the irreligion of the politicians, and the
injustice of the rich in the capital.   The poison which
weakened the nation's blood had its source in their
heart.   There had the evil gathered which was shaking
the state to dissolution.

This section of the Book of Micah, whether it be by
that prophet or not, describes no features of Jerusalem's
life which were not present in the eighth century ;
and it may be considered as the detailed picture of
the evils Micah had summarily denounced.   This is
one of the most poignant criticisms of a commercial
community which have appeared in literature.   In
equal relief we see the meanest instruments and the
most prominent agents of covetousness—the scant
measure, false weights, unscrupulous prince and venal
judge.   And although some sins are denounced which
are impossible in our civilisation, yet falsehood, squalid
fraud, pitilessness of the struggle for life are exposed
as we see them about ourselves.   Through the prophet's ancient and often obscure eloquence we feel
those shocks and sharp edges which still break through
our Christian civilisation.   Let us remember that the
community addressed by the prophet was, like our own,
professedly religious.

The widespread sin with which the prophet charges
Jerusalem in those days of her commercial activity
is falsehood :   *Her inhabitants speak lies, and their
tongue is deceit in their mouth.*   In Mr. Lecky's *History
of European Morals* we find the opinion that ' the one

respect in which the growth of industrial life has exercised a favourable influence on morals has been in the promotion of truth.' The tribute is just. The exigencies of commerce and industry are fatal to many of the conventional pretences and flatteries which grow up in all kinds of society. In commercial life, more perhaps than in any other, a man is taken, and has to be taken, at his inherent worth. Business, the life which is called *par excellence* Busy-ness, wears off every mask, all veneer and unction, and leaves no time for the cant and parade which are rife in other professions. Moreover the soul of commerce is credit. Men have to show that they can be trusted before other men will traffic with them, at least upon that scale on which alone the great undertakings of commerce can be conducted. When we look back upon trade and industry, and see how they have created an atmosphere in which men must seem what they really are ; how they are of their needs replacing the jealousies, and intrigues, which once were deemed indispensable to the relations of different peoples, by large international credit and trust ; how they break through the conventions that divide class from class, we must do homage to them, as among the instruments of the truth which maketh free.

But to this there is another side. If commerce has exploded much conventional insincerity, it has developed a species of the genus which is quite its own. In our days nothing can lie like an advertisement. The saying ' the tricks of the trade ' has become proverbial. Every one knows that the strain of commercial life is largely due to the amount of falseness that still exists. The haste to be rich, the pitiless competition, have developed a carelessness of the rights of others to the truth from ourselves, with a capacity

for subterfuge which reminds us of nothing so much
as that state of barbarian war out of which it was the
glory of commerce to have assisted mankind to rise.
Are the prophet's words about Jerusalem too strong
for portions of our own commercial communities?
Men who know these best will not say that they are.
But let us cherish rather the powers of commerce
which make for truth. Let us tell men who engage
in trade that there are none for whom it is more easy
to be clean and straight, that lies, whether of action
or of speech, only increase the mental expense and the
moral strain of life ; and that the health, capacity,
foresight, and opportunities of a merchant depend on
his resolve to be true and on the courage with which
he sticks to the truth.

One habit of falseness on which the prophet dwells
is the use of unjust scales and short measures. The
hoards or fortunes of his day are *hoards of wickedness*,
accumulated by the use of the *lean ephah*, the *balances of
wrong* and *the bag of false weights*. These evils are more
common in the East than with us : western government
makes them almost impossible. But, all the same, ours
is the sin of the scant measure, and the more so in
proportion to the greater speed and rivalry of our
commercial life. The prophet's name for it, *measure
of leanness*, of *consumption* or *shrinkage*, is a symbol of
those duties and offices of man to man, the full and
generous discharge of which is diminished by the haste
and the grudge of a prevalent selfishness. The speed
of modern life tends to shorten the time expended on
a piece of work, and to turn this out untempered
and incomplete. The struggle for life in commerce,
the organised rivalry between labour and capital, not
only puts every man on his guard against giving others
more than their due, but tempts him to scamp his

own service and output. You hear men defend this
parsimony as if it were a law. They say that business
is impossible without the temper which they call
' sharpness ' or the habit which they call ' cutting it
fine.' But such character and conduct are the decay
of society. The shrinkage of the units must always
mean the disintegration of the mass. A society whose
members strive to come short of their duties is a society
which cannot continue to cohere. Selfishness may be
firmness, but it is the firmness of the rigour of death.
Only unselfish excess of duty, only generous loyalty
to others, give society compactness and indissolubleness.
Who is responsible for the enmity of classes, and the
mutual distrust of capital and labour ? It is the workman whose aim is to secure the largest wages for the
smallest work, and who will, in blind pursuit of that,
wreck the trade of a town or a district ; it is the employer who believes he has no duties to his men beyond
paying them the least he can induce them to take ;
it is the customer who only and ever looks to the cheap-
ness of an article—procurer in that prostitution of
talent to scamping which kills art, and joy, and pity
for the bodies and souls of our brothers. These are
the real anarchists. On their methods social coherence
and harmony are impossible. No organism can thrive
whose various limbs ever shrink in on themselves.
There is no true life except by living to others.

But the prophet covers the evil when he says that
the *leal are perished out of the land*. The original means
the man distinguished by ' hesedh,' that word which we
have on several occasions translated *leal love*, because
it implies not only an affection but loyalty to a relation.
And, as the use of the word frequently reminds us,
' hesedh ' is love and loyalty both to God and to our
fellow-men. We cannot dissociate these : they are

one. But here it is the human direction in which the word looks. It means a character which fulfils the relations of society with the fidelity, generosity, and grace that are the proper affection of man to man. Such a character, says the prophet of his time, is perished from the land. Every man lives for himself, and in consequence preys upon his brother. *They all lie in wait for blood ; they hunt every man his brother with a net.* This is not murder but the reckless, pitiless competition of the new conditions of life developed in Judah by the long peace and commerce of the eighth century. And the prophet carries this selfishness into a striking figure in ver. 4 : *The best of them are as briars, the most upright a prickly hedge.* He realises what we mean by sharpness and sharp-dealing : bristling self-interest, all points ; splendid in its own defence, but barren of fruit, and without covert for any life.

CHAPTER XXXI

OUR MOTHER OF SORROWS

MICAH VII. 7–20

AFTER so stern a charge, so condign a sentence,
confession is natural, and, with prayer for forgiveness and praise to the mercy of God, it fitly closes
the Book. As we have seen,[1] the passage is a cento
of fragments, from different periods in the history of
Israel. One allusion suits the Syrian wars; another
can only refer to the day of Jerusalem's ruin. In
spirit and language the Confessions resemble the prayers
of the Exile. The Doxology has echoes of several
Scriptures.[2]

But from these fragments, it may be of many centuries, rises clear the One Essential Figure: Israel,
her secular woes upon her; our Mother of Sorrows,
at whose knees men have learned their prayers of
confession and penitence. Other nations have been our
teachers in art, wisdom, and government. But she
is our mistress in pain and in patience, teaching men
with what conscience they should bear the chastening
of the Almighty, with what hope and humility they
should wait for their God. Surely not less lovable,

---

[1] Above, pp. 398 ff.
[2] Cf. with it Exod. xxxiv. 6, 7 (J); Jer. iii. 5, l. 20; Isa. lvii. 16;
Psalms ciii. 9, cv. 9, 10.

but only more human, that her cheeks flush for a moment with the hate of the enemy and the assurance of revenge. Her passion is soon gone, for she feels her own guilt to be greater ; and, seeking forgiveness, her last word is what man's must ever be, praise to the grace and mercy of God.

Israel speaks :—

vii. 7. *But I will look out for Yahweh,*
    I will wait for God my Saviour,[1]
    My God will hear me !

  8. *Rejoice not upon me, my foe,*[2]
    Though I be fallen I rise,
    Though I sit in the dark, Yahweh is my light.[3]

  9. *The anger of Yahweh I bear—*
    Because I have sinned against Him—
    Until He shall plead my cause,
    And effect my right,
    Bring me forth to the light
    To gaze on His righteousness.

 10. *And my foe* [2] *shall see,*
    And shame shall cover her,
    She that keeps saying to me
    Where is Yahweh thy God ?
    Mine eyes shall fasten upon her,
    Already she is for trampling ! [4]

[1] So LXX ; Heb. *God of my salvation.*

[2] Feminine both in Heb and LXX.

[3] On the syntax of ver. 8 see A. B. Davidson's *Hebrew Syntax*, § 130, R 4, § 132, R 2.

[4] Heb. and LXX, *like mire in the streets*, which Marti, J. M. P. Smith and other moderns take as a gloss from Ps. xviii. 43 ; probably rightly as it makes a line too much in the otherwise regular stanzas. Duhm would rather omit *mine eyes shall fasten on her.*

A prophet speaks :—

11. *One day thy walls shall be built,*
    That day shall thy border be broad ; [1]
12. *That day unto thee they shall come*
    From Asshûr even to Egypt,
    And from Egypt on to the River,
    To sea from sea and mountain from mountain. [2]
13. *While earth* [3] *grows waste because of her dwellers,*
    Because of the fruit of their doings.

An Ancient Prayer in the Ḳinah rhythm :—

14. *Shepherd Thy folk with Thy staff,*
    The flock of Thy heritage.
    Dwelling alone in woodland,
    In the midst of garden, [4]
    May they pasture in Bashan and Gilead,
    As in days of yore,
15. *As in days of Thy marching from Egypt*
    Show to us [5] *wonders.*
16. *Nations shall see and be shamed*
    Of all their might,
    They shall put the hand to the mouth,
    Their ears shall be stunned.

---

[1] יַרְחֶק־חֹק , note the assonance, it explains the unusual choice of
חֹק for *border ;* LXX, *thy border ;* Heb. omits *thy.* But Ewald renders
distant the date. LXX also takes into ver. 11 the הוּא יוֹם of ver. 12.

[2] For Heb. הָהָר read with LXX מֵהָר.

[3] Rather than *the land.*

[4] Literally *jungle in the midst of gardenland* or *Carmel.* Plausible
as it would be to take the proper name Carmel along with Bashan and
Gilead (see *Hist. Geog.*, p. 338), the connection prefers the common noun
garden or *gardenland.* Perhaps the clause needs rearrangement. Yet
compare יַעַר כַּרְמִלּוֹ , 2 Kings xix. 23 ; Isa. xxxvii. 24

[5] So read instead of Heb. *I will show him.*

vii. 17. *Dust shall they lick like serpents,*
            Like worms of the earth.
        Trembling they come from their fastnesses,
            [To Yahweh our God.] [1]
            Tremble and fear before Thee.

A Doxology in the Ḳinah rhythm :—

18. *Who is a God like Thyself,*
        Removing iniquity,
    And passing over transgression,
        To the rest of His heritage.
    He holdeth not His anger for ever,
        But His pleasure is mercy.
19. *He will return, He will us pity,*
        Tread down our iniquities.
    Yea, Thou wilt cast to the depths
        Of the sea all our sins.
20. *Thou wilt show forth troth unto Jacob,*
        Leal love to Abraham,
    As to our fathers Thou swarest
        From days of yore.

[1] This line, which disturbs the metre and is unnecessary to the sense, may be a later addition.

INDEX OF PASSAGES AND TEXTS

A single text will always be found treated in the exposition of the passage to which it belongs. Only the other important references to it are given in this index. In the second of the columns Roman numerals indicate the chapters, Arabic numerals the pages, of this volume.

Date Due

de 4386-04, CLS-4, Broadman Supplies, Nashville, Tenn.,
inted in U.S.A.